GHOST OF WAR

GHOST OF WAR

The Sinking of the *Awa maru*

and Japanese-American

Relations, 1945–1995

Roger Dingman

Naval Institute Press
Annapolis, Maryland

Library of Congress Cataloging-in-Publication Data

Dingman, Roger,

    Ghost of war : the sinking of the Awa maru and Japanese-American
relations, 1945–1995 / Roger Dingman.

      p.   cm.

    Includes bibliographical references and index.

    ISBN 1-55750-159-9 (alk. paper)

    1. Awa Maru (Ship) 2. World War, 1939–1945—Naval operations,
Japanese. 3. World War, 1939–1945—Naval operations—Submarine.
4. World War, 1939–1945—Naval operations, American. 5. Shipwrecks.
6. Japan—Foreign relations—United States. 7. United States—
Foreign relations—Japan. I. Title.

D777.5A92D56 1997

940.54'5952—DC21   97-25742

Printed in the United States of America on acid-free paper ⊚
04 03 02 01 00 99 98 97 9 8 7 6 5 4 3 2
First printing

For Linda

Contents

Illustrations

Preface

ON THE NIGHT of 1 April 1945, the American submarine *Queenfish* (SS 393) sank the Japanese passenger-cargo ship *Awa maru* in the Taiwan Strait, off the coast of China. The *Awa maru* was returning home under a guarantee of safe passage after delivering relief supplies to American and Allied prisoners of war and civilians in Japanese custody. More than two thousand people, most of them noncombatants, perished instantly—more than had died on the *Lusitania*, the *Titanic*, or any other non-naval vessel since 1916.

This book is about the *Awa maru* tragedy. It attempts to explain how and why so catastrophic an incident could have occurred. It describes how the Japanese and American governments dealt with the immediate consequences of the sinking during and after the Pacific War. It also traces the development, change, and death of memories of this event in popular American and Japanese remembrances of the larger war in which it took place. The book concludes with an account of the salvaging of the *Awa maru* more than thirty years after her sinking.

The pages that follow can be read in different ways. They tell a compelling human story: of individuals caught up in a war that was not of their own making; of the risks they faced and the tragedies they endured; and of their postwar efforts to come to grips with, and find meaning in, what they had experienced.

What follows can also be read as a chapter in the larger history of Japanese-American relations over the last half-century. Washington promised during the war to indemnify Tokyo for the loss of life and property on the *Awa maru*, but it managed after the war to avoid making any such payment. The

United States also used negotiations over the sinking to compel Japan to promise repayment for the full costs of the military occupation that followed on its defeat. That triggered talks that dragged on for years and laid bare the inner dynamic of relations between the two governments.

This book can also be read as a study in the construction of public memory. It reveals how both attackers and victims tried to explain what happened to the *Awa maru*. Going beyond that, it shows how larger forces at work in governments, the media, and popular culture combined to produce quite different American and Japanese understandings of the *Awa maru* incident and the larger war in which it occurred.

But for me, the story that follows is first and foremost a tale of war. The *Awa maru* incident raises in microcosm larger questions about organized violence between nations, questions that have for centuries perplexed those who engage in such violence. How and why does error—or accident—intrude upon the designs of those who would employ war to achieve rational political ends? Can human beings use war for just purposes without, in turn, creating new injustices? How and why does war in memory become so very different from what it was in actual experience? Can those who were enemies ever agree on a common understanding of their past that will allow them to escape from it? I cannot promise to give definitive answers to those questions in this book, but I can tell an important tale that, fifty years after the event, remains virtually unknown to Americans. I can resolve some, but not all, of the riddles that attend both the destruction of the *Awa maru* and her eventual recovery. And, I would hope, I can offer substantial food for thought about how individuals, governments, and peoples deal with issues that war raises for us all.

This book is the end product of four years of research specifically devoted to its subject, but it builds upon many more years' experience of studying and teaching naval history and Japanese-American relations. In the course of working on it I have drawn upon the talents and assistance of many people acknowledged elsewhere in the pages that follow. Some proved so vital to the completion of this work, however, as to deserve special mention and thanks at its beginning: Dean Allard, Bernard Cavalcante, and Ed Marolda of the Naval Historical Center, Washington D.C.; Alice Creighton, Special Collections and Archives Division, Nimitz Library, U.S. Naval Academy, Annapolis, Maryland; Milton Gustafson, Kathy Nicastro, John Taylor, and

Barry Zerbe, U.S. National Archives, Washington, D.C.; John E. Bennett and Frank N. Shamer, both retired U.S. Navy captains living in San Diego, California; Harry Hall, Moberly, Missouri; Cdr. Chihaya Masataka, IJN (Ret.), and Cdr. Seno Sadao, JMSDF (Ret.), of Tokyo and Hayama, Japan; Mrs. Tōkō Takeko, Tokyo; Miss Koide Izumi, International House of Japan, Tokyo; Professor Hata Ikuhiko, Chiba University, Chiba, Japan; Professor Takahashi Hisashi, formerly of the Office of War History, National Defense Institute, and currently at Sophia University, Tokyo; Nonomura Masao, Iwama Kazuko, and Saitō Kiyoko of the *Awa maru* Bereaved Families Association, Tokyo; Matsui Kakushin, *Asahi shimbun*, Tokyo; Kogo Eiki, NHK Broadcast Culture Institute, Tokyo; Shimotsuma Kakuho, Chief Priest of Renjōji Temple, Nara; and Arai Shigeru, Osaka, Japan.

Dr. Edwin DeYoung of the Geographic Information Systems Laboratory, University of Southern California, generated the maps that accompany the text. I alone, however, am responsible for interpretations—and any errors—in this book. My words have come into print with apparently so few errors because of the efforts of Paul Wilderson, executive editor of the Naval Institute Press, and its managing editor, J. Randall Baldini, along with Linda O'Doughda and other members of their staff. Pelham G. Boyer also helped by providing careful and insightful copyediting. That I persisted in transforming ideas and aspirations into this story is due in substantial degree to the support and encouragement of my wife, Linda. This book is dedicated to her.

A Note on Orthography

Individual Japanese names are given in the normal Japanese order, that is, surname followed by personal name. I have used the normal American order for the names of Japanese-Americans.

With the exception of the capital cities Tokyo and Beijing, I have romanized place and personal names in the following manner: For the Japanese I have used the Hepburn system, with appropriate macrons; for the Chinese I have used the Wade-Giles method; and for the Korean I have used the McCune-Reischauer system.

GHOST OF WAR

1

The Greatest Submarine Error

SUNDAY NIGHT, 1 April 1945, was murky off the China coast. As so often happened in the spring, a thick fog cast its weightless veil over the waters of the Taiwan Strait, blotting out their surface. Only occasionally did the moon peek through to send its shimmering light down onto the sea.[1]

A long, dark object sliced the surface, its leading edge sending wavelets outward to contend with the chop that marred the gently undulating sea. The USS *Queenfish* (SS 393) was moving slowly to the southwest, charging the batteries that enabled her to operate far beneath the ocean's surface. The *Queenfish,* as her photograph reveals, was sleek—311 ½ feet long with only 27 ¼ feet of beam. She was also fast. Although gliding that night through the water at four knots, a speed yachtsmen would consider barely respectable, her four Fairbanks-Morse engines could skim her along the surface at twenty knots. Beneath the waves, she could move at nine knots, fast enough to agilely move in on unsuspecting Japanese merchant ships or to maneuver so as to avoid enemy depth charges.[2]

This cigar-shaped gray, black, and white boat was crammed with weapons and electronic devices that made her lethal to anything Japanese. The ten-centimeter surface radar could locate and track objects up to thirty miles away. State-of-the-art sonar supplied low-frequency passive (listening) bearings and emitted high-frequency sound impulses that, echoing back as "pings," provided range information on potential targets. A periscope with the finest optics available allowed the *Queenfish,* when submerged just below the surface, to spot targets visually and thus confirm what the electronic gear reported. The boat could fire twenty 1-inch electric torpedoes from her ten tubes. These weapons, originally "Chinese-copied" from German models and then modified on the basis of combat experience, could be directed with almost unfailing accuracy at anything that moved on or in the sea.[3]

The *Queenfish*'s most important weapon, however, was her crew. Her captain, Cdr. Charles Elliott Loughlin, and five of the nine other officers on board were "plankowners," having ridden the ship from the moment she had slipped into Atlantic waters little more than a year earlier at Portsmouth, New Hampshire.[4] They knew most of the boat's fifty-seven enlisted crewmen well. Some among the crew, like Joe Parks—who, as the senior enlisted man on board, was known as the "chief of the boat"—were longtime companions who had manned the *Queenfish* and kept her complex machinery in tip-top condition since she had been commissioned.[5] Others were newcomers, replacements picked up when the submarine had gone to Pearl Harbor the preceding January for refitting, resupply, and relaxation.[6]

These men had all volunteered for the kind of life they shared on board the *Queenfish.* They lived cheek-by-jowl in cramped quarters that took up barely a fourth of the sub's interior space. The smell of their sweat, the cigarettes they smoked, and the food they ate combined with that of paint and diesel fuel to give the very air they breathed a distinct odor. If their food was a bit better than that provided for surface sailors, they suffered from a shortage of freshwater more severe than that which plagued every man who went to war at sea. Even though the *Queenfish*'s evaporators provided a steady supply of distilled water for her main storage batteries, there never seemed to be enough for individual use. Officers shared close but comfortable quarters, but at least some of the enlisted men had to "hot bunk"—that is, climb into the beds of men who had relieved them after four weary hours of standing watch.[7]

Shared risk, no less than physical closeness, bound these sixty-six men together psychologically. They knew that death stalked them constantly. Everyone on board remembered former classmates or shipmates who had gone down with one of the forty-five subs lost in the Pacific since Pearl Harbor.[8] Submariners perished at a rate higher than that for any other element of the United States armed forces in World War II: more than one out of every five who departed on a submarine war patrol never returned.[9] Unlike Marines, who fell one by one when they hit the beaches of enemy-held islands and atolls, these men would all die together if Japanese torpedoes or depth charges found the *Queenfish* when she was traveling under the sea. The knowledge that one man's error—a hatch improperly closed, a navigational aid or radar screen incorrectly read, a torpedo carelessly handled— could seal the fate of all haunted these men as well, spurring them on to the highest levels of proficiency in keeping the *Queenfish* on patrol.

Pride also helped forge them into a team of hunter-killers. They and their boat wore decorations that attested to excellence. Dolphins on their chests, gold for officers and silver for enlisted, and beards on a few faces set them apart from the average U.S. Navy man. They were proud of their skipper, Commander Loughlin, whose decisions might determine whether they lived or died, or whether they would rank as successes or failures in the eyes of their peers. He brought to his job techniques of team play and leadership learned as an all-American basketball player at the U.S. Naval Academy.[10] He wore two Navy Crosses for having sunk more than one hundred thousand tons of enemy shipping. The crew was proud of the *Queenfish* too. She had won a Presidential Unit Citation for performance on her first war patrol, when she sank nearly fifty thousand tons of enemy shipping and rescued eighteen Australian and British prisoners of war who might otherwise have perished with a Japanese transport sunk by another American submarine.[11]

On that murky April night, a commitment to find and kill the enemy bound the *Queenfish*'s officers and men still more tightly together. On two previous war patrols they had bagged far more than a normal share of prey.[12] Their third foray, by contrast, had proven nearly fruitless. Thirty-two long days and nights alone in the Western Pacific had apparently gotten them but one "kill."[13] That was not good in the highly competitive Pacific submarine force in which, as they all knew, "inefficient" skippers could be plucked from

The USS *Queenfish* (SS 393) undergoes sea trials. *The USS* Bowfin *Museum, Honolulu, from National Archives 80-G-233791*

command and "unproductive" crews might be ruthlessly reshuffled.[14] Now, twenty-four days after leaving Saipan, having made and lost contact with five enemy ships, the *Queenfish* still had nothing to her credit.[15]

For the men on board her on that April Sunday evening, the past twenty-four hours had been routine—boring and somewhat frustrating. The *Queenfish* had not made contact with anything other than a single aircraft, which might even have been friendly.[16] The only other boat in her "wolfpack," the USS *Sea Fox* (SS 402), had at least found a little excitement, firing six torpedoes at, and then scurrying away from, what appeared to have been a Japanese convoy.[17] No gray-green blips signifying the presence of a potential target had disrupted the harmony of the waves that darted across the *Queenfish*'s radar. No propeller beats had struck the ears of sonarmen listening for sounds that might betray the presence of an enemy. Life on board the *Queenfish* on 1 April 1945 was monotonous, just like it was most days at sea.

Suddenly, at 2200 (ten o'clock in the evening) the *Queenfish*'s senior radar technician, Charlie Moore, reported over the sound-powered communication circuit known as the 7MC that he had a contact at seventeen thousand yards.[18] At that moment, the *Queenfish*'s skipper was sitting in the wardroom (a small lounge for officers) with Lt. Cdr. Frank Nickols Shamer, a prospective commanding officer who might eventually replace him, and the submarine's assistant torpedo data computer operator and first lieutenant, Lt. (jg)

Edwin A. Desmond. They hurried to the conning tower, where Lt. John E. Bennett and Ens. Howard "Shorty" Evans were waiting.[19] After checking that initial reported range of the target, Loughlin gave the order, "Tracking party, man your stations." He then sent Lieutenant Commander Shamer back to officers' country to make sure everyone there had gotten the word to man their tracking stations. Shamer found Lt. Harold E. Rice, who had just jumped out of the officers' shower, drying and dressing as quickly as he could so as to be able to dash to the conning tower, where he would serve as torpedo data computer operator.[20]

When Shamer returned to the control room, Loughlin handed him a message for the *Queenfish*'s "sister wolf," the *Sea Fox*.[21] It reported initial radar contact with a possible target—bearing 230 degrees, at a range of seventeen thousand yards. Unhappy over the *Sea Fox*'s failure earlier in the day to report immediately her initial contact with a Japanese convoy, Loughlin was determined to do better.[22]

By the time Shamer returned, Loughlin, followed by Ensign Evans, had clambered up the ladder to go "topside" (to the bridge), where the officer of the deck (OOD), Lt. (jg) John F.M. Davison, was waiting. Shamer exchanged a few words with Loughlin and was sent to the conning tower to help supervise the attack team. The submarine's gunnery officer, Lt. (jg) Edward J. Berghausen, relieved Davison as OOD so that he, as the *Queenfish*'s torpedo officer, might go below to oversee preparation of the weapons to be used against the presumed enemy vessel. That left six sets of eyes—from the bridge, Loughlin's, Berghausen's, and those of Quartermaster Second Class John A. Massey; the two lookouts in the periscope supports; and Evans's from the "cigarette deck" aft of the conning tower—to peer through the fog in search of further clues as to the target's location. With visibility reduced to no more than two hundred yards, they saw nothing.[23]

Instead, to get a good fix on the potential prey, Loughlin had to rely on what men and machinery told him. For an hour, all on board the *Queenfish* strained to do so. When first contact was made, the submarine had been slightly northeast of the predicted track of its target, which presented a pip on the radar screen with just the right size and aspect for a destroyer or destroyer escort. Loughlin gave orders to take up a position one thousand yards off that track to determine whether the target was zigzagging to reduce the risk of submarine attack. But the surface ship turned only once, sharply to port. So did the *Queenfish*. Radarmen then anxiously checked their scopes to determine if the surface ship's sudden maneuvers suggested that it had targeted their boat. They saw no sign of that.[24]

The submarine then closed to within thirty-six hundred yards of the target. On the bridge, Loughlin gave orders to slow the *Queenfish* to four knots. Below, Lieutenant Desmond relayed the necessary numbers from the torpedo data computer to the torpedomen. In these last moments before the attack, sonarmen listened for sounds of the target's propellers churning through the dark waters; what they heard were sounds characteristic of heavy screws—just the sort that would enable an enemy destroyer or destroyer escort to race through the night. Still, Lieutenant Rice questioned that identification of the target, just as the *Queenfish* was approaching the firing point, but Shamer did not report those doubts to his skipper. He saw no reason to "screw up" what seemed likely to be a perfect attack.[25]

As the *Queenfish* swung to the right (starboard) into attack position, her stern tubes ready to shoot along a track perpendicular to that of the target, four "fish" were readied to swim. They would travel at about thirty knots, aimed to hit three feet below the surface. Desmond set them in a spread with one and a half degrees between each, guaranteeing that they would strike along a 290-foot length of the target's track.[26]

At 2300 (eleven o'clock), still unable to see the target but apprised electronically of its speed, character, and course, Loughlin gave orders to fire the "fish." They swam perfectly. He—and Lieutenant Berghausen and Evans—knew that when they saw the flash of the torpedo explosions through the fog.[27] At three minutes after the hour, Loughlin ordered increased speed and, with bearings provided by the torpedo data computer, turned the *Queenfish* back toward the attack position.[28] Before she got there, the radarmen and Shamer saw the target pip split in two and vanish—a sure sign that all four *Queenfish* torpedoes had hit their mark.[29]

At that moment the tensions that had been building over the preceding hour effervesced into a wave of joy that swept over everyone on board the *Queenfish*. Unable to contain his elation, Shamer, who had been peering over Rice's shoulder during the last moments before the attack, bent over and kissed the startled torpedo data control operator on the temple. The gesture befitted a perfect score: four of the torpedoes the *Queenfish* fired had struck the target.[30]

The submariners had their "kill!"

Their prize, however, was bigger than anyone on board the *Queenfish* imagined. They thought they had sunk an Imperial Japanese Navy destroyer or destroyer escort, a ship that normally carried a crew of ninety to one hundred men.[31] In fact, their torpedoes had hit the *Awa maru*, a passenger-cargo ship crammed with more than two thousand men, women, and children. All but one of them went down with the ship.[32]

The *Queenfish*'s kill set a record. Her Mark XVIII-2 torpedoes sent more human beings to their deaths in the depths of the Taiwan Strait than had the single German torpedo that had sunk the SS *Lusitania* off the coast of Ireland nearly thirty years earlier, during World War I. The SS *Titanic* had plunged three-quarters as many victims into the North Atlantic when she struck an iceberg in 1912. Only one other American submarine in the Pacific War up to that point had killed in one blow so many Japanese on board a noncombatant vessel.[33]

But the *Queenfish*'s victims had been on a ship traveling under an American guarantee of safe passage. The *Awa maru* wore white crosses and was festooned with lights to signify her special character: she was a relief vessel authorized to carry Red Cross packages of food and medicine to American and Allied prisoners and civilian internees in Japanese hands. On that foggy night of 1 April 1945, the ship was homeward bound, traveling along a prearranged course. Word of her protected status and projected course and schedule had been broadcast repeatedly to American submarines.[34]

In sinking the *Awa maru*, the *Queenfish* committed the "greatest submarine error in World War II."[35]

How could such a tragedy have happened? How would the U.S. Navy and the governments of Japan and the United States deal with it? And why, in time, would Americans and Japanese come to remember it, and the war in which it occurred, in radically different ways?

2

Relief to the Prisoners

THE CHAIN OF EVENTS that culminated in the sinking of the *Awa maru* began on land, not at sea. When Adm. Harold Stark, Chief of Naval Operations (CNO), telephoned the White House on the afternoon of 7 December 1941 to report on the Pearl Harbor attack, he read to President Franklin D. Roosevelt a draft telegram ordering Pacific commanders to commence unrestricted air and submarine warfare against Japan. The president readily approved it.[1] That order provided the rationale for building the *Queenfish*, sending her across the Pacific, and training her officers and men to sink everything that flew the Japanese ensign.

That same day, officials in Japan and the United States began interning each other's diplomats and resident aliens—men and women once considered harmless but now regarded as potentially dangerous enemies.[2] Within seventy-two hours of the Pearl Harbor attack, each side began taking the other's soldiers prisoner. Six months later, Japan and the United States found themselves burdened with the responsibility of caring for hundreds of thousands of prisoners of war (POWs) and civilian internees. Efforts to exchange them or, that failing, to provide better treatment for them gave rise to negotiations that involved not only America and Japan but also Great Britain, Switzerland, and the Soviet Union. These roundabout talks took less than seven months to shape an accord for the exchange of diplomats and some other civilians. But it would be October 1944 before the two sides reached conditional agreement on safe passage for ships carrying relief supplies to American and Allied nationals in Japanese custody.[3] That accord set the stage for the voyage of the *Awa maru*.

Why did it take more than three years to reach that agreement? What prompted the negotiators to take up and then abandon positions that had for so long blocked an accord? How did the men who shaped it hope to keep error from destroying it?

War upsets the moral compass in human affairs. Killing, which is forbidden in every society, suddenly becomes not only licit but imperative. The rules of behavior change so rapidly that, before long, individuals, societies, and nations are treating one another in ways scarcely imaginable in peacetime. Actions planned and events unforeseen disrupt the norms of international behavior. That complicates life for those who try to confine the violence that attends war. In trying to set reasonable limits to it, they inevitably clash with others who insist that whatever needs to be done to win the war must be done. Because passions have risen and normal lines of communication are down, defining the most limited and obviously humane agreement even on something like the provision of relief to those held prisoner becomes terribly difficult.

During the first six months of war, prewar norms of behavior fell aside rapidly enough to stun both Japanese and Americans. The attack on Pearl Harbor left the latter willing to do almost anything to defeat what they universally regarded as an unparalleled act of treachery. Within hours of that attack, President Roosevelt approved the implementation of plans for action in the event of war against Japan, plans that had taken shape over the preceding nine months: Pacific area air and naval commanders were told, "Execute against Japan unrestricted air and submarine warfare."[4] Shortly thereafter, nine new Japanese ocean-cruising subs were ordered to take up station on the American West Coast to sink enemy merchantmen. Although these first boats had no success, Japanese submariners elsewhere soon began attacking American merchant vessels without warning.[5] Both sides had followed Nazi

Germany's lead in violating a treaty they had signed eleven years earlier that had made such actions illegal.[6] Tokyo denounced what Washington did even as President Roosevelt spurred Americans to do what "must be done" to defeat Japan.[7]

That imperative soon came to include seizing large numbers of enemy citizens—soldiers and civilians alike. As defeat and disaster rained down upon the United States and its allies during the first six months of the war, the numbers of those who fell into Japanese hands swelled. At first those numbers were in the hundreds, as garrisons at Guam, Wake, and Hong Kong surrendered to Japanese invaders.[8] But they soon grew exponentially. When Singapore fell on 15 February 1942, more than 130,000 Australian, British, and New Zealand soldiers became POWs. Three weeks later, when the Imperial Japanese Army completed the conquest of Java, sixty thousand Dutchmen met a similar fate.[9] American defenders held out on Corregidor and the Bataan peninsula for another two months, but when they surrendered on 6 May 1942 another eleven thousand fighting men and additional hundreds of civilians became prisoners of the Japanese.[10]

During these same bitter months Americans scooped up and jailed Japanese nationals. Within twenty-four hours of the Pearl Harbor attack, the FBI had seized 345 "dangerous enemy aliens" in Hawaii. In the first days of the fighting in the Philippines, Japanese businessmen in Manila were incarcerated; in Davao, on the southern island of Mindanao, some of their compatriots were herded into camps and killed by Filipino policemen. In the United States itself, by 10 December 1941 U.S. Army and Border Patrol detention centers held hundreds of persons of Japanese ancestry that Mexico had rounded up and delivered to American authorities. In April 1942 Washington began cooperating with South American governments in "ethnic purification" programs that sent more than two thousand Japanese to internment camps in the United States.[11] The most sizable and shameful seizure of civilian internees occurred when the U.S. Army began "relocating" Japanese and Japanese-Americans away from the West Coast under the terms of Executive Order 9066, which President Roosevelt signed on 19 February 1942. In time that decree put nearly forty thousand Japanese nationals and twice as many Americans of Japanese ancestry in camps scattered from the deserts of eastern California to the rice fields of Arkansas.[12]

By late 1942 these seizures were producing a problem that neither side had fully anticipated and both found difficult to manage. The Americans and Japanese now held tens of thousands of each other's nationals as prisoners or civilian internees. However, there was a decided imbalance in their holdings. The Japanese had far more POWs overall, thanks to their triumphs over British, Australian, and Dutch forces in Southeast Asia; Americans, however, had imprisoned or interned more than three times as many Japanese.[13] The result was a forced mixing of peoples of different race, culture, and standards of living that was bound to produce trouble.

In theory, that ought not to have been the case. The United States and Japan had signed the 1907 Hague Convention, which guaranteed prisoners of war freedom from violence, set limits on the work they could be required to perform, and obliged their captors to provide food, medicine, and supplies adequate for a humane standard of life. In 1929 both nations participated in negotiations at Geneva, where it was agreed that neutral powers would be allowed to send representatives to inspect prison camps and freely question those incarcerated about their living conditions.[14] While the United States readily signed and ratified the resulting convention, Japanese delegates to the conference were loath to do so, either because their government opposed the very idea of keeping prisoners happy or because they feared that feeding non-Japanese prisoners the same rations as soldiers would produce complaints certain to embarrass Japan. Only after an American delegate to the conference pointedly reminded them that failure to sign the agreement "would place . . . [their] nation in an unfortunate light" did the Japanese representatives to the conference seek and obtain permission to sign it.[15]

The Japanese Diet failed to ratify the 1929 Geneva Convention, but five years later Tokyo hosted a meeting of the International Committee of the Red Cross (ICRC), at which delegates drafted and approved an accord for the protection of enemy civilians in belligerent countries. It urged the Swiss government to summon a formal diplomatic conference that would make the agreement part of international law. The outbreak of fighting, first in China and then in Europe, frustrated this effort.[16]

Concern over the fate of civilians caught in the crossfire of Japan's advancing forces prompted the U.S. State Department, on 18 December 1941, to press Japan to extend to civilian internees the same guarantees of equitable treatment that the 1929 Geneva Convention promised to prisoners of war. A little more than two months later, perhaps in response to ICRC suggestions but more probably out of concern for their own nationals already interned and likely to be "relocated" with masses of Japanese-Americans, Tokyo officials agreed to apply the provisions of the 1929 Geneva Convention to civilian internees.[17] They also acknowledged that the 1934 draft Red Cross rules for treatment of civilian internees should apply to the noncombatants they held.[18]

No one in Washington expected mere words to protect Americans in Japanese custody. Even if Tokyo honored its February 1942 pledge to treat civilian internees according to the standards that applied to prisoners of war, their fare would be poor indeed. Prisoners were supposed to be fed a diet equivalent to that of the Japanese soldier; if what former American residents of Japan reported was correct, that peasant in uniform got pickles, rice, and bits of fish.[19] In particular, food of that sort would certainly not sustain the men and women of "good and best New England, Middle Atlantic, or Southern families" who had gone to East Asia as agents or employees of firms and organizations of "substance . . . and financial weight" but were now prisoners of the Japanese. State Department officials quickly recognized that these peoples' political importance was "out of all proportion" to their numbers. American diplomats knew everything possible must be done to assure their survival and well-being.[20]

Three factors, however, complicated the task of aiding those in Japanese custody. One was structural. Diplomats on both sides of the Pacific who sought to aid their imprisoned or interned compatriots had to deal with many agencies of their own government before they could negotiate with their counterparts. There were many captors and jailers—army and navy, *kempeitai* and FBI agents, border patrol officers and local police—in Japan, the United States, China, and Southeast Asia. As the prisoner count swelled, each government created still more organizations, notably the War Relocation Authority in the United States and Prisoner of War Information and Administration bureaus within the Japanese war ministry, to deal with those in custody.[21] That complicated life for diplomats working in the State Department's Special War Problems Division (SWPD) and the Central Liaison Office (CLO) of the Ministry of Foreign Affairs in Tokyo, who dealt with prisoner and internee matters.[22] Lacking clout within as well as outside their own organizations, they had to struggle to build bureaucratic consensus on each step they proposed to take. That was bound to retard progress in getting relief to those held by the enemy.

Communication problems also slowed things down. With relations severed, diplomats had to rely on intermediaries—at first Spain for Japan and Switzerland for the United States, then the Swiss for both.[23] Messages between Washington and Tokyo had to go by way of Madrid or Bern, where they were accepted for delivery by Spanish or Swiss diplomats to the State Department or foreign ministry. The involvement of the ICRC also complicated matters. It was not just an agency for implementation of what American and Japanese diplomats agreed upon but an independent organization with aid programs of its own. Its communications network was sometimes helpful, sometimes maddeningly slow and imperfect.[24]

But the attitudes of senior government officials posed the most serious obstacle to getting aid to prisoners and internees. Lower-level State Department officials in the SWPD correctly surmised that Tokyo, in determining how to handle American prisoners of war and civilian internees, would carefully watch how Washington treated Japanese nationals, but some members of the Roosevelt cabinet, and the president himself, ignored that link. They failed to realize how deeply the internment of Japanese and Japanese-Americans wounded Japan's pride.[25] They either forgot or ignored the fact that reciprocity smoothes relations between nations, even when they are at war with one another.

The Japanese government was no more consistent than the American in its attitudes toward prisoners and internees. While his diplomats insisted upon reciprocity in negotiations concerning them, Tōjō Hideki, who served concurrently as prime minister and war minister and thus had direct responsibility in this matter, took an extraordinarily harsh attitude toward enemy nationals. Completely insensitive to American concern for those in Japanese custody, he took a month to reply to Washington's first inquiry as to whether Japan would abide by the terms of the 1929 Geneva Convention governing the treatment of prisoners of war. Tōjō interpreted very loosely its provisions regulating work by those in custody. "No work, no food!" was the policy he laid down.[26] When in the summer of 1942 the Red Cross sought permission to deliver quinine to Americans in the Philippines, he refused, saying it would be wrong to treat the defeated any better than Japanese troops

in the islands, who were suffering similar hardships and diseases.[27] The prime
minister's tough line echoed what one of Japan's most eminent international
legal scholars had argued: enemy aliens in this war need not be treated as
well as Russians and Germans in earlier conflicts. They were not guests.[28]

Attitudes of that sort guaranteed the failure of initial American efforts to
get food and medicine to those in Japanese custody. In the spring of 1942, relying upon international legal norms that allowed a neutral ship under International Red Cross auspices and traveling with a safe-conduct to carry relief
supplies to those in enemy custody, Washington tried to have the Swedish
ship *Vasaland* take parcels to American prisoners. Japan's ally, Germany,
blocked her departure from the Baltic.[29] Shortly thereafter, relief supplies
were loaded aboard the *Gripsholm*, a vessel which Washington and Tokyo
agreed would exchange high-ranking diplomats and some other internees at
a Portuguese East African port in July 1942.[30] Because she could not carry
both exchangees and a substantial cargo, the American Red Cross chartered
a second vessel, the *Kanangoora*, to take relief supplies for those held prisoner. Washington then asked Tokyo to let the ship transfer those materials to
a Japanese Red Cross vessel when the exchange of interned officials took
place. The Japanese spurned that proposal, declined to send a counterpart
vessel, and refused "for strategic reasons" to let any American Red Cross
ship cross the Pacific.[31]

Assistant Secretary of State Breckinridge Long, the white-haired Missouri
politician who supervised the SWPD, suspected the proposal to send the
Kanangoora would fail even before it was made.[32] The day after the *Gripsholm*
disgorged her load of exchangees, he called in American Red Cross officials
to help draft a message about getting food and medicine to those who
remained in Japanese custody. Long sent that appeal but regarded it as "a
vain effort, . . . principally 'for the record,'" because he was convinced that
"the Japs will not do it."[33]

Long was right. Prime Minister Tōjō did not want Red Cross minions
snooping around in Japan's new empire in the south under the guise of
delivering relief to enemy nations.[34] But the diplomat was wrong to place all
of the blame for failure on the Japanese; American behavior also contributed
to that result. Washington simply would not give anything to get what it
wanted in negotiations with Tokyo. The Americans balked at a second
exchange of persons, which would have been based on a list of names Japan

Cross packets of vitamin-fortified edibles—and medicines. The goods, eleven-pound packages, could be stockpiled at Vladivostok for later transfer to Japanese authorities, either on the Manchurian border or at some other place of Tokyo and Moscow's choosing. They could then eventually be distributed to needy American and Allied prisoners and internees.[43]

Appealing for help from Moscow was a long shot in January 1943. The Soviet-Japanese Neutrality Pact signed two years earlier was allowing Joseph Stalin to fight a one-front war that was far from over.[44] One of Hitler's armies faced defeat at Stalingrad, but two others were besieging Leningrad (St. Petersburg) and Moscow.[45] Stalin had therefore avoided actions that might provoke Japan; for instance, Moscow had protested, but without threatening the use of force, Japanese searches and seizures of Soviet ships transiting the Sea of Japan. Nine months after Jimmy Doolittle's raiders bombed Tokyo, the Russians still held four of his men.[46]

The Soviets also showed slight concern for prisoners of war. They had not signed the 1929 Geneva Convention. They spurned International Red Cross pleas to respect its provisions in dealing with masses of German POWs captured in the Battle of Stalingrad. Their behavior had prompted the American Red Cross representative in Moscow to remark that "considerations of happiness, health, and even of human lives . . . have never been allowed to interfere with decisions and attitudes thought advisable" by the Soviet government.[47] The discovery, barely ninety days after Washington sent its first tentative inquiry to Moscow, of the corpses of hundreds of Polish Army officers who had been shot and buried in a mass grave in the Katyn Forest—presumably by the Red Army—made the chances for Soviet cooperation on any prisoner of war matter look even less promising.[48]

Despite the long odds on success, Washington hoped that its ambassador in the Soviet Union, William H. Standley, might persuade the Russians to transport and stockpile relief supplies for those held by the Japanese. Standley was a seventy-one-year-old retired admiral, not a professional diplomat. He had no love for the Russians. The admiral/ambassador remembered how they had embarrassed him in 1896 by drinking to excess when he (as a midshipman) had visited Vladivostok on a fleet visit celebrating the coronation of Tsar Nicholas II. As chief of naval operations many years later, he complained that Soviet military and naval attachés were "the most avid seekers after information that I have ever seen[,] . . . more earnest and zealous than

had provided.[35] They also helped Peru cleanse itself
and schemed to seize the last unrepatriated senior J
South America.[36] American actions left Japanese fore
with little incentive to try to win concessions on reli
prime minister and the military. They would not give ur

Thus, as the first year of war drew to a close, Amer
Japanese custody while negotiations to get help to them

As 1943 opened, American diplomats realized that that d
be allowed to continue. Although Long, their supervising a
had sunk into a torpor induced by doubt that Tokyo woul
second exchange of persons, SWPD officials felt they must
show the public that they were doing everything possible to
being of those held by the Japanese.[37] Ordinary America
a great deal about the captives' mistreatment from accoun
Gripsholm returnees late in 1942. None was more striking
than the story of Shanghai newspaper editor John B. Powell.
told it with two photographs in its 7 September 1942 issue: one
Pearl Harbor, showed him standing smiling at a cocktail par
depicted him lying in a hospital bed, a bony leg and toeless
toward the camera. After confiscating his shoes, the Japanese ha
an unheated cell and neglected his frozen feet until gangrene se
they amputated all of his toes.[38] A month later Powell publish
story in the magazine *Nation,* and in November 1942 the *Readers*
it before millions more readers.[39]

Anxious to prevent the recurrence of tragedies like Powell's,
by their inability to resolve differences with the War Departmer
Japanese over passenger lists for a second exchange ship, and eager t
strate their own efficacy, SWPD officials turned in desperation to tl
Union for help.[40] They asked Moscow if it would object in principle
dling small quantities of relief supplies destined for American and
prisoners and civilian internees held by the Japanese.[41] The Russian
with America and Britain in the fight against Germany and Italy but
in the war against Japan, seemed logical candidates to play the role of
mediary.[42] State Department officials thought that Soviet cargo ships s
from the American West Coast could be loaded with "food from hom

the Japanese." Only a strong sense of duty had prompted the admiral to accept Roosevelt's offer to become ambassador to the Soviet Union.[49]

His first year there had not gone well. Standley had to shuttle back and forth between Moscow and Kuibyshev (Samara) six hundred miles to the east, on the Volga, because the Russians had moved their Commissariat of Foreign Affairs there when the Germans besieged Moscow.[50] His official residence in the capital was cold and dilapidated; his Kuibyshev home was little more than a cottage. The Russians proved difficult to deal with on even the most petty issues, and their restrictions on his movement made the admiral feel like a prisoner. By early 1943 Standley was bored and chagrined. He had expected to exhaust himself in the service of his country, but President Roosevelt often bypassed him on issues of major significance for the prosecution of the war and the sustenance of the Anglo-Soviet-American coalition. That left the admiral/ambassador with little to do but play gin rummy, billiards, and cribbage with his staff; watch movies and listen to war news on the radio; and write long letters to his wife half a world away in San Diego, California.[51]

Admiral Standley probably welcomed Washington's February 1943 orders to raise with the Russians the question of transporting and stockpiling relief supplies for POWs.[52] At last he had something important to do. His first encounter, however, with the vice-commissar of foreign affairs, Andrei Vyshinski, was hardly encouraging. Vyshinski sidestepped the issue by suggesting that the International Red Cross might be a better intermediary for the purpose than his government.[53] Although Standley pressed for "an expeditious reply" to his request for help, two weeks later nothing had happened. Vyshinski's deputy claimed ignorance of the matter.[54]

When the admiral/ambassador broached the subject a month later in Moscow with Foreign Minister Vyacheslav Molotov, the man who had signed the Nazi-Soviet Non-Aggression Pact of August 1939 and the Soviet-Japanese Neutrality Treaty in April 1941 simply said he "wasn't acquainted" with it.[55] Standley fared no better even in April 1943, when the Japanese hinted that they might consider a plan to send materials for American prisoners and internees via the Soviet Union. Molotov put Standley off again, saying the Commissariat of Foreign Trade would have to consider the matter. He hinted at his reluctance by suggesting relief supplies might better be sent across the Atlantic to Murmansk or Archangel for rail shipment to the Soviet-Manchurian border.[56]

President Franklin D. Roosevelt greets his ambassador, Adm. William H. Standley, while the chief of naval operations, Adm. Ernest J. King, looks on. *Hearst Collection, Los Angeles Examiner photographs, Regional History Center, University of Southern California*

Soviet evasiveness prompted Standley's superiors in Washington to back away from anything that smacked of immediate action. They ordered him to try simply to get Moscow's agreement "in principle" to cooperate in the relief effort.[57] The Soviets agreed to that, provided that Washington and Tokyo reached "a suitable understanding."[58] That was hardly likely when America and Japan were mired in disagreement over who might be exchanged on a second *Gripsholm* voyage.

After three more attempts failed to achieve Soviet cooperation, State Department officials tried to bluff Moscow into it.[59] That proved counter-productive. On 5 August 1943 Standley received a formal diplomatic note from the Commissariat of Foreign Affairs saying that the question of Moscow's approaching Tokyo about transporting and stockpiling relief shipments for POWs "should be considered closed."[60]

Although he had already decided to resign, neither Standley nor his superiors were prepared to accept that answer. Pleading, polite inquiries, and bluff having failed, State Department officials, pressured by the Pentagon to do more, decided to try threats.[61] Admiral Standley was told that he might, in his farewell call on Stalin, link continuation of Lend-Lease aid to the Soviet Union with Russian cooperation in getting food and medicine to Americans in Japanese hands. The ambassador did so gladly. He told Stalin that the American people could not understand why Soviet ships could carry aid from America for Russians but not return the favor by transporting relief parcels to be stockpiled in the Soviet Far East. "Increasing public pressure [from] relatives and friends" of those held by the Japanese, Standley told Stalin, was becoming "politically embarrassing" to the Roosevelt administration. There was a real possibility that the American people would criticize the Soviet Union for "not cooperating" in the effort to get relief to the prisoners. Moscow, he suggested, need not do so openly; the cargoes of vessels carrying such aid could be kept secret from the Japanese until the Red Cross relief parcels had been off-loaded at Vladivostok.[62]

A few days later the State Department made Standley's implicit threat explicit. Moscow was told that the administration felt it "vitally necessary" to demonstrate that "all feasible arrangements, however preliminary," were being made to get help to those in Japanese custody as soon as possible. Consequently, the Soviet Union would be required to sign an agreement, in conjunction with its endorsement of the third Lend-Lease protocol, to load

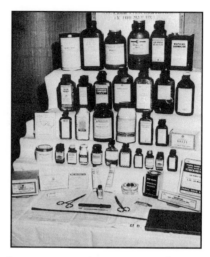

The Red Cross medical relief packets that the *Awa maru* took to prisoners of war.
Author's photograph, from Harry N. Pence collection, University of California San Diego

fifteen hundred tons of Red Cross relief supplies aboard Russian ships departing the American West Coast for Siberia—no Soviet cooperation, no American aid. The Russians would not be held responsible for spoilage or deterioration of these materials while they awaited transshipment to the Japanese for delivery to American and Allied prisoners. Washington simply wanted to get the goods moving—immediately—to Vladivostok.[63]

Stalin was no student of the influence of public opinion on American foreign policy, but he cannot have mistaken Washington's message. Barely two weeks after his final meeting with Standley, the dictator signaled his willingness to cooperate. On 26 August 1943 the head of the Soviet Purchasing Mission in Washington told the chief of the War Department's International Aid Division that the Russians were ready to help deliver relief supplies to Americans in Japanese custody. He asked when and in what volume the Red Cross parcels could be delivered to Portland, Oregon, for shipment across the Pacific on Soviet merchant vessels.[64] A few days later Foreign Minister Molotov made Moscow's willingness to cooperate official. His government would sign a single agreement for American provision of more Lend-Lease aid and Soviet carriage and stockpiling of Red Cross parcels—even though, as he added in a final fillip to Admiral Standley, he really saw no connection between the two actions.[65]

That remark strengthened the departing ambassador's negative feelings about the Russians and also his determination to get home as quickly as possible. Telling his wife "the party is over," he left the Soviet Union in September 1943 doubting that his diplomatic mission had been a success.[66] But the admiral/ambassador could take pride in what he had done to help those held by the Japanese. Within a few days of his return to Washington, two Soviet ships loaded with Lend-Lease goods and Red Cross relief parcels sailed from Portland, Oregon, bound for Vladivostok. A week later a third vessel departed, and ten days after that yet another. At the end of December 1943, when a fifth Soviet ship left Portland, American Red Cross officials estimated that nearly twenty-five hundred tons of relief supplies were on their way to those who so desperately needed them.[67]

That was a thousand tons more than the Soviets had agreed to accept. Moscow now summarily informed Washington that no more relief parcels could be accommodated until the Japanese agreed to transship them.[68] When that would be, no one at the end of 1943 knew. For while Washington had cajoled and threatened Moscow into cooperation, American officials as yet had no idea of how they might persuade Tokyo to pick up and deliver what was now on Soviet soil to those held prisoner. Diplomacy among allies at war, especially when one needs aid from the other to continue the fight, is much simpler than that between enemies.

It took a long time for the cooperation that Washington had wrung out of Moscow to bear fruit. Thirteen months passed before the State Department announced that the Japanese had agreed to pick up relief supplies meant for prisoners and internees in their custody. Nearly two months more slipped away before a small Japanese ship appeared in Soviet waters to take aboard those supplies.[69] What caused that delay? And by what alchemy did diplomats find a way to end it?

More than forty years later, the son of an American POW who died in captivity blamed Japanese pride: the Japanese government would not allow improvements in prisoners' diets when ordinary citizens' living standards were plummeting. When an agreement was finally reached in October 1944, State Department officials claimed that their restraint in criticizing Japan's mistreatment of prisoners had elicited Tokyo's cooperation in getting succor to Americans in Japanese custody.[70] Neither of those explanations was correct, and both were too simple. Each presumed that action by one of the parties had produced success, when in fact a combination of changes—in American negotiating strategy, in Soviet behavior, and in Japan's military and political circumstances—brought about the agreement that would lead to the voyage of the *Awa maru*.

At the beginning of 1944 the Roosevelt administration made a disastrous shift in its POW public-information policy and negotiating strategy. Unable to keep secret any longer the details of what had befallen American captives of the Japanese, Washington tried to shame Tokyo into cooperating in their relief. The State Department fired off an eighteen-page message to the Japanese foreign ministry that hinted, for the first time, that the United States and its allies would hold Japan responsible after the war for any mistreatment of their nationals in Japanese custody.[71] That threat was followed by dramatic disclosures about the sufferings of those captured in the Philippines and the harrowing adventures of a few who escaped their Japanese jailers. The White House was acting to preempt leakage of these grisly facts to the press, but their release prompted congressional inquiries as to why the administration had kept them secret for so long.[72] President Roosevelt barely got off the hook by saying that silence had been the price paid to get Red Cross relief parcels delivered to prisoners via the *Gripsholm* exchanges. He also angrily repeated Secretary of State Cordell Hull's pledge that Japanese who mistreated American prisoners would eventually be brought to justice.[73]

Then the administration stoked the fires of public fury it had ignited. A War Department poster that depicted "the Japan way"—the "cold-blooded murder" of captured Doolittle Raid airmen—was distributed all over the nation. Former ambassador Joseph C. Grew, whose long years of residence in Tokyo gave him a reputation for "understanding" the Japanese, expressed "fiery rage" at the "Tokyo war lords'" brutality. He reminded them of their promise to respect the terms of the 1929 Geneva Convention. Breckinridge Long told House investigators that thousands of American nationals held by the Japanese faced death from malnutrition. That prompted the relatives of POWs to announce plans for a march on Washington.[74]

None of these charges of mistreatment and expressions of outrage had the desired effect on Japan. Tokyo had already stiffened its position on prisoners. Modified foreign currency exchange procedures had reduced internees' ability to buy supplies on local markets.[75] The Foreign Ministry had refused to discuss delivering relief packages until Washington responded to its own protests of alleged American attacks on hospital ships.[76] Now Tokyo made it clear that Japan was not going to be coerced into cooperation. *Dōmei*, the official Japanese news agency, labeled stories of prisoner mistreatment "vicious propaganda."[77] The Foreign Ministry sent the State Department a sixty-eight-page refutation of those charges that also enumerated all the wrongs Americans had done to interned Japanese and Japanese-Americans.[78] Claiming they had a "complete plan" for picking up and delivering relief parcels to American and Allied prisoners and internees, Tokyo officials blamed Washington for the delay in its implementation.[79]

Charges hurled back and forth across the Pacific produced deadlock once more. How was it to be broken? Some Americans called for drastic action. Congressional Democrats pressed the president and his subordinates.[80] A captured airman's wife who became vice president of a national POW families association begged President Roosevelt to use his fabled powers of persuasion to get Stalin to intercede with the Japanese on behalf of "those starving, suffering wrecks, our own American boys."[81] Secretary of State Hull put an even more extreme suggestion before the president: he should cut the Gordian knot by freeing Japanese and Japanese-American internees. That would deprive Tokyo of its pretext for refusing to negotiate further exchanges of nationals and the delivery of relief supplies to Americans held prisoner.[82] Hull's proposal was not sheer fantasy. Some Japanese had already left the camps for college or work;[83] the assistant secretary of war, for his part, saw no real security need to keep Japanese-Americans away from the West Coast any longer. Roosevelt's own attorney general was inclined to think that the Japanese-Americans who filed suit challenging the legality of their internment would win. The president, however, was not about to alter internment policies, even though his diplomats thought they constituted a major obstacle to agreement on exchanging or getting help to those held prisoner. In an election year, with passions against the Japanese running high, Roosevelt was just not going to "do anything sudden or drastic."[84]

The president's caution forced State Department officials to look for other ways to break the deadlock. Externally, they turned once again to the Russians for help. Early in April 1944 they prevailed upon Moscow to tell Tokyo that the Soviet Union hoped Japan would give favorable consideration to various American proposals for a third exchange of persons and delivery of relief supplies.[85] Internally, SWPD officials tried to get their superiors to stop trying to "shame" Japan into cooperation by publicizing atrocities committed against POWs. Although the White House initially refused their request, the Pentagon agreed that further release of such horror stories would have a "most unfortunate" influence on efforts to get relief to those in Japanese custody.[86]

That created a more receptive climate for Tokyo's 10 May 1944 proposal. Foreign Minister Shigemitsu Mamoru indicated that Japan would agree to a monthly exchange of mail and relief supplies at Vladivostok—but the Soviet Union, as well as America and Japan, would have to guarantee safe passage for the ships used in that transaction. Moreover, the country sending relief would have to pay all of the costs involved; further, before one parcel left the dock at Vladivostok, Washington would have to promise to deliver "such relief supplies as Japan may send to its subjects interned in the United States."[87] Tokyo, as always, would not give unless it got.

Foreign Minister Shigemitsu apparently wanted this proposal to succeed, for he told Washington, through the Swiss, that he hoped no new anti-Japanese publicity campaign would "thwart" his efforts to get aid to the prisoners.[88] SWPD officials, however, read it as an invitation to press the Soviets for more help in forging an agreement. The diplomats fired off messages to Moscow, sent notes to the Soviet embassy, and even asked the British to urge the Russians to cooperate.[89]

The Soviets, however, remained skeptical and cautious. Vyshinsky told the Japan expert on the staff of the American embassy in Moscow that Tokyo had proposed Vladivostok, a closed military port whose harbor had been mined, knowing full well that the Soviet Union could not agree to its use. When Washington pressed Moscow to consider an alternative port, Vyshinski was at first noncommittal, then hinted that transfer of the goods would be better done at some point on the Soviet-Manchurian border. Eventually, he conceded that "special consideration" might be given for a one-time-only exchange at Nakhodka.[90]

It was the end of May 1944, however, before Ambassador Andrei Gromyko told Secretary of State Hull that Moscow had offered Tokyo the use of that tiny port, which lay some sixty miles by air, and nearly a hundred by rail, south and east of Vladivostok. Any future transfers of mail and relief supplies would have to take place in some harbor on the remote Kamchatka

Peninsula, as far to the north and distant from Vladivostok as Boston is from New Orleans.[91] Despite that proviso, Hull's subordinates liked Moscow's "reasonable counter-offer" and urged its publication so that the Japanese would "find it awkward" to refuse. When Stalin proved reluctant to do so, American diplomats seized the initiative. On D-Day, 6 June 1944, as American and Allied troops were wading ashore at Normandy, Washington announced its acceptance of Tokyo's proposal, with the proviso that Nakhodka, rather than Vladivostok, would be the point of transfer for mail, food, and medicines destined for those in Japanese custody.[92]

That news confronted Tokyo with a hard choice. Should Japan proceed along the lines Washington and Moscow were suggesting? Or would it be preferable to stand firm on principle and refuse to pick up relief supplies destined for enemy nationals until the Americans stopped issuing threats, publicizing atrocity charges, and treating the Japanese they held in bafflingly obnoxious ways?[93] Tokyo officials apparently found it difficult to decide what to do, for they took nearly four months to craft a tentative, conditional proposal to pick up and deliver relief supplies to American and Allied prisoners and internees.

Their reasons for finally agreeing were complex and remain less than completely clear. Diplomats cloaked their motives by saying that the decision was taken "from a long range point of view."[94] Some of them may have concluded that since comprehensive settlement of prisoner and internee problems was impossible, step-by-step progress toward that goal was the only realistic course of action. Others, sensing the depth of American anger over Japan's treatment of prisoners and internees, may have favored picking up and delivering the relief supplies as a way of lessening its backlash when the war ended.

Still other diplomats may have seen the relief agreement as a precautionary measure needed to protect the Japanese held by Americans. While they debated what to do, the fighting was turning decidedly against Japan. More and more prisoners, combatants and civilians alike, fell into enemy hands. In Burma, 40 percent of the troops fighting the British at Imphal surrendered.[95] Gen. Douglas MacArthur took increasing numbers of prisoners as he advanced westward in New Guinea;[96] other American forces captured thirty-five thousand Japanese civilians, including senior officials, when they conquered Guam and the northern Marianas.[97] Helping the Americans get relief to those in Japanese custody, Tokyo diplomats may have reasoned, might make them willing to let assistance reach the Japanese they held themselves.

Japanese military and naval men had their own reasons in the summer and early fall of 1944 for accepting an agreement to pick up and deliver relief supplies to enemy prisoners and internees. Senior-staff-level thinking about POWs had begun to change even before the fall of Saipan caused Tōjō, the original advocate of harsh treatment for enemy persons, to resign as prime minister and war minister.[98] Several months before he left office, one of his more imaginative subordinates, the vice-director of the Army's Prisoner of War Bureau, proposed shipping POWs from Southeast Asia to the Japanese home islands.[99] If, as senior army and navy officials continued to hope in the early summer of 1944, the war was to end with Japanese victory in a decisive battle that forced the enemy to the negotiating table, these men might be valuable—live hostages were worth more than dead men's bones as bargaining chips.[100] That line of thinking figured in the decision to begin shipping POWs to Japan in June 1944.[101] It may also have strengthened the argument for agreeing to send a ship to pick up relief supplies for them.

Concern for narrow military advantage, however, probably clinched the case. While the debate over what to do continued in Tokyo, American submarines were having an increasingly deadly effect. On 29 June 1944, the USS *Sturgeon* (SS 187) sank a transport carrying the 44th Independent Mixed Brigade to Okinawa; fifty-six hundred troops died. A month later, the *Bowfin* (SS 287) torpedoed a freighter carrying evacuees from that island; fifteen hundred women and children perished.[102] By the time the debate ended, American submariners' sinkings of Japanese merchantmen had climbed to an all-time high; also, in October 1944, losses to Yankee surface ships and aircraft reached their second-highest point in the war.[103] If picking up several hundred tons of relief supplies from a Soviet port for transfer to Japan and eventual delivery to prisoners and internees would purchase safe passage for a vessel or vessels laden with materials needed to support Japan's war effort, then an agreement might be worthwhile.

But would a safe-passage agreement prove effective? Skeptics in Tokyo had reason to doubt that it would. Americans, as they saw them, were not particularly law abiding or careful foes. Their attacks on Japanese hospital ships had already drawn protests from Tokyo;[104] they had torpedoed ships carrying their own POWs;[105] and in July 1944, American submarines had broken into the Sea of Okhotsk and attacked indiscriminately, sinking a neutral Soviet vessel as well as a Japanese transport.[106] Skeptics may well have doubted that Americans would honor a safe-passage agreement, even if it was meant to protect a ship carrying food and medicine to their fellow countrymen. The doubters may also have wondered if enemy commanders had sufficient control over their subordinates to prevent an attack, whether deliberate or accidental, on the protected vessel.

The advocates of a safe-passage agreement appear to have overcome the skeptics' objections in two ways. First, Japan demanded an ironclad guarantee of safe passage in terms that were without precedent in international law: Japan could use the vessel carrying relief supplies as it saw fit, loading whomever and whatever it wanted; the United States had to promise to keep its ships and submarines away from the vessel; Americans could not board and search the ship, even if they suspected that her holds carried contraband war materials.[107] The ship would thus be free from the threat of enemy attack and better able to serve Japan's own purposes.

Second, Tokyo officials proposed a series of relief voyages rather than a single journey. One large ship could have gone to Nakhodka, taken on the more than two thousand tons of food and medicines there, and then carried them to needy prisoners in Japan, China, and Southeast Asia. At this point, Tokyo offered simply to dispatch a vessel to the Soviet port, load it with the relief packets stockpiled there, and carry them back to Japan.[108] Whether or not additional ships took those goods to China and beyond would depend upon the enemy's behavior. If the first ship crossed the Sea of Japan and returned home safely, then a second and perhaps a third might be allowed to hazard a voyage through more distant, submarine-infested waters. What Japanese diplomats proposed was, in today's diplomatic parlance, the first of a series of "confidence-building" measures.

This procedure had an additional advantage that may have helped overcome military and naval skepticism: it gave Japan the option of using vessels with carrying capacities far greater than was needed for the relief supplies. That meant, in effect, that a small amount of enemy cargo bought safe passage for an ever-increasing volume of Japanese goods. Relief to the prisoners could thus be transformed into resupply for Japanese forces in China and the southern reaches of the empire. The balance of advantage, heavily weighted in Japan's favor, thus outweighed the dangers inherent in risking increasingly scarce merchant marine vessels to carry relief supplies to enemy personnel.

Tokyo officials struggled from June to October 1944 to hammer out consensus on this cautious but unequal counterproposal. Their Washington counterparts accepted it in seventy-two hours. American officials did so because they felt they had no other choice. When they first unscrambled Tokyo's proposal, they may have been momentarily outraged.[109] The Japanese were pressing for military advantage even when engaged in a supposedly humanitarian act. Tokyo was showing no respect for the normal provisions of international law governing guarantees of safe passage. Finally, Japan's promise of delivery of relief supplies to starving American prisoners and internees was implicit, not explicit.

But objections of that sort, as members of the Interdepartmental Prisoner of War Board knew, could not be allowed to block acceptance of the Japanese proposal.[110] Their primary concern was to save American lives. They knew prisoners and internees were struggling to survive in desperate circumstances. They reasoned that the value of contraband that the Japanese might secret aboard a relief vessel paled in comparison to the lives that might be lost by further delay in receiving food and medicine. State, War, and Navy Department officials also wanted to silence critics furious at the Japanese for their mistreatment of prisoners and only slightly less angry at these agencies for not doing more to help POWs and internees.[111] Getting the relief packages moving toward their intended recipients would at least slake those critics' thirst for action. Thus, having hinted that a breakthrough in the negotiations was at hand, a delighted State Department spokesman announced on 24 October 1944 that Tokyo had agreed to dispatch a ship across the Sea of Japan, from Niigata to Nakhodka, to pick up relief supplies destined for American and Allied prisoners and internees.[112]

What had finally produced that accord? American circumspection had something to do with it. State Department officials certainly claimed that it had; they told President Roosevelt, through Adm. William D. Leahy, his naval aide, that the agreement was due "in some measure" to the cessation since May 1944 of official releases about Japanese atrocities against POWs.[113] They also thought reciprocity had something to do with their success in fashioning an accord; by urging the Japanese to include in the ship's cargo relief supplies for Japanese held by the United States and its allies, Washington had signaled its acceptance of that principle, so vital to Tokyo.[114] Deep in their hearts, one suspects, Americans who fashioned the agreement that would eventually send the *Awa maru* on her fateful voyage recognized a bitter truth: though they had pressured the Soviet Union into cooperating in the relief endeavor, they had had to yield to the extraordinary Japanese terms to start the flow of relief supplies. Concession had proven the key to obtaining Japan's agreement to pick up and (they hoped) deliver food and medicine to the POWs and internees who so desperately needed both.

That was true, tactically speaking. But in broader perspective, Japan's agreement to begin delivering relief supplies to prisoners appears to have grown out of its worsening circumstances. The tide of war turned against Japan between May and October 1944, while its diplomats and military men were struggling to decide what to do. It pushed Tōjō Hideki from power. It sent more and more men to enemy prison camps. Tokyo could not, as Foreign Minister Shigemitsu made clear, remain indifferent to their welfare. The new circumstances made live POWs of increasing value to Japan—no longer as pawns in peace negotiations that would follow a great Japanese victory, but as hedges against complete defeat. Conserving the lives of enemy nationals thus became something that would serve Japan's national interest no less than the desires of its enemies. In the final analysis, however, the needs of war dictated Japan's tentative cooperation in getting relief to prisoners and internees. Despite what diplomats or clever uniformed men may have thought about the long-term benefits of working with the Americans on relief matters, what Tokyo most needed in the autumn of 1944 was safe passage for whoever or whatever would strengthen Japan's chances for success in battle. In the end, then, it was the desire to get fighting men and combat matériel safely across the seas of the Western Pacific that brought Tokyo to agreement with Washington on moving food and medicine toward prisoners and internees.

Thus, as 1944 neared its end, those who fashioned the relief-to-prisoners accord, Japanese and Americans alike, faced a single, daunting question: Could that agreement be made to work?

3

Mission of Mercy

THE MEN WHO had shaped the relief-to-the-prisoners agreement hoped the answer to that question was yes, but they understood how fragile the accord was. What they had labored so long to create might be destroyed in an instant. Accidental action by some American in uniform might violate the safe-passage agreement and sink a ship carrying relief supplies to prisoners and internees. Anger stirred by some battlefield event, by the death or condition of POWs, or by clashes between Japanese internees and their captors might prompt either Washington or Tokyo to terminate the agreement. Also, abuse might intervene; Japanese officials anxious to make the accord work to the empire's advantage might so corrupt its original purpose as to make it null and void in American eyes. That could lead to an attack on the vessel carrying relief supplies. Between November 1944 and March 1945, diplomats on both sides of the Pacific labored to remove these threats to the October accord. They worked with military and naval men to reduce the likelihood of accidental destruction of the accord and the vessels implementing it. They tried to protect the agreement from new fires of hatred stoked by American bombing of Tokyo and by fresh disclosures about the horrors American and Allied prisoners had suffered at Japanese hands. They succeeded in getting the *Awa maru* under way on her mission of mercy to those held captive in China and Southeast Asia.

As they watched, they saw her mission transformed. Japanese military men—and some diplomats—extracted a price for implementing the extraordinary agreement of October 1944. They insisted that the *Awa maru* serve Japan's military and diplomatic purposes even as she carried out a diplomatically defined humanitarian mission. As they altered the ship, her course, and her schedule to meet those needs, Tokyo officials posed a difficult question to their Washington counterparts: Did Japan's use of the *Awa maru* for its own purposes constitute an abuse of the safe-passage agreement so great as to warrant her destruction?

That question had not yet occurred to anyone on either side of the Pacific in the autumn of 1944. Japanese and American officials concentrated then on trying to make work the agreement it had taken so long to fashion. On 21 October Tokyo informed Washington of the proposed route and schedule for the first ship to be used in implementing the relief accord, the *Hakusan maru*. The 4,300-ton Japan Sea Steamship Company vessel, as the solid line on the map shows, would depart from Niigata and proceed to Nakhodka by way of Najin in northeastern Korea. At Nakhodka the ship would pick up the relief materials previously shipped to, and stockpiled by, the Soviets. After stopping in Najin again on her homeward-bound voyage, she would call at Moji before completing her mission at Ōsaka.[1] Two days later, the U.S. Navy having assented to that schedule, SWPD diplomat Eldred Kuppinger proposed that Washington broadcast it by short-wave radio, to reassure Tokyo.[2] When, later, the Japanese altered the ship's schedule, their message to Washington arrived in time for Kuppinger to get confirmation from the Navy Department that the revised track and times had been broadcast to the fleet.[3]

The Russians also helped American officials monitor the *Hakusan maru*'s progress. Three days after Washington received the first change to her schedule, the Soviet Ministry of Foreign Affairs telephoned the American embassy in Moscow to report that the ship had departed Nakhodka four days ahead of that revised schedule; a full report from the American consul general in Vladivostok confirmed it.[4] But long before the details were known, the

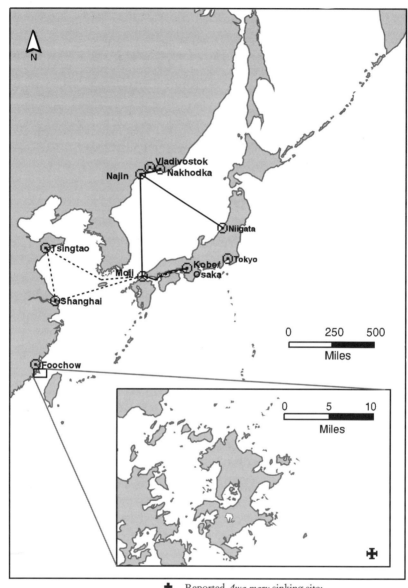

+ Reported *Awa maru* sinking site:
latitude 25 degrees 25'1" north,
longitude 120 degrees 07'1" east

Voyages of the *Hakusan maru* (solid line) and the *Hoshi maru* (broken line).

Americans had been told of the *Hakusan maru*'s movements, first by the Bureau of Information spokesman in Tokyo, Iguchi Sadao, then by Soviet foreign ministry officials in Moscow.[5]

American officials who got these reports of her journey may well have become angry and suspicious as they read them. The Japanese clearly were using the *Hakusan maru* as much or more for their own purposes as for carrying relief supplies. Ninety-one passengers rode her across the Sea of Japan. She carried five bags of mail, seventy-three cases of books, and thirty-two tons of Japanese tea to Nakhodka for transshipment to Japanese interned in Australia, Britain, and the United States.[6] She spent only thirty-six hours in Nakhodka, and her captain grumbled about having to take so many tons of relief supplies aboard there.[7] His ship had stopped for three days at Najin on the outward voyage, however, whereas he tarried less than a day at that northern Korean port on the return trip, off-loading a mere hundred tons of relief supplies for internees held in Korea.[8] The *Hakusan maru* also failed to follow the revised schedule that Tokyo had warned Washington to respect. She did not reach Kobe until 11 November, a day after Iguchi Sadao had said she would.[9] Had she taken some particularly valuable cargo to Korea? Had she brought back something needed to fuel munitions factories in western Japan? American officials could only guess at answers to such questions.

Despite their doubts, diplomats on both sides of the Pacific refused to let discrepancies between what Tokyo said the *Hakusan maru* would do and what she did disrupt the relief-to-prisoners accord. Ten days after her voyage ended, the SWPD official responsible for relief matters urged his superiors to commend Japan for its cooperation, so as to elicit more good behavior in the future.[10] On the same day (22 November, Japan time) a Japanese foreign ministry official handed Swiss Minister Camille Gorge a message for Washington that proclaimed the first relief ship's voyage a success and announced that two other ships would be used to deliver what she had picked up to prisoners in China and Southeast Asia. The ICRC delegate in Japan had watched as stevedores off-loaded nineteen hundred tons of relief supplies at Kobe. Eight hundred tons of those materials were already on their way to those held in the Japanese home islands. Tokyo hoped to be able to get the remainder to prisoners and internees in China and Southeast Asia before Christmas.

The Japanese insisted, however, that the two ships to be used for that purpose be given the same protection that the *Hakusan maru* had enjoyed. Washington must promise that they would be free from "any attack, visit, or any interference whatever" by American or Allied forces.[11] Delighted by Tokyo's indication that the relief agreement was working, Washington readily assented to those conditions. SWPD officials were now so confident that the arrangement would work that they began pressuring Moscow to allow further transshipments of relief supplies at Soviet ports. They also reassured Tokyo that the *Hakusan maru*'s cargo of goods meant for Japanese internees had arrived safely in San Francisco and would soon be delivered to its consignees.[12]

The *Hakusan maru*'s apparent success set the stage for the voyage of the *Hoshi maru*. Two days before Christmas 1944, Tokyo announced that this small vessel, only two-thirds the size of the first relief ship, would take about 275 tons of food and medicines from Japan to prisoners and internees in China. She would go, as the broken line on the map indicates, from Kobe to Shanghai and Tsingtao by way of Moji, departing from that harbor on the southern (Kyūshū) side of the Shimonoseki Strait in western Japan a week after the new year—1945—began. Her voyage would end at Moji on 28 January.[13]

Once again, officials on both sides of the Pacific were nervous about the voyage of a relief vessel. Tokyo planned for the ship to creep across the East China Sea, hoping her slow movement would identify her in the eyes of American submarine captains as a specially protected vessel. They warned port officials in China to pay "strict attention" so that nothing meant for prisoners and internees would be pilfered.[14] In Washington, SWPD officials interrupted the New Year's holiday to get Navy Department approval for transmission to Tokyo of an acknowledgment of the *Hoshi maru*'s projected course and schedule. Because she would be traversing waters frequented by American submarines, they also warned Tokyo that the ship must maintain "strict adherence" to that track; there could be "no deviation" from it, except for reasons beyond the *Hoshi maru*'s master's control—which, if they occurred, must be immediately reported to Washington.[15]

Japanese officials did just that, both to prevent an attack on the ship and to facilitate her use for their own purposes. The *Hoshi maru* left Kobe laden with fifteen tons of gold bullion destined for the Yokohama Specie Bank branch in Shanghai. Her departure from Moji was delayed by a day to allow her to take aboard 7½ billion Chinese yuan in central bank reserve notes as well. The gold and notes were desperately needed to prop up the faltering paper currency that Japan used in occupied China.[16] Tokyo informed Washington of this delay and told the captain of the *Hoshi maru* that it was "absolutely necessary" to stick to this new schedule so as to ensure the safety of his ship.[17]

Nevertheless, he drove her across the submarine-infested East China Sea faster than planned, arriving in Shanghai a day early. Worried Japanese diplomats asked that he be given "stringent instructions" to keep the *Hoshi maru* on her announced course and schedule for the remainder of her voyage.[18] Despite that warning, he did not do so; the *Hoshi maru* left Shanghai a day earlier than the Americans had been told she would.[19] She arrived at Tsingtao without relief supplies for prisoners held elsewhere in north China and took aboard contraband goods.[20] Washington learned from intercepted and decrypted messages that on the return voyage to Japan her holds would be full of coal and pig iron, commodities the army considered more vital than the aluminous shale the navy wanted. And the *Hoshi maru* ended her voyage at Kobe rather than Moji, in order to deliver looted whiskey and opium destined for senior officials of the Ministry of Greater East Asia Affairs.[21]

The ship's departures from her announced course and schedule worried Japanese officials; nonetheless, the Americans did not take advantage of them to attack and destroy the *Hoshi maru*. Nor did Japanese politicians, angered by the first B-29 bombing raids on Tokyo, demand termination of the relief agreement in retaliation.[22] Emboldened by potential critics' quiescence and encouraged by the *Hoshi maru*'s safe return, Japanese officials on 1 February 1945 announced that a third relief vessel, the *Awa maru*, would take the remaining relief packages to American and Allied prisoners in Hong Kong, Indochina, and the former Dutch East Indies. Just as they had for the *Hakusan maru* and the *Hoshi maru*, they demanded that Washington reaffirm its pledge not to subject the ship to "any attack[,] visit[,] or any interference whatsoever" on either her outward- or homeward-bound voyages.[23]

That third request for confirmation of the safe-passage guarantee reached Washington at a time when anger was threatening to destroy the arrangement. New and alarming information about Americans held prisoner by the Japanese had ignited it. On the day the *Hoshi maru* left Moji for Shanghai,

General MacArthur's Sixth Army waded ashore at Lingayen Gulf—the exact spot from which Japanese forces had begun their conquest of Luzon—and began rushing south toward Manila.[24] By the time the ship returned to Kobe, American troops had liberated more than five thousand "Bataan death march" survivors from Japanese prison camps. News photographs and stories of these starving men and of emaciated civilian internees freed from Manila's University of Santo Tomas camp enraged the American public.[25]

Forward-looking SWPD diplomats, anticipating such an outburst when more became known about Japanese maltreatment of Americans in their custody, had tried, with indifferent success, to forestall it. They sought complete control over the official release of new information about POWs but got only grudging agreement from the Pentagon to coordinate its disclosure.[26] They failed utterly to keep the British government from revealing that fifteen thousand Allied prisoners had died while building a railroad from Thailand to Burma.[27] Although they insisted that getting relief to prisoners should take priority over condemning their captors' misdeeds, their new superior, Secretary of State Edward Stettinius, told President Roosevelt and his cabinet colleagues that publicizing Japanese atrocities from time to time was "probably a good thing."[28]

Fortunately for the advocates of the relief-to-prisoners accord, the president and his secretary of state were away—at Yalta, trying to persuade Stalin to enter the war against Japan—when these stories of POW maltreatment began to appear.[29] The acting secretary of state, Joseph C. Grew, a returned internee who had previously fanned the administration's public relations campaign against Japanese atrocities, now realized that getting help to those still held by the enemy must be America's first priority. He sought to use "good" news from Tokyo—the offer to send the *Awa maru* southward—to counteract the "bad" news from Southeast Asia that might otherwise have destroyed the relief accord. On 7 February 1945 Grew announced that a ship laden with food and medicine for prisoners and internees in Taiwan, Hong Kong, and Southeast Asia would depart Japan in ten days' time.[30] That bit of good news helped dampen the flames of public anger that liberated prisoners' tales of maltreatment had ignited.

Japanese officials paid little attention to those that continued to burn. They did not respond to enemy anger over their treatment of prisoners and

internees by canceling the voyage of the *Awa maru*. By February 1945, canceling the trip in retaliation for what was being said about Japan abroad would
have been a luxury that could no longer be afforded. For, Tokyo officials—
diplomats and military men alike—realized that the ship's voyage could be
made to serve Japan's interests even more than the needs of enemy prisoners
and internees. Army Transport Command officers had chosen the *Awa maru*
to complete this third phase of the relief agreement because she was one of
the few remaining large, fast, and reliable vessels that could serve their needs
as well as those of diplomats and the enemy. By February 1945 American
submarines had decimated Japan's merchant marine. The Rising Sun ensign
had flown over six million tons of merchant shipping when Pearl Harbor was
attacked, and over the next four years four million tons more were added.
But by early 1945 the U.S. Navy was well on its way to sinking more than
nine out of those ten million tons of Japanese merchant shipping.[31] The *Awa
maru* had survived that holocaust.

The ship was big. A little more than 508 feet long and 41 feet wide, she
displaced 11,249 tons.[32] Her holds could carry far more than the approximately eight hundred tons of relief supplies for prisoners warehoused in
Kobe.[33] She was fast too. Her 14,000 hp Mitsubishi diesel engine could push
her through the water at speeds of up to seventeen knots.[34]

The *Awa maru* was also a creature of war, designed to carry out its tasks.
The last passenger-cargo ship to be built during the war with private capital,
she had been laid down by her owner, Nippon Yūsen Kaisha (NYK), at the
Mitsubishi Heavy Industries Shipyard in Nagasaki. Shōda Jūyaku, a scion
of one of the founding families of the Mitsubishi *zaibatsu* (large financial
combine) had presided over her launching on 24 August 1942.[35] He named
her for Awa Province, the mountainous section of Shikoku bordering the
eastern entrance to the Inland Sea that is today's Tokushima Prefecture.[36]
Over the next six months shipyard workers, including some who may have
been American and Allied prisoners of war, transformed what was to have
been a cargo-liner on NYK's Australia route into a Southeast Asian war
workhorse.[37] The *Awa maru* had fewer passenger cabins than her elegant sister ship, the *Angei maru*. They were fitted with simple furnishings appropriate to the war austerity that the Japanese government forced on all of its
citizens. The ship wore a coat of drab gray paint. She was completed early in
March 1943;[38] by that time, she had been armed with two deck guns, an

The *Awa maru*. *Nonomura Masao,* Awa maru *Bereaved Families Association*

antiaircraft gun, and four depth charges that could be launched from her stern.[39]

The ship never operated as a normal merchant vessel. Instead, she became a munitions carrier whose every move was directed by the Imperial Japanese Army. On her maiden voyage she hauled arms from Moji to Singapore, the metropolis of the Southern Region; she brought home Southeast Asian raw materials to fuel war-driven industries. Success in this and other such voyages won her a nickname—"the arsenal that moves across the seas" —and made it necessary for her to carry an armed guard of two dozen men to man her weapons and fend off possible enemy boarding parties.[40]

Army Transport Command officials also chose the *Awa maru* to implement the relief-to-prisoners agreement because her captain and crew were reliable. Capt. Hamada Matsutarō, whose Hitleresque moustache suggested he was a man attuned to the times, lived in Kobe and had served NYK for many years. He had shaped the 148 men under his command into an efficient and proficient crew.[41] Hamada had commanded the ship, almost without incident, through several dangerous episodes. In November 1943 saboteurs had put mines under her stern while she was anchored off Singapore's West Docks, but the *Awa maru* was not harmed. En route home a few days later, she narrowly escaped two torpedo attacks. Maneuvering to avoid the American "fish," the ship struck another vessel in her convoy and damaged her stern. Nonetheless, she returned home safely.[42]

The *Awa maru* came closest to disaster on 18 August 1944. By that time Captain Hamada's skill had earned the ship the designation as pacesetter for convoy HI-71, which was ferrying men, munitions, and other war matériel to Manila for use against an expected American reinvasion of the Philippine Islands. The escort carrier *Ōtaka* was assigned to accompany and provide air cover for the convoy. But the "great hawk" became the bait that lured the *Rasher* (SS 269) to the southward-moving Japanese ships. After sinking the carrier, the submarine fired sixteen more torpedoes at the ships in convoy HI-71, destroying three of them. The *Awa maru*, shrewdly maneuvered by Hamada, evaded the fish and led the surviving ships in the convoy to Manila, where she off-loaded her cargo of munitions.[43]

Convinced that the *Awa maru* could do the job of taking relief supplies to prisoners and internees in China and Southeast Asia, Imperial Japanese Army officials modified her to carry out that mission and serve their own purposes. At Kobe, the ship acquired a new coat of green paint, and her sides, decks, and funnel were marked with large white crosses; special lights were affixed to illuminate those protective markings.[44] While stevedores loaded nearly eight hundred tons of crated relief supplies, shipwrights installed special safes, which would contain a ton of gold bullion destined for Thailand.[45] That precious cargo and the relief supplies had barely been taken aboard when B-29s made their first daylight incendiary-bomb attack on the Kansai region.[46] To escape it, the *Awa maru* fled Kobe a day earlier than planned and headed west through the Inland Sea to Ujina.

At that historic military transportation center on the southeastern side of Hiroshima harbor, her armed guards departed.[47] Her defensive armaments were removed; in their place technicians installed devices that could be used to blow up the *Awa maru* to prevent her boarding or capture by enemy forces.[48] After these modifications were completed, the ship took aboard aircraft parts and other munitions the Imperial Japanese Army needed for use in Indochina, Malaya, and Burma.[49] Once more, the arsenal that moves across the seas headed west toward the narrow Shimonoseki Strait that separates Honshū and Kyūshū and entered Moji harbor. There, local officials altered her cargo so as to give her an additional humanitarian mission. Reducing the amount of machinery she was originally ordered to carry, they made more room in her holds for sugar and salt from Taiwan—commodities the Japanese in Southeast Asia desperately needed.[50]

At Moji, the *Awa maru* also welcomed aboard her last southbound passengers. Some were minor minions of empire; they brought only dreams and a few personal possessions with them. Seventeen-year-old Kitamura Tetsutarō, for example, was a onetime art student who had grown bored of war work in the homeland. He had volunteered to work for a Mitsubishi-related firm in Sumatra in hopes of furthering his dream of becoming an engineer.[51]

Others were men of high rank from Tokyo who gave the *Awa maru* a diplomatic mission. Three senior officials—Vice Minister Takeuchi Shimpei and Southern Region General Affairs Division Chief Tōkō Takezō of the Ministry for Greater East Asian Affairs, and Foreign Ministry Research Bureau Chief Yamada Kantarō—were going south to patch up relations between Tokyo and Bangkok and to help manage the transfer of gold to the Thai government.[52]

As final preparations for her departure from Japan neared completion, the men who would ride the *Awa maru* south showed no outward signs of concern for her safety.[53] Hamada went about his duties in his usual brisk and efficient manner. Vice Minister Takeuchi, in a letter written the morning of the ship's sailing, described the preceding night's farewell party at a hot spring resort near Shimonoseki, just across the strait from Moji, as if it were simply another ritual in the routine of official life. The teenager Kitamura was too excited about leaving to worry about dangers that might lie ahead.[54]

At least some on board the ship harbored doubts about the *Awa maru*'s safe return, however. The ship's chief engineer gave his pocket watch to a friend to deliver to his wife in the event something happened to him. Vice Minister Takeuchi tried to suppress the anxieties he felt in a farewell letter to his wife and family that mixed admonition, gaiety, and bravado. Living in Tokyo, they should look first to their own safety if, as was likely, B-29s continued to bomb the capital. He said he might even be safer than they were, for the *Awa maru* was large and pleasant enough to remind him of the ship that in earlier, more peaceful times had carried them all to Europe. She bore white crosses on her sides, deck, and funnel, just as had been specified in the safe-passage agreement with America. Thus there was no reason to worry about him.[55]

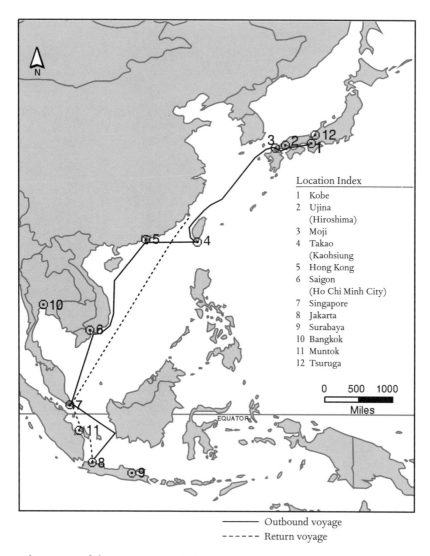

Location Index
1 Kobe
2 Ujina
  (Hiroshima)
3 Moji
4 Takao
  (Kaohsiung
5 Hong Kong
6 Saigon
  (Ho Chi Minh City)
7 Singapore
8 Jakarta
9 Surabaya
10 Bangkok
11 Muntok
12 Tsuruga

—————— Outbound voyage
- - - - - Return voyage

The voyage of the *Awa maru*, 17 February–1 April 1945

So, on 17 February 1945, when the *Awa maru* headed west out of Moji and turned south into the East China Sea, she was a ship of hope.[56] Americans hoped she would bring life-sustaining food and medicine to those held prisoner; the Japanese hoped she would fulfill the missions they had given her—carrying munitions to the frontiers of empire in the south, taking food to its defenders, delivering diplomats to smooth relations with an ally, and bringing back commodities needed for the defense of the homeland. And everyone—the Japanese as well as the Americans—trusted that those white crosses she wore, glowing with lights in the gathering darkness, would protect the *Awa maru* from any attack. Little did they suspect that a strange combination of circumstances yet to unfold would render those talismans of safe passage meaningless.

With but one exception, the *Awa maru* carried out her relief-to-prisoners missions without incident. After leaving twenty-two tons of relief supplies at Takao [Kaohsiung], she left that southwestern Taiwan port early to escape American bombing.[57] Then the ship headed southwest across the South China Sea to occupied Hong Kong. There, just as the diplomats had agreed, dockworkers on 22 February 1945 off-loaded forty-one tons of relief supplies for British, Canadian, Australian, and American prisoners and civilian internees held nearby. Stevedores at other ports repeated that task two days later at Saigon. A week after that, at Singapore, dockworkers took 70 percent of the cargo destined for those in Japanese custody there. Two weeks later the *Awa maru* off-loaded the last of the relief supplies she had taken aboard at Kobe into small craft that ferried them to Jakarta.[58]

Most, but not all, of these life-sustaining materials were then taken to camps for distribution to the detainees for whom they were intended. Some were pilfered. The official in charge of the West Docks at Singapore where the *Awa maru* off-loaded her cargo sampled the chocolate—an item that had long since vanished from his diet—that the relief packages contained and enjoyed the taste of a Lucky Strike cigarette for the first time. Other items meant for those at the huge Changi Prison Camp nearby ended up in the hands of Chinese children, who hawked them in Singapore's black market.[59] Nonetheless, the bulk of the food and medicines the *Awa maru* carried did reach American and Allied prisoners and internees. The ship completed the mission that entitled her to safe passage essentially as the architects of the relief accord intended.

She also succeeded in delivering the munitions that, in a strict interpretation of international law, stripped her of her specially protected status.[60] At Saigon, some seventeen hundred crates of vehicle parts, two thousand crates each of munitions and aircraft parts, and six hundred tons of various other military supplies were removed from her holds.[61] On 28 February the *Awa maru* left the city once known as "the Pearl of the Orient" lightened of most of the burden that might have given the enemy license to destroy her. By the time she reached Singapore four days later, the ship had completed the first phase of her military mission.[62]

Meeting the demands that Japanese diplomats had placed on her proved much more complicated. The three senior diplomats who had taken passage on the ship—Takeuchi Shimpei, Yamada Kantarō, and Tōkō Takezō—had a mission that was both general and particular. On the one hand, they were to confer with Japanese ambassadors to Burma, French Indochina, and Thailand and with the senior military commander in the region about improving the three countries' integration into the Greater East Asia Co-Prosperity Sphere.[63] On the other, they sought to improve Thai-Japanese relations by reaffirming that the ton of gold bullion the *Awa maru* carried would be delivered.[64]

Strained relations between Tokyo and Bangkok made fulfillment of those tasks difficult. Although Japan and Thailand had signed an offensive-defensive alliance late in December 1941, and Prime Minister Tōjō Hideki had visited Bangkok in July 1943, the two nations were at best uneasy partners in what had become a losing war against the United States and its allies. Japanese troops had occupied the Thai capital, and over the ensuing years they had become burdensome to the local people and their economy. In 1943 they confiscated and melted down for their own use all of the copper coins in circulation in Thailand. Tokyo also squeezed loans out of Bangkok that by 1944 amounted to nearly double the Thai government's regular revenues. That prompted the Thai premier to propose, in jest, to his cabinet colleagues that they invite the ranking Japanese in Bangkok to a banquet and appear naked so as to dramatize their government's financial situation. In an effort to ameliorate the situation, Tokyo had promised to begin repaying a portion of the loans in gold. To that end, a ton of gold bullion had been loaded aboard the *Awa maru*.[65]

Vice Minister Takeuchi and his fellow diplomats left the ship at Saigon on 28 February to fly to Bangkok.[66] When, four days later, they met with Thai Foreign Minister Phraya Shinsena and Prime Minister Khuang Aphaiwongse, the best they could offer was partial compliance with the pledge that had been made. In March 1944 Tokyo had proposed selling 50 million yen in gold to Bangkok: 20 million in the first year, and then a sum worth between 5 and 10 million yen annually thereafter. But the gold on the *Awa maru* was worth barely 2 ¼ million yen. To make matters still worse, Tokyo had insisted that the Thais bear the risk if the bullion were lost in transit to their country.[67]

That risk was very real, for worsening war conditions made it increasingly difficult for the Japanese to deliver the gold and freshly minted *baht* notes that the *Awa maru* carried. Tokyo officials had originally planned to off-load both at Saigon and ship the crates of currency and bullion by rail across Vietnam and Cambodia to the Thai capital. Nonetheless, allegations of their own military's confiscation of goods in transit and worries lest French colonial officials in Indochina discover the gold prompted them to suggest off-loading at Singapore and shipping by rail to Bangkok.[68] But by early February 1945, when they made that proposal, guerrillas had attacked along that line, and enemy bombers had taken out the Chao Phraya River bridge, which a train traveling from Singapore to Bangkok would have to cross.[69] Accordingly, Japanese diplomats in the Thai capital asked, later in the month, that the gold be flown in from Singapore.[70]

Whether it was delivered that way or over the hazardous rail route from Singapore remains unclear. By mid-March, however, the *Awa maru* had completed her diplomatic mission. The newly minted currency arrived in the Thai capital—only to be greeted by complaints over its coloration—on 13 March.[71] Three days later, forty boxes containing the gold she had carried from Japan arrived in Bangkok.[72]

By that time, the *Awa maru*'s outward voyage was over. On 23 February 1945 Tokyo officials had shortened it so as to make Jakarta (Batavia), rather than Surabaya, hundreds of miles farther east on Java, her southernmost port of call. The ship stayed an extra two days at the capital of the onetime Dutch East Indies.[73] Just what she did there, after off-loading 175 tons of relief supplies for prisoners and internees in camps in nearby Bandung and at five other unknown locations on Java, remains unclear.[74] Wary port officials, intent on keeping her identity and cargo secret, insisted that the ship remain moored offshore rather than docking alongside a pier.[75]

At Jakarta, however, the *Awa maru* began the final phase of the mission that was most important to her masters in Tokyo: bringing home men and matériel needed for the defense of the homeland. At Saigon she had taken aboard 480 merchant mariners who had survived the sinking of fourteen vessels, and rice and electrical machinery had been lowered into her holds.[76] At Jakarta she loaded as much as several thousand tons of rubber.[77] On the morning of 18 March she headed north, bound for Muntok on the island of Bangka, which hugged the eastern coast of Sumatra roughly halfway between Singapore and Jakarta.[78] Tarrying there for three days, she took on what was perhaps the most vital war commodity of all, nearly twenty-five hundred tons of refined and crude oil from the nearby Palembang field. Thousands of tons of oil drilling machinery, tin ingots, and tungsten were also placed in her holds.[79] Then, on 23 March 1945, the *Awa maru* sailed for a second time to Singapore.[80] Port authorities there, acting in response to a flurry of telegrams from Tokyo, gave priority to filling remaining space in the ship's holds with tin and rubber.[81]

But the most precious cargo that awaited her as she neared the capital of the crumbling Southern Region was human. When the *Awa maru* approached the Singapore Central Docks, an anxious crowd clamored to get aboard her. During the weeks since her previous departure, enemy bombs had fallen on the city, heightening the sense of unease and insecurity that its Japanese residents felt. Somehow, words to the effect that the *Awa maru* would be "the last boat home" had spread among them. The individuals who watched the ship approach thought her most important mission should be to take them home.[82]

That, however, was not how it was to be. Tokyo officials had long since defined priorities for repatriation, rules that privileged those who could best contribute, in one way or another, to the coming defense of the homeland. It had taken them more than a month to agree on a final passenger list, and even then Singapore officials made last-minute changes to it.[83] Military and naval officials appear to have won the battle to determine who should board the *Awa maru*. On the eve of her departure, nearly half of those on board had some connection with the Imperial Japanese Navy. Another 38 percent served the army or were mobilized civilians attached to it. Barely one out of every twenty either worked for or was sponsored by the foreign ministry or its sister diplomatic service, the Greater East Asia Ministry.[84]

Those figures hid a more important truth about the *Awa maru*'s passengers, however. The vast majority of them were noncombatants, men and women who represented a cross section of the human capital that Japan had invested in the acquisition, exploitation, and protection of its southern empire. Nearly five hundred of the passengers were merchant mariners who had sailed its seas on ships laden with the region's wealth.[85] Approximately 150 were managers and engineers who ran mining operations for the state-directed Shōwa Electric and Japan Light Metals corporations. They had boarded the ship at Muntok.[86]

Another 450 were the remnant of a corps of nearly five thousand physicists, chemists, engineers, and geologists who had been drawn from universities, research institutes, and private industry to go south and exploit the conquered region's resources. Only a third of them had volunteered to go.[87] Some of them, like the brilliant young geologist Aochi Kiyohiko, aged twenty-five, had found the experience exciting and professionally rewarding. Others, like fifty-nine-year-old Professor Chiya Yoshinosuke, who in prewar days had represented Japan at an International Geological Society conference in Washington, D.C., had found it exhausting. He was being invalided home after having served the Imperial Japanese Navy as a consultant on fuels development policy.[88] Still others among the passengers were survivors of a group of prospecting geologists sent by the navy to New Guinea and Borneo late in February 1944. Half of them had gone to the island of Biak, just below the equator off the northern coast of New Guinea, which they helped fortify in expectation of an attack by General MacArthur's forces. By the time that fight was over, only eighteen of the eighty-nine geologists dispatched to Biak had survived. Less than three out of ten among those who had gone to Borneo had lived. A mere forty from more than three hundred men who had been mobilized from the former North Sakhalin Oil Company and sent south had survived and made their way to Singapore to board the *Awa maru*.[89]

On the eve of her departure for home, the ship's cabins and passageways were also crowded with ordinary working men who had done their best to develop the southern region for Japan's benefit. Arai Shigeo was a shipwright who had worked for NYK, the *Awa maru*'s owner, and had then been mobilized by the navy to work in the Singapore shipyard.[90] Hirao Toshiya had left his prewar architectural and construction firm to become a construction administrator at Balikpapan and Surabaya in the former Dutch East Indies.[91] Yamanaka Toshio, a railroad engineer, and Motomura Hiroki, a leather tradesman, had been mobilized by the army and navy, respectively, to work in the south.[92] Abe Chūzō, a hospital administrator and longtime employee of the Furukawa Mining Company, was a former internee who was returning home for a second time.[93]

Talented men of rank and influence also fought for and won berths on the safe-passage ship. The army put senior military advisers to Southeast Asian states on her.[94] Gen. Iwahashi Kazuo, who as chief of staff of the Third Maritime Transport Command had supervised army port operations at Singapore for two years, got a cabin because he was slated to take command of the Imperial Japanese Army's Fifteenth Flotilla—a group of small craft that presumably would be used in the final defense of the home islands.[95] A former chairman of NHK, the Japanese government broadcasting service and television network, and its ranking representative in Singapore also came aboard.[96] Diplomats, by pleading with their army opposites in Tokyo and striking bargains with individual military men in Singapore, more than doubled their original allotment of berths on the ship. That enabled them to put senior officials from Rangoon, Bangkok, Singapore, and Jakarta, including family members, aboard the *Awa maru*.[97] They also got berths for two young leaders of the pro-Japanese Indian independence movement, by claiming that the men had to be in Tokyo for a second conference of Greater East Asia leaders set to open early in April 1945.[98]

By the evening of 27 March 1945, the struggle to determine who should go home on the *Awa maru* was over. But as she sat bulging with that precious human load, low in the water off Singapore, her cargo was not yet complete. That night small boats carrying the last of it came alongside her. That secret, and perhaps even deadly, cargo never appeared on the ship's manifest. Just what it was remains unclear. It may have been special weapons— "chibi" poison gas bottles or a cluster-fragmenting type of grenade, both of which had been employed against the British in Burma—intended for use in the final defense of the homeland.[99] One soldier of the Eleventh Hiroshima Corps stationed in Singapore at the time recalled spending two days offloading boxes labeled "red powder" from the ship and stowing in their place containers marked "tin" that were large enough to contain special weapons.[100]

The secret cargo may also have been loot. Another Eleventh Hiroshima Corps veteran told of going to the Southern Regional Development Bank in the dark of night, picking up more than six hundred very heavy boxes, and convoying them by truck to the Singapore docks. Unfortunately he could not read their labels, which were written in the Roman alphabet.[101] The general who headed the Third Maritime Transport Command, which was responsible for final selection of the *Awa maru*'s cargo, recalled that Capt. Hidaka Shinsaku, chief of the Singapore naval intelligence office, had had some of his toughs load something secret on board the ship. Hidaka himself later claimed that the boxes had contained gold, British and American currency, and industrial diamonds—all of which had been deposited in three specially constructed safes on board the ship.[102]

Once that secret cargo had been stowed, the *Awa maru* was ready to depart for home.

On Wednesday morning, 28 March 1945, the *Awa maru* weighed anchor and began her voyage back to Japan.[103] Her passengers considered themselves lucky. Refugees from a crumbling Southeast Asian empire, they thought they were headed home on a ship whose safe passage the enemy had guaranteed. Their presence on the ship and the cargo she carried had altered the balance of purpose for her journey. When she departed Japan, her primary goal had been to bring succor to those interned or imprisoned; now she functioned as an agent of mercy not for Americans but for Japanese who might otherwise have been stranded in conquered lands about to fall from the emperor's grasp. The *Awa maru* passengers had good reason to feel thankful and to begin to relax. When one of the women on board gave birth to a daughter shortly after the ship left Singapore, they crowded around to congratulate her.[104]

The Japanese officials who had sent the ship to Southeast Asia had every reason to be pleased with her performance and with the agreement that made it possible. In return for taking two thousand tons of relief supplies to enemy prisoners and internees, they had gotten safe passage for three vessels that, by the time the *Awa maru* returned, would have brought nearly twenty-nine thousand tons of badly needed commodities and almost twenty-five hundred of the best, brightest, and most useful officials, technicians, and fighting men back from the far reaches of empire.[105] The enemy had not violated the safe-passage agreement, even though the ships' captains and the port officials who controlled the movements of the vessels had departed from their announced courses and schedules. The belief that the *Awa maru* would return home safely was well founded.

To ensure that she did so, Tokyo officials changed her course and schedule once more. Originally, the *Awa maru* had been ordered to reach Mutsure, a small island approximately one and a half nautical miles north and west of the entrance to the Shimonoseki Strait, by the afternoon of 4 April 1945. She would then proceed to Moji harbor the next morning.[106] On the eve of her departure from Singapore, however, 105 American planes dropped mines into the Shimonoseki Strait.[107] That made return to Moji impossible. So Tokyo ordered Captain Hamada to alter the *Awa maru*'s track so as to reach Tsuruga, nearly three hundred nautical miles north and east of Mutsure, by the afternoon of 5 April.[108] At that more distant port on the Sea of Japan she was less likely to be attacked by American B-29 bombers. The ship would also be much closer to Nakhodka, the Soviet port that Japanese diplomats expected she would eventually revisit to pick up a second cargo of food, medicine, and mail for enemy prisoners and internees.[109]

Thus, as March 1945 came to an end, Japanese officials had every reason to regard the homeward-bound *Awa maru* as a symbol of success. Her voyage and those of the *Hakusan maru* and *Hoshi maru* appeared likely to vindicate the wisdom of their judgment in concluding the relief agreement and implementing it in ways that served Japan's needs. The mission of mercy— outward for the benefit of enemy nationals, homeward for the Japanese— looked to Tokyo like a diplomatic and military triumph.

But in war, perhaps even more than in peace, appearances can be deceiving. What looked like a triumph was about to become a tragedy.

4

The *Queenfish* Gets Her Kill

SHORTLY AFTER the *Awa maru* left Singapore, two American aircraft flew over her.[1] It was probably they who took a photograph that shows her plowing through the waves, low in the water thanks to her heavy load of passengers and cargo. That image, together with intercepted and decrypted messages about her voyage that American diplomatic and naval officials read, raised a troublesome question: Had the Japanese, by using her for their own purposes, stripped the *Awa maru* of the special protection promised by the relief-to-prisoners accord?

Ironically, the man in Washington who had probably worked hardest to make the relief agreement a reality was the first to pose that question. Eldred Kuppinger, chief of the SWPD's Relief Section, was outraged by mounting evidence that the Japanese were using the *Awa maru* to repatriate high-ranking officials.[2] He understood enough of international law, from his many exchanges with State Department legal experts, to know that a safe-passage guarantee could be withdrawn. Doing so was legitimate "not only when the grantee abuses the protection [it provides]," but also for reasons of "military expediency."[3]

But when Kuppinger asked his War and Navy Department opposite numbers if the Japanese, by their actions, had so abused the safe-passage guarantee as to warrant destruction of the *Awa maru,* their answer was "no." That judgment, in which Kuppinger quickly concurred, did not rest upon close international legal analysis of what the Japanese had done.[4] Neither was it an emotional response of the sort that intelligence officers felt as they read decrypted messages about the ship. At first they wanted to sink her because she had carried munitions and aircraft parts on her outward voyage and was crammed with contraband by the time she left Singapore. Upon reflection, however, they realized that breaking a promise of safe passage would be unwise.[5] Kuppinger and his colleagues had anticipated that the Japanese might use the *Awa maru* for military purposes, and now they thought it more important to continue shipping relief supplies to prisoners and internees than to sink a vessel that had abused its guarantee of safe passage.[6] Washington was not about to order the destruction of the *Awa maru.*

Decisions made in capital cities far from the scene of action in war do not, however, necessarily determine what happens within it. Half a world away on Guam, Vice Adm. Charles Andrews Lockwood, Jr., Commander, Submarine Force, Pacific (ComSubPac), and his staff read the same decrypted and translated intercepts that State and Navy Department officials in Washington did. They drew a very different conclusion from them: that the *Awa maru* should be sunk. She deserved destruction because she had transported machinery and munitions meant to kill Americans and their allies. That act, in Admiral Lockwood's view, stripped Japan of any right to claim safe passage for the ship.

Lockwood asked Adm. Chester W. Nimitz, Commander in Chief, Pacific Fleet (CinCPacFlt), for permission for one of the submarines under his command to sink the *Awa maru.* But Nimitz turned a deaf ear to ComSubPac's request.[7] He may have done so because he no longer believed that decisions in war could be made according to some absolute standard of right and wrong behavior.[8] In the Pacific War, he and all those under his command were doing what they had to in order to defeat the enemy. The Japanese were simply trying to do the same thing.

Nimitz may also have rejected Lockwood's request for the same reason Washington officials declined to destroy the *Awa maru*—concern for the fate of those still in Japanese hands. If the ship were sunk, Tokyo could hardly be expected to continue the arrangement to get food, medicine, and mail to them; and the masters of prison and internment camps might even take reprisals against them. Sinking the *Awa maru* might provide those who ordered it a moment of moral self-satisfaction, but it could also spell death for those whose need for succor her voyage was supposed to meet.

Consequently, the *Awa maru* continued her homeward-bound voyage still protected by a guarantee of safe passage. She would not be sunk as an act of policy. Indeed, American diplomatic and naval officials continued to cooperate with the Japanese in efforts to prevent her deliberate or accidental destruction. Three times, on three successive nights early in March, they broadcast the ship's revised course and schedule to the entire Pacific submarine fleet.[9] On 30 March, before Washington had received Tokyo's final changes to her projected track but after Nimitz rejected Lockwood's request to destroy her, ComSubPac sent an admonition to all submarines under his command. Those operating in the Western Pacific north of Hong Kong were told that the *Awa maru*, carrying "POW supplies," was now northbound en route to Moji. "Lighted at night and plastered with white crosses," she would pass "through your areas between now and 4 April." Sub commanders were ordered to "let it [the ship] go by safely."[10]

Why, then, did the *Queenfish* torpedo the *Awa maru* barely forty-eight hours after ComSubPac ordered her not to do so?

The answers to that question are to be found in the history of the *Queenfish* and the nature of the war she fought. On 24 February 1945, a week after the *Awa maru* left Moji, SS 393 slipped down the channel from Pearl Harbor into the open Pacific.[11] As she began what was to be her fourth war patrol, most of the men on board probably thought about the dangers of war that lay ahead or the pleasures of Hawaii just past rather than about previous departures from other ports. Yet what they and their submarine would do on this patrol was shaped by what had followed each of those departures. What was past for the *Queenfish* and her crew was truly prologue to the fateful events that lay ahead.

Perhaps only one among them, the *Queenfish*'s skipper, Cdr. Charles Elliott Loughlin, thought back to her very first departure, nearly a year earlier. On that cold March day at Portsmouth, New Hampshire, he, appropriately enough, had been the center of attention. For Elliott Loughlin, as he preferred

The *Queenfish*'s skipper, Elliott Loughlin, reads his orders at her commissioning on 11 March 1944. *Capt. John E. Bennett, USN (Ret.)*

to be called, had been named to command the *Queenfish* even before her keel had been laid.[12] He had watched, on 30 November 1943, when Mrs. Robert A. Theobald, wife of the unlucky admiral whose force failed to prevent Japan's seizure of two Aleutian islands, performed the traditional launching ceremony.[13] Breaking a bottle of champagne over the new vessel's bow, she named it "Queenfish" after a small edible fish that swam in waters off America's Pacific Coast.[14] On 11 March 1944, as a photograph taken on the occasion shows, Elliott Loughlin, surrounded by the officers and men who were the *Queenfish*'s "plankowners," or original crew, read aloud as tradition dictated his orders to take command of the newly commissioned submarine.[15]

That ceremony was entirely appropriate, for as her captain, he—more than anyone else—bore responsibility for fusing the men and machinery under his command into a finely honed instrument of war. Loughlin certainly had what it took to do so. The lanky North Carolinian had been an All-American basketball player and tennis champion at the U.S. Naval Academy.[16] The drive and determination he showed on the courts served him well when, as an ensign on the battleship *New Mexico* (BB 40), he worked for

Hyman Rickover, the ship's engineering officer. From that submariner-to-be, who would later become famous as "the father of the nuclear navy," Loughlin acquired an absolute devotion to duty and a passion for mastery of detail that served him well for years to come.[17] He also must have had an independent streak of character, for in 1938, when flight training seemed to hold the greatest promise of naval eminence, he opted for submarine service. Trained on board the *S-35*, one of the type of World War I vessel that caused ordinary sailors to dub submarines "pigboats," Loughlin took command of an even older boat, the *S-14*, early in 1942.[18] For the next fifteen months, while others took on more exciting combat missions, he trained her crew on defensive patrols in the Caribbean and western Atlantic.[19]

That experience was vital, however, to the shaping of the *Queenfish* and her crew. Solid performance earned Loughlin command of her, and he personally selected the best of *S-14*'s petty officers and enlisted men to become plankowners of the sleek new boat being built at the Portsmouth [New Hampshire] Navy Yard.[20] When she was finished, he and they celebrated at a lively party at the Club Pannaway just outside the shipyard. As they danced and drank the evening away, one sailor, Seaman Earl Symonds, "liberated" a stuffed deer's head from the hall. The next morning, as the *Queenfish* headed out into the Atlantic for three months of training, the trophy found a permanent home crammed between some pipes in the forward torpedo room. By the time the sub reached Pearl Harbor in July 1944, that remembrance of her beginnings had become a mascot with which no one on board was willing to part.[21]

On 24 February 1945, as the *Queenfish* began her fourth war patrol, some among the six officers and thirty-eight enlisted men who had been crewmen when she headed toward combat for the first time early in August 1944 may have thought back to her first war patrol.[22] What they had experienced on that longest, most exciting, and most successful of the boat's voyages to date had bonded them indelibly to the *Queenfish*. Strong memories of it lingered, in part, because that voyage had been one of "firsts."

On 31 August 1944 they had experienced for the first time the instantaneous mix of exhilaration and anxiety that gave submarine warfare its distinctive character. On that night, while patrolling on the surface, the *Queenfish* spotted her first prey—a large passenger-cargo vessel and an oiler traveling in convoy with two other ships and three escorts. An approaching aircraft forced her to dive, but a few minutes later her torpedomen, responding to Loughlin's orders, fired six fish, four of which found their targets.[23] Crew members argued over whether they had sunk one or two ships, but that didn't matter. What counted, as Loughlin noted, was the feeling of confidence that spread throughout the ship.[24]

Moments later that exhilaration turned to anxiety as the *Queenfish* dove deeper in an attempt to escape the first depth charges the convoy's escorts hurled at her. An experienced submariner like Loughlin did not consider the thirty-two that boomed around his boat an "intensive or persistent" attack.[25] But for others on the *Queenfish* that night the depth charges were—and would always be—terrifying. One chief petty officer had the foresight to keep a bucket at his battle station; after one of those depth charges violently shook the boat he would vomit into it, much to the disgust of shipmates close at hand. Nonetheless, he, like they, went right on with his duties.[26]

That kind of determination helped the *Queenfish* survive that attack, make four others of her own, and send two Japanese transports and a torpedo boat to the bottom before her first war patrol came to an end.[27] Nearly a year later, however, those triumphs were perhaps less memorable and significant in welding men on board the *Queenfish* into an effective fighting team than was an act of mercy they had performed on that same, maiden combat voyage.

A little more than two weeks after the submarine drew her first blood, she conducted her first rescue. Shortly after 1300 (one o'clock in the afternoon) on 14 September 1944, lookouts spotted two men on a raft.[28] The *Queenfish* turned toward them and saw others clinging to rafts that were being tossed up and hurled down in rough seas. They were "the most horrible human beings you've ever seen," Loughlin later recalled. Weakened by exposure, some among them were "like driftwood," incapable of grasping the lifelines tossed to them from the *Queenfish*.[29]

Within minutes, officers and men from the sub plunged into the water to rescue these men. Lt. John Edward "Jack" Bennett, of Riverdale, Illinois, was first among them. Quick action in moments of danger seemed to come naturally to him. On 7 December 1941, at Pearl Harbor, he had caught some Japanese shrapnel while scurrying from his ship, the cruiser *San Francisco* (CA 38) to her sister ship, the *New Orleans* (CA 32), in an attempt to help put more antiaircraft fire in the air. Months later, on board the *San Francisco* off Guadalcanal, he had been wounded by Japanese shells that demolished her bridge, but he had dashed to the ship's stern to man antiaircraft guns against the attackers.[30] Along with Bennett, the most junior officer on the *Queenfish*, Ens. Ed "Desperate" Desmond of Dorchester, Massachusetts, also dove into the waves to take a lifeline to men on the rafts. Robert J. "Boats" Reed, the submarine's body-building chief boatswain's mate, Quartermaster O.B. "Tex" Hendricks, who sported a gold diamond-studded star in one earlobe, and three other men also jumped in to help pull survivors on board the *Queenfish*.[31]

One of the castaways, despite being shoved by the high seas against the sub's hull, had the strength and aplomb after being taken aboard to say smartly, "Able Seaman Arthur Bancroft, HMAS *Perth*. What ship, sir?" Told "American submarine *Queenfish*, welcome aboard!" he was helped below and taken to the forward torpedo room.[32] There the *Queenfish*'s engineering officer, Lt.(jg) John H. Epps, and Pharmacist's Mate Harold Dixon gave him and the seventeen others taken aboard water, hot soup, brandy, and medical treatment. After a swabbing with fuel oil to loosen from their skins a coating of oil from the Japanese transport they had escaped, the men were scrubbed in hot showers and given clean clothes.[33] These ministrations, however, did not save two of the Australians and Britons, who died over the next two days. They were buried at sea in the traditional manner—sewn into canvas bags weighted with a 4-inch shell to carry to them to the depths.[34]

What the survivors told the submarine's crewmen steeled their minds still harder against the enemy whose ships they sought to sink. The survivors were POWs who had been forced by their Japanese captors to help build a jungle railway from Thailand into eastern Burma. Having endured the barbarous treatment and inhumane living conditions later made infamous by *The Bridge on the River Kwai* (both a film and a book), they had been among thirteen hundred prisoners crammed into the steerage of the *Rakuyo maru* for shipment to Japan as slave laborers. The *Sealion* (SS 315) had torpedoed their ship, which caught fire but did not sink immediately, allowing them to make an "orderly evacuation" onto rafts. Japanese escorts came by later to pick up their countrymen, but they drove the POWs away with revolver fire. Nonetheless the Australians and British survived, thanks to a melon they found and rain that provided drinking water, until the *Queenfish* came upon the rafts to which they had lashed themselves.[35]

Rescuing these men made the submarine's crew, mere boys in the eyes of those whom they saved, feel like manly heroes.[36] Their captain derived the "greatest satisfaction" from what they had done.[37] His superiors saw to it that Washington found out about the rescue, and the navy subsequently recognized the crew's bravery by awarding the *Queenfish* the Presidential Unit Citation, a pennant flown proudly from her mast.[38] That decoration attested to the skill, bravery, and most importantly, the unity of purpose with which the submarine and crew had acted on this first war patrol.

The *Queenfish*'s second patrol was more routine but no less important in influencing what her crew would do in April 1945. After routine refitting at Majuro in the Central Pacific Marshall Islands, which Japan had once ruled as a League of Nations mandate, she headed late in October 1944 for Saipan, in the northern Marianas.[39] Only recently taken at the cost of more than three thousand American and in excess of twenty-seven thousand Japanese lives, the island had become advanced headquarters for the boat's type commander, Admiral Lockwood, whose flag flew on the submarine tender *Fulton* (AS 11).[40] At his direction, the *Queenfish* headed west through the Tokara Strait, a gap in the string of islands that looped southward from Kyūshū to Okinawa, and into the East China Sea.[41] Her task was to find and sink as many ships as possible from precisely the sort of convoy plying back and forth between Japan and the conquered Southern Region in which the *Awa maru* normally operated.

The man who gave the *Queenfish* that mission embodied the U.S. Navy's understanding of submarine warfare and the service's acceptance of what it had become since Pearl Harbor. Although initially reluctant to join the pigboat navy, Lockwood had spent most of his professional life since leaving the Naval Academy in 1912 working on or for submarines. After completing Submarine School in the last days of World War I, he opted for sea duty in a submarine rather than more schooling. By the late 1920s, after having commanded five different boats—one of which was the *S-14* that Loughlin skippered from 1942 to 1944—Lockwood came to Washington to run the "submarine desk" in the office of the CNO.[42] In that billet he fought hard to get the navy and Congress to approve construction of the *Tambor* (SS 198) class of fleet submarine. He saw these boats, which were designed for trans-Pacific operations, not just as eyes for scouting an advancing enemy surface fleet but also as fists capable of independent operations against the presumed Japanese foe.[43] When Pearl Harbor came, Lockwood was in London working out details for bringing American submarines across the Atlantic to operate under British command against German U-boats.[44]

Lockwood began changing the undersea war against Japan almost from the moment he took command of one of the two American submarine forces based in Australia. Short, energetic, and greedy for quick results, he challenged the Navy Department's Bureau of Ordnance by conducting tests to prove that poorly performing torpedoes rather than timorous or incompetent skippers were responsible for the meager results of early submarine forays against Japanese ships.[45] When a plane crash took the life of the Pacific sub force commander in January 1943, Lockwood feigned disinterest in the job but then delighted in accepting it and using it to revolutionize the undersea war against Japan.[46]

Lockwood turned that struggle into a ruthless drive to sweep from the Pacific everything that flew the Rising Sun ensign. The title of his postwar autobiographical account—*Sink 'Em All! Submarine Warfare in the Pacific*—captured his view of what had to be done to those whom he called "y.b.'s"—yellow bastards.[47] He fought Washington bureaucrats to get more accurate torpedoes and better exploders, going so far as to tell submarine officers in the capital, "If the Bureau of Ordnance can't provide us with torpedoes that will run and explode, then for God's sake get the Bureau of Ships to design a boat hook with which we can rip the plates off a target's sides."[48] He pushed CinCPac to let him move submarine bases and his own operational headquarters forward, first to Majuro, then to Saipan, so as to be closer to and better able to fight the undersea war against Japan.[49] He introduced wolfpacking, hoping that this technique of encircling prey, used with such deadly effect early in the war by Germany in the Atlantic and roundly condemned by Washington, might prove even more lethal to Japanese naval and merchant marine ships.[50]

Lockwood's drive and determination got him a "spot" promotion to vice admiral barely nine months after he became ComSubPac.[51] But rank did not separate him from the men who fought under his command. Scarcely old enough to have fathered sub skippers of Loughlin's class and age, he felt " a twinge of sorrow and . . . soul-searching" every time he saw boats shove off on war patrol.[52] Whenever he could, he welcomed in person the "lads" who manned them when they returned from patrol. His obvious concern earned Lockwood the nickname "Uncle Charley."[53] But as commander he functioned more like a coach than a friendly relative: Lockwood organized his boats into teams; kept track of their skippers' kills; and then broadcast "the Pacific score," along with news and even doggerel verse, to those under his command.[54] That built morale and elicited even greater effort from the men who served under him.

So the crew of the *Queenfish* left Saipan on her second war patrol determined to make Admiral Lockwood even more proud of them than he already was. They got the kills he wanted, putting torpedoes in six Japanese ships—a subchaser, a gunboat, a transport, two cargo ships, and what was presumed to be an escort aircraft carrier—in the week of 8–15 November 1944.[55] However, the *Queenfish* and her wolfpack mates, the *Barb* (SS 220) and *Picuda* (SS 382), who also sunk enemy ships, did not operate with the kind of close coordination that Lockwood desired.[56] Each boat was her own star performer, and every captain found it difficult to identify the type of enemy craft destroyed. Loughlin was certain, for example, that debris that banged against the *Queenfish* on 9 November 1944 came from an oiler; the only kill eventually confirmed in that night's attack, however, was a patrol craft.[57] Six days later, *Queenfish* torpedoes struck what Loughlin and his crew thought was a *Chitose*-class escort carrier. In fact, the ship they sent to the bottom turned out to be a much smaller aircraft ferry.[58]

Target misidentification of this sort and imperfect coordination with wolfpack mates would prove crucial in the *Queenfish*'s later attack on the *Awa maru*. But at this point in the war, larger achievements overshadowed seemingly small mistakes. By early December 1944, when Commander Loughlin and his crew returned to Guam, they had sunk four sizable enemy ships, one out of every two with which they had come into contact. They could take pride in the fact that eleven of the twenty-two fish they had fired hit targets, a batting average that would make any baseball player—or submarine captain —jealous.[59]

Indeed, their successes on this second war patrol and the recognition accorded them immediately after it were vital to sustaining their willingness to risk their lives far from home in pursuit of enemy ships and eventual victory. Admiral Lockwood recognized that when he praised the *Queenfish*'s attacks as "perfectly executed, . . . outstanding" models of "excellent teamwork."[60] He also sent her officers and crew a poignant Christmas message that acknowledged the loneliness of their task and called attention to the

The *Queenfish* crew relaxes at Camp Dealey, Guam. *Capt. John E. Bennett, USN (Ret.)*

pride their families felt in them.[61] To complete this shower of praise, his deputy, Rear Adm. John H. Brown, came to Camp Dealey, a rest and recreation center on Guam, where the submarine's crew relaxed while their boat was reprovisioned, to hand out individual decorations for the heroism they had shown in rescuing the shipwrecked British and Australian POWs on the *Queenfish*'s first war patrol.[62]

Recognition of that sort reinforced the natural aggressiveness of the sub's young crew when, on 29 December 1944, they departed Guam for their third war patrol in the East China Sea and northern reaches of the Formosa Strait. Loughlin too had new reasons to find and sink prey, for he had been named to command the wolfpack that included the *Barb*, *Picuda*, and *Queenfish*. That determination was manifested on New Year's Day 1945, when the three ships used 4-inch guns and 20- and 40-mm fire to sink a presumed Japanese patrol craft that turned out to be a weather ship.[63]

While that success seemed to augur triumph ahead, in fact failure and frustration were the principal results of the *Queenfish*'s third war patrol. A week later, on a very dark and overcast night, the wolfpack made its first coordinated attack against a Japanese convoy. Loughlin and his crew meticulously tracked an oiler and a transport, fired sixteen torpedoes, and found to their dismay that only two had struck their targets.[64] "Queerfish," as the *Barb*'s captain, then-Cdr. Eugene B. "Gene" Fluckey, dubbed his wolfpack mate, had made "incredible misses!"[65] Loughlin had to admit that while the attack as a whole demonstrated the value of close coordination among wolf-pack mates, he and his men had "contributed but little" to the destruction of that convoy.[66]

Eight days later, on 16 January 1945, near the twenty-fathom curve south of Turnabout Light on Niu Shan [Cow Mountain] Island off the China coast —the same general area in which the *Queenfish* would sink the *Awa maru*— Loughlin and his crew suffered what was probably their most humiliating experience of the war to that date. In another night surface encounter, they made three attacks on a Japanese convoy: all eight of the torpedoes they fired missed their targets. Such failure was "a complete mystery" to Loughlin, for the *Queenfish*'s fire control party could not find any evidence that the torpedo control director had malfunctioned. Surmising that the torpedoes, for some unknown reason, "must have run erratic," he could only scrawl "Nuts!!!" in his war patrol log.[67] That uncharacteristic expression of personal feeling gives support to now-retired Admiral Fluckey's assertion that, given the great risks a submarine commander and crew took in attacking, misses were "crushing" to morale.[68]

Commander Loughlin then ordered the *Queenfish* to move away from the scene of her humiliation and head back to base to reload her empty torpedo tubes. Instead, the submarine was ordered to Pearl Harbor, giving him and his men ten long days to ponder what might account for their "disappointing and depressing performance" on the *Queenfish*'s third and shortest war patrol.[69]

What happened in Hawaii raised their spirits and increased the probabilities of success on their next war patrol. After six months' absence, every man on board the *Queenfish* was eager to partake of Hawaii's wartime pleasures. Turning the ship over to a refitting crew, they hurried ashore.[70] Some went straight to the Royal Hawaiian Hotel, commandeered by the navy, where they could sleep in clean white-sheeted beds and dance with hostesses who had volunteered to salve their loneliness. Others headed downtown for Hotel Street, were sex was readily for sale.[71] A few of the ship's officers tasted the islands' more refined pleasures. They went to Molokai at the invitation of George R. Cooke, master of one of the so-called Big Five firms that dominated Hawaii's economy and set the rules for its society. There they rode horses on Cooke's fifty-five-thousand-acre ranch, watched his seventy-seven-year-old wife, Sophie, dance the hula, and entertained lusty thoughts about her beautiful Okinawan maid. Loughlin, as was customary for a submarine captain, stayed ashore near the *Queenfish* and kept his own counsel about what he did on this much-needed break from the tensions of war.[72]

While he and his men were ashore, crews at the submarine base made changes to the *Queenfish* that would make her an even more lethal instrument. They took off a 4-inch 50-caliber gun forward and emplaced a 5.25-inch gun aft. They installed an ST radar in the number one periscope position and Mark VIII target-bearing tracking equipment in the control room. Sailors also loaded new Mark XVIII-2 torpedoes, with corresponding new warheads and exploders, to replace the mixed-part Mark XVIIIs that had performed so poorly on the third war patrol. They modified the bow planes to allow diving at a shallower angle. Also, to provide more safety when the *Queenfish* might next come under attack, they added a muffler to silence one of the boat's blowers.[73]

When Loughlin returned to his boat, he discovered that her crew had been changed as well. A prospective commanding officer (not necessarily for the *Queenfish*) would accompany him as skipper-in-training.[74] Loughlin could easily relate to Frank Nickols Shamer, four years his junior at the Naval Academy, and a fellow varsity basketball player. Although two collisions had marred Shamer's career, he had shown himself to be a most capable trainer of submariners-to-be while captain of the *Cachalot* (SS 170). The fact that he had already been on five war patrols added to his professional stature, and his technical expertise and sunny disposition guaranteed that Loughlin would find Shamer a most valuable addition to the *Queenfish*'s crew.[75]

Other personnel changes made in his absence may, however, have given Loughlin a moment's concern. Two grizzled officer plankowners left the *Queenfish*, and their places were taken by two reserve officers, Lt. (jg) Edward J. Berghausen of Cincinnati, Ohio, and Shorty Evans, a curly-headed ensign for whom the coming war patrol would be the very first taste of combat. Nearly a quarter of the *Queenfish*'s original enlisted crew—including four highly valued chief petty officers—were gone too, their places taken by less-experienced men.[76] Loughlin could only hope that the long voyage westward from Pearl Harbor to Saipan would provide sufficient time and opportunity to integrate these new men into the crew already bonded to the *Queenfish.*

Fortunately, the submarine's thirty-two-hundred-mile voyage to the forward base from which her fourth war patrol would begin did just that. It was more like a peacetime training mission than a journey toward combat, for by late February 1945 the U.S. Navy had all but swept the Japanese enemy from the Central Pacific. Indeed, the very day the *Queenfish* departed Pearl Harbor, U.S. Marines raised the flag on Mt. Suribachi on Iwo Jima, producing one of the most dramatic and long-lived images of the entire war.[77] By 6 March, when lusty cheers from her new wolfpack mates on the *Spot* (SS 413) and *Sea Fox* (SS 402) greeted the sub as she moored alongside the tender *Fulton* at Saipan, General MacArthur's forces had retaken Manila, Corregidor, and Bataan, scenes of their humiliation and surrender three years earlier.[78] The larger tides of war, no less than the particular changes that had come to the *Queenfish,* pointed toward a victory against Japan that could not be too far off.

Spirits were thus high on board the submarine when, three days later, early on the morning of 9 March 1945, the *Queenfish* got under way for her fourth war patrol.[79] For Loughlin and the plankowners, the chance to restore a reputation tarnished by the failures of their last patrol loomed ahead; for the newest members of the submarine's crew, ahead lay the chance to prove their manhood in war. Little did any of them, from Loughlin down to the greenest seaman, suspect that the *Queenfish* was setting out on her most fateful voyage yet.

When she departed Saipan the *Queenfish* carried a warning message that might have kept her from sinking the *Awa maru.* It was a clear-language text advising that Tokyo had changed the specially protected ship's course and schedule in a way that would pull her away from the eastern side of the Taiwan Strait to run close to the Chinese mainland. Her revised track put the *Awa maru* squarely in the area the *Queenfish* had been ordered to patrol.[80]

The submarine did not get that message in the usual way. Because she was alongside the tender *Fulton* on all three of the nights on which the message was broadcast, her radiomen had not copied it. Instead, the *Queenfish*'s communications officer, Lt. (jg) John Tayman Geer, brought it aboard in a sheaf of routine unclassified messages he had picked up on the *Fulton*.[81]

Lieutenant Geer, who came from Brookhaven, Mississippi, was perhaps the most colorful and certainly the most star-crossed junior officer among the crew. A former University of Texas varsity wrestler, he tipped the scales at more than two hundred pounds and (not surprisingly) bore the nickname "Bull." His shipmates knew when he was approaching, even if they could not see him, for the smoke of the cigars he loved preceded his arrival.[82] They generally welcomed his presence. Geer was a genial and generous officer who got along well with the radiomen who worked under his direction. He had even lent one man a pair of officer's shorts and took him along on a target-shooting expedition in Hawaii.[83]

The *Queenfish*'s communicator was also the butt of a good-natured practical joke that was often replayed. Bull frequently got up in the middle of the night for a snack of bread smothered in tabasco sauce. When he went back to sleep, the sub's navigator would get hold of his web belt and trim a half-inch off of it. When Geer got up and tried to buckle his belt, he found it tighter than ever. His struggles to secure it around his ample girth prompted poker-faced fellow officers to warn him about eating too much and getting too fat.[84]

Geer found nothing striking about the message concerning the *Awa maru*'s intended track. He initialed it and routed it up the command "ladder" to the *Queenfish*'s navigator and executive officer, Lieutenant Bennett. When Bennett flipped through the pile of routine radio traffic that contained this admonition, he too failed to see anything special about it. He initialed it but did not call it to Commander Loughlin's attention. The skipper apparently never saw this message. Further, during the busy days and nights of war patrol that followed, neither the radiomen who maintained the message file nor Geer noticed that the *Queenfish*'s captain had not read and initialed what appeared to be just another insignificant message.[85]

That lapse in communication set the submarine and her crew on course to committing a disastrous error. Nearly a month later, ComSubPac sent the *Queenfish* (and all other boats under his command) a second admonition, this time encoded, about the *Awa maru*. It ordered them to let the Japanese ship "go by safely," because she was carrying "POW supplies."[86] That factual error hinted that the message was hastily and poorly drawn. Normally, Cdr. Richard G. Voge, Admiral Lockwood's precise and efficient assistant chief of staff for operations, would have drafted or checked it. But in late March 1945 he happened to be away on temporary duty in the Philippines. His assistant, who wrote the order *not* to attack the *Awa maru*, neither referred to the earlier unclassified messages about her nor specified her expected noon positions.[87] He may have thought omission of any reference to a specific position was necessary to preserve cryptographic security; one was not supposed to repeat in coded form what had been previously broadcast in clear language. As a result, ComSubPac's warning order simply informed his lads that the *Awa maru* would be passing "thru your areas."[88]

That vagueness stripped Admiral Lockwood's admonition of its intended force, at least insofar as Loughlin and his crew were concerned. Not having seen the previous message, which definitely put the *Awa maru* on a track passing through the *Queenfish*'s war patrol area, the sub skipper could not make sense of ComSubPac's latest warning. "This is the most stupid [*sic*] dispatch I've ever seen in my life!" he muttered to himself.[89] Had he read, or had his fellow officers remembered, the earlier, unclassified message about the *Awa maru*, someone on board the *Queenfish* might have made the connection and kept her from committing a terrible error. In fact, no one did. No one was looking for, or expected to find, an enemy vessel "lighted at night and plastered with white crosses" that were meant to stay the hands of an American submarine commander.[90]

So, when just before 2300 (eleven o'clock at night) on 1 April 1945, a pip indicating the presence of a possible target at seventeen thousand yards appeared on the *Queenfish*'s SJ radar, Loughlin and his crew sprung into preparations for an attack. Their experiences on this fourth war patrol to date were such that even a much more explicit admonition about the *Awa maru* might not have stopped them; the preceding two weeks had been full of frustration and empty of triumph. The *Queenfish* had spotted ten possible targets during that period, but each time, either weather or other unfavorable factors had ruled out going to battle stations for attack. She herself had as often been prey as predator. Eight times in the preceding seven days the sub had been forced to dive to escape planes that might have attacked her. Not once had her torpedoes been readied for firing, and the new 5.25-inch gun on her deck was still a virgin.[91] Little wonder, then, that Commander

Loughlin and the fire control party on the *Queenfish* were predisposed to see that pip as the "kill" they so very much needed and wanted to make.

But the adrenaline flowing through their bodies was not the only reason they did so. That pip carried the characteristics of a destroyer or destroyer escort; it moved across the screen at a speed more appropriate for a warship than for a merchant vessel pressed into military service. It did so in part because Imperial Japanese Army officials at various ports of call had burdened the *Awa maru* far beyond normal limits with cargo and passengers. Low in the water as a result of her overloading, the ship presented a smaller than usual radar image not unlike that of a destroyer.[92] She moved at a speed more appropriate for a warship than a merchant vessel because Captain Hamada, having been ordered to reach Tsuruga, nearly three hundred miles beyond Moji, his ship's original destination, was pushing the *Awa maru* through the foggy night at top speed.[93] As a result, from what Loughlin and his crew—blinded by fog, misled by their electronic sensors, and imperfectly informed by their superiors—could see, that pip was a target that must be attacked.

An hour later they fired four torpedoes that sank the *Awa maru* within four minutes.[94] "One-two-three-four hits out of four, batting one hundred!" a radioman in the conning tower joyously jotted on a scrap of paper that would become part of his diary.[95] Ens. Howard "Shorty" Evans, the junior officer of the deck (JOOD), observing the torpedo firing from the cigarette deck, appeared to jump with glee. When asked by one of the lookouts if he had leaped for joy, he retorted, "Hell, no! The torpedo explosion threw me up."[96]

Only moments before the Japanese ship plunged, stern first, into the murky sea, Commander Loughlin gave orders for the *Queenfish* to turn around and head at increased speed toward the position where the doomed vessel was. Eight minutes later the sub slowed to a stop in the midst of a large oil slick that reeked of gasoline. Lookouts spotted survivors clinging to bits of wreckage bobbing up and down in the rising seas.[97] Ensign Evans pointed a Marine Corps automatic rifle toward them, his finger uneasy on the safety.[98] He and the men of the *Queenfish* were about to see the human face of their enemy for the first time.

But precisely how many of those faces they saw will remain forever

unclear. Later, Loughlin would write in his personal log that a "total of perhaps twenty" Japanese could be seen; he revised the number to "not more
than fifteen or twenty" in the *Queenfish*'s patrol report.[99] Radioman John
Goberville recorded that the sub "ran into a thousand men in the water,
hollering, screaming, and really raising hell."[100] Boats Reed was called up
on deck just after the attack. He recalled hearing "a lot of people in the water
. . . screamin' and hollerin.'" Although he couldn't see them too well, their
cries were something that, he said, "I'll never forget as long as I live."[101] In
a few minutes the faces from which those cries came would slip beneath the
waves forever.

Before they did, however, Loughlin ordered that lines with life rings
attached be tossed toward those who had survived the torpedoing of the
Awa maru.[102] Reed recalled throwing a small yellow line with a ring on its
end toward people floating on bales of rubber from the ship's cargo. When
the ring hit them, however, "they'd jump over the side."[103] All but one, that
is; one man raised his arm and yelled. He caught the life ring, held onto it,
and was pulled toward the *Queenfish*. When he drew near her, just aft of the
conning tower, the seas thrust him under her hull and against her sides. He
suffered "terrific punishment" from this battering.[104]

Reed had a hard time pulling the man up out of the water. Because it was
dark and dangerous, Loughlin did not want anyone to go over the side, as
some had done in rescuing POWs on the *Queenfish*'s first war patrol. Reed
called for help, and fellow boatswain Paul Johnson arrived just in time to
keep him from falling overboard. Finally, they succeeded in "jerking" the
man aboard. Reed, schooled by stories about how the Japanese fought desperately in close quarters, grabbed the man. Throwing him "real macho" on
the deck, he put his knee in the captive's back, and grabbed his hair. Then he
asked Johnson to hold the man and make sure the enemy did not have a
weapon.[105]

In fact, the sole survivor of the *Awa maru* was in no shape to harm anyone. As he later recounted the story of what befell him on that dark Sunday
night, he had been hurled by the force of the torpedo explosion from his
ship's deck into the water. Stunned, he swallowed large quantities of oil-
darkened seawater while struggling for his life. Somehow, he managed to
swim away from the sinking *Awa maru*. When he saw the *Queenfish* close at

hand, he raised his arm and shouted for help;[106] that was what drew Reed's lifeline to him.

Some forty minutes later, Loughlin judged it was time to give up trying to recover any more survivors or salvage any of the *Awa maru*'s cargo that was floating nearby. Rising seas made it "impracticable and undesirable" to "forcibly rescue" those in the water who spurned assistance. In time, Loughlin judged, the man just taken aboard could identify the ship that had been sunk and provide more details about her cargo.[107]

Hours passed before that surmise, which now prompted Loughlin to head the *Queenfish* eastward toward her originally assigned patrol area, proved true.[108] The survivor was taken below to the after torpedo room, but not without further trauma along the way. As Reed opened a hatch to push him through, a sailor startled by the sight of a Japanese picked up a wrench in a threatening manner and shouted, "Keep your eye on that sonofabitch. I don't trust him!" Reed shackled the man he and others regarded as an enemy prisoner to an empty torpedo skid in the after torpedo room—the very spot from which one of the four fish that sank the poor man's ship had come.[109] Crewmen then cleaned him off with fuel oil and gave him a "depth-charge ration" (about fifteen ounces) of brandy to speed his recovery from the trauma he had suffered. Once he appeared to revive, they summoned Bennett, the *Queenfish*'s executive officer, to question him.

After the crew secured from battle stations, Bennett had gone to the wardroom, where he found a Japanese-English dictionary and a phrase book. From them he copied out, in romanized Japanese words and large *katakana* —the more formal of the two Japanese syllabaries derived from simplified Chinese characters—a few words and phrases he thought might be useful in questioning the man just pulled aboard. But when Bennett went to the aft torpedo room, they turned out not to be as vital as he had thought; the Japanese survivor understood a little English and spoke a few words. Seeing that the man was shaking, Bennett ordered that he be unshackled from the torpedo skid.[110] Obviously, he was not fit to undergo extensive questioning at this point.

Bennett did, however, ask him the most immediately pressing question: What was the name of his ship? The man managed to scrawl in katakana a four-syllable answer: "A-wa ma-ru." The lieutenant then sent someone to the sub's radio "shack" to see if any messages or information about the *Awa maru* could be found. Eventually, a man returned carrying a copy of the most recently received and decoded warning from ComSubPac. Once he read it, Bennett realized that the vessel the *Queenfish* had just sunk had been not a warship but a passenger-cargo vessel traveling under some sort of special protection.[111]

Shortly before dawn, the *Queenfish*'s executive officer became the proverbial Persian messenger. Going to Loughlin's bunk, he awakened his commanding officer and told him the bad news: the *Queenfish* crew had just sunk the very ship that Admiral Lockwood had directed them to "let . . . go by safely." Hearing that, the sub's skipper exclaimed, "Oh, Christ!"—a most uncharacteristic outburst for the usually unflappable North Carolinian.[112]

The epithet was perfectly appropriate at that moment. Loughlin now suddenly realized that he and his men had committed an error of monumental proportions. Acting in what seemed to them the most reasonable and professional manner possible, they had done the unthinkable. At that instant, the *Queenfish* skipper must have wondered how he and his men could have made such a mistake.

That question would haunt Elliott Loughlin and his crew for the rest of their lives. It would later trigger impassioned charges in Japan that the sinking of the *Awa maru* was anything but accidental. Some there, many years after the war had ended, even implied that senior American officers had rigged events on the night of 1 April 1945 so as to make what was deliberate appear accidental.[113]

Those speculative allegations were untrue, in both particular and general terms. They ignored one of the grimmest truths that war presents to all who engage in it: the constant threat, real presence, and terrible consequence of human error. War may, as the great Prussian theorist Carl Maria von Clausewitz claimed, be the reasoned pursuit of political objectives by military means; but it is also, as he pointed out, the kingdom of chance—one in which the possibilities of error are far greater than in more peaceful times.[114]

Consequently, to war is to err. Fallible human beings who find themselves trying to kill one another are bound, by the very nature of the enterprise in which they are engaged, to make decisions that seem correct yet yield disastrous results. The "fog of war" does not necessarily dim the reason of men in combat. But it most certainly clouds their vision and allows them to take otherwise unthinkable actions, which can have tragic, unintended consequences.

In this instance that fog blinded Japanese and Americans alike. Tokyo officials were perhaps a bit too clever and certainly unmindful of the potential consequences when they demanded unconditional safe passage for the *Awa maru*. They were so blinded by their desire to use the ship for other than the principal stated purpose of her safe-passage guarantee that they underestimated the possibility of her being sunk despite the precautions taken to protect her. Japanese officials in Singapore, by overloading the ship with human and material cargo, grasped too hard at the "straw" promise of safe passage home. Had she not been so low in the water, the *Awa maru* might not have seemed to resemble a destroyer to those who scanned the radar screens on board the *Queenfish*. Captain Hamada likewise fell prey to the temptation to concentrate on immediate orders and overlook the possibility of unseen dangers. Racing through fog-shrouded waters known to be frequented by enemy submarines without either sounding his ship's horn or zigzagging to reduce the likelihood that an enemy torpedo would find its way to the *Awa maru*'s bottom was, to say the least, risky behavior.

Yet all of these decisions, each of which heightened the possibility that the ship might be sunk in error, appeared sensible to the Japanese officials who made them. Indeed, given their empire's deteriorating circumstances and their sense of duty, which impelled them to do everything possible to prevent its defeat, could they have chosen to act other than as they did?

The same can be said for the Americans, who were much more directly responsible for the destruction of the *Awa maru* and of all but one of the lives of those on her. They too fell victim to error, time and again, amidst the fog of war. Their central aim—to defeat Japan promptly by whatever means necessary—justified, in their eyes, the campaign of unrestricted submarine warfare that sent the *Awa maru* to the bottom of the Taiwan Strait. The very magnitude of their endeavor, however, guaranteed that error would attend its execution. The *Queenfish*'s failure to identify fully her target before sinking it was not a unique event but one of many such happenings. One need only glance at the parallel columns of American claims, Japanese verifications, and the blank spaces signifying uncorrelated submarine sinkings of merchant vessels in the Pacific to realize how common was imperfect target identification. Such lists, when read a half-century after the events of 1 April 1945, make the sinking of the *Awa maru* seem less extraordinary, if not more nearly normal.[115]

The same can, with equal justice, be said about the imperfect communications that failed to instill greater caution in the *Queenfish* crew before they sank the *Awa maru*. In later years Elliott Loughlin, musing over the might-have-beens, lamented that the pre-patrol briefing officer at Saipan had failed to mention the Japanese ship's impending transit of his submarine's assigned area.[116] In the grand scheme of things, however, the significance of that failure was minuscule. Similarly, for an assistant on the ComSubPac staff to have sent out a less carefully drafted and more vague message than his superior would have written seems more an ordinary than an exceptional occurrence. The mishandling of the warning messages on board the *Queenfish* is equally comprehensible. If one considers, even for a moment, how many thousands of messages that Jack Bennett, "Bull" Geer, and the *Queenfish* radiomen handled, the fact that one—however vital for the lives of those on the *Awa maru*—was not called to Loughlin's attention appears anything but unusual. Error in war is omnipresent.

Even if all of the admonitory messages had gotten through to the *Queenfish*'s skipper, would Loughlin have behaved any differently than he did on that fateful Sunday evening in April 1945? Probably not. For in every other instance in which an American sub skipper had held his fire rather than attack a protected Japanese vessel, such as a hospital ship or one traveling under guarantee of safe passage, the clues pointing to the correctness of that decision were obvious at the time. The captains of the *Hoe* (SS 258) and *Caiman* (SS 323), who had spotted the *Awa maru* earlier in her voyage, had been deterred by her special markings.[117] So too had the skipper of the *Crevalle* (SS 291), who had tracked the ship barely twenty-four hours before she was sunk.[118] Only ten days before the *Awa maru*'s demise, Loughlin himself had decided against firing torpedoes at a properly lighted hospital ship.[119]

When the reverse was true, and American sub captains did sink Japanese hospital ships—a tragedy that occurred on at least three prior occasions—they had been unable, due to tactical conditions or the enemy's failure to illuminate properly the protected vessels, to see their prey.[120] That was what happened on the night of 1 April 1945. Captain Hamada kept blazing the lights that identified the *Awa maru* as a special ship.[121] In this instance, the fog of war was real—and thick enough to blind Loughlin and his men to her protected character.

Their eyes told them—through an electronic intermediary—that the *Awa maru* was a legitimate target. The mix of reason, passion, and determination that kept them at their dangerous job demanded that they try to sink her. To have done otherwise was unthinkable.

But now, thanks to the lone survivor they had pulled aboard, they knew that they had done the unimaginable. How could they explain their actions to their superiors? And how would the navy, the administration, and the nation ultimately responsible for their actions judge them?

5

Court-Martial: "A Damned Shame"

I N THE WEE HOURS of Tuesday, 3 April 1945, Vice Adm. Charles Andrews Lockwood, Jr., found a quiet moment on board the *Bonefish* (SS 223) in which to write his wife, Phyllis. "Had a bit of hard luck yesterday," he wrote. The *Queenfish* sank the *Awa maru,* her safe-conduct pass to the contrary notwithstanding. In the fog, "the Q," as he put it, mistook the Japanese ship for a destroyer that was part of a nearby convoy. "The y.b.'s will swear we did it intentionally. Actually," the admiral continued, he had sought permission to sink the *Awa maru* since spies in Singapore reported that she had unloaded ammunition and weapons including two 155-mm cannon. But "Mr. N" [Fleet Adm. Chester W. Nimitz, Commander in Chief, Pacific Fleet (CinCPac)] said "No!" So, Lockwood ruefully concluded, "he probably thinks I did it on purpose. The fact is," he asserted defiantly, "I'm not a damned bit sorry!"[1]

The conflicting tones of Admiral Lockwood's letter captured precisely the complexity of the dilemma that he, Elliott Loughlin and the *Queenfish* crew, and their naval superiors now faced: how to cope with error—in this case, a mistake of tragic proportions for its victims and potentially terrible

Vice Adm. Charles
Andrews Lockwood, Jr.
*Naval Historical Foundation col-
lection, from National Archives
80-G-398230*

consequences for its perpetrators. At one level, they found a quick and easy answer to that dilemma: less than three weeks after the *Queenfish* sank the *Awa maru,* a naval court-martial found Cdr. Charles Elliott Loughlin guilty of negligence. But at a deeper level, that verdict provided no really satisfactory answers to the more basic questions that attended the conduct of the Pacific submarine war. What was the relationship between national policy and individual action? Who or what was responsible for the deaths resulting from a policy of unrestricted submarine warfare? And what of error? How could its presence be reconciled with the professionalism and pride of the U.S. Navy? In their efforts to deal with the *Awa maru* tragedy during the spring of 1945, American naval officials demonstrated how very difficult it was for them to reach even tentative answers to those questions.

From the first moment on Monday morning, 2 April 1945, when Admiral Lockwood learned what the *Queenfish* had done, there was a real chance that the U.S. Navy might try to keep the sinking of the *Awa maru* secret. That would have been quite consistent with a policy of saying as little as possible about what "the silent service" fighting the war under the Pacific was doing. It was also quite practical, for the sole survivor of the tragedy remained in custody on board the *Queenfish*. Officers on Lockwood's staff may have considered such an approach, for six hours of a normal working day passed between their receipt of the submarine's initial report on the sinking and dispatch of a message to CinCPac headquarters about it. Admiral Lockwood sent that information to Nimitz, expressing "deep regret" for what had occurred.[2]

CinCPac was loath to rush to judgment about what should be done. His thoughts were focused on the battle for Okinawa, which had begun the very day that the *Queenfish* sank the *Awa maru*. Nimitz thus sent a personal message to the CNO, Fleet Adm. Ernest J. King, that suggested discreet delay in doing anything about the sinking. Taking a line of "plausible deniability" when the Japanese, as they inevitably would, protested the destruction of the *Awa maru* might be the best course of action.[3] If, as first reports hinted, the ship had been wildly off her previously announced course and schedule, had Commander Loughlin been wrong to attack her? The sole survivor of the sinking was in naval custody, and if Tokyo raised questions about what had occurred, the Japanese could simply be told that the *Awa maru* had struck a mine.[4]

That approach to the sinking did not appeal at all to Admiral King. The CNO was an irascible but conscientious commander who demanded accountability from all of his subordinates; he was angered and upset by what had happened. His deputy, Vice Adm. Richard S. "Dickie" Edwards, suggested saying nothing until more details of the incident were known. King rejected that counsel and reported the sinking to Secretary of the Navy James Forrestal.[5] Twenty-four hours slipped by. Then, even before State Department officials agreed on how best to proceed, King fired off orders to CinCPac: despite Admiral Lockwood's expression of "deep regret" over the sinking of a ship whose safe passage the United States had guaranteed, the incident was "of such importance" that Nimitz must "relieve [the] captain of the *Queenfish* from command and bring him to trial by General Court Martial." Those actions were necessary, King continued, so that "the record may be clear."[6]

But clarifying the record did not prove easy for any of the American naval officers directly concerned with the sinking of the *Awa maru*. Their attitudes toward error complicated the task of carrying out King's order.

Nimitz and Lockwood complied with that command—if slowly and not without reluctance. Although the CNO had asked for immediate confirmation of the position and time of the *Awa maru*'s destruction, more than eighteen hours passed before Nimitz sent that information on to Washington. Moreover, he concurred in Lockwood's decision to keep the *Queenfish* on war patrol for another ten days and then allow eight more for the return voyage to Guam.[7] That choice guaranteed that nearly three weeks would pass before Loughlin, the defendant-to-be, reached the site of the court-martial King had ordered. Clearly, Loughlin's superiors wanted to buy time for preparation of his defense.

Lockwood began that process only minutes after sending his first report on the sinking to Nimitz, by ordering the *Queenfish* and the *Sea Fox* to return to the site to search for evidence of the cargo the *Awa maru* had been carrying.[8] Although she got there first, the *Sea Fox* had to cut short her search in order to rush a seaman, wounded in a bizarre shooting by a fellow crewman, to the *Tench* (SS 417).[9] Loughlin searched all afternoon on 3 April and by nightfall was convinced that "no survivors remained." His "continuous examination" of debris scattered over a wide area, however, revealed something of potential importance to his own defense. The *Awa maru* had carried thousands of bales of rubber and a large number of carefully packed tin boxes that contained "a dark granulated material," which he and his crew could not identify. Her holds had thus been crammed with contraband—war-related materials that normally deprived the vessel carrying them of any guarantee of safe passage. The next morning, after reporting that discovery to ComSubPac, the *Queenfish* returned, at Lockwood's direction, to normal war patrol duties, temporarily taking over those of her wolfpack mate, the *Sea Fox*.[10]

Doing so gave the *Queenfish* crew a brief but welcome return to the normal routines of war at sea. Men who had been "afraid we would catch hell [for] sinking a ship that was supposed to be taking supplies to POWs in Japan" began to feel a little better.[11] Of course, the sole survivor was there to remind them of their destruction of the *Awa maru*, but in their cramped environment even he became a normal presence. On the night he was hauled aboard, a crewman fearful of the enemy had menaced him with a wrench; but now, dressed in a shirt one of the torpedomen had provided, the captive was at work doing laundry and allowed to move relatively freely around the sub. Later, Shorty Evans would remember the sole *Awa maru* survivor as "a very nice person—the only one who had courage [enough] to come aboard the *Queenfish*."[12] Crewmen even came to refer to him by name—Shimoda Kantarō.

After recovering from the immediate trauma he had suffered, Shimoda began to provide more information about himself and his ship to his captors. Some of what he said was true. He was a forty-six-year-old steward first class who had served on board NYK ships for years. He had a wife who had borne him five children. The oldest was a nineteen-year-old girl, who sewed parachutes; his older sons worked in a sugar-processing factory. The children were Christians, having studied at missionary-run schools, while he and his wife were Buddhists.

Speaking in halting English about his own wartime experiences, Shimoda may even have drawn some sympathy from his captors. He had narrowly escaped death three times previously when the ships on which he served had been torpedoed. One of them was the *Teia maru*, which had taken Americans interned in Japan to the *Gripsholm* for its second exchange and then carried Red Cross relief supplies to American and Allied POWs in Japanese custody.[13] Perhaps these earlier brushes with death had given him the strength and tenacity to hold onto the life ring until he was pulled aboard the *Queenfish*.

Shimoda also said a good deal that was either untrue, beyond his power to know with certainty, or designed to flatter his captors. With the exception of thirty-six women and fourteen small children, he said, most of the passengers on board the *Awa maru* had been survivors of ships previously sunk in the southwest Pacific; in fact, only about 20 percent were men of that sort. He recalled that thirty tankers had been sunk near Singapore within the past five months and claimed that fourteen transports had been sunk at Takao and another forty at Saigon. He also said that people in Japan were suffering from the ravages of the American submarine blockade; even butter (a commodity most Japanese would never have used) was in short supply! Indeed, as Shimoda saw it, American subs, unlike their worthless Japanese counterparts, would end the war within two years by sinking all of Japan's ships.[14]

On Saturday evening, 7 April, this interlude of relative calm came to a sudden end. Although Loughlin had requested an extension of time in the *Queenfish* and *Sea Fox*'s new area, Lockwood ordered him to terminate the war patrol and return to Guam.[15] That order, sent after he and Nimitz had delayed implementing King's directive to hold a court-martial, made no mention of a trial.[16] But Loughlin and his crew probably sensed that a reckoning of sorts for their attack on the *Awa maru* lay ahead. Why else, with sixteen torpedoes left in the racks, fuel enough to stay on war patrol longer, and but one enemy ship sunk, would ComSubPac have ordered the *Queenfish* back to Guam?[17]

That surmise may have prompted Loughlin, probably with assistance from Lieutenant Bennett, to complete his official report on the *Queenfish*'s sinking of the *Awa maru*. Apart from what Bennett had gleaned in follow-up interviews with Shimoda, most of what it said was by now old and unexceptional news. The report rehearsed in detail what had happened on the night of 1 April, summarized what Shimoda had said about the *Awa maru*'s cargo, and detailed efforts over the past few days to locate, recover, and identify materials from the sunken ship.

Its concluding paragraph, however, was a stirring defense of the *Queenfish*'s actions. Loughlin said he "deeply regret[ted]" the sinking of the *Awa maru* but quickly added that he had done so "in the sincere belief" that she was "a legitimate target." He readily admitted his own error in evaluating "factors which tended to identify the ship as other than the *Awa maru*" but contended that the "mistaken identity" was "excusable" and the ensuing attack "justified." In Loughlin's view it seemed "incredible" that a ship "protected by lights, markings, and advance notice guaranteeing safe passage" would race through an area known to be patrolled by hostile submarines at a speed which, in the prevailing weather conditions, would "obviously" preclude "close observation" of her protective markings. Such action would place the submarine tracking such a ship in "an untenable and dangerous" position. Given the submarine force's thorough indoctrination in "aggressive tactics" and the *Queenfish*'s previous efforts to perform accordingly in areas where "normally any contact is a legitimate target," he had simply acted reasonably in attacking the *Awa maru*. "Considering the circumstances surrounding this attack," Loughlin concluded, he would find it "most difficult to justify and explain any other action" that might have allowed "this unidentified ship" to proceed "unmolested."[18]

That was the essence of the *Queenfish* skipper's defense of her sinking the *Awa maru*. Four days later, Loughlin seized an unexpected opportunity to bolster that defense and compensate for the error he and his men had committed. On the morning of 11 April, the *Queenfish* sighted a friendly PB4Y-2 Liberator aircraft. About an hour later her radiomen decoded a message reporting that two life rafts with thirteen men on board had been found. But it did not give any position. That evening the *Queenfish* received orders to help recover the men but had to backtrack 170 miles to do so. A little before 0200 (two o'clock the next morning), her lookouts spotted flares and a bobbing white light in the rough seas. Forty-five minutes later, the sub approached the two life rafts. The *Queenfish*'s "strong-armed boatswain" had to hang over the side to pull the thirteen men on board, as the waves began filling their boats with water. Bennett then tried, but failed, to sink the rafts by slashing their watertight compartments. Then, worried lest the sub's searchlight, which had been on for more than thirty minutes, betray her position to the enemy, Loughlin decided that the *Queenfish* must clear the area.[19]

He also sensed that the rescuees, crewmen from the PB4Y-2 sighted the preceding morning, might provide valuable evidence of his crew's bravery and professionalism. Three hours later the sub closed the destroyer *Cassin* (DD 372); in the normal course of events, those rescued would have been transferred to the larger vessel for medical examination and transportation to the nearest port. But Loughlin, who recalled the value of returning from the *Queenfish*'s first war patrol with rescued victims on board, declined to put them on the destroyer. His stated reason for not doing so—reluctance to interrupt their "primary treatment," sleep—rang hollow; while they had come aboard "extremely weary" after eighty-one hours crammed into life rafts, once fed, treated for minor ailments, and given a chance to rest, they appeared free of "excessive anxiety" and "neurosis."[20]

Loughlin's decision guaranteed that the *Queenfish* would enter Apra harbor carrying thirteen witnesses to her crew's prowess and but one reminder, Shimoda Kantarō, of their error in sinking the *Awa maru*. That gave the crew reason to hope that they would be received with something like the cheers that had greeted them when they arrived at Saipan at the beginning of this, their fourth war patrol. Such hopes were not entirely unrealistic, for Lockwood had told them of the *Queenfish*'s nomination for a Presidential Unit Citation for her first war patrol and had commended them for "nice work" in a "most expeditious" night rescue of the downed PB4Y-2 crew.[21] Indeed, had they not sunk the *Awa maru*, the men of the *Queenfish* might have been praised in a *Life* magazine article about a submarine war patrol that photojournalists (and former prisoners of the Japanese) Carl and Shelly Mydans had come to Guam to produce.[22]

Instead, a swarm of stern-faced visitors greeted them. Well before the *Queenfish* moored alongside the *Bowfin* (SS 287), which nestled in the shadow of the tender *Apollo* (AS 25), Marine guards came out and took Shimoda Kantarō away in a small boat. No sooner had the last of the lines been secured than Admiral Lockwood came aboard.[23] That in itself was not unusual, for Uncle Charley liked to greet his lads returning from war patrol. The youngest vice admiral in the fleet knew how important personal gestures of appreciation were to sustaining the morale of the men who served under him.[24]

But this time the admiral was not smiles and handshakes. He had bad news for Elliott Loughlin, news which he had concealed for eleven days: the *Queenfish* skipper was to be relieved of his command and brought before a general court-martial for having sunk the *Awa maru.*[25]

That moment was perhaps the lowest in both men's naval careers. Lockwood approached it feeling like Dr. Jekyll and Mr. Hyde. With one hand he would be commending Loughlin and the *Queenfish* for rescuing the downed aviators; he also knew that CNO King had approved a Presidential Unit Citation for her first war patrol. With the other he would, in effect, be punishing Loughlin and his crew for an action that he personally thought was entirely justifiable. To relieve and court-martial Loughlin, as he confided to his wife in a letter written earlier that day, was just "a damned shame all the way through."[26]

Loughlin was stunned by what Lockwood had to say. "I just feel that we ain't been done right!" he replied slowly, in words tinged with the drawl of his native North Carolina. Then he spoke in his own and his men's defense: the third warning message—directed to all subs under Admiral Lockwood's command—had not specified just where the *Awa maru* might be. Furthermore, the briefing officer who had spoken to him just prior to the *Queenfish's* departure from Saipan had said nothing about a ship that would be traveling through his boat's war patrol area with a guarantee of safe passage.[27]

That disclaimer sent Commander Voge and Cdr. William D. Irvin, Lockwood's staff operations and communications officers, respectively, scurrying below to search message files in the *Queenfish's* radio shack. What they found there removed any doubts about the need to proceed with a court-that photojournalists (and former prisoners of the Japanese) Carl and Shelly Mydans had come to Guam to produce.[22]

Instead, a swarm of stern-faced visitors greeted them. Well before the *Queenfish* moored alongside the *Bowfin* (SS 287), which nestled in the shadow of the tender *Apollo* (AS 25), Marine guards came out and took Shimoda Kantarō away in a small boat. No sooner had the last of the lines been secured than Admiral Lockwood came aboard.[23] That in itself was not unusual, for Uncle Charley liked to greet his lads returning from war patrol. The youngest vice admiral in the fleet knew how important personal gestures of appreciation were to sustaining the morale of the men who served under him.[24]

But this time the admiral was not smiles and handshakes. He had bad news for Elliott Loughlin, news which he had concealed for eleven days: the *Queenfish* skipper was to be relieved of his command and brought before a general court-martial for having sunk the *Awa maru*.[25]

That moment was perhaps the lowest in both men's naval careers. Lockwood approached it feeling like Dr. Jekyll and Mr. Hyde. With one hand he would be commending Loughlin and the *Queenfish* for rescuing the downed aviators; he also knew that CNO King had approved a Presidential Unit Citation for her first war patrol. With the other he would, in effect, be punishing Loughlin and his crew for an action that he personally thought was entirely justifiable. To relieve and court-martial Loughlin, as he confided to his wife in a letter written earlier that day, was just "a damned shame all the way through."[26]

Loughlin was stunned by what Lockwood had to say. "I just feel that we ain't been done right!" he replied slowly, in words tinged with the drawl of his native North Carolina. Then he spoke in his own and his men's defense: the third warning message—directed to all subs under Admiral Lockwood's command—had not specified just where the *Awa maru* might be. Furthermore, the briefing officer who had spoken to him just prior to the *Queenfish*'s departure from Saipan had said nothing about a ship that would be traveling through his boat's war patrol area with a guarantee of safe passage.[27]

That disclaimer sent Commander Voge and Cdr. William D. Irvin, Lockwood's staff operations and communications officers, respectively, scurrying below to search message files in the *Queenfish*'s radio shack. What they found there removed any doubts about the need to proceed with a court-

sub. Later, Shorty Evans would remember the sole *Awa maru* survivor as "a very nice person—the only one who had courage [enough] to come aboard the *Queenfish*."[12] Crewmen even came to refer to him by name—Shimoda Kantarō.

After recovering from the immediate trauma he had suffered, Shimoda began to provide more information about himself and his ship to his captors. Some of what he said was true. He was a forty-six-year-old steward first class who had served on board NYK ships for years. He had a wife who had borne him five children. The oldest was a nineteen-year-old girl, who sewed parachutes; his older sons worked in a sugar-processing factory. The children were Christians, having studied at missionary-run schools, while he and his wife were Buddhists.

Speaking in halting English about his own wartime experiences, Shimoda may even have drawn some sympathy from his captors. He had narrowly escaped death three times previously when the ships on which he served had been torpedoed. One of them was the *Teia maru*, which had taken Americans interned in Japan to the *Gripsholm* for its second exchange and then carried Red Cross relief supplies to American and Allied POWs in Japanese custody.[13] Perhaps these earlier brushes with death had given him the strength and tenacity to hold onto the life ring until he was pulled aboard the *Queenfish*.

Shimoda also said a good deal that was either untrue, beyond his power to know with certainty, or designed to flatter his captors. With the exception of thirty-six women and fourteen small children, he said, most of the passengers on board the *Awa maru* had been survivors of ships previously sunk in the southwest Pacific; in fact, only about 20 percent were men of that sort. He recalled that thirty tankers had been sunk near Singapore within the past five months and claimed that fourteen transports had been sunk at Takao and another forty at Saigon. He also said that people in Japan were suffering from the ravages of the American submarine blockade; even butter (a commodity most Japanese would never have used) was in short supply! Indeed, as Shimoda saw it, American subs, unlike their worthless Japanese counterparts, would end the war within two years by sinking all of Japan's ships.[14]

On Saturday evening, 7 April, this interlude of relative calm came to a sudden end. Although Loughlin had requested an extension of time in the *Queenfish* and *Sea Fox*'s new area, Lockwood ordered him to terminate the war patrol and return to Guam.[15] That order, sent after he and Nimitz had delayed implementing King's directive to hold a court-martial, made no mention of a trial.[16] But Loughlin and his crew probably sensed that a reckoning of sorts for their attack on the *Awa maru* lay ahead. Why else, with sixteen torpedoes left in the racks, fuel enough to stay on war patrol longer, and but one enemy ship sunk, would ComSubPac have ordered the *Queenfish* back to Guam?[17]

That surmise may have prompted Loughlin, probably with assistance from Lieutenant Bennett, to complete his official report on the *Queenfish*'s sinking of the *Awa maru*. Apart from what Bennett had gleaned in follow-up interviews with Shimoda, most of what it said was by now old and unexceptional news. The report rehearsed in detail what had happened on the night of 1 April, summarized what Shimoda had said about the *Awa maru*'s cargo, and detailed efforts over the past few days to locate, recover, and identify materials from the sunken ship.

Its concluding paragraph, however, was a stirring defense of the *Queenfish*'s actions. Loughlin said he "deeply regret[ted]" the sinking of the *Awa maru* but quickly added that he had done so "in the sincere belief" that she was "a legitimate target." He readily admitted his own error in evaluating "factors which tended to identify the ship as other than the *Awa maru*" but contended that the "mistaken identity" was "excusable" and the ensuing attack "justified." In Loughlin's view it seemed "incredible" that a ship "protected by lights, markings, and advance notice guaranteeing safe passage" would race through an area known to be patrolled by hostile submarines at a speed which, in the prevailing weather conditions, would "obviously" preclude "close observation" of her protective markings. Such action would place the submarine tracking such a ship in "an untenable and dangerous" position. Given the submarine force's thorough indoctrination in "aggressive tactics" and the *Queenfish*'s previous efforts to perform accordingly in areas where "normally any contact is a legitimate target," he had simply acted reasonably in attacking the *Awa maru*. "Considering the circumstances surrounding this attack," Loughlin concluded, he would find it "most difficult to justify and explain any other action" that might have allowed "this unidentified ship" to proceed "unmolested."[18]

That was the essence of the *Queenfish* skipper's defense of her sinking the *Awa maru*. Four days later, Loughlin seized an unexpected opportunity to bolster that defense and compensate for the error he and his men had com-

mitted. On the morning of 11 April, the *Queenfish* sighted a frien[d] Liberator aircraft. About an hour later her radiomen decoded reporting that two life rafts with thirteen men on board had been it did not give any position. That evening the *Queenfish* receive[d] help recover the men but had to backtrack 170 miles to do so. A li[t] 0200 (two o'clock the next morning), her lookouts spotted fla[sh]bobbing white light in the rough seas. Forty-five minutes later, approached the two life rafts. The *Queenfish*'s "strong-armed bo[ys]" had to hang over the side to pull the thirteen men on board, as th[ese] began filling their boats with water. Bennett then tried, but failed, to rafts by slashing their watertight compartments. Then, worried lest t[he] searchlight, which had been on for more than thirty minutes, betray h[er] tion to the enemy, Loughlin decided that the *Queenfish* must clear the

He also sensed that the rescuees, crewmen from the PB4Y-2 sight[ed] preceding morning, might provide valuable evidence of his crew's br[avery] and professionalism. Three hours later the sub closed the destroyer [ ] (DD 372); in the normal course of events, those rescued would have transferred to the larger vessel for medical examination and transport[ation] to the nearest port. But Loughlin, who recalled the value of returning f[rom] the *Queenfish*'s first war patrol with rescued victims on board, declined to them on the destroyer. His stated reason for not doing so—reluctance interrupt their "primary treatment," sleep—rang hollow; while they [had] come aboard "extremely weary" after eighty-one hours crammed into [the] rafts, once fed, treated for minor ailments, and given a chance to rest, th[ey] appeared free of "excessive anxiety" and "neurosis."[20]

Loughlin's decision guaranteed that the *Queenfish* would enter Apra ha[r]bor carrying thirteen witnesses to her crew's prowess and but one reminde[r] Shimoda Kantarō, of their error in sinking the *Awa maru*. That gave the crew reason to hope that they would be received with something like the cheers that had greeted them when they arrived at Saipan at the beginning of this, their fourth war patrol. Such hopes were not entirely unrealistic, for Lockwood had told them of the *Queenfish*'s nomination for a Presidential Unit Citation for her first war patrol and had commended them for "nice work" in a "most expeditious" night rescue of the downed PB4Y-2 crew.[21] Indeed, had they not sunk the *Awa maru*, the men of the *Queenfish* might have been praised in a *Life* magazine article about a submarine war patrol

Cdr. Charles Elliott Loughlin: a hero one day, on trial the next. *Mrs. Lynn Elliott Duval*

martial. The sub had received the two previous plain-language messages about the projected course and schedule of the *Awa maru*; together with the encoded warning of 30 March, they should have alerted the *Queenfish* to her proximity and prevented an attack on her. That Elliott Loughlin's initials did not appear in the routing box to indicate that he had seen those first two messages did not matter.[28] Once they were received, he, as commanding officer, was responsible under Navy Regulations for seeing that the *Queenfish* responded properly to those warnings. Thus, there was at least a technical case to be brought against Loughlin. After he saw that evidence, Lockwood stayed on board the *Queenfish* for nearly an hour trying to explain to Loughlin why there was no alternative to a court-martial. In an effort to assuage the sub skipper's obviously hurt pride, the admiral invited him to dinner that evening. But nothing Lockwood said then or later could dispel Loughlin's "sullen and remorseful" feelings.[29]

The events of the next few days made Loughlin and his men feel even worse. They spent Sunday, 15 April, on board the *Queenfish*, shifting her mooring to allow the *Bowfin* to get under way, and off-loading torpedoes to the *Apollo* in preparation for a refit. Early the next morning the crew was mustered to witness a sad ceremony: Lt. Cdr. Frank Shamer relieved their plankowner skipper, Elliott Loughlin, of command of the *Queenfish*. Commanding officers came and went in the life of every submarine, but to see this man, whom they liked and respected and who had been with their boat since before she slid off the ways into the Atlantic so many months ago, depart under the cloud of an impending court-martial must have pained the *Queenfish* officers and crew. Once the change of command ceremony ended, they departed for a bittersweet spell of "rest and recreation" behind the fences of Camp Dealey.[30] Loughlin was left alone to face the court-martial he felt he should not have to stand.

While these unhappy events took place, preparations for that trial went forward. Admiral Lockwood approached the event with decidedly mixed feelings. Twelve days earlier he had agonized over it and its probable result. "I hate to see this trial held," he confided to his wife. Even if Commander Loughlin were acquitted, there would always be a "blemish" on his record. "I can't help but blame myself a little," he admitted, for not having foreseen the possibility of a mistaken attack in the fogs so common to the Taiwan Strait in the spring of the year. Lockwood's burden of guilt was even heavier because he knew he would not be able to testify in person in Loughlin's defense; by the time the court-martial proceedings began, the admiral would be on his way to Pearl Harbor, Washington, and San Diego for conferences about new and more daring submarine operations against Japan. He was also scheduled to pause for a long-delayed reunion with his wife and young sons in San Diego's beautiful, mountainous backcountry.[31] The thought of that prospective pleasure—something denied to his lads, one of whom was about to be, in his view, unjustly court-martialed—must have stirred the admiral's conscience most unpleasantly.

Lockwood had long since decided to alleviate the twinges of guilt he felt by doing everything possible to see that Elliott Loughlin would be cleared of any wrongdoing. Well before the *Queenfish* entered Apra harbor he vowed, "I intend to leave no stone unturned to obtain a full and honorable acquittal." The admiral recognized that that might be rather difficult, given the "international angle and national honor involved"; "getting some very outstanding legal talent" was the first step toward achieving that goal.[32] Over the next ten days he and his chief of staff at the Pearl Harbor submarine base, Como. Merrill E. Comstock, did everything they could to enlist such talent.

Lockwood asked Nimitz to order a rear admiral to head the defense team, and when that proposal was rejected he wrote to the submarine detailing officer in the Navy Department's Bureau of Personnel asking for help in locating a second candidate for the job. When that specific individual proved unavailable, Comstock suggested appealing directly to the Secretary Forrestal or CNO King for help. Lockwood was not prepared to make so blatant a request for top-level assistance, but he did ask that a senior submariner who was also an attorney temporarily assigned to the CNO's staff be named defense counsel. When King spurned that proposal, Comstock persuaded CinCPac to let Capt. Henry C. Bruton, a highly decorated former commander of the *Greenling* (SS 213) and a lawyer currently serving as chief of staff at the Pacific Fleet Submarine Training Command, head the defense team. He would be assisted by a fellow George Washington Law School graduate, Marine Lt. Col. John H. Coffman, and if possible, a third officer.[33]

Although Lockwood's spirits were buoyed by the confidence that Bruton exuded when the two men met on the morning of the *Queenfish*'s arrival at Apra harbor, he was not prepared to leave matters solely in the defense counsel's hands.[34] Before he left Guam, the admiral took three more steps to influence the outcome of the pending court-martial. One was normal enough: Lockwood left the deposition that he had promised. In it he admitted that the orders under which the *Queenfish* operated had not been "sufficiently adequate" to cover "all conditions of visibility." They had not specified what action should be taken when visibility was poor against unidentifiable surface vessels "which might reasonably be believed" to be hospital ships or vessels traveling under a grant of safe passage.

Lockwood also contrasted the *Queenfish* skipper's professionalism with the less-than-perfect performance of the *Awa maru*'s captain. He praised Elliott Loughlin as "a fine example of an officer and a gentleman," asserting that his record demonstrated that he was "a fearless and daring leader" who made "skillful and aggressive" attacks. The sub captain was "most careful" in ascertaining and implementing his orders. He had demonstrated proper initiative, as well as "speed, intuition, and skill" in search-and-rescue operations. Captain Hamada, however, had not done all he should have to protect his ship on the night of 1 April. By not sounding her horn in the dense fog that enveloped her, he took on a heavy measure of responsibility for the loss of the *Awa maru*.[35]

Lockwood's second step was to appeal to Nimitz, the convenor of the impending court-martial, on Loughlin's behalf. In his endorsement of the *Queenfish*'s official report on the sinking of the *Awa maru,* Lockwood downplayed the notion of American culpability. Loughlin had simply been doing his job, obeying orders to conduct "unrestricted submarine warfare" against all enemy vessels except hospital ships and those granted safe passage. Hamada had both violated the rules of the road and disregarded his orders —by "apparently" not sounding fog signals and racing his ship eleven miles off the prearranged course and eighteen miles ahead of schedule. Loughlin, Lockwood insisted, could not have brought the *Queenfish* close enough to determine the *Awa maru*'s identity without laying her open to destruction by what he believed was an enemy destroyer. Thus, Lockwood informed Nimitz, "this tragic incident" was not the result of culpably negligent behavior by Loughlin but rather an "unavoidable accident of war."[36] Those words constituted a plea to the superior who could modify the findings and sentence of the court-martial so as to find Elliott Loughlin innocent.

Lockwood's third step on the *Queenfish* skipper's behalf was to try to influence one of the members of the court. That individual was Rear Adm. John H. Brown, Jr.—known in his midshipman days as "Babe" the football star—his deputy in Hawaii, who was flying out to take command of the submarine force while Lockwood was away. In a "list of pending items" left for his deputy, Lockwood said he "naturally" wanted to obtain "full and honorable acquittal" for Cdr. Elliott Loughlin. The admiral told his subordinate about the deposition he had left with the defense counsel. He also said he was prepared to share in the blame if the coming investigation found that he, personally, or any element in his organization was at fault. Lockwood wanted all the facts brought out so as to "to clear [Commander Loughlin] and to avoid future mistakes" like those made in sinking the *Awa maru.*[37] When Admiral Brown took his seat on the coming court-martial, he would know exactly what *his* immediate superior wanted him to do.

Admiral Nimitz, under whose authority the trial would be convened, held too exalted a position on the chain of command to take such obviously partisan steps as Lockwood had. He knew exactly where King stood on this matter. He—or members of his staff who helped prepare for the court-martial proceedings—knew Washington had sent a skeptical yet responsible reply to Tokyo's initial pleas for any information about the fate of the *Awa maru.* It promised that the navy would "in all sincerity and good faith" conduct an investigation to resolve any "degree of uncertainty" that remained as to the "actual identity" of the sunken vessel.[38] That statement, published two days before the *Queenfish* reached Guam, left little doubt that the navy was under pressure from politicians and diplomats to find out how and why she had sunk the *Awa maru.*[39]

But CinCPac could influence the outcome of that inquiry indirectly, by the choices he made in setting it up. Two were of fundamental importance and could be interpreted as favoring the defendant. Nimitz limited the scope of the investigation by bringing only narrowly defined charges against Loughlin. None raised the broader international legal and ethical issues posed by his sinking the *Awa maru.*[40] No American naval officer in the midst of a war to the death against a fierce enemy was prepared to discuss the "abstract" issue of whether or not the unrestricted submarine warfare in which that event took place was illegal. As a result, Loughlin would face only very specific, albeit serious, allegations: culpable inefficiency in performance of duty, disobedience of a lawful order, and negligence in obeying orders.[41]

The Pacific Fleet commander also tilted the balance of advantage slightly toward the defense by creating a panel of judges of extraordinary rank and naming a minimally competent prosecutor to present the case against Elliott Loughlin. The former were extremely strong—high in rank, deep in experience, and certainly not without understanding of what undersea warfare was all about. Never before—at least in this war—had so many and such senior officers been assembled to pass judgment on the actions of a single submarine commander and his crew.[42] Nimitz named Vice Adm. John H. Hoover, known as "genial John" for the severity of his demeanor, as the most senior member of the court.[43] Vice Adm. Jesse Oldendorf, under whom Loughlin had served in the Caribbean earlier in the war, came next in rank.[44] Two rear admirals followed—Ernest L. Gunther, a naval aviator, and John Brown, Lockwood's deputy and replacement.[45] Two captains, Archer M.R. Allen and Lewis S. Parks, rounded out the panel of judges.[46]

These men were well qualified by experience to understand the predicament that Elliott Loughlin confronted in sinking the *Awa maru* without prior identification of the target. Four of them were qualified submariners. Three had commanded boats.[47] One of the oldest had been on a transport sunk by a German submarine in World War I.[48] The youngest, Captain Parks, knew firsthand of the perils and frustrations, the rewards and errors of undersea war against the Japanese. As skipper of the *Pompano* (SS 181) he had pioneered through-the-periscope photography and come under mistaken attack by an American carrier-based dive-bomber. One of the first sub skippers to attack a target escorted by ships having effective sonar gear, he had later in the war experienced the virtually fruitless kind of patrol that had so frustrated the *Queenfish* early in 1945.[49]

The man Nimitz named judge advocate general, or prosecutor, was, by contrast, an expeditious but weak choice. Nimitz had allowed Lockwood to reach back to the much bigger pool of naval legal talent at Pearl Harbor to find defenders for Loughlin; for a prosecutor he and his staff looked only locally on Guam and fixed upon Capt. John McCutchen. McCutchen was not a submariner but the commanding officer of the *Apollo*, at whose side the *Queenfish* was moored.[50] Although he was senior to the defense counsel, he lacked any legal training.[51] Indeed only at the last minute did Nimitz provide him with an assistant counsel—a gesture, it would seem, that was essential to offset the obvious imbalance of strength between the defense and prosecution legal teams.[52]

That decision suggested that Nimitz felt that he too was under the gun as a consequence of the *Queenfish*'s sinking the *Awa maru*. While he empathized with Loughlin, turned a blind eye to Lockwood's efforts on the sub skipper's behalf, and named judges likely to understand the situation the *Queenfish* commander had faced on the night of 1 April 1945, Nimitz recognized that the U.S. government appeared to have violated its word. That alone demanded that the court-martial about to begin be thorough and fair.

But would it be so?

At precisely 1000 (ten o'clock in the morning) on Thursday, 19 April 1945, Cdr. Charles Elliott Loughlin was brought before those who were to judge his conduct in the sinking of the *Awa maru*. Their shoulders heavy with the gold of high rank, the four admirals and two captains selected by Admiral Nimitz sat behind a table at the end of a long, narrow room in one of Guam's many hastily built temporary buildings. They watched silently as the proceedings began with the required ritual. Commander Loughlin first requested recognition of Captain Bruton and Lieutenant Colonel Coffman as his counsel; the judge advocate, Captain McCutchen, then read the three charges and specifications brought against the *Queenfish* skipper. The first accused him of "culpable inefficiency in the performance of duty." It stated that despite his submarine's receipt of all three warning messages concerning the *Awa maru*, Loughlin had failed "to make proper investigation, identification, and observation" of the target. Therefore, he had made an "improper attack."

The second charge asserted that Loughlin had disobeyed Admiral Lockwood's "lawful order," contained in the message of 30 March 1945, to "let pass safely" the *Awa maru*.

The third and final charge alleged that the *Queenfish* skipper had been guilty of "negligence in obeying orders" by failing to proceed "with due caution and circumspection" in trying to identify the *Awa maru* before sinking her.

Asked how he pleaded to each of these charges, Loughlin responded clearly and firmly, "Not guilty."[53]

McCutchen then began presenting the case against him. He got off to a rough start. The first prosecution witness, the *Queenfish*'s new skipper, Lt. Cdr. Frank Shamer, was obviously reluctant to testify against his predecessor.[54] McCutchen bumbled in interrogating him. Three times he questioned Shamer about what Loughlin had said; each time Bruton objected that any reply would be hearsay; and every time the court sustained those objections.[55]

McCutchen also hesitated to go for the jugular in questioning Shamer. The then-prospective commanding officer admitted that at least one of the three messages warning of the *Awa maru*'s protected character and possible presence in the *Queenfish*'s operating area had been received aboard the sub. McCutchen also got Shamer to admit that he had spoken with Loughlin about the possibility of encountering an enemy ship traveling under safe passage. But he declined to pursue the much more significant question of why the other two messages had not come before the *Queenfish* skipper's eyes. Doing so might have added weight to charges of culpable negligence and willful disobedience of an order.[56]

Bruton then seized the opportunity of cross-examining Shamer to refute those allegations. Shamer said the warning message of which Loughlin was aware had been addressed broadly— "generally to all submarines on patrol" —rather than directly in a manner that specified and alerted the *Queenfish*. Bruton then led Shamer on with questions designed to demonstrate how carefully Loughlin had observed the rules of engagement in identifying and attacking targets. Had any distinctive lights on the *Awa maru* been visible on the night of the attack? "No," Shamer replied. But then he went on to say that a week before the attack, when Loughlin had spotted a Japanese hospital ship that was illuminated with lights signifying her protected character, the *Queenfish* skipper had "turned away . . . and allowed her to go unmolested." Would so cautious a sub commander have acted precipitously or negligently on the night of 1 April 1945?[57]

A member of the court then interrupted the interrogation with a question of his own. How, he asked Shamer, had he (and by implication Loughlin) known that the target vessel was a warship? Shamer shot back that *he* knew so because the ship was moving "at high speed in greatly reduced visibility." To do so, she would have to have had either instruments such as those on board a warship or "a terrific desire" to get to "some scene of [battle] action." A merchant vessel would have had neither. That response allowed the defense counsel to prompt Shamer into providing still more exculpatory evidence. He revealed that earlier in the day, the *Sea Fox* had attacked a convoy about fifteen miles north of the contact point with the target—precisely the spot toward which the *Awa maru* appeared to be rushing.[58] Her behavior provided yet another plausible reason for Loughlin and his crew to presume that the vessel whose pip danced across their radar screen was in fact a warship, and thus a legitimate target for attack.

That exchange prompted McCutchen to shift the focus of his questioning to the narrower and less serious charge of negligence. Once again, he stumbled. He drew a damaging admission from the one subordinate that Loughlin believed to have been genuinely negligent—John Geer.[59] The hapless communications officer produced a copy of the warning message of 30 March and stated that to his knowledge the target had not been identified before the *Queenfish*'s torpedoes were fired. But Bruton pounced on that remark. What was Geer's battle station? "Assistant plot officer," the communicator replied. In that position, Bruton inquired, had he been able to know whether or not a particular target was identified? "No, sir," Geer stated, utterly destroying the value of his testimony.[60]

McCutchen was not prepared to give up his attack after that faux pas, however. He quizzed one *Queenfish* officer after another in an attempt to demonstrate that negligence in target identification was responsible for the wrongful sinking of the *Awa maru*. He rehearsed with each man just where he had been during the approach and probed for information as to what he had known about the possibility of a protected enemy vessel being in the submarine's operating area. Despite their reluctance to say anything harmful to Loughlin, McCutchen drew some potentially damaging remarks from them. He got Lieutenant Bennett, the executive officer and navigator, to admit that the radar pips on which the *Queenfish* crewmen had relied so heavily for target identification were not "invariably correct or adequate predictors" of a ship's size or type.[61] He drew admissions from four other officers that Commander Loughlin had neither given oral instructions nor written anything in his captain's night orders about the *Awa maru*—despite receipt of the warning message of 30 March.[62]

But for each of these thrusts Captain Bruton had an appropriate parry. He got Bennett to say that radar pips did provide some measure of target identification. In cross-examining each of the other four officers, he elicited opinions that, under the circumstances then prevailing, written night orders would have been superfluous. In preparations for a surface attack, a sub captain would have been on the bridge. Loughlin was there—wide awake, quite capable of giving necessary and appropriate orders.[63] That obviated the need for any night orders and diminished the importance of their absence.

That exchange brought the prosecution to what might have been a dramatic moment in the presentation of its case. McCutchen called the sole survivor, Shimoda Kantarō, accompanied by an interpreter, to testify.[64] Although he was technically a civilian internee, Shimoda had been taken to a prisoner-of-war camp that held about six hundred men, built after the retaking of Guam.[65] He had probably been interrogated there in preparation for the court-martial.

The judge advocate could conceivably have asked him questions that would have reminded the court of the enormous cost in human lives of the *Queenfish*'s erroneous sinking of the *Awa maru*. He could also have pressed inquiries that would have cast doubt on the submariners' accounts of what had happened on 1 April 1945. Was, for example, visibility on that night in fact as poor as they had said it was? Had very many others been able, like Shimoda, to race from their rooms to the deck as the torpedoes struck and escape from the doomed ship? Why was he, of all the other potential survivors in the water, the only one to have been pulled aboard the *Queenfish*?

Captain McCutchen ignored all such questions and stuck narrowly to the facts. The only thing of value he got from Shimoda was acknowledgment that the lights on the white crosses on the *Awa maru*'s sides and stacks had been illuminated at ten o'clock, an hour before *Queenfish* encountered her. He failed utterly to follow up when the defense counsel got Shimoda to admit that he had not heard the ship's foghorns that evening—even though the absence of that sound might well signify the absence of the fog that the men of the *Queenfish* claimed had precluded visual identification of the target.[66]

Instead, just before he formally rested the prosecution's case, McCutchen stood by while a member of the court got Shimoda to provide potentially mitigating evidence. What, he asked, had the *Awa maru* been carrying? Tin, rubber, and sugar in her holds, and victims of previous merchant ship sinkings in her passenger compartments, the Japanese replied through his interpreter. Those who had loaded the *Awa maru* with contraband had violated the customary provisions of a safe-passage guarantee. Should not that Japanese wrongdoing be taken into account in weighing the American sub commander's guilt or innocence? No one said a word about that, and McCutchen abruptly rested the prosecution's case.[67]

Captain Bruton then began his questioning for the defense. He could certainly empathize with Commander Loughlin, for he himself, as skipper of the *Greenling*, had in August 1942 sunk the *Brazil maru*, a vessel almost the same size as the *Awa maru*; that ship had been carrying six hundred passengers, only one of whom survived.[68] But plotting a strategy for Loughlin's defense had not been easy. The *Queenfish* skipper, convinced he had done no wrong and bitter after his relief from command, had wanted to speak in his own defense.[69] But Bruton insisted it would be better for Loughlin not to testify. The former *Queenfish* skipper was still emotionally upset. Moreover, since both sides admitted that the warning messages about the *Awa maru* had been received on the *Queenfish*, he might be snared into admitting that it had been his responsibility as captain to obey all of them. That would be sufficient, in technical terms, to convict Loughlin by words from his own mouth. That prospect—and Bruton's reminder that the prosecution had to *prove* he had done wrong—apparently convinced the former *Queenfish* captain that he had best remain silent.[70]

Bruton turned instead to other, presumably more credible, witnesses to make the case for Loughlin's innocence. His first premise quickly became clear: the *Awa maru* had created the circumstances that led to her misidentification by being off her announced course, schedule, and track. Lieutenant Bennett attested to that, and an independent witness, the navigator of Admiral Lockwood's flagship, the sub tender *Holland* (AS 3), agreed. Her speed and movement toward the point where the *Sea Fox* had been involved in an engagement earlier on 1 April 1945 gave her pursuers good reason to suppose that she was a warship.[71]

Bruton used a similar combination of *Queenfish* crewmen and independent witnesses to develop his second line of argument: the *Awa maru* had shed whatever immunity from attack she may have had by carrying contraband. Robert Reed, the sub's chief boatswain's mate, made that point dramatically by gesturing toward a pile of rubber and several airtight cans filled with an unidentified "black stuff" that had been placed in a front corner of the tiny room. The prosecution objected to that, arguing that there was no proof that these materials came from the *Awa maru*. The court, much to Bruton's chagrin, sustained that objection.[72]

When the court reassembled the next morning, the defense counsel struck back by recalling Shimoda Kantarō to the witness chair. The sole survivor reaffirmed that the *Awa maru* had carried contraband and admitted that she had already off-loaded all of the Red Cross supplies intended for POWs.[73] To clinch his main point, Bruton had Lockwood's staff operations and combat intelligence officer, Commander Voge, paraphrase a dispatch that revealed how the Japanese ship had off-loaded six hundred tons of ammunition, two thousand bombs, and twenty crated planes at Saigon.[74]

The defense counsel then turned to another independent witness, Cdr. Russell Kefauver, to argue that on the night of 1 April, Loughlin had simply done what any normally aggressive, successful sub skipper would have done. Kefauver, captain of the *Springer* (SS 414), who had been in command on five of his eleven war patrols, explained why Loughlin's behavior was logical rather than criminal or negligent. He said it was reasonable for Commander Loughlin to assume, at the seventeen-thousand-yard range at which the *Awa maru* first appeared on his sub's SJ radar, that the target was a destroyer or small merchant vessel rather than the much larger ship she was. When questioned, he affirmed that with the information Loughlin had had at hand, he, Kefauver, would have set the torpedoes at a depth and spread appropriate for a 250- to 300-foot-long destroyer—which was exactly what the *Queenfish* skipper had done.[75] Bruton thus got Kefauver to make, in technical terms, the essence of the defense argument: Commander Loughlin's professional expertise, rather than disobedience or negligence, was the taproot of the *Queenfish*'s destruction of the *Awa maru*.

To clinch that argument, Bruton turned to witnesses who were not there. He had his counterpart, McCutchen, read Lockwood's deposition, which insisted that circumstantially driven error rather than culpable negligence had caused the tragedy.[76] He then introduced, despite prosecution objections overruled by the court, one document after another that attested to the professionalism of Loughlin and his crew. The members of the court heard endorsements commending the submarine's performance on previous war patrols; her Presidential Unit Award citation; and various statements that accompanied Loughlin's personal commendations and awards. Having heard so much about the accused's professionalism, Bruton surmised, how could members of the court possibly find the onetime *Queenfish* skipper guilty of anything resembling culpable negligence, willful disobedience of orders, or even mere sloppiness in the attack on the *Awa maru?*

With that, he rested the case for the defense.[77]

Late on the morning of Friday, 20 April 1945, the opposing counsels summed up their cases. Captain McCutchen led off with a very brief, narrowly legalistic, simple statement to the effect that Commander Loughlin was guilty of all three charges brought against him. Captain Bruton responded with a much longer and more impassioned argument. He insisted that the *Awa maru* was not a cartel (specially protected) ship in international legal terms. No one had demonstrated that she had ever transported relief items for American and Allied prisoners of war. Nonetheless, the evidence for her having carried contraband, thereby shedding her protected status, was overwhelming.

Bruton argued that the *Awa maru*'s journey was not a mission of mercy but an act of treachery—the latest in a line of Japanese deceptions that stretched back to the bombing of the American gunboat *Panay* (PR 5) on the Yangtze River in December 1937, and the "sneak" attack on Pearl Harbor four years later. He argued that Tokyo had initially routed the *Awa maru* through a minefield north of Taiwan so as to lure American ships to destruction there; the Japanese had changed her course and schedule at the last minute in order to save the ship. Captain Hamada, however, had unintentionally disrupted this plot by imprudently speeding silently and directly (rather than zigzag-ging) through fog-shrouded, submarine-infested waters. The Japanese cap-tain's negligence and Loughlin's professional competence had thus drawn the *Queenfish* and the *Awa maru* to their fateful encounter.[78]

Bruton further argued that Loughlin's actions on the night of 1 April 1945 were reasonable and prudent under the circumstances. The *Queenfish* crew had drawn proper conclusions from the electronic means of target identifica-tion at their disposal. For Loughlin to have taken the *Queenfish* any closer to the *Awa maru* would have been "not only highly imprudent" but "unjustifi-ably dangerous." The *Awa maru* had shed her special character by carrying contraband and thus was no different from any other enemy merchant vessel. Hence, attacking and sinking her was not only "proper and lawful" but also "an important stroke toward the winning of the war against the Japanese."

That powerful line of argument was meant to overshadow Bruton's far weaker responses to the second and third charges brought against Elliott Loughlin. The defense counsel danced around the fact that the last warning message had been received aboard the *Queenfish,* asserting that if disobedi-ence had occurred it was unintentional rather than willful. Moreover, even Admiral Lockwood, under whose authority the admonition had been sent, admitted that that message was vaguely worded. Bruton seized upon its exact words to make the admittedly "somewhat tenuous" argument that Loughlin had never attacked an *Awa maru* "carrying prisoner of war sup-plies" but only a ship "loaded with war supplies and seamen."

In an attempt to refute the negligence charge, Bruton reminded the court of Loughlin's previously demonstrated prudence and service reputation. It would have been utter folly, he insisted, for the commander to have hazarded both by bringing the *Queenfish* closer to what he reasonably presumed was an enemy warship capable of destroying her. The defense counsel closed his argument by stressing the omnipresence of error in war. Those who fought it were, after all, human. Bruton reminded the members of the court of the "relative youth and inexperience" of the *Queenfish* officers who had appeared before them. Perhaps Loughlin had erred by relying on the information and judgments they fed him, but could he have done otherwise?

Bruton also pointed to the fragility of memory as a source of error. More than three weeks passed between the *Queenfish*'s receipt of the first two warn-ing messages and that of the third admonition, which depended upon familiarity with its predecessors for its force. Failure to make that connection paled in comparison with Japanese treachery and error as a cause of the erroneous sinking of the *Awa maru*. Her Tokyo masters' deceit and her captain's negligence, Bruton concluded, put her athwart the *Queenfish*'s torpedoes.[79]

After a break for lunch, McCutchen presented his rebuttal of the defense's case. His counterarguments were simple: two wrongs do not make a right, and ignorance does not absolve an individual of responsibility. McCutchen held that the nature of the *Awa maru*'s cargo, which Bruton claimed had violated her duties under international law and made her liable to sinking or seizure, was irrelevant. The issues before the court-martial were matters of military, not international, law. Moreover, Commander Loughlin had no knowledge of the *Awa maru*'s possible violation of normal terms of a safe-passage guarantee before he sank her. The defense's implicit argument that two wrongs—Japan's abuse of that guarantee and the *Queenfish*'s sinking of the *Awa maru*—added up to a right, contradicted all of the "standards of ethical conduct" that the United States as a nation embraced. Loughlin had been negligent, McCutchen concluded, because "mere belief" as to the identity of a target was not enough; a responsible submarine skipper was required by the orders and information he had received to know what his prey was before sinking it. Thus, Loughlin's negligence must be given greater weight than any errors Captain Hamada may have committed in explaining how and why the *Awa maru* was sunk.[80]

After McCutchen fell silent, he and everyone but the six members of the court left the room so that they, acting alone, could make their decision. Shortly thereafter, as custom dictated, the judge advocate general was recalled and directed to record the court's findings: not guilty on the first two charges, but guilty on the third and least serious. The four admirals and two captains did think Charles Elliott Loughlin had been guilty of negligence in obeying orders. They had him returned to the room, informed him of their decision, and then dismissed him so that they might determine an appropriate sentence.[81]

The punishment they settled upon reflected their own mixed feelings about the proceedings just concluded. Some members of the court, as their often friendly and sometimes leading questions had hinted over the past two days, appeared predisposed to find the commander innocent of all charges.[82] Others had hewed more strictly to the letter of Navy Regulations in a manner that would require them to find Elliott Loughlin guilty.[83] Now they appeared to strike a balance between those two positions by settling upon what looked like a compromise punishment. The court could have directed that the *Queenfish* skipper receive something as serious as a letter of reprimand from the Secretary of the Navy; it could have merely slapped his wrists, by directing that he be censured by his commanding officer. Instead, these six men decided that Charles Elliott Loughlin be given a letter of admonition from the Secretary of the Navy.[84]

That verdict prompted very different assessments of the court-martial. Years later, reflecting on it, Loughlin said that its result was "a foregone conclusion." Once his counsel had admitted that the message warning of the *Awa maru*'s possible presence had been received by the *Queenfish*, "school was out." He was guilty, in a technical sense, of not doing more to try to identify the *Awa maru* before sinking her. So the verdict "had to be negligence." The members of the court had "had to find us [the *Queenfish* crew] guilty of something."[85] The trial had been a setup. A few years after Loughlin voiced that opinion, a Japanese television docudrama about the sinking of the *Awa maru* hinted at precisely the opposite conclusion: the court-martial had been a whitewash. The prosecution had simply scratched around on the surface, politely questioning the *Queenfish* crew without ever challenging their version of events.[86]

Neither of those judgments was quite correct. Despite his efforts to get Loughlin acquitted, Lockwood knew that the larger logic of the situation demanded a conviction of some sort. The possibility could not be ignored that Japanese reprisals would be taken against American prisoners if some punishment were not handed down to the perpetrator of so great an error. The hapless Captain McCutchen was determined to get a conviction. However, he did not probe as deeply or carefully as he might have into the basic elements of the *Queenfish* officers and crew's explanation of just what led to the sinking of the *Awa maru*. The court-martial was, in the end, an imperfect but nevertheless genuine attempt to fix responsibility for torpedoing the ship.

In 1945 no one of significance within the navy was satisfied with the verdict. Loughlin, left on Guam without any meaningful duty for two weeks before being ordered to ride the *Pogy* (SS 266) back to Pearl Harbor, felt he had been victimized.[87] Brooding over what had happened and what lay ahead, he thought his career was ruined. In the normal course of events a court-martial conviction would reduce his chances for further advancement in rank and probably keep him from ever commanding a submarine again.[88] Hoping to salvage what he could of his future, he wrote to Lockwood that he was "keenly aware" of the impact of the *Queenfish*'s error on the submarine service's reputation and that he had come to "deeply regret" what had occurred. Perhaps those words of contrition, written while he waited on temporary duty at the submarine training command in Pearl Harbor, would convince the admiral to let him remain in the submarine service.[89]

Loughlin's worries were exaggerated, however, for his superiors did everything possible to minimize the effects of the court-martial verdict. The *Queenfish*'s squadron and division commanders wrote glowing endorsements on the report of the patrol during which the submarine sank the *Awa maru*. The latter, after summarizing the defense arguments in the case, commented wryly that while he did not know the provisions of the safe-passage guarantee, the cargo of the Japanese ship appeared to be "a mighty strange one" for a ship so protected.[90]

While in Washington, Admiral Lockwood saw to it that "everyone concerned," including King, his deputy, Admiral Edwards, and Secretary of the Navy Forrestal, knew that the sinking of the *Awa maru* was "a mistake for which I feel that I was equally responsible." When he returned to Guam he wrote to Loughlin, advising him to make arrangements when in Washington to pay his respects, and tell his story, to the CNO. He urged the former *Queenfish* skipper not to let the conviction—"a bad blow"—get him down. "Take it in your stride," he advised in a fatherly tone, and "it won't be long before your outstanding ability will get you back into full favor."[91]

Admiral Nimitz did not feel the same way as Lockwood. He bore the responsibility of reviewing the court-martial's findings and sentence; under the Navy Regulations then in effect, he, as the convening authority, had the power, if dissatisfied, to change one or both—but only in a manner favorable to the defendant. But when his staff legal officers reviewed the court-martial transcript, they concluded that Commander Loughlin should have been convicted of culpable inefficiency as well as negligence in performance of his duty. They also reported that the members of the court had usurped the function of higher authorities by imposing a "totally inadequate" sentence on the *Queenfish* captain.[92]

Years later, Loughlin, *Queenfish* crewmen, and some officers on Admiral Lockwood's staff claimed that the verdict had so infuriated Nimitz, he ordered that members of the court be given letters of reprimand for having imposed so light a sentence. Some said Nimitz had wanted a stiffer sentence either because it would have softened Admiral King's initial anger at the sinking, or because it would have allowed CinCPac to express his own feelings about the sinking by reducing the sentence. No reprimand, however, is to be found in the service record of the court-martial's youngest member—who went on to achieve flag rank.[93] Instead, Nimitz grudgingly accepted the court-martial's findings and sentence, so that Loughlin would not "entirely escape all punishment," and informed Washington of his decision.[94]

There, King backed down from his initially tough position on the sinking of the *Awa maru*. He may have softened a bit after hearing what Lockwood had to say about it.[95] He may simply have followed the advice of the Judge Advocate of the Navy, Vice Adm. Thomas L. Gatch, who was Lockwood's Naval Academy classmate. Gatch typed his own reaction to the sinking of the *Awa maru* in a memorandum attached to the court-martial record. He believed that Commander Loughlin had been "in a very tough spot"; he had had "no time" to verify what the target was; and if he had let a prey escape he would have "neglected his duty." King may also have felt, after reading Gatch's memorandum, that having held the court-martial and informed the State Department of its result, the navy had done all that was needed to "clear the record."[96]

Certainly he and other senior Navy Department officials did everything they could to protect Loughlin from the consequences of his error. Forrestal did not reveal his name when, more than a month after the trial ended, he told Secretary of State Edward Reilly Stettinius, Jr., that "disciplinary action" had been taken against Loughlin.[97] Someone in the Navy Department, piqued by that result, tried to reverse it in the court of public opinion by telling Walter Winchell, a nationally syndicated Washington columnist and radio broadcaster, about it. Winchell then attacked the new Truman administration for allowing diplomats to "push around" submariners, "every one of whom was a hero."[98] One of his listeners responded by writing his senator, complaining that it was outrageous for "an honest mistake" to become the cause of a court-martial.[99]

After this flurry of protest, Navy Secretary Forrestal waited a bit longer to issue the letter of admonition. When he finally did so he explained that "extenuating circumstances" on the night of the sinking accounted for the *Queenfish* skipper's actions.[100] Loughlin's name was not revealed to the press until after the Japanese surrender, and in that account he was portrayed simply as a hero who had made a mistake.[101]

That was how Loughlin was treated when, after having taken leave to visit his wife and new baby daughter, he went to Washington to see the submarine detailing officer in the Bureau of Personnel. Capt. (later Vice Adm.) Frank Watkins handed him the letter of admonition. Some of its words must have alarmed the sub skipper; his "gross negligence," he read, had caused the U.S. government "extreme embarrassment" in its conduct of the war. Other language that suggested his conduct on the night of 1 April 1945 had been "totally at variance" with his previous record as a "successful naval officer," however, hinted that not all of his superiors thought he deserved punishment.[102] When, after reading the letter, he was asked what he wanted to do next, Loughlin momentarily lost his composure. Although he wanted to be assigned to supervise construction of a new boat, he humbly replied, "Gee, Captain Watkins, I just don't know. This [reprimand] is a plain disaster to me after having done pretty well for three war patrols."

In fact, it was not. Admiral Edwards, then vice CNO, had told Watkins to "see that the young man gets a good job." The detailing officer asked Loughlin if he would like to be operations officer on the staff of Commander Submarine Force Atlantic. The former *Queenfish* skipper leapt at the chance to work for Admiral Lockwood's Atlantic counterpart in a position that would also bring him to the attention of the Commander in Chief, Atlantic Fleet.[103]

That exchange put Elliott Loughlin back on track toward flag rank. By the time it occurred, Lockwood had decided to return the *Queenfish* to normal undersea warfare. On 2 June 1945, under her new skipper, Shamer, she departed Guam on what was to be her last and least eventful war patrol.[104] The destruction of the *Awa maru* was behind her, and the U.S. Navy had done everything possible to put that unhappy event behind it.

The process of doing so had been agonizing for all of those directly involved. Loughlin and the *Queenfish* officers and crew did come to feel remorse and regret for what had occurred. Those who passed judgment on their actions did so with a heavy heart, for they saw only technical error, not morally culpable guilt, in the *Queenfish*'s sinking of the *Awa maru*. However wrong her action may have been, in their eyes it could not compare with the wicked deeds of a treacherous enemy. For them the sinking was, as Lockwood put it, just "a damned shame."[105]

Nonetheless, he and those above him in the naval hierarchy recognized that war has its own imperatives. Going through with the court-martial was one of them. There had to be a trial in order to prevent reprisals against those in Japanese custody and to keep alive the hope of getting additional relief supplies to them. Yet their consciences told the men who sat in judgment on Charles Elliott Loughlin, reviewed his sentence, and determined his next assignment that neither he nor any of those who served under him were truly guilty. Justice in the larger sense, as these men saw it, precluded stiff punishment.

Thus, as the war drew to its end, the U.S. Navy washed its hands of the sinking of the *Awa maru*. What had happened on the night of 1 April 1945 was something to be forgotten—quickly. But neither the government of Japan nor that of the United States was willing or able to forget that tragedy.

6

Promises Made, Promises Unkept

ON 10 APRIL 1945, ten days after the *Awa maru* was sunk, Tokyo radio broadcast a plea for any information about her. The ship was five days overdue from her projected arrival at Tsuruga, her revised final destination, and Japanese officials had begun to fear the worst.[1] She might never return. A broadcast certain to be monitored by Japan's enemies might at least provide some clue to her fate. If it brought no response, then Japanese officials could reasonably presume that the ship had succumbed to some natural peril of the sea. But if the enemy replied, then Tokyo would know whom to blame for the loss of the ship.

The broadcast was the first step in the time-honored process by which governments deal with error committed in their name. Normally, the offended party—the victim—presses the offending state—the victimizer—to investigate what happened and to acknowledge responsibility for what has occurred. If the offending state does so, the victimized state prepares and presents a claim for repayment of the loss it had suffered. The two sides then negotiate a settlement of that claim. The incident is closed when the victimizer sends monies to the victim for distribution to those who have suffered direct loss arising from the error committed.

The *Awa maru,* however, had not been a normal merchant ship. Her destruction was not an ordinary event. And nothing was usual about the settlement of claims arising from her destruction. For the first and only time during the war, the U.S. government acknowledged responsibility for the wrongful sinking of a Japanese ship, offered to replace it, and promised full indemnification after the war. That was extraordinary.

What followed was even more unusual: Washington never paid Tokyo a cent in compensation for the *Queenfish*'s destruction of the *Awa maru.* Having promised to pay, the United States began searching, barely ninety days after the fighting stopped, to find some way to get Japan to compensate its own citizens for the losses they had suffered on the night of 1 April 1945. Three years later, American diplomats who counted themselves friends of Japan devised a claims settlement scheme by which Washington, in effect, reneged on its promise to indemnify Tokyo for the sinking of the *Awa maru.*

What strange twist of events produced such extraordinary, inconsistent, and seemingly amoral American behavior?

The first sign that resolving claims arising from the destruction of the *Awa maru* would not proceed normally came on 10 April 1945, the very day the Japanese broadcast their appeal for information about her fate. Washington sent Tokyo a bland, disingenuous reply. The Americans said they had information about a ship's sinking approximately forty miles off the estimated track of the *Awa maru.* No special lights or special illumination as provided in the safe-passage agreement had been seen on that vessel, yet the sole survivor claimed she had been the *Awa maru.* If the ship sunk was the *Awa maru,* then the United States "deeply regretted" what had occurred. However, because "a degree of uncertainty" remained as to the "actual identity" of the vessel destroyed, Washington was conducting, "in all sincerity and good faith," an investigation into where "primary responsibility" for the sinking might lie. Having clouded the probable truth in such diplomatic language, the American message concluded by expressing the hope that nothing would disrupt plans for further delivery of relief supplies to prisoners of war.[2]

That message stunned and infuriated officials in Tokyo. They knew the truth even if the Americans declined to face up to it. The *Awa maru* and more than two thousand Japanese lives had been lost. That grim news was a finger of war that touched them personally; among the dead were friends, relatives, and some of their best colleagues. Military and diplomatic officials cannot have escaped the feeling that they bore some responsibility for those deaths. After all, they had fought over who should be given a berth on board the *Awa maru* on her supposedly safe voyage home. Army Ministry officials had ordered Gen. Iwahashi Kazuo, chief of the Third Transport Command responsible for shipping control at Singapore, and other officers needed for the coming decisive defense of the homeland to board the ill-fated ship.[3] Senior diplomats had wangled space on board her so that some of the best younger diplomats and their families could join Vice Minister Takeuchi, Bureau Director Yamada, and Tōkō Takezō in returning home safely from the collapsing Southern Region. They had hoped she would bring eager pro-Japanese nationalists from South and Southeast Asia to a Second Greater East Asia Conference to be held in Tokyo.[4]

Now these officials knew that all had met a horrible death; they were numb with grief. The Japanese ambassador in Bangkok summed up what they felt: "The news we have received about the *Awa maru* disaster is unbearable," he wired Tokyo. He asked his colleagues there to convey "heartfelt sympathies" to the families of his recent high-ranking visitors and to relatives of those from his embassy who had perished.[5] Nonetheless, the ambassador and his superiors knew that words could not possibly compensate the bereaved for the loved ones lost on the *Awa maru*.

More than two weeks passed before Tokyo responded to Washington's admission that the ship had been sunk. Grief, bureaucratic caution following the formation of Adm. Suzuki Kantarō's new cabinet, and disagreement over what to say produced that delay.[6] What finally emerged were two responses, radically different in substance and tone. On 25 April 1945 Iguchi Sadao presented the first of them; he had been the counselor of the Japanese embassy in Washington in December 1941, had been interned and then exchanged on the *Gripsholm*, and was now the spokesman for the Board of Information.[7] He spoke in a wounded but magnanimous tone to reporters. The empire, he said, had suffered a particularly painful loss. A large number of women and children as well as the vice-minister for Greater East Asian

Affairs, senior Ministry of Foreign Affairs officials who had previously served in Great Britain and the United States, and a onetime minister of commerce and industry had perished with the *Awa maru.*

But Japan was not vindictive. While some had urged retaliation through cessation of delivery of the relief supplies the ship had carried, the headquarters of the Japanese Expeditionary Forces in the Southern Region had ordered prison camp authorities to distribute those materials. Needed food and medicines had in fact gotten to the prisoners.[8]

The second response, contained in an official note of protest dated 26 April 1945, took a much harder line. It rejected as specious what Washington had said about the sinking, terminated the agreement to deliver relief supplies, and hinted ominously at retribution. This communication, dispatched the day after Iguchi spoke, insisted that messages received from the *Awa maru* just prior to her sinking revealed that she had been in her scheduled position. Moreover, her distinctive lights signifying her protected character had been illuminated on the night of 1 April. Yet an American submarine had attacked her.

That being the case, Japan could only conclude that the United States had abandoned its "former desire[s] concerning the treatment of prisoners and civilian internees." The American government, therefore, bore full responsibility for "this . . . most outrageous act of treachery unparalleled in the world history of the war." Tokyo demanded that Washington accept "whole responsibility" for a "disgraceful act" committed in violation of "fundamental principles of humanity and international law." The protest note concluded ominously by reserving Japan's right to take any measures necessary to cope with "such perfidious action" by the United States.[9]

When they read what was coming out of Tokyo, officials in Washington must have shuddered. Japan was striking back. There would be reprisals against Americans in Japanese custody. They could only imagine what would happen to prisoners. In fact, Gen. Jonathan Wainwright, the highest-ranking American held by the Japanese, was told he and his men would get no more Red Cross supplies because an American sub had sunk a ship loaded with them.[10] An imprisoned member of the U.S. Marine Detachment in Beijing was informed by his "delighted" captors that no further relief would be coming because of the sinking.[11] In time, American officials learned just what the sinking of the *Awa maru* meant for civilian internees: Tokyo had limited the number of International Red Cross officials' visits to their camps, saying that her destruction justified the reduction.[12]

Fears for the safety and well-being of those in Japanese custody were only one of several factors that shaped Washington's decision over what to do next. From the moment they learned that the *Awa maru* had been destroyed, State and Navy Department officials had disagreed over how best to proceed. CNO King and Secretary Forrestal had wanted to admit what had occurred and proceed quickly with a court-martial inquiry. State Department officials, worried about having to indemnify Japan, preferred, for their own (contradictory) reasons, to move slowly. The more legalistic among them felt that prompt and public acceptance of responsibility for the sinking would be like "entering our defense before being charged with a crime."[13] SWPD negotiators, steeled by years of bargaining with Tokyo over personnel exchanges and what now looked like a disastrous attempt to provide relief to the prisoners, took an even more pessimistic view. They insisted that "nothing" the United States could do was likely to have "any important effect" on the position the Japanese would take on indemnification. Tokyo would "squeeze" Washington for everything it could get, just as Americans would have pressed the Japanese if they had been the victims and not the victimizers in an incident of this sort.[14]

That difference of opinion produced the evasions in Washington's first response to Tokyo's initial inquiries about the fate of the *Awa maru*. It guaranteed that debate would follow when, in mid-May 1945, Tokyo's second formal protest note reached Washington. The document's contents were predictable. The Japanese demanded an official apology for the sinking; notification of the punishment of those responsible for it; and payment of an indemnity of unspecified size for lives lost, injury to the sole survivor, and destruction of the ship and her cargo.[15] But no one in Washington expected that the debate over how to respond to Tokyo's demands would run on for seven weeks.

It proceeded fitfully, in an extraordinarily disjointed manner. At first, diplomats stood firm against any admission of guilt to the Japanese. Although Under Secretary of State Joseph C. Grew had told Navy Secretary Forrestal and Secretary of War Henry L. Stimson that reaching agreement on a response to Tokyo's protest was a matter of "high urgency," his SWPD subordinates preferred to go slow.[16] Some acted on the premise that delay would force the Japanese to admit that the *Awa maru* had carried contraband. That would weaken the eventual Japanese case for indemnification.[17] Others made a distinction between carrying contraband and evacuating "large numbers" of Japanese, including senior officials. They insisted that the safe conduct granted the *Awa maru* had not been so broad as to allow use of the ship "for any purpose whatsoever."[18] That posture produced another evasive reply to Tokyo's protest. More than a month after the Loughlin court-martial, which constituted the navy's official inquiry into the cause of the erroneous sinking, had ended, Washington told Tokyo that the United States regretted the heavy loss of life on the *Awa maru* but could not accept responsibility for the sinking "pending the outcome of further inquiries."[19]

That vague statement troubled officials and ordinary citizens worried about the fate of prisoners and internees in Japanese hands. The liberation of Manila in February 1945 revealed that by December 1944 those held there had been getting less than half the protein, about a third of the carbohydrates, and barely a quarter of the total number of calories required by men doing light work.[20] POW parents, already alarmed by that news and afraid that the sinking of the *Awa maru* might disrupt the flow of vitally needed food and medicine to their sons, protested. One of them, a Montrose, Colorado, father whose son had been "a slave of the Japs . . . for over three years" wrote President Truman, saying that he feared the State Department was botching the job of keeping those supplies moving toward the prisoners.[21] Another, angered by the vagueness of Washington's public statements about the *Awa maru* sinking, asked the president to consider how those in Japanese custody might feel about the fact that their government was apparently not concerned enough about their plight to make "any amends to lighten their burdens."[22]

Allegations of that sort prompted the diplomats to press the Navy and War Departments to agree to provide Japan a replacement ship for the *Awa maru*. The idea originated in SWPD only hours after the first news of her sinking reached Washington;[23] three weeks later, Under Secretary of State Grew asked Navy and War officials to consider it.[24] By early May, American Red Cross officials were thinking along similar lines. One of them, who monitored relief efforts for Americans held by the Japanese, drafted an appeal to the secretary of state urging him to offer Tokyo a replacement ship.[25] His boss, President Roosevelt's onetime law partner, stepped up the pressure for action by reporting that the International Red Cross representative in Tokyo believed a replacement ship offer would be appropriate if it were shown that an American submarine had sunk the *Awa maru* in violation of the terms of the safe-passage agreement.[26]

External pressure of that sort and hopes of continuing to provide relief to Americans held by the Japanese helped move the replacement ship proposal swiftly through the Washington bureaucracy. The Joint Chiefs of Staff referred it to a subordinate committee, which concluded, just when State Department officials were declining to admit responsibility for the sinking, that there was "no ground" on which the United States could refuse to do so. That group advised that transferring a comparable ship to the Japanese was the best way to keep badly needed food and medicines flowing to prisoners and internees. They recommended approval of the replacement ship scheme to the Joint Chiefs of Staff, who in turn forwarded it to the State-War-Navy Coordinating Committee. That body sent it on to the service secretaries and the secretary of state, and those three men quickly agreed to it.[27] Grew, now acting secretary of state, then presented the plan to President Truman, who promptly approved it late in June 1945.[28] A few days later, the Joint Military Logistics Command, the interagency body that controlled shipping, agreed, albeit reluctantly, to transfer to Japan an American-built merchant ship of roughly the same size and characteristics as the *Awa maru*.[29]

That unprecedented decision was taken only a few days after diplomats finally decided that the United States must acknowledge its responsibility for sinking her.[30] They did so with the greatest reluctance. Not until two weeks after their first message to that effect was sent to Tokyo did they publicly disclose what the United States was prepared to do. Washington would negotiate an indemnity payment, but only after the fighting stopped. The sole Japanese survivor of the tragedy would be returned—in conjunction with future exchanges of personnel that SWPD officers already knew Tokyo was unwilling to make.[31] That admission was accompanied by Secretary Forrestal's equally reluctant acknowledgment that the submarine captain who sank the *Awa maru* (Commander Loughlin's name was not revealed) had been court-martialed and relieved of command.[32]

But nothing was said about a replacement ship, either to Tokyo or to the American public. State Department officials, still smarting from Walter

Winchell's (misguided) attack on them for the court-martialing of Elliott Loughlin, were of two minds. Under Secretary Grew, although eager to resolve the *Awa maru* matter quickly, fretted over the "unfortunate effect" on public feeling if it became known that Washington was "giving" Tokyo a replacement vessel. He thought it best to do so secretly, saying nothing about the transfer unless forced to do so.[33] The Assistant Secretary of State for Public and Congressional Affairs, Archibald MacLeish, favored a slightly more open but nonetheless delicately nuanced approach. On 26 July 1945, the day President Truman and the British prime minister, Clement Attlee, issued the Potsdam Declaration calling upon Japan to surrender, he endorsed the idea of broadcasting to Tokyo the offer of a replacement ship, coupled with a warning.[34]

That brought two naval officers into the picture as scriptwriters for the proposed broadcast. Capt. Harry L. Pence, who had retired and become the American Red Cross coordinator for East Asian prisoner of war relief on the very day the *Queenfish* sank the *Awa maru*, provided its basic ideas.[35] Capt. Ellis M. Zacharias, one of Admiral Lockwood's classmates, who had become a pioneering Japanese linguist and Japan specialist in the Office of Naval Intelligence, refined the text.[36] The script they crafted struck a delicate balance between acceptance and evasion of American responsibility for the sinking. It mixed appeal and admonition to the Japanese. Pence and Zacharias insisted that the destruction of the *Awa maru* had been a genuine mistake, not a "willful" or "deliberate" violation of the safe-passage agreement. Washington was thus offering a replacement ship not as indemnity, but as an outright gift.

The script went on to suggest that Japan was obliged to accept that offer and continue delivering relief supplies to prisoners—for two quite different reasons. Payback was one of them. Japan had an obligation to repay the United States for its humanitarian gestures in the past. The United States had provided relief to the victims of the great Kantō earthquake in 1923, returned the remains of a former Japanese ambassador on board the cruiser *Astoria* (CA 34) in 1939, and, more recently, had permitted evacuation of the starving Japanese garrison from Wake Island. Prudence was another. Tokyo should seize this "last opportunity" to improve its prisoner of war treatment record. If the Japanese did not do so, then the American public's anger over their refusal to facilitate delivery of food and medicine to those in custody would poison trans-Pacific relations for years to come. Time in which to avoid that unhappy development, the script concluded ominously, was "running short."[37]

Indeed it was. What Pence and Zacharias wrote never reached the ears of Japanese listeners because the war ended four days before its scheduled broadcast.[38] Washington's last wartime communication to Tokyo about the sinking of the *Awa maru* was not their balanced appeal but a bluntly worded diplomatic note that restated the American position on indemnification and the return of the sole survivor, and it added the offer of a replacement ship. It drew a sharp distinction between the latter, an unconditional offer for immediate action, and the former, qualified steps of indemnification and exchange that might be taken later.[39] Worried to the last about appearing "soft" on the enemy, State Department officials made it clear that the replacement ship was not an indemnity offered "in an apologetic mood"; it was simply a means of enabling the Japanese to resume delivery of relief supplies to those in their custody.[40]

On 6 August 1945, the very day the *Enola Gay* dropped the first atomic bomb on Hiroshima, Swiss Minister Camille Gorge forwarded Washington's message to the Japanese foreign ministry from Karuizawa, the summer resort village to which he had gone to escape the heat, food shortages, and destruction of Tokyo.[41] Diplomats there took four days to draft and deliver to the Swiss for transmission to Washington their uncompromising reply. Bitter and defiant to the end, they protested the U.S. Navy's failure to impose "severe punishment" on those responsible for sinking the *Awa maru*. They insisted that her destruction was a "unique case" in which the issue was so "absolutely clear and simple" that immediate payment should be made to those who had suffered loss from it. They repeated their demand for Shimoda Kantarō's immediate return, rejecting Washington's claim that he could not be handed over until other POW matters were resolved. Most importantly, their final wartime statement all but rejected the replacement ship proposal. Japanese diplomats refused to consider it until the United States accepted their previous demands, provided answers to their questions about the *Queenfish*'s failure to rescue more survivors, and agreed to pay an indemnity of 226 million yen for the loss of life and property on board the *Awa maru*. Any "substitute" ship dispatched across the Pacific would have to be equivalent to her.[42]

President Harry S Truman read the essence of that message on Tuesday afternoon, 14 August 1945. It came to him as a bitter disappointment. Newspapers that morning had reported that the Japanese legation in Bern had received a very long message from Tokyo. The president was hoping and praying that that communication was Japan's formal offer to surrender. But when he read the daily summary of MAGIC-intercepted and decrypted messages that an officer brought to him, the president discovered that that long message was Tokyo's demand for 226 million yen in indemnification for the sinking of the *Awa maru*. As he read its summary, the president noticed a marginal note scrawled alongside it: Tokyo was not demanding repayment for the munitions the Japanese "hospital ship" was carrying.[43]

That bitterly sarcastic comment may have drawn an understanding smile from Harry Truman, a man not known for charity toward his enemies. It certainly augured ill for resolution of the *Awa maru* affair. Washington and Tokyo had initiated the diplomatic dialogue normally used to craft a settlement, but a yawning gap in attitudes and expectations separated the two sides. American officials had acknowledged responsibility for the sinking and had offered, under the duress of war, to make eventual amends. Their heads told them that the Japanese case for indemnification was technically correct; but in their hearts they agreed with what had been written for the president's benefit in the margin: Tokyo had no moral or legal grounds on which to demand repayment for the death and destruction resulting from the sinking of the *Awa maru*.[44] Japanese officials, by contrast, thought they had laid firm foundations for an eventual settlement in their favor. The Americans had admitted responsibility for the sinking and offered to make restitution for it. Tokyo diplomats believed that the United States would eventually pay the bill for what the *Queenfish* had done to the *Awa maru*.

In August 1945 no one in Washington or Tokyo could imagine how very, very long it would take to close that gap and settle the *Awa maru* claims.

The very day his diplomats sent their demand for payment for the destruction of the *Awa maru* to Washington, Emperor Hirohito broadcast his words of surrender. Suddenly the war was over. Americans who had fought it under the seas were stunned, confused, and elated by that news. Admiral Lockwood felt "limp as a rag" and unsure of his emotions. He was delighted not to have to send any more "splendid lads" out to possible death; but he felt

The *Queenfish* returns from her last (fifth) war patrol. *Capt. John E. Bennett, USN (Ret.)*

"very sad" about having to break up the submarine force under his command.[45] News of the Japanese surrender caught the *Queenfish* in the middle of a training exercise off Midway. Commander Shamer insisted on finishing it, then headed the sub back to port, where "yowling and screaming" sounds of a victory celebration already under way greeted him. Once ashore, his crew kept the party going until six hours beyond the normal closing time for the beer hall there.[46] Two weeks later, Admiral Lockwood stood alongside Admiral Nimitz, General MacArthur, and Gen. Jonathan Wainwright, the most senior American prisoner of war in the Pacific, on board the USS *Missouri* (BB 63) in Tokyo Bay. In a moment of supreme triumph, they watched Japanese military, naval, and diplomatic officials sign the document of surrender.[47]

That same moment was, for the Japanese, one of supreme humiliation. But Foreign Minister Shigemitsu Mamoru and his subordinates were only bowed, not broken, by defeat. Despite their haughty rejection of Washington's conditional offer to provide a replacement ship for the *Awa maru,* they determined to ensure that the United States would honor its pledge to indemnify those who had suffered loss as a consequence of her destruction. Barely six weeks after the surrender ceremony, they joined relatives of diplomats who had gone down on the ship in a memorial service for their deceased colleagues. That same day, the Foreign Ministry issued a statement promising continued efforts to secure compensation for those bereaved by the sinking of the ship.[48]

Harsh new realities, however, limited what they could do. Defeat and the return of prisoners and internees to American and Allied hands deprived them of any real bargaining power. Far more urgent tasks than claims resolution absorbed their energies and attention. Developing effective liaison with Supreme Commander Allied Powers (SCAP) officials, preventing their excessive interference in Japanese internal affairs, and even planning for a peace settlement took precedence over trying to resolve claims arising from the war just ended.[49] Japanese diplomats thus proceeded slowly and cautiously in trying to settle the *Awa maru* claims.

They began in October 1945 by seeking what Washington had promised a year earlier, before the ship set out on her fateful journey: full reimbursement of the costs of transporting and delivering relief supplies to prisoners and internees.[50] SCAP officials, through whom all Japanese communications to Washington now went, responded by demanding a full accounting in support of what was to be a final claim. Iguchi Sadao, the wartime public information spokesman and now the director of the General Affairs Bureau of the Central Liaison Office, which dealt with American occupation authorities, replied with a memorandum that detailed precisely what Japan expected to receive. It indicated that Washington owed Tokyo 728,400 of the original 1.3 million yen spent in getting relief supplies to the prisoners.[51] (The remainder had already been sent to Japan through the Swiss, during the war.) SCAP officials, anxious to put such war-related matters behind them, dutifully forwarded this seemingly innocuous claim to Washington.[52]

When it reached State Department officials early in January 1946, they responded as if it were a blast from the first snowstorm of the year—something expected but nonetheless thoroughly unpleasant.[53] Assistant Secretary of State for Administration Donald Russell, a former law partner of Secretary of State James Byrnes and a fellow South Carolinian, reacted very negatively. He complained that the United States had already paid Japan $188,000 during the war, under duress, and was unlikely to recover those funds. Whether or not the balance supposedly due could be "considered" in connection with reparations Tokyo was expected to pay Washington was not yet clear.[54] That guarded response suggested that Russell was looking for some way to avoid paying Japan anything in hard cash. He put off responding to the Japanese request until his subordinates had examined all of the claims arising from the sinking of the *Awa maru*.

Two days later, on 4 January 1946, Special War Plans Division officials completed a study that did just that. They reaffirmed the American obligation to compensate Japan for loss of the ship, her cargo, and the lives of those on board her. They warned, nonetheless, that Tokyo was trying to squeeze too much out of Uncle Sam. The monies demanded the preceding August had been exorbitant. Rather than compensating for the loss of life according to the four-tiered system the Japanese had proposed, they suggested that Washington should simply pay a flat five thousand dollars for the death and personal property of each victim of the sinking.[55]

When State Department officials met on 28 January to review this study and the Japanese request for repayment of transshipment costs, they made two significant decisions. The latter would eventually be "paid," just as Assistant Secretary Russell had suggested, in the form of a credit against reparations Japan owed the United States. However, resolution of the larger questions arising from Japan's earlier demand for indemnification for the loss of the *Awa maru*, her cargo, and the lives and property of those who went down with her would have to wait until some future, unspecified date.[56]

The reasons for those timorous bureaucratic decisions are not difficult to discern. No one doubted the legal obligation of the United States to compensate Japan for sinking a ship traveling under guarantee of safe passage. Everyone had reason to believe, just after President Truman's special representative had completed an on-the-spot assessment of Japan's ability to pay, that substantial reparations monies would become available.[57] These funds could be used as a source of credit with which to "pay" the *Awa maru* claims. That would avoid what Under Secretary Grew had feared the preceding summer—appearing to "give" the Japanese anything. It would also make it unnecessary for State Department officials to go before Congress seeking funds for payment of an indemnity to the Japanese.

Their reluctance to do so was understandable. Passions stirred by greater knowledge of Japanese treatment of prisoners and internees ran very high.

In between their preparation of a report that recommended "payment" of the *Awa maru* claims via offsetting funds, and its acceptance, State Department officials, along with army, navy, and Red Cross representatives, heard chilling reports of what had befallen those in Japanese custody. An ICRC official told them how those unfortunates had gotten only a tenth as much food and medicine from the Red Cross as prisoners held in Europe. Rear Adm. Joel Boone, Admiral Nimitz's staff medical officer, gave them grisly details of conditions at the Omori POW camp near Tokyo, which he had visited immediately after the Japanese surrender. Although he was a physician and a born Quaker, he confessed that "nobody came out of Japan hating the Japs more than I did."[58]

Words of that sort uttered in private only echoed what State Department officials knew the American people felt. Polls taken shortly after the fighting stopped showed that 85 percent of Americans approved the atomic bombing of Hiroshima and Nagasaki, and 60 percent thought the United States was not being "tough enough" on the Japanese.[59] Magazine articles portrayed them as 70 million "unregenerate . . . problem children."[60] And a cascade of reports on Japanese mistreatment of prisoners of war and civilian internees fanned hatred of the defeated enemy. Beginning with the State Department's revelation of the burning and murder of prisoners in the Philippines and the navy's disclosure that downed fliers had been killed in Borneo, the public read tales of the beating, starvation, beheading, and crucifixion of American POWs and of the mass execution of civilian internees. First reports of gruesome medical experiments performed by the infamous Gen. Ishii Shirō on prisoners in Manchuria strengthened the public's anti-Japanese feelings.[61] In January 1946, no one in Washington was prepared to repay anything to a nation that had treated prisoners that way.

But Washington officials were ready to return the sole survivor of the sinking of the *Awa maru*. Two days before a State Department committee decided to postpone and offset through Japanese reparation payments whatever Washington might owe Tokyo for that act, Eldred Kuppinger of SWPD asked Capt. Thomas Tonseth, of the office of the assistant chief of naval operations for administration, about Shimoda Kantarō. Where was he? When and how might he be returned to Japan? On 28 January 1946 Tonseth replied that Shimoda had been taken from Guam to Tinian, where he was being held in a camp for civilian internees. He could be returned to

Japan if and when the State Department asked the navy to do so.[62] Barely a week after that exchange, Under Secretary of State Dean Acheson wrote Navy Secretary James Forrestal requesting that the sole survivor be sent home as soon as transportation was available.[63]

Many years later, some Japanese read ulterior motives into Shimoda's treatment at American hands. At a time when millions of war repatriates traveled in slow, seagoing vessels of all kinds, Shimoda flew back to Japan in the company of two navy captains.[64] He arrived in Tokyo on 22 February 1946 and was turned over to Ministry of Foreign Affairs officials the next day.[65] He subsequently told of staying in a downtown Tokyo hotel and meeting General MacArthur.[66] Three days later he met with relatives of *Awa maru* victims at the Ministry of Foreign Affairs, and one of the latter recalled his saying that SCAP had given him money—presumably to keep quiet about what had befallen him. That he subsequently took a job as a houseboy in the home of an American army officer and vanished into obscurity seemed further evidence of Washington's determination to ensure that the sole survivor said nothing about the sinking of the *Awa maru*.[67]

In fact, however, no such complicated motives determined Shimoda's treatment. By early 1946 humanity and common sense—qualities that Dean Acheson and Eldred Kuppinger possessed in ample measure—suggested that he ought to be returned to Japan. He was of no value to the United States; with American POWs returned, whatever bargaining leverage he might have provided State Department negotiators had long since vanished. What he knew about the sinking of the *Awa maru* was, as his testimony in the Loughlin court-martial had suggested, very little and of no great import. He may never have met MacArthur, and no record survives of SCAP appointments for 22 February, the Washington's Birthday holiday, that might confirm or disprove his claim to have done so.[68]

That he went to work for an American officer's family was not at all unusual in occupied Japan for a former ship's steward who spoke some English. Personal reasons, not American policy, probably kept him out of the spotlight upon his return to Tokyo. Shimoda had fallen in love with a nurse's aide on Tinian, and he may not have been ready to confront his wife and children with that emotionally painful news.[69] Vanishing into the obscurity of postwar Japanese society was a logical choice for the sole survivor to have made on his own.

After Shimoda disappeared from public view, American officials turned their attention to other aspects of the *Awa maru* tragedy. At one level, they set out to guarantee that neither the circumstances that had made the voyage of the unfortunate ship necessary nor those that had brought about her destruction reoccurred. At the U.S. Naval War College in Newport, Rhode Island, future naval leaders studied the sinking as an international law case.[70] It posed significant questions for debate as to how they might behave if they found themselves in circumstances similar to those that confronted Loughlin on the night of 1 April 1945. In Washington, State Department and American Red Cross officials began efforts to revise provisions of the 1929 Geneva Convention governing treatment of and access to prisoners of war and civilian internees, as well as those on the usage and marking of hospital ships. In the spring of 1946 some of them traveled to Paris for negotiations that resulted three years later in a greatly revised and expanded Geneva Convention addressing those aspects of the laws of war.[71]

At another level, American diplomats reaffirmed the validity of the wartime pledge to indemnify those harmed by the sinking of the *Awa maru*. A small amount of food and other supplies destined for the French and Swiss embassies in Tokyo had gone down on the ship.[72] While the postwar Gaullist government apparently declined to press a claim for indemnification on behalf of its collaborationist Vichy predecessor, the Swiss sought repayment for what they had lost.[73] The navy had no authority to make such payment, and so Sen. Arthur Vandenberg, a Republican from Michigan, with the cooperation of State Department officials, introduced a resolution providing $425 to satisfy the Swiss claim.[74] He shepherded it along quickly, and in March 1947 the resolution was approved by voice vote in both houses of Congress.[75] With President Truman's approval, the Swiss, who had proven so central in getting relief to American and Allied prisoners and internees, were repaid for what they had lost on board the *Awa maru*.

The trouble-free passage of that resolution suggested that legislators, no less than officials of the executive branch, recognized at least in principle Washington's obligation to indemnify Japan for losses suffered as a consequence of the sinking. But in practice, repaying the Swiss and compensating the Japanese were two entirely different matters. In December 1946, just before the congressional resolution authorizing payment to the Swiss was introduced in Washington, Central Liaison officials in Tokyo submitted their second postwar request for indemnification. It appealed for early action and repayment on humanitarian and economic grounds. Families bereaved by the sinking of the *Awa maru* were suffering, and her owners—the NYK shipping firm—faced serious financial difficulties.[76] The document implied that the United States should regard Japan's claim as yet another way of promoting her economic recovery and reconstruction. Indemnifying the bereaved families and the shipowner would help reduce Japan's dependency upon the United States.

That argument left the State Department unmoved. When a committee composed of officials from the SWPD, its Legal Affairs Office, and Japan experts from its Far Eastern Division reviewed the Japanese request, they in effect tabled it by asking for more detailed information in support of the claim.[77] Five months later Tokyo tried again, forwarding a detailed accounting in support of its earlier claims for indemnification. That document simply vanished into a void of bureaucratic inattention at Foggy Bottom.[78]

American diplomats turned a deaf ear to the Japanese requests for a variety of reasons. They remained chary of the strong anti-Japanese feeling in the public at large. They also sensed that Tokyo's December 1946 plea was supremely ill timed in terms of American domestic politics. The preceding month voters returned a Republican majority to Congress for the first time since 1930;[79] fiscally conservative GOP legislators were not likely to approve a request to repay the still-hated Japanese for an error American submariners had committed.

Tokyo's request for indemnification also arrived at a time when the State Department lacked the leadership needed to overcome congressional and popular resistance to paying the Japanese anything. Although *Time* magazine named Secretary of State James Byrnes "Man of the Year" for his European peacemaking efforts, President Truman, tired of what he perceived as the one-upmanship of a man who might be his rival for the 1948 Democratic presidential nomination, decided to replace Byrnes with General of the Army George C. Marshall.[80] But the president delayed making that change until January 1947, leaving junior State Department officials bereft of the support they needed to act on the *Awa maru* claims.[81]

By early summer 1947, when the second and more fully documented Japanese request for indemnification reached Washington, diplomats were simply too busy with other matters of high policy to pay any attention to it.

General Marshall and his inner corps of advisers focused on containing the Soviet threat they perceived in Europe. All of their energies went into implementing the Truman Doctrine and building support for what became the Marshall Plan for the economic reconstruction of Western Europe.[82] State Department Japan experts—and General MacArthur—were caught up in what turned out to be a premature effort to conclude a Japanese peace treaty. The diplomats were too preoccupied with trying to overcome Soviet, British, Australian, and Chinese Nationalist objections to a "soft" peace with Japan to devote any serious attention to Tokyo's request for indemnification.[83]

Thus, America's commitment to repay Japan for the sinking of the *Awa maru* survived the tumultuous changes of the first two postwar years without so much as a penny in indemnification monies crossing the Pacific.

As 1947 drew to a close, State Department officials grew worried about what they regarded as stagnated American policy for Japan. Polls suggested that the public thought Japan was the only major non-American country in which conditions were improving;[84] American diplomats were not so sure. Washington's efforts to negotiate an early peace treaty had foundered on the rocks of discord among Japan's former enemies—and had deeply disappointed the Japanese. American-imposed political and economic reforms initially opposed by Japanese leaders had yet to bring about economic recovery. Tokyo officials resented SCAP's heavy-handed intervention, but neither General MacArthur nor the Pentagon was willing to reduce its size or role in Japanese life.[85] Indeed, the Department of the Army was seeking a 40 percent increase in appropriations for its administration of occupied Japan. That jump was certain to catch the attention of tightfisted members of Congress, possibly making Japan policy an object of partisan debate in the coming election year.[86] Anxious to avoid that and eager to draw Japanese leaders to America's side in the deepening Cold War, diplomats felt something had to be done to stop the dangerous drift in Japan policy.

One way of doing so was to remove emotion-stirring, war-related issues from the agenda of Japanese-American relations. Early in January 1948, Robert A. Fearey of the Division of Northeast Asian Affairs proposed settling the *Awa maru* claims so as to improve the situation. Fearey was a young but important figure in the State Department's so-called Japan Crowd, that is, those who favored lenient treatment of the former enemy. After graduating from Harvard in June 1941, he had gone to Tokyo to serve as private secretary to Ambassador Joseph Grew.[87] Interned after Pearl Harbor, he returned home in August 1942 on the first *Gripsholm* exchange. Fearey took a more positive attitude than many of his colleagues (and most Americans) toward the Japanese because he had a more balanced view of the origins of the Pacific War than they did. He had overheard a shouting match between Ambassador Grew and Secretary of State Hull over the rights and wrongs of American policy just before the Pearl Harbor attack.[88] Also, Fearey had spent the war neither fighting the Japanese nor dueling with them in frustrating negotiations over prisoner and internee matters; instead, he had worked on what became the key American planning documents for the occupation of their homeland.[89]

Late in 1945, he returned to Japan to see the devastation wrought by war and size up the possibilities for the nation's reforming its polity and economy. Fearey helped assemble lists of those to be rounded up and tried as war criminals, but he favored constructive rather than punitive treatment of Japan.[90] As early as April 1946 he recognized that the United States had enduring security interests in Northeast Asia that might require keeping American forces in Japan after its occupation ended.[91] Having supported the attempt to negotiate a peace settlement in the spring of 1947, he was concerned about the negative psychological impact of its demise upon the Japanese people and their leaders.[92] As Fearey and other Japan experts in the State Department saw matters, a putative ally deserved better than the ride on an emotional roller coaster that the failed peace effort had given it.

By January 1948, the Department of the Army was asking Congress to appropriate 1.2 billion dollars, a figure equal to about 20 percent of the Marshall Plan funds for Western Europe, for relief and reconstruction in Japan over the next five years. Nearly half of that amount was sought for use during the first year.[93] At the time, however, both the Republican Congress and Democratic President Harry Truman, who faced an uphill struggle for election in his own right, were looking for ways to cut the budget.[94] To have asked them to appropriate additional monies to compensate Japan for the sinking of the *Awa maru* would have been foolhardy.

Consequently, Fearey resuscitated the notion of "paying" Japan without spending any money.[95] Two years earlier, reparations had seemed the logical source of funds to be credited to Tokyo's account. By early 1948, however, the prospects of obtaining any such payments from Japan had shrunk to near zero. The United States and its wartime allies disagreed vehemently over the amount and character of reparations Japan should pay. The Soviet Union wanted to take them from current production, but the United States believed doing that ran counter to the goal of rebuilding the Japanese economy.[96] So, Fearey looked elsewhere for "funny money" with which to "pay" the *Awa maru* claims. He found it in a strange place—military housing built to assure the comfort of occupation forces living in devastated Japan. Over the preceding twenty-seven months, the United States had shipped more than 6 million dollars' worth of materials across the Pacific to construct these buildings. Fearey presumed that these structures would revert to Japanese control when a peace treaty was concluded. Using them as the asset with which to "pay" the *Awa maru* claims appeared to him to be a painless approach:[97] Washington would be giving up only what it expected to lose anyway, and Tokyo would get some tangible assets as compensation for the sinking of the passenger-cargo vessel.

Fearey had not yet spelled out his proposal in detail when William Joseph Sebald, acting political adviser to SCAP, broached with General MacArthur the idea of settling the *Awa maru* claims. The old general, as he often did when confronted with a new idea, scoffed at the proposal; he thought paying the Japanese anything now for something done during the war was ridiculous. Japan had surrendered unconditionally, and the United States had more than met its moral obligation to compensate for the destruction of Japanese lives and property by providing hundreds of millions of dollars' worth of food and relief since the war's end. Indeed, MacArthur snapped, the Japanese government would do well to drop the *Awa maru* claims altogether.[98]

Sebald knew enough not to take the general's remarks as outright rejection of the idea of negotiating a settlement of those claims. That left the door open for Fearey, two weeks later, to forward a second and more refined version of his original proposal. He disliked the bargain implicit in MacArthur's remarks, that is, offsetting what Washington owed Tokyo for sinking the *Awa maru* with monies Japan was supposed to repay the United States for the costs of its occupation. In his view, those costs would "never be met in full." But he recognized the general's importance in settling the claims. Perhaps, Fearey suggested, MacArthur, whose vanity was well known, might change his attitude toward a settlement if he were asked to serve as a go-between in bringing it about. He might act now even if the conclusion of a formal peace treaty with Japan had to wait until some still-unknown time in the future.[99]

On 31 January 1948, Sebald took that proposal to MacArthur. SCAP, who harbored hopes of becoming the Republican nominee for president, warmed to the idea of playing peacemaker. But having failed the previous spring in his effort to prod Japan's former enemies into making peace, he was reluctant to go out on a limb now. Japan, he suggested, might gain international goodwill if Tokyo appeared to take the initiative in offering to drop its claims, as a gesture of appreciation to the United States for aid received since 1945. That would be better than any kind of offset arrangement. MacArthur even suggested a way how the Japanese political leaders might avoid criticism for giving them up. The ideal time for the Japanese government to make that offer would be just after the Congress approved the Department of the Army's appropriation for the coming year—which presumably would include 40 percent more aid for Japan than in preceding years.[100] Tokyo would be giving up a little at a point in time when it was getting a lot.

MacArthur's suggestion both delighted and dismayed Fearey and his State Department colleagues. If SCAP was willing to broker a settlement, so much the better. However, the linkage between *Awa maru* claims and repayment of occupation costs was potentially very dangerous. Fearey did not want MacArthur to say anything that might compromise a position that he himself knew to be factually false but was politically and diplomatically essential. It would be disastrous if the general implied that Tokyo was unlikely to meet its obligation, under the terms of the Potsdam Declaration, to repay in full the costs of military occupation. If he said anything of that sort, the Japanese would seize upon his words and try to wriggle out of their obligation to pay. Worse still, SCAP would in effect be contradicting what Department of the Army spokesmen had already told congressional appropriations committees. Thus, Fearey cautioned that MacArthur, in trying to broker a settlement of the *Awa maru* claims, must not say anything that might compromise Washington's official position on repayment: namely, that occupation costs were a "valid debt owed by Japan to the United States, reducible only by decision of the United States."[101]

That proviso helped Fearey get the approval of senior State Department officials, two weeks later, for negotiating an official end to the *Awa maru* affair. But before he sent instructions to MacArthur's acting political adviser in Tokyo, Fearey added a second provision that revealed his sensitivity to the moral issues involved in indemnification. People, not governments, were the ones who had been harmed by the *Queenfish*'s erroneous acts on the night of 1 April 1945. MacArthur should speak on their behalf, even as he moved to resolve the claims at the governmental level. Fearey suggested that the general ask senior Japanese government leaders if those who had suffered bereavement or loss as a consequence of the sinking had been, or would be, paid some compensation. Such a question, coming from so lofty a source, he presumed, would put pressure on Tokyo officials to pay the families of the dead and the owners of the ship.

Once General MacArthur had obtained assurances on that point, talks with the Japanese to settle the *Awa maru* claims might begin at the earliest date he considered "propitious."[102] With those words, the stage was set for something quite extraordinary: the first formal negotiations between Washington and Tokyo in the postwar era.

By January 1948 American diplomats had traveled a long way from the position they had taken shortly after the Japanese surrender. Two years earlier, certain State Department officials had considered reneging on the promise of indemnification they had made with such great reluctance in the summer of 1945. Now they took a different attitude toward the *Awa maru*. She was not simply a reminder of a bargain concluded under the duress of war or of an error committed in its fog. Laying her to official rest might help move the United States and Japan to a much broader settlement that would restore peace to the Pacific.

The diplomats who proposed to settle the *Awa maru* claims in advance of that peace recognized that doing so might put them at odds with a public and a Congress less forgiving of the past or less aware of Japan's value as a Cold War ally than they were. And so they fashioned a bargain that they insisted was not a trade: Tokyo would offer to abandon its *Awa maru* claims against the United States and commit itself to paying the real victims of the sinking; Washington would provide more aid on top of the millions it had already given and accept, in private, the fact that Japan would never fully repay that aid—even as it insisted that Tokyo publicly reaffirm that commitment. Both sides would treat this bargain as a step toward conclusion of a formal peace settlement.

Was this convoluted proposal simply camouflage for America's breaking its earlier promise to pay for the sinking of the *Awa maru?* To this day, some members of families bereaved by that tragedy believe that to be the case. They see it as proof positive of the moral bankruptcy of cynical Yankee diplomats.[103] In their view, the United States behaved like a party responsible for an automobile accident who at the time of its occurrence admits fault but later refuses to pay for the damage he has caused.

However, that view of American behavior between 1945 and 1948 in dealing with the *Awa maru* claims fails to take account of the difference between individuals and states. The standards of behavior and judgment for the latter are not, as even the ancient Greeks recognized, the same as those for the former. States must make decisions and act on the basis of interest, not in accordance with unchanging standards of personal morality.[104] Their understanding of what it is in their interest to do—or not do—changes over time. International agreements are therefore considered valid and binding upon those who make them *rebus sic stantibus*—that is, so long as the fundamental circumstances that gave rise to them remain unchanged.[105]

By the beginning of 1948, American officials most directly concerned with Japan realized that the situation they faced differed radically from that of the summer of 1945. Japan, an enemy then, was a putative ally now. Preserving and strengthening Tokyo's ties with Washington demanded laying the ghost of war to rest. The best, the most logical, and indeed, as they saw it, the only immediate way of moving forward toward that goal was to persuade the government of Japan to drop its claims against the United States for the sinking of the *Awa maru* and to agree to pay to the victims of that tragedy the indemnity monies that Washington had once said it would send to Tokyo.

The proposal was sound in the abstract, suited to current American domestic political realities, and strategically sensible. But could Washington persuade Tokyo that it was in Japan's best interest to accept it?

7

Laying the Ghost of War to Rest

EN. DOUGLAS MACARTHUR was not at all sure that Washington could do it. On 27 July 1948, six months after his State Department superiors directed him to proceed with negotiations to settle the *Awa maru* claims, William Sebald brought a draft agreement to the general. MacArthur read the brief text. Its five articles waived all Japanese claims arising from the destruction of the *Awa maru,* committed the Japanese government to "endeavor to provide adequate treatment" for the families of her victims and her owners, offered America's "deep regret" for the sinking, and expressed Japan's gratitude to the United States for aid received since the end of the war. A supplementary "agreed terms of understanding" embodied Washington's *sine qua non*: that Tokyo acknowledge the validity of Japan's obligation to repay occupation costs, loans, and credits received to the United States, whose government had the sole power to reduce or alter that debt.

Putting the paper down, MacArthur agreed to its terms and authorized Sebald to go ahead with negotiations to secure its final approval. But then, looking his visitor in the eye, he added a word of warning to the diplomat: "You will be lucky if you put that one across."[1]

The remark demonstrated the supreme commander's prescience and his understanding of the Japanese. Nine months would pass before, in another meeting in his office, MacArthur, Sebald, and Japanese Prime Minister Yoshida Shigeru signed an *Awa maru* claims resolution agreement.[2] More than two years would go by before the Japanese Diet appropriated funds to provide compensatory payments to NYK and to the families of those bereaved by the sinking of the ship.[3] Indeed, not until nearly fifteen years later did American and Japanese diplomats finally agree on the full meaning of *Awa maru* claims resolution agreement.[4]

That result was virtually unimaginable to the men who negotiated it. They believed that their words and deeds could, in significant measure, lay the ghost of war to rest. By settling the *Awa maru* claims, they could move on to shape peace and security agreements that would guarantee friendship and cooperation between the United States and Japan over the long term. That was their shared intent. As they discovered in these, the first genuine postwar negotiations between their two countries, however, defining an agreement based on shared intent was not easy. The ghost of war, symbolized by the *Awa maru* claims, would not go quietly.

A little more than ninety days before he took the proposed claims settlement agreement to General MacArthur, William Sebald hosted a stag dinner party for Prime Minister Ashida Hitoshi, three of his cabinet officers, the heads of three key administrative agencies, and the probable Japanese manager of any negotiations, Vice Minister of Foreign Affairs Yoshizawa Seijirō. He wanted the evening to seem a purely social occasion, so he instructed his juniors to limit their usual probing questions. The guests were to enjoy the good food, drink, and conversation at his official residence, which had once been Baron Maeda's mansion. Perhaps seeing the cherry trees just starting to bloom on the palatial grounds, and being treated as friends rather than former foes or subordinates, would "butter up" Prime Minister Ashida and put his guests in the mood to talk—later—about the *Awa maru* claims and other pending issues.[5]

The evening went well.[6] Sebald directed one of his younger subordinates, Richard B. Finn, to draft outlines for a settlement, responses to questions

William J. Sebald with Prime Minister Yoshida Shigeru. *William J. Sebald collection, U.S. Naval Academy Library*

that the Japanese could be expected to ask, and the text of an agreement.[7] He himself decided on a strategy for getting MacArthur and his own superiors in Foggy Bottom to agree on something. He knew that the supreme commander was "not fond" of "complicated agreements" and would chafe at State Department instructions in a matter whose resolution had presumably been left to his discretion. It would be best, Sebald told his Washington superior, John M. Allison (chief of the Division of Northeast Asian Affairs), to communicate via airmail rather than official cable when dealing with the *Awa maru* matter. Using that "back channel" would keep MacArthur's protective but nosey uniformed subordinates from interfering in negotiations on its settlement. Sebald wanted to push for an agreement within the next couple of months because, as he confided to Allison, "I fear for [Prime Minister] Ashida's tenure."[8]

That remark, the careful thought given to communications procedure, the dinner at his home, and his encounter with MacArthur all suggested that Sebald was absolutely the right man to try to strike a bargain with the Japanese for resolution of the *Awa maru* claims. A tragic accident—the death of George Atcheson, Jr., in a plane crash the preceding September—had made him acting political adviser to General MacArthur.[9] But any personnel officer would have been hard pressed to find a man better qualified to make that attempt. Sebald had all of the right experiences, connections, and motivations necessary to make him an effective negotiator in the search for an official end to the *Awa maru* tragedy.

The acting political adviser was an old navy hand. Born in Baltimore forty-seven years earlier, he had graduated from the U.S. Naval Academy in 1922 and served as a junior officer on the battleships *Texas* (BB 35) and *Oklahoma* (BB 37) and the light cruiser *Cincinnati* (CL 6).[10] Sebald left the navy in 1930, returning a week after Pearl Harbor to the Office of Naval Intelligence as a Japan expert. After working in code breaking for a time, he shifted to the office of the Commander in Chief, U.S. Fleet, or COMINCH, where he established a combat intelligence division and headed its Pacific section. Awarded a Legion of Merit and promoted to captain, U.S. Naval Reserve, for his wartime service, he left the navy for a second time in November 1945.[11]

Sebald was also an old Japan hand who knew members of the State and Navy Department "Japan crowds" as friends and mentors of his youth. He had first crossed the Pacific in 1925 as a navy language student. In Japan his linguistic abilities grew quickly, winning high praise from then–assistant naval attaché Ellis Zacharias, later coauthor of the proposed broadcast appeal for improved Japanese treatment of prisoners (mentioned in chapter

in that he was intimately familiar with the circumstances that had given rise
to the dispatch and demise of the ship. He had felt intensely the need to get
relief to those in Japanese custody, for his wife's sister and brother-in-law
had been imprisoned by the Japanese in Manila's University of Santo Tomas
camp for three years.[19] Access to decrypted messages may have allowed him
to see how Japanese officials used the ill-fated ship for purposes other than
relief on her final voyage. Sebald had immediately recognized the broader
significance of the sinking when it occurred; as head of the Pacific Section,
Combat Intelligence Division, COMINCH, he had been the first to suspect
that the vessel reported sunk by the *Queenfish* was the *Awa maru*. When a former classmate then working at Admiral Nimitz's Joint Intelligence Center
confirmed that surmise, Sebald was "flabbergasted." He urged his navy superiors to inform the State Department immediately; the Japanese, he insisted,
would certainly raise "a ruckus about this."[20] That prediction proved true for
a much longer time than Sebald could have imagined.

In January 1946, having left the navy for a second time, the negotiator-
to-be traveled to Tokyo as an auxiliary member of the Foreign Service, to
take a job as special assistant to the acting political adviser to General
MacArthur.[21] Although it was painful to have to leave his wife behind in
Washington (dependents were not then allowed in occupied Japan, and she
had to resolve her own citizenship status), ambition beckoned Sebald back to
Japan.[22] Over the next two years he had ample opportunity to develop skills
vital for success in negotiating an amicable end to the *Awa maru* affair. Sebald
came to know and understand how the elites jostling for power in occupied
Japan worked. At first cautiously and privately, then more publicly, he let
himself become the point of contact for Japanese diplomats, businessmen,
and intellectuals who sought to soften the impact of occupation policies
upon themselves, their firms, or their families. The names of members of the
imperial family, scions of the zaibatsu, court officials, and the rising generation of "new" diplomats—as well as old prewar Japanese friends and
acquaintances like Admiral (and Ambassador) Nomura—crowded the pages
of his daily diaries. Through them and with the help of his wife, who joined
him in 1947, Sebald became an unusually astute observer and reporter of the
Tokyo political scene.[23]

The acting political adviser also came to know and admire Gen. Douglas
MacArthur as perhaps no other State Department official of the day did. No

6).[12] His amorous intentions toward Edith deBecker, the beautiful bu
strong daughter of an English barrister who had married into a Jap
family of some social standing, also blossomed.[13] After their marriage in
Sebald returned to the U.S. East Coast where, in addition to his regular di
on board the *Oklahoma*, he served as aide and speechwriter for Adm. Nom
Kichisaburō, who came with the Imperial Japanese Navy Training Squadr
in 1929 to visit America's northeastern port cities.[14]

Edith Sebald, however, grew lonesome during her husband's frequen
absences and chafed under her German-speaking mother-in-law's watchful
eye. She pleaded with Sebald to take up a career whose rewards were com-
mensurate with his talents and ambitions. In July 1930, after bad bets in the
declining stock market cut their income, he left the navy for law school at the
University of Maryland.[15] Three years later, having received his degree and
been admitted to the Maryland bar, he left for Japan to take over his father-
in-law's legal practice.[16]

Over the next six years Sebald gained experiences that sharpened skills
needed to broker a settlement of the *Awa maru* claims. Barred as a foreigner
from representing clients in court, he built a substantial practice in Kobe
interpreting Japanese law and commercial regulations for major non-Japanese corporations. He translated and published Japan's civil, criminal, and tax
codes, and produced a compendium of emergency legislation enacted after
war between China and Japan broke out in 1937. He represented a major
French shipping firm in a collision and wrongful-death suit, brokering a
compromise on indemnification with the Japanese bureaucracies involved.
Indeed, Sebald grew fairly wealthy representing various non-Japanese individuals and firms as they tried to cope with increasingly strict regulations
imposed by ever more nationalistic bureaucrats.[17]

Eventually, he was forced to leave Japan by rules of that sort, which made
his legal practice difficult and financially unrewarding. He returned in June
1939 to Washington, D.C., where he formed a legal partnership and began to
represent major Japanese trading firms who were trying to deal with export
controls imposed after Washington abrogated the U.S.–Japan Commercial
Treaty of 1911 to express its displeasure with Japan's actions in China. In
that capacity he secretly passed along to old naval intelligence friends information about his clients' commercial and maritime activities.[18]

Sebald was also the right man to handle the *Awa maru* claims negotiations

nonmilitary member of the SCAP staff saw the general more often than Sebald. He was frequently the proverbial Persian messenger, bearing bad tidings about the reaction of Foggy Bottom to something SCAP had said or done. Sebald, schooled by service under crotchety and sometimes inconsistent naval superiors, was savvy enough to remain silent when the general burst out in tirades against Washington officials. He was shrewd enough to return later, at a calmer moment, when MacArthur might be persuaded to shift his position.[24] Sebald also gained credibility in SCAP's eyes by talking tough to the Russians—or tactfully but firmly to the Australians—as presiding officer of the Allied Council for Japan.[25] While it would be an exaggeration to say that Sebald knew he could manipulate MacArthur for his own purposes, he had certainly, by 1948, honed the skills needed to get the general to back the *Awa maru* claims settlement he hoped to conclude.

Finally, Sebald had one other quality necessary for success in these negotiations: ambition. He was childless; his professional career was his life. He had come late to the Foreign Service, yet nearly a year after the political adviser's death he remained merely an acting successor. Sebald wanted to advance to the top of the professional diplomatic ranks, and he believed he had the background, linguistic ability, and social skills needed to become America's first postwar ambassador to Japan.[26] Success in these first genuine American-Japanese negotiations since the war might be a harbinger of still greater things to come.

Sebald launched the negotiations intended to lay the *Awa maru* incident to rest on 22 April 1948, when he met with Prime Minister Ashida (who also served as foreign minister) and his deputy at Kasumigaseki (site of the Ministry of Foreign Affairs), Vice Minister Yoshizawa.[27] Both men were particularly well qualified to deal with the claims problem. Ashida was a professional diplomat, scholar, journalist, and, most importantly, an extraordinarily supple and durable politician. Then sixty, he had spent seventeen years abroad before resigning from the Foreign Ministry in 1932 in protest over the Kwantung Army's conquest of Manchuria. Over the next decade, in addition to being elected a Seiyūkai Party member of the Diet, he served as editor of the English-language *Japan Times*, traveled to Europe and America to defend Japan's China policies, acquired a doctorate from Keio University, and published five books.[28] Although American firebombs destroyed his Tokyo home, he survived the war unscathed as a Diet member representing his native Kyoto.[29] What he had written and said in defense of Japan's prewar expansionist policies might well have gotten him purged from postwar political activity, but the American committee reviewing his record concluded that his words had not contributed in any significant way to the war effort.[30]

After the war Ashida rose quickly to political prominence. His initial success came in part because other, more senior politicians were purged by occupation authorities, in part because of old Foreign Ministry bureaucratic ties, and in part because his command of the English language needed to deal with those authorities was so extensive. In October 1945 he became Minister of Health and Welfare in a cabinet headed by the old "liberal" prewar foreign minister, Shidehara Kijūrō.[31] Ashida also demonstrated that he knew how to walk the line between cooperation and subservience when dealing with Japan's American occupiers. In the summer of 1946, he chaired the Diet subcommittee that reviewed the American-originated draft for a new Japanese constitution. Ashida modified the language of its "no-war" Article Nine with words that recognized his nation's right to self-defense.[32] Success in that endeavor prefigured more adroit political maneuvering that over the next two years made Ashida first the head of his own Democratic Party, then foreign minister in a Socialist cabinet, and finally, in March 1948, prime minister.[33]

By that time, Ashida had clearly established himself as a friend of the United States. As foreign minister, he had engineered a series of behind-the-scenes initiatives for conclusion of an early peace treaty. They had failed to achieve their immediate purpose, but through them Ashida conveyed Japan's willingness to side with the United States against the Soviet Union in the deepening Cold War and to allow American forces to remain in Japan after a peace agreement was concluded.[34] Ashida had also dispelled SCAP's initial suspicions of him. Although General MacArthur himself had in the fall of 1947 termed him "an ambitious schemer" who was "more anti-Anglo-Saxon" than any other Japanese politician, Ashida convinced MacArthur's chief of staff to endorse, and SCAP to accept, his candidacy for the premiership.[35] Ashida also used his English-language skills and social graces to get to know Sebald. He entertained him officially and became a frequent guest at the American's intimate dinner parties for former zaibatsu, court officials, and Japanese royalty.[36]

Prime Minister Ashida
Hitoshi. *Iwanami Shoten*

In Yoshizawa Seijirō Ashida had a deputy quite capable of managing claims negotiations with Americans. He knew them firsthand. He had two years' prewar service at the Japanese embassy in Washington. They had charge of him when, as ambassador to Canada, he was interned in the United States and then returned home on the *Gripsholm* in 1942.[37] Yoshizawa also had hands-on experience with indemnity negotiations. In December 1937, as head of the Foreign Ministry's America Bureau, he had managed talks that resulted in quick payment of American claims arising from Japanese attacks on the *Panay* on the Yangtze River.[38] Furthermore, Yoshizawa had shown himself capable of dealing firmly but tactfully with American occupiers. When, in January 1948, SCAP insisted on moving the Central Liaison Office from the Foreign Ministry to the prime minister's office, thus depriving senior Japanese diplomats of direct contact with General MacArthur's subordinates, Yoshizawa complied but protested the unwisdom of that change.[39]

Sebald presented his outline for an *Awa maru* settlement to Ashida and

Yoshizawa on 22 January 1948. Neither man seemed keen to talk about it. The prime minister, like MacArthur earlier, expressed surprise that the Potsdam Declaration had not forced Japan to drop all claims against the United States and its allies.[40] Sebald responded by leading the two men, clause by clause, through his draft settlement text. He then zeroed in on what was for him the most crucial point: that Japan must drop its *Awa maru* claims unconditionally. Tokyo must, as the last of five articles proposed, recognize that occupation costs, loans, and credits received from Washington were "valid debts . . . reducible only by the decision of the United States." Without such an acknowledgment, he argued, the public might wrongly conclude that the settlement was a kind of *quid pro quo* for continued American aid, rather than the complete and unconditional abandonment of claims that his Washington superiors wanted.[41]

At first Ashida responded politely to the proposal, saying he would have it studied and considered by his cabinet. But then he hinted at opposition to what Sebald was offering. Should not the United States offer some compensation to families of the bereaved? Without it, he feared, the proposed settlement might occasion considerable debate in Japan. If, however, Washington were in some way to offer payment to those families, the Japanese would regard the settlement as a magnanimous gesture. Perhaps, the prime minister hinted, America and Japan could find a way to put the sinking of the *Awa maru,* a tragedy that symbolized their former enmity, behind them graciously. Sebald immediately rejected that idea. Knowing well that war passions had not yet died at home, he said that if a settlement involving payment to the Japanese were proposed to the Congress, the American people would probably recoil in disgust. He could not imagine any good results coming out of doing that. Stung by the sharpness of Sebald's retort, Ashida quickly retreated into what appeared to be polite compliance with the American's wishes. While his official reply would have to follow cabinet discussion, he said, he personally expected formal acceptance of what Sebald had proposed.[42]

The differences that surfaced in this first negotiating encounter hinted at underlying disagreement between the United States and Japan over how to resolve the *Awa maru* claims. Washington wanted to avoid making any direct payment to Tokyo, while the Japanese still felt that America had a moral responsibility to compensate those who had suffered as a consequence of the sinking of the ship. Sebald chose to ignore that difference. He quickly got his Washington superiors to approve both the draft settlement and continuation of his efforts to secure prompt Japanese acceptance of it.[43] Ashida, by contrast, did nothing. He did not raise the *Awa maru* claims issue with his cabinet, as he had said he would; he let Yoshizawa and his subordinates take their time in studying Sebald's proposal. Not until nearly two months later, early in June 1948, after the American had broached the matter informally and followed up with a phone call to spur his memory, did Ashida tell Yoshizawa to do something to stave off the impatient Sebald.[44]

When the Japanese diplomat came to the acting political adviser's office, he offered one technical objection after another to the American's proposal. Yoshizawa said Foreign Ministry lawyers objected to the proposed third article of the agreement because it committed his government to providing "adequate and fair treatment in accordance with Japanese law" to those who suffered loss as a consequence of the sinking of the *Awa maru*. There was no such law, he insisted, and if this provision were included in the agreement, the government would be subjected to costly lawsuits seeking indemnification. Yoshizawa was "practically certain" that NYK, the ship's owner, would file such a suit.

Sebald responded that the United States was not "inflexible" on the language of that article. Washington had simply wanted to address the moral issue of compensation for families of the victims of the sinking. Yoshizawa then objected that there was no basis in Japanese law for the common law concept of equity that underlay the American proposal. Japanese law derived from Roman law, in which there was no such notion.

He then raised his most crucial objection, which was procedural. Foreign Ministry legal experts, Yoshizawa reported, thought that Article 73 (3) of the new, American-imposed constitution required Diet approval of the proposed settlement. They felt legislators might vote on the agreement either before or after it was signed. But, Yoshizawa added, Prime Minister Ashida did not want to put an *Awa maru* settlement before the Diet during its current session, which would continue until the end of June. Sensing that Yoshizawa's last point rested on political, rather than constitutional, concerns, Sebald dismissed them. There was no need to involve either the American Congress or the Japanese Diet in the settlement, he said. What he had proposed would be an executive agreement, not a treaty requiring legislative sanction in either country. Quick resolution of the *Awa maru* claims was what really mattered. Sebald warned Yoshizawa that "a fairly long delay" might result if they did not seize the present opportunity to lay to rest the tragedy that had given rise to them. MacArthur, who could have "weighty beneficial effects" on public acceptance of an agreement on both sides of the Pacific, might not remain in Japan for long. And if, as some political observers surmised, the Ashida cabinet were to resign in the near future, he and Yoshizawa would have to make "a complete re-start" of the negotiations.

While the Japanese diplomat probably did not welcome that prospect, he had to respect Prime Minister Ashida's "firm" view that no agreement should be concluded while the Diet was in session. The best Yoshizawa could do was a weak offer to keep working to define an agreement. His staff would begin talking with Sebald's subordinates to prepare an agreed-upon text. Action could be taken on that document shortly thereafter.[45]

Sebald suspected that the Japanese were once again resisting, even as they appeared to comply with American wishes. He doubted the arguments Yoshizawa had presented and correctly surmised that politics was the real reason for Ashida's reluctance to conclude an agreement quickly. That very morning an *Asahi shimbun* cartoonist portrayed the prime minister as a *jin-ricksha* man sweating under a hot sun that bore the face of his chief rival, Yoshida Shigeru.[46] Sebald suspected that Ashida did not want to give his opponents any ammunition with which to attack him in the Diet. Abandonment of Japan's claim to indemnification for the sinking of the *Awa maru* might indeed trigger just such an attack.

When, a few days later, Sebald briefed MacArthur on his conversations with Ashida and Yoshizawa, the general listened patiently to the report of their objections to the proposed agreement. Immediately recognizing their political basis, he set limits to what he would do as intermediary. MacArthur was not about to hazard the popularity he enjoyed as SCAP by letting Ashida make it seem that he had forced a distasteful settlement upon the Japanese government. The general told his acting political adviser he would sign an agreement—but not in his official capacity as supreme commander.[47]

That did not bother the diplomat, and over the next month he had one of his subordinates, a young Harvard-trained lawyer and former Naval Reserve officer, Richard B. Finn, work with Yoshizawa's representative, Asakai Koichirō, a former Central Liaison Office official skilled in pleasing and spying upon Americans, to draft terms for a settlement.[48] By the third week of July 1948 the two younger men had produced the text, described earlier; Sebald took it to MacArthur for approval and comment.

The general's doubts of its acceptability to the Japanese proved accurate; two days after Sebald thought they had approved it, Yoshizawa came seeking another change. He said that separating its fifth article, which committed Japan to repay occupation costs, from the text and making it an ancillary agreement would strengthen the government's hand in dealing with the Diet. Sebald initially opposed that idea strongly, but then he agreed. It would make the resultant agreement look more like a genuine accord between Americans and Japanese than like some "dictation" forced by the former on the latter.[49]

That concession to Ashida's political sensitivities was not sufficient to bring about an agreement, however. The prime minister presided over a weak coalition government comprising members of his own Democratic Party, more conservative People's Cooperative Party members, and Socialists— who held a plurality of seats in the Diet but were split into Left and Right factions.[50] He alternated between periods of Hamlet-like indecision, in which he felt that the many problems facing his government precluded any positive action, and moments of optimistic determination, in which he voiced faith in gritty persistence.[51] The last thing he wanted was to appear to bow before American demands. Yet on 22 July 1948 SCAP demanded that he deny public employees the right to strike—a move certain to deepen divisions among his Socialist coalition partners.[52] That came on top of mounting pressure from Washington to cease deficit spending, reduce dependence on American assistance, and cut the number of government employees.[53] Struggling to cope with these much larger problems, Ashida, understandably, dragged his feet in dealing with the *Awa maru* claims.

Delay worried Sebald. He had returned to Japan more than two years earlier as convinced as any American that the defeated Japanese must be changed and their government reformed if they were to regain full sovereignty.[54] Now he wondered "whether the whole Occupation will not, in the long run . . . have been a futile undertaking." The Japanese would revert to nationalism, display all of the "objectionable attributes" they had shown before the war, and throw off occupation-imposed restraints and changes. If all of that were so—and America's strategic objective was to keep Japan on its side in the Cold War—then the time had come to make friends with "the people who in any event will be in control in Japan eventually."[55] That would require putting disputes arising from the unhappy past—things like the *Awa maru* claims—to rest as quickly and quietly as possible.

Seizing the moment, Sebald on 24 August 1948 persuaded MacArthur to intervene in the negotiations. The general summoned Ashida from a cabinet meeting to his general headquarters. For an hour and a quarter the supreme commander heard the prime minister and Sebald debate over how best to settle the *Awa maru* claims. Ashida began by insisting that his objections to the proposed agreement were procedural, not substantial. Even though others who suffered as a consequence of the war might reasonably claim that the victims of a single ship sinking were being accorded special treatment, his government stood ready to do what it could to pay them consolation monies —sums that would not be formal indemnity payments. The objections of that small group would not matter. The Diet would certainly approve an accord "blessed by the intermediation . . . of the Supreme Commander," even though crude Communists might criticize the United States.

But if a claims renunciation agreement were presented to the legislators simply as a fait accompli, it would certainly be "severely criticized" by them; the ensuing debate might even have "serious repercussions" in both Japan and the United States. Consequently, Ashida concluded, the proper course of action was the democratic procedure spelled out in Article 73 of the constitution—that is, to go to the Diet for approval of the agreement.

Sebald mustered every argument he could against what Ashida had said. There was, in his view, a real risk of "unwarranted and embarrassing" criticism of the proposed agreement in the Diet. Nonetheless, Ashida's government had no legal obligation to put it before that body before signing it. Article 73 of the new constitution did not apply, because the proposed agreement was not a treaty—a point that MacArthur immediately seconded by saying that if it were, *he* certainly would have no authority to allow its signature. Furthermore, Sebald suggested, the Ashida government could go to the Diet later when seeking funds to implement the agreement—without necessarily committing the legislators to explicit approval of its terms.

After this jousting between the negotiators, MacArthur proposed, and Ashida and Sebald accepted, an elaborate procedural agreement for what was to be done. At "a propitious time" when the Diet returned to meet in special session, the prime minister would "undertake to obtain" cabinet approval for the agreement. Immediately thereafter he would summon party leaders either to get their agreement that the government had the authority to sign a settlement agreement without prior Diet approval, or if they rejected that proposition, their approval of such an agreement when it was presented to the legislature. When party leaders agreed to that procedure, resolutions in support of the agreement would be introduced into both houses of the Diet. In the meantime, however, both the details of the negotiations that had produced the proposed agreement and its text were to be kept secret.[56]

Ashida left SCAP General Headquarters pleased with that resolution of the issue. He could rightfully claim that the Americans had acknowledged the principle of Diet participation in conclusion of an *Awa maru* claims-abandonment agreement. If and when he went to the Diet with such a proposal, he would be protected from nationalistic critics both by SCAP's blessing and by either his partisan opponents' prior concurrence in the accord or by their acknowledgment that they had no right to demand it. Moreover, he would control the timing of any attempt to put a formal end to the *Awa maru* tragedy.

A month after the meeting with MacArthur, Ashida appeared ready to proceed. Sebald invited the prime minister to his home for a chat. While they sat in lawn chairs overlooking its spacious garden, he pressed his visitor for a date on which the *Awa maru* matter would be presented to the Diet. The two men apparently agreed on one, and Sebald, in a gesture of thanks, said that he was prepared to take up the question of rehabilitating zaibatsu officials—men whose talents were now needed to hasten Japan's economic recovery—with his superiors in Washington. Ashida left feeling satisfied, and upon returning to his official residence, he told Yoshizawa what had transpired. His deputy too was pleased by the prospect of an early settlement of the *Awa maru* matter.[57]

But Ashida's partisan foes, the very men whose support he would need to get Diet acquiescence in a settlement, had other ideas. As September turned into October, they stepped up their attacks on his weak coalition government. They alleged that he had caved in to American dictates for revision of the National Public Service Employees law. The public prosecutor then indicted Ashida's Socialist vice-premier, charging that he had taken bribes in what became known as the Shōwa Denkō affair. That cast a shadow over

Ashida as well, and by the end of the first week of October he felt he had no choice but to "take responsibility" for the scandal and resign.[58]

His decision to do so, made public on 7 October 1948, threw the Japanese political world into turmoil and buried for the time being the chances for a quick settlement of the *Awa maru* claims issue. Perhaps that was appropriate, for throughout the preceding months of talks fear of public scrutiny had shaped Japanese and American negotiators' behavior. Ashida and Sebald recognized that putting the *Awa maru* claims—a reminder of their nations' former enmity—behind them was in their common interest. But because both men realized that their readiness to do so exceeded that of most of their fellow citizens, neither was willing to take real risks. Ashida used the new American-imposed constitution to stave off pressure for quick action; Sebald opposed a more open and democratic review of the proposed settlement, because he feared criticism in Japan that might turn popular and congressional opinion at home even further against the defeated enemy. As he and his Washington superiors saw matters, the only way Japan could gain stature it needed to appear ready for a peace treaty in the eyes of the American people was to renounce voluntarily its *Awa maru* claims.

To achieve that goal he moderated his pressure on Japanese leaders so as to accommodate their political needs. Sebald's skill in doing so may have contributed to his promotion, a few days before Ashida's resignation, to the rank of minister.[59] As the summer of 1948 turned to autumn, however, no amount of American sensitivity to Japanese needs could produce a settlement of the *Awa maru* claims.

On Thursday, 14 April 1949, more than six months after Ashida Hitoshi resigned as Japan's prime minister, the man who finally brought about that resolution came to Douglas MacArthur's office on the seventh floor of the Dai-Ichi Building, opposite the Imperial Palace. When he arrived, promptly at eleven that morning, Minister-Counselor Sebald and the supreme commander were waiting for him. Yoshida and Sebald signed the claims settlement agreement, and then General MacArthur added his name to it as witness. At long last, negotiations between the United States and Japan arising from the sinking of the *Awa maru* more than four years earlier had come to an end.[60]

The document they signed read just like what Finn had drafted a year earlier. Nothing of substance had changed. Nor did the tiny, plump Yoshida seem any more courageous than his thin predecessor in assuming responsibility for abandonment of Japan's legitimate claims. As he prepared to leave, the prime minister asked MacArthur and Sebald not to say anything about the signing until an "appropriate" time came for him to report it to the Diet.[61] In fact, a great deal of change, embodied in the person of Prime Minister Yoshida, had swept over politics in Japan and over relations between Tokyo and Washington during the preceding six months. Those shifts enabled Yoshida, MacArthur, and Sebald to lay the *Awa maru* claims to official rest.

On Saturday, 16 October 1948, only two days after he was chosen prime minister for a second time, Yoshida paid a courtesy call on Sebald. He assured Sebald that he had the *Awa maru* matter "in hand" and would negotiate with the acting political adviser "later on." Sebald, momentarily taken aback by the prime minister's bold manner, cautioned him against making "a premature leak" to the press. What Yoshida said in reply left the American with the impression that the new prime minister "apparently" would attempt to handle the matter as the United States desired.[62]

That brief exchange reflected the new spirit that Prime Minister Yoshida brought to the task of resolving the *Awa maru* claims problem. He knew he could not change what had already been agreed to, but he was determined to acquiesce in the Americans' desires only on his own terms. Indeed, he would accept them only in a way that made it appear that he was doing so in Japan's best interest. That posture was entirely consistent with his personality, his career up to 1945, and his prior dealings with the American occupiers. Despite his small physical stature, Yoshida was a vigorous, strong-willed, and often abrasive personality.[63] He had always stood out among his peers. The son of a geisha and a member of the very first Diet, he had been adopted as a teenager by a Yokohama merchant, who made him independently wealthy. Yoshida graduated from Tokyo Imperial University, entered the foreign service, and married into the family of one of the leaders of the Meiji Restoration.[64] His professional life was marked both by quick accession to highly desirable posts—London, Rome, and a place on the Japanese delegation to the Paris Peace Conference of 1919—and by stunning failures. The military had kept him from becoming foreign minister in 1936, in a cabinet headed by his friend Hirota Kōki—a man who barely two months after Yoshida's second accession to the prime ministry would go to the gallows as a class-A war criminal. Over the next three years, as ambassador to England, he slowed but failed to prevent Japan's drift into alliance with Nazi Germany and Fascist Italy. In the closing months of the war, Yoshida's efforts to persuade the Japanese government to make peace so as to preserve the imperial system landed him in the custody of the dreaded *kempeitai*, or special police.[65]

Spectacular success followed on that failure. Barely two weeks after Japan's surrender, Yoshida became foreign minister. Less than nine months later he became prime minister for the first time, even though he was not an elected member of the Diet.[66] In those positions he had to get along with Americans, but his first encounters with occupation officials were not promising. He laughed at SCAP when MacArthur, in his customary manner, lectured him while pacing up and down in his office. He greeted one of the most powerful and ardent American reformers by saying, "So you're the man who's going to make us democratic. Ha, ha!"[67]

Yoshida gradually learned that success in early postwar diplomacy meant striking a balance between accommodating and defying American wishes. He cultivated MacArthur and sought his support through frequent visits and numerous polite letters. Yet he also struggled to avoid being labeled an American puppet. Late in 1946 that meant reversing his position on who should take responsibility for a further purge of Japanese political and economic leaders. Having failed to get MacArthur to do so, Yoshida realized that it would be best for his government to appear to act spontaneously in carrying out the dismissals.[68]

In the autumn of 1948, Yoshida found himself in a similar position. He knew what the Americans wanted in an *Awa maru* claims settlement. He also knew his own position was not strong. SCAP officials had looked deep into his own party for an alternative to him as prime minister, and had found one, only to see that individual decline to serve. Nearly half the Diet ballots just cast for his election to that office had been blank. His cabinet was weak and his party faction ridden.[69] Once again the situation seemed to demand accommodation, clothed in the guise of independent action.

To achieve that goal Yoshida adopted Ashida's tactic. Two weeks after he first spoke with Sebald about the *Awa maru*, the prime minister drew him aside at a garden party and outlined his plan for building formal consensus on a claims-abandonment agreement. He would get both houses of the Diet to pass resolutions asking the government to negotiate an accord "forgiving the claim."[70] That would insulate him from any serious criticism. Although Sebald still harbored reservations about the feasibility of this procedure, he went along with Yoshida's proposal. Keeping his fingers crossed, he bet that the wily old man would succeed behind the scenes, by greasing all the slides needed to assure easy Diet passage of such resolutions.[71]

Nonetheless, over the next month Yoshida failed to deliver what he had promised. The secret of an impending deal to resolve the *Awa maru* claims got out, and Sebald had to staunch the leak.[72] No sooner was that done than Yoshida interposed himself in a conflict between SCAP officials and his own subordinates over implementation of the National Public Service Law that had caused Ashida so much trouble. His purpose then, just as it had been in 1946, was to get the Americans to bear some responsibility for the consequences of their demands. He also wanted to get SCAP's sanction for calling elections that he had wanted all along.[73] The struggle went on until 23 December 1948, the very day that former Prime Minister Tōjō and six other major war criminals were executed.[74] Only then, after brokering a compromise between SCAP and opposition party leaders, did Yoshida agree to end the life of his second cabinet and set elections for one month later.[75]

That poll revolutionized the Japanese political landscape. Yoshida's party gained an absolute majority of seats in the lower house of the Diet, while Ashida's Democrats and former coalition partners in the Socialist Party suffered devastating defeats.[76] Yoshida strengthened his own position within the conservative fold by running former bureaucrats as Diet candidates and bringing them into his cabinet. He seized upon this victory to assert his personal, "one-man," dictatorial style of leadership.[77] That proved essential in persuading first his cabinet and then the Diet to sanction a budget that completely reversed his campaign pledges and toed the tough deflationary lines that Joseph E. Dodge, General MacArthur's new financial adviser, demanded.[78]

Once he succeeded in that endeavor, Yoshida was ready to tackle the *Awa maru* claims. He (or his political minions) persuaded eight leading members of each of the two houses of the Diet to cosponsor resolutions calling upon his government to abandon them.[79] By early April 1949 the time seemed right to press for the resolutions' approval; the scent of international change was in the spring air. In Washington, the North Atlantic Treaty was about to be signed. Mao Tse-tung's communist troops were poised to cross the Yangtze and complete their conquest of China.[80] And in Tokyo, Yoshida had what Ashida had lacked: the raw political power to assure Diet approval of the *Awa maru* resolutions.

On a cloudy Wednesday, 6 April 1949, he had his handpicked Vice Minister of Foreign Affairs, Okazaki Katsuo, speak in defense of a resolution approving his government's decision to abandon the *Awa maru* claims.[81] The resolution acknowledged, as Sebald and his State Department superiors desired, Japan's "incalculable debt of gratitude" to the United States for the aid it had received. But that statement was preceded by language that looked to the future: Japan was making progress in "reconstruction dedicated to peace." It was followed by words that signalized the once-defeated nation's recovery of autonomy: Tokyo was "spontaneously and unconditionally" waiving its right to claim damages arising from the *Queenfish*'s destruction of the *Awa maru*.[82] Language of that sort reflected Yoshida's determination to make concession seem the magnanimous gesture of a people well on the way to recovery of full independence.

Okazaki also symbolized that determination. Late in 1947 SCAP had demanded his resignation as vice minister after details of the Foreign Ministry's planning for a peace treaty were prematurely disclosed.[83] Yoshida had brought him back, and now he defended an American-sponsored settlement of the *Awa maru* claims against critics on the Left. Communist Nashimoto Sakujirō taunted him with what were, in effect, his own subordinates' words. Expecting a negotiated rather than an imposed peace treaty, they were compiling documents in defense of claims for losses caused by American attacks, including the atomic bombing of Hiroshima and Nagasaki.[84] Why, Nashimoto asked, was the government so anxious to settle the *Awa maru* affair now when the claims would have to be reconsidered in peace treaty negotiations?[85] A Socialist Diet member joined in the attack, saying that the government should not throw away ordinary people's rights to indemnification, especially when doing so meant bowing before superior American military power.[86]

Okazaki responded first with an argument that Sebald and his superiors had hoped would never be made: by abandoning the *Awa maru* claims and voicing appreciation for prior aid, the Diet would help convince the American Congress to vote still more money for Japanese relief and economic reconstruction. He then added a more personal plea, one his subordinates had often made in the past: putting off resolution of the claims until a peace treaty was negotiated would hurt those who had already suffered as a consequence of the *Awa maru* tragedy. The bereaved and the ship's owners deserved prompt consolation.[87]

Those arguments did not prove entirely convincing to Diet members. Sebald, who went to the lower house to observe the proceedings, noticed that when they voted—by standing rather than by formal recording of their preferences—Socialists as well as Communists opposed the resolution. Others reported that the number of those opposed to the claims-abandonment resolution was even greater in the upper chamber, where Yoshida lacked a majority. Nevertheless, the resolution passed.

Sebald was so delighted by the result that immediately after leaving the Diet building he issued a press statement; hoping to strengthen Yoshida's hand, he said he had been "deeply impressed" by the Japanese expression of gratitude for past aid. He then fired off a telegram to Washington that recorded the precise moment at which the successful vote had been taken in each of the Diet chambers.[88]

The charade of spontaneous concession that Yoshida and Sebald pulled off did not fool many Japanese. The prime minister and his political allies swallowed claims abandonment as a small but necessary step toward formal peace. However, press commentators across the political spectrum thought otherwise. The Communist *Akahata* (Red Flag) attacked the government for seeking passage of such a resolution. One of the lesser sheets retold Shimoda Kantarō's story, as if to elicit renewed sympathy for victims of the *Awa maru* sinking. The popular but anonymous front-page commentator in the *Asahi shimbun* strongly criticized the settlement; it was "unconscionable," he argued, to link claims abandonment and American aid in a way that made one seem a precondition for continuation of the other. To burden Japan with a huge debt for repayment of aid and occupation costs after a peace treaty had been concluded was even more unwise.[89]

These signs of opposition prompted Yoshida to pause. He exchanged and published flowery congratulatory letters with Sebald four days after the Diet vote, but four more passed before the two men signed the claims-abandonment agreement, with MacArthur as witness. Yoshida asked them to keep its signature secret, and it remained so for nearly two weeks more.[90] That gave him time to shepherd the coming year's painfully deflationary, American-designed budget through the lower house of the Diet. His government also accepted the new, fixed exchange rate that Washington wanted—something that fellow conservatives like Ashida thought would slow Japan's economic recovery and reentry into world markets.[91] The prime minister did not make his formal, official report to the Diet on conclusion of the *Awa maru* claims-abandonment agreement until 26 April 1949.[92]

Its sugary language barely concealed the fact that Japan was eating the crow of defeat and promising to pay the American eagle much more than had been lost in the sinking of the *Awa maru*. That did not bother sophisticated diplomats and seasoned politicians like Yoshida Shigeru and Ashida Hitoshi. They grasped what their critics then and later failed to understand: justice in the wake of a war is almost impossible to attain. Pursuit of national interest, even if it means sacrificing particular goals, is much more important. Thus, Yoshida and Ashida accepted what Sebald proposed because they believed conclusion of an *Awa maru* claims-renunciation agreement moved Japan a step closer to formal peace and recovery of independence. They concluded what was a morally flawed agreement in hopes of building a lasting peaceful relationship between Japan and the United States. Convinced that the two nations must stand together in the Cold War, Tokyo dropped legitimate claims against Washington for the *Queenfish*'s destruction of the *Awa maru*.

Before she could be completely and officially forgotten, however, Japanese officials had to "endeavor" to provide consolation monies to the bereaved and the ship's owner, NYK.[93] They took fifteen months to define and initiate a payment program. By November 1949 Foreign and Finance Ministry bureaucrats had deadlocked over how much to ask for *Awa maru* claims payments. The new Vice Minister of Foreign Affairs, Ohta Ichirō, told Sebald that the issue was money. His ministry had requested an appropriation in the coming year's budget of 200 million yen (approximately what Tokyo had demanded from Washington as indemnity in August 1945) for consolation payments. But Finance Ministry officials, who had to implement the tough, budget-balancing, deflationary policy that Washington now insisted upon, wanted to cap payments at no more than 130 million yen—about two-thirds of what Tokyo had originally demanded from Washington.

Once Sebald indicated that he had no objection to reductions in the 1945 figures, however, two conflicting principles of fairness, both of which worked to the disadvantage of those who were supposed to receive consolation payments, pitted diplomats against financiers.[94] Foreign Ministry officials dropped their original scheme of compensation according to the rank of the victim, but they wanted to keep their 1945 valuation figures as the basis for any payments. They proposed paying bereaved families 100,000 yen for each person who had gone down with the *Awa maru*.[95] That approach, however, completely disregarded the ravages of inflation over the preceding four years.

Finance Ministry officials, on the other hand, were reluctant to make substantial payment to those harmed by the loss of the ship because they feared that doing so might set a dangerous and expensive precedent. As yet, not a single yen had been authorized for payment to millions of others who had suffered human or material loss as a consequence of the war.[96] Foreign pressure—from the United States—required treating the *Awa maru* victims as a special group, which was unfair. Nonetheless, there was no reason to compound that injustice by paying them handsomely.

This debate ended in a compromise of sorts in the spring of 1950. The diplomats got the budgeteers to increase per capita payments to families of victims 10 percent over the original Finance Ministry proposal; the resultant amount, however, was only 70 percent of what they themselves had first sought.[97] Finance Ministry officials, mindful of the government's basic policy of economic recovery through export promotion, demanded a drastic increase in payments to NYK. The shipping firm wanted enough money to build a five-thousand-ton replacement vessel, the maximum permitted Japan under currently prevailing Occupation restrictions. That would be less than half the size of the lost *Awa maru*. Foreign Ministry officials wanted to give individual bereaved families priority over shipowners, and they proposed paying NYK only enough to build a vessel a tenth her size.[98] But in the end, the shipping firm got nearly 18 million yen—a sum equal to the 1945 insured value of the *Awa maru* plus interest on that amount over the preceding five years.[99]

When, late in July 1950, the Diet considered the government's compensation proposal, power rather than principle determined the final result. Prime Minister Yoshida had tightened his grip on Japanese domestic politics.

Although his party had not won an absolute majority in upper-house elections the preceding month, the prime minister had benefited from General MacArthur's purging of his archenemies in the Japanese Communist Party from further participation in politics.[100] He had strength enough to ram through legislation authorizing consolation payments to those victimized by the sinking of the *Awa maru*.

But he did not need to do so, for two reasons. Legislators were as anxious as he was to make progress toward conclusion of a peace treaty that would restore Japan's independence. Yoshida's diplomatic strategy of cooperating with the United States on other matters had begun to bear fruit. He had sent special envoys to Washington to signal his readiness to make security and economic concessions in order to get a peace treaty. The Americans, in turn, dispatched John Foster Dulles, who would be their designated principal negotiator, to Tokyo to consult with Yoshida.[101] No one wanted to rock the diplomatic boat by questioning the wisdom or fairness of the *Awa maru* claims-abandonment agreement.

The outbreak of war in Korea in June 1950 also reduced the matter's domestic political significance. That conflict forced Japanese to turn their thoughts from the lost war to what this new conflict might mean for their future. Businessmen and Finance Ministry officials sensed that supplying American and other United Nations forces fighting in Korea would bring handsome profits to Japan. Yoshida's opponents on the Left took as their summons to battle General MacArthur's call for the creation of a National Police Reserve to replace American troops who had gone to Korea; for them, rearmament was a much more important issue than the government's use of Japanese monies to compensate victims of an erroneous American attack.[102] In short, the new war sucked the life out of the old one, destroying at the same time the political saliency of the *Awa maru* settlement.

So it was that the Yoshida government and the Diet quietly washed their hands of the *Awa maru* tragedy. They passed legislation that gave its victims six months in which to request consolation payments. What bereaved families got for a loved one was a pittance—from fifty to seventy thousand yen per person, depending upon the number of individuals in a single family who had perished. That, at the current exchange rate, came to between $138 and $194. NYK, as noted above, did only slightly better: the shipping firm got 17.8 million yen ($49,500).

These payments were not enough to make up for what those victimized by the sinking of the *Awa maru* had lost. They were made, however, at a time when Occupation decrees forbade compensatory payments to the families of war dead and to soldiers returning from the lost war. Those who suffered loss from the sinking of the *Awa maru* got something, when other war victims got nothing.[103]

The ship was, after death—as she had been in life—an exception to the rule.

The Diet's passage of legislation providing for the compensation of the victims was the last act but one in the settlement of the *Awa maru* claims. When Yoshida Shigeru came to San Francisco in September 1951 to sign a peace treaty, he assented to its nineteenth article, by which Japan abandoned all claims against its former enemies arising from the conduct of the Pacific War. That provision in the peace treaty confirmed what Japanese and American officials had agreed upon two years earlier.[104] It guaranteed that the *Awa maru* would never again rise from the depths of the Taiwan Strait to trouble formal relations between the United States and Japan.

That was precisely what Ashida and Yoshida, and Sebald and MacArthur, wanted. Much like the navy officials who court-martialed Charles Elliott Loughlin, they were satisfied to meet the demands of form without resolving all of the questions of substance that attended the sinking of the *Awa maru*. Why had they behaved in that way?

A dozen years after the Diet passed legislation authorizing payment of compensation to the victims of that tragedy, Prime Minister Ikeda Hayato gave a flip answer to that question. Responding to a Socialist legislator who insisted that the 1949 claims-renunciation agreement had not committed Tokyo to repay Washington for postwar aid received, he insisted that it most certainly had. Ikeda, who had been Yoshida's finance minister, then claimed that Tokyo had struck a good bargain with Washington in 1949: in return for dropping *Awa maru* claims worth a few millions, Japan got nearly 2 billion dollars in aid from the United States.[105]

Ikeda's answer may have been good politics in 1962, but it was bad history, for the men who negotiated the *Awa maru* claims settlement a dozen years earlier had not been interested in settling accounts. They were charting a course toward a new future, and they were prepared to treat the *Awa maru* as a ghost of the past. They looked ahead with greater prescience—and anxiety—than did legislators and ordinary citizens, in whom passions born of war lingered longer and more strongly. These leaders were more concerned with shaping a new relationship, one in which the United States and Japan would stand together against Soviet Russia and Communist China, than with righting the wrongs of the past. William Sebald and his State Department superiors had crafted a settlement formula that slighted justice in the abstract so as to avoid provoking congressional opposition to providing more economic and moral support to Japan. Ashida and Yoshida maneuvered, with imperfect success, to find some way to abandon legitimate claims without appearing to have danced to Washington's tune. In the end, both sides realized that laying the *Awa maru* officially to rest through a claims agreement was the lesser evil that must be accepted if the greater good of mutually beneficial relations in a peaceful future was to be achieved.

To that end they consigned the *Awa maru*—and, with her, any thought of the greatest error of the Pacific submarine war—to the depths of official oblivion.

But would that ill-fated ship remain on the bottom of the Taiwan Strait forever, whether in memory or in reality?

8

Heroes

THIRTY YEARS AFTER Japanese and American diplomats officially buried
the *Awa maru,* Chinese salvagers found her. News of their discovery
was flashed to the world, bringing to the attention of millions unborn
in 1945 the story of "the greatest submarine error of the Second World War."[1]
But by 1979, that story had become quite different on opposite sides of the
Pacific, for sharply divergent public memories of the Pacific War, its submarine element, and the sinking of the *Awa maru* had developed in America and
Japan. In the United States, what had been freely acknowledged as a tragic
error of huge proportions had shrunk to the point of insignificance. The
Awa maru story was all but forgotten in America, where World War II submariners had come to be regarded as heroes in "the good war."[2] In Japan,
this particular error had become emblematic of tragedies of even greater
size. The Japanese knew and enshrined in their public memory an *Awa maru*
story that reinforced an image of themselves as the ultimate victims in the
Pacific War.

How did Americans and Japanese come to see the same event in the same
war in such radically different ways? How did that difference of perspective

shape their behavior as competitors in a protracted race to find and salvage the *Awa maru?* What, indeed, does their behavior suggest about the chances for reconciling conflicting national public memories and truly laying the ghost of war to rest?

At first glance, the answer to the puzzle of diverging American and Japanese public memories of the sinking of the *Awa maru* and of the war in which it occurred seems quite simple: roles determine memories. The Japanese were victims in the attack, and their government's postwar abandonment of the rights of indemnification simply reinforced that conviction. As a result, what became imbedded in Japan's public memory was a story of double victimization in a lost war. Although they were accidental victimizers in the sinking of the *Awa maru*, Americans, by contrast, were victors in the larger war in which it occurred. How natural, how very human it was for them simply to forget an incident whose tragic overtones conflicted with the triumphant strains of victory in a "good" war.

Logical though it may seem, and valid though it may be for the individuals who participated in, or those whose lives were transformed by, the sinking of the *Awa maru*, a role-based explanation cannot solve the puzzle of divergent American and Japanese public memories of that event and the war in which it occurred. For public memory—that is, what a people collectively remember about some event in the past—is not the same as individual memory. Individual memory is an artifact of the event, either as experienced by its participants or as reconstructed by the historian from documents, participants' recollections, and his or her own feelings about the past. Its expression is singular in form—the words of a participant or the book created by an author.

Public memory, by contrast, is plural in origins and expression. It is formed by forces that come into play long after the event. The needs of states in their interactions with one another, the interests of different individuals and groups in societies, and even culturally conditioned, distinctive value systems all interact in shaping what a people understands about the past. While the substance of public memory is singular and coherent, it manifests itself in many different forms—not just in the written word but also in art and advertisements, films and television programs, and public monuments.[3]

But the forces that produce nations' public memories and create differences between them are not blindly impersonal. To comprehend how they work, one cannot simply rely on logical inference or accept without question seeming axioms about national behavior. Instead, this ghost of war must be pursued by tracing the development of different *Awa maru* stories on opposite sides of the Pacific. One way of doing so is to walk in the footsteps of those who shaped those tales, considering what they said, how and why they said it when they did, and why their versions of the *Awa maru* story became imbedded in, or vanished from, public memory of the Pacific War.

In the United States, the story of the *Awa maru* story begins and ends with Vice Adm. Charles Andrews Lockwood, Jr. No one did more to shape American public memory of the sinking of the *Awa maru* and the submarine war in which it occurred than the man who was ComSubPac in April 1945. He defined the central narrative thread of the tale and its ethical framework even before its details became public knowledge. He broadcast the story and infused it with policy significance during the immediate postwar years. And Admiral Lockwood unwittingly facilitated its shrinkage and eventual disappearance from public memory by helping translate the larger Pacific submarine war story from verbal to visual form.

Lockwood's desire to put that story before the public grew out of his forced silence during all but the last few months of the war. Bursting with pride at the accomplishments of the men he sent out to sink anything and everything Japanese, he longed to tell the world of their exploits. But he could not, lest he jeopardize their safety by inadvertently providing the enemy with valuable operational information—just what a loose-tongued congressman had done early in the war by announcing that the Japanese were setting depth charges too shallow to destroy American submarines.[4] Lockwood also had to protect the secret process that enabled his men to find their targets, which was the decrypting of Japanese radio messages. He was not about to discuss the unrestricted submarine warfare they fought in the Pacific at a time when America had declared German U-boat warfare in the Atlantic illegal.[5] All the frustrated admiral could do was pour out his innermost thoughts about the undersea war against Japan in letters to his wife.[6]

The sinking of the *Awa maru*, however, gave Lockwood a perfect opportunity to break the navy's official silence about that war. Tokyo's vehement public protests over the incident had to be answered, and on 2 May 1945 the admiral, who was then in Washington, held his first press conference. He spoke at length about the submarine's successes in the war against Japan but said not a word about the *Awa maru* tragedy.[7] His words on this occasion set the stage for a second press conference, held two months later, when his men's success in driving the Rising Sun ensign from the seas had greatly diminished the risk of speaking out. On 4 July 1945 Lockwood proudly told reporters about the success of Operation Barney, in which nine of his boats, protected by primitive "stealth" technology, had penetrated the mine barrage guarding the entrances of the Sea of Japan and destroyed twenty-eight enemy ships.[8]

Admiral Lockwood's press conferences were but one aspect of his efforts, late in the struggle, to shape public understanding of what had been in effect a secret war against Japan. He also allowed reporter Robert Trumbull to conduct extensive interviews with the skipper and crew of the *Silversides* (SS 236). These formed the basis of what became the first book-length account of an American submarine's exploits against the Japanese.[9] Lockwood also let Hollywood cameramen come aboard subs to teach skippers how to film sinkings through periscopes. That technique provided immediately useful training aids and valuable visual proof of the submarine's effectiveness for later public use.[10] The admiral also directed his chief of staff for operations, then-captain Richard Voge, to begin preparing official histories for the benefit of future submariners and historians.[11]

The motive underlying all of these actions was simple. Admiral Lockwood wanted his countrymen and the world to know of the great deeds his "lads" had performed. He wanted everyone to acknowledge that unrestricted submarine warfare against Japan—despite errors like the sinking of the *Awa maru*—had been a legitimate and ethically acceptable tactic in a war fought to repay the Japanese for the attack on Pearl Harbor. That belief imbued his first postwar speech, a eulogy for lost submariners and their boats delivered with great moral force at Cleveland, Ohio, on Navy Day 1945.[12]

But when Admiral Lockwood followed his wartime boss, Admiral Nimitz, whom President Truman had named chief of naval operations, back to Washington in January 1946, he brought with him a second, more policy-relevant motive for telling the Pacific submarine war story.[13] He had sensed long before the fight was finished that a storm over service roles and missions was brewing.[14] Lockwood wanted to make certain that the submarine service retained a prominent place in the American arsenal, whatever the result of that struggle. Indeed, he wanted Nimitz to create the post of deputy chief of naval operations for submarines and give him that job.[15] Nimitz, though an old pigboat sailor who had assumed and relinquished command of the Pacific Fleet on board a submarine, declined to oblige.[16] He had surrounded himself with undersea warriors, including personal aides who knew the *Awa maru* story almost firsthand;[17] the new CNO probably did not want to appear too partisan to one element of the naval service. So he named Lockwood inspector-general of the navy.[18]

Lockwood turned that drab position into a platform upon which he became spokesman-general for submarine warfare. By early 1946 he had recognized that the harmony and euphoria that had marked victory celebrations —ranging from a triumphant presidential naval review in New York harbor to the *Queenfish* crew's "Welcome Home Heroes" party in San Francisco— had vanished.[19] The war *after* the war had begun in earnest, and it was even worse than he had anticipated. Congress was probing the Pearl Harbor attack, considering various schemes for reorganizing the armed services, and preparing to wield its budgetary knife in a manner that might well cut beyond the fat to the very bone of the defense budget.[20] In these circumstances, the navy had to put the story of its past accomplishments before Congress and the public if it was to survive as an effective fighting force. Lifting the veil of secrecy that had enshrouded "the silent service" in the Pacific thus became an urgent, policy-relevant matter.

Lockwood went about it with great skill. In his waning days as ComSubPac, he had ordered preparation of a memorial to those who had died in the undersea warfare against Japan. It came out early in 1946 as a handsome government publication in which appeared the name of every submariner who had perished and the story of every boat lost.[21] The material in it prefigured what became the navy's first official account of the submarine war against Japan, made public on 2 February 1946. Not surprisingly, Admiral Lockwood was the man who appeared before reporters to explain and comment on those two press releases.[22]

He called their attention to three key points in them. First, unrestricted submarine warfare, although outlawed by the 1930 London Naval Treaty, was legitimate. The "impossibility" of distinguishing between Japanese merchant and naval auxiliary vessels had justified sinking whatever flew the enemy flag. Second, submarine warfare was extremely efficient. At a cost of

Heroes return: Cdr. Frank N. Shamer and his crew celebrate the *Queenfish*'s home-coming in San Francisco in October 1945. *Capt. John E. Bennett, USN (Ret.)*

3,500 lives and fifty-two boats, American submariners sent 276,000 Japanese (more than one-third of whom were civilians) to their deaths. They put more than nineteen hundred ships (nine out of ten of which were merchant craft) on the bottom. Third, America's undersea warriors were true heroes —daring in intruding into enemy home waters; noble in sacrificing their own lives at a rate greater than that for any other element of the armed services; and truly heroic in rescuing more than five hundred downed aviators.

Lockwood said nothing of error in general or the sinking of the *Awa maru* in particular, for on that winter's day his focus was more on the future than the past. By telling the story of the Pacific submarine war, the admiral was in effect refuting a recent Herblock cartoon that had appeared in the *Washington Post*. It depicted a boy named "Atom" gazing at a row of ships at anchor and asking approaching admirals, "Is this that junk you were telling me about?" Rejecting the notion that atomic air war would replace conventional conflict on land and sea, Lockwood told the reporters that atomic-powered submarines, whose "rockets" would have nuclear warheads, would be "an extremely desirable development."[23] His remarks thus made the link obvious between past success in the submarine war against Japan and the future needs of the navy.

Over the remaining twenty months of his active duty in Washington, Admiral Lockwood continued to make the Pacific submarine war story the handmaiden of current naval policy. Within the navy, he persuaded Admiral Nimitz to name a coordinator for submarine research and warfare in the office of the CNO.[24] He provided vital support for the production of massive official histories of the American submarine effort in World War II.[25] He also backed communications intelligence experts in their efforts to secure adequate funding for continuation of code breaking like that which had enabled his submariners to find so many Japanese targets.[26]

Lockwood's public activities made the link between past and present even more obvious. Insisting that history must not be allowed to repeat itself, he told a Senate committee that the navy must keep eighty boats on active service and another hundred in reserve.[27] He traveled around the country to inform veterans groups, local political leaders, and students about submariners' great deeds in the war against Japan. In contrast to the enemy, who had made only a halfhearted and wasteful submarine warfare effort, his men had fought like prize-fighters, "without gloves, without a referee, and with no time out between rounds," to destroy anything, everywhere that flew the Rising Sun ensign. They were heroes who deserved praise, remembrance, and emulation as models of leadership and teamwork.[28] But Americans must, Lockwood wrote, recognize that their weapons—boats like the *Queenfish* and the torpedoes she carried—were already obsolete. Fleet submarines must be modernized, and radically new craft—costly atomic-powered boats armed with nuclear missiles—must be built.[29]

In telling the Pacific submarine war story and drawing such policy-relevant conclusions from it, Lockwood made no mention of the sinking of the *Awa maru*. Perhaps he felt that an error of that magnitude had best go unmentioned when the future of the submarine seemed in doubt. After settling into retirement, however, in the home he built in the California coastal range near San Jose, Lockwood decided to speak out as a private citizen, and he changed his account of the Pacific submarine war to give the *Awa maru* story a prominent place.[30] He spoke of the sinking publicly for the first time on an auspicious anniversary, Pearl Harbor Day 1948.[31] His remarks on that occasion provided the template from which he fashioned seventeen other speeches delivered before San Francisco Bay area naval, civic, and religious groups over the next year; three *Saturday Evening Post* articles published in the summer of 1949; and an autobiographical book about the Pacific submarine war, which appeared in March 1951.[32]

By the end of 1948 Lockwood had compelling reasons for speaking out about the submarine war and the sinking of the *Awa maru*. Once again forces within and outside the navy appeared to threaten the future of the submarine. The new CNO, Adm. Louis Denfeld, had triggered Lockwood's retirement by rejecting yet another appeal to establish a deputy chief of naval operations for submarines.[33] The voters in November 1948 returned a president and a Congress committed to still further cuts in defense spending.[34] Admiral Denfeld locked horns with air force generals over construction of a super-carrier, triggering even more bitter interservice clashes that culminated in President Truman's decision to relieve him as chief of naval operations.[35] The intensity of what Lockwood perceived as threats to the future of the submarine demanded that he tell the Pacific submarine war story, including its *Awa maru* chapter, at the very moment American and Japanese diplomats were completing the claims-abandonment agreement they hoped would foster amnesia about the war.

When Lockwood told the *Awa maru* story publicly for the first time, he opened it with a defense of the morality of the Pacific submarine war. What Japan had done at Pearl Harbor justified what Americans later did to Japanese everywhere. Tokyo's German ally had stripped Japanese vessels of whatever protection the 1930 London Naval Treaty might have afforded them by waging unlimited submarine warfare in the Atlantic and arming merchant ships. Consequently, American submarine skippers like Elliott Loughlin had had to be aggressive in pursuing and destroying enemy ships. In a war of the scope they fought, mistakes were bound to happen. The sinking of the *Awa maru* was simply the biggest among them.

That error occurred, according to Admiral Lockwood, because Americans played by the rules and the Japanese did not. He himself had been tempted to sink the *Awa maru* when intelligence intercepts revealed that she was carrying contraband cargo. But Admiral Nimitz had refused his request for permission to do so, demonstrating that broad moral principle governed the U.S. Navy's conduct of submarine warfare. Similarly, Admiral King had been right to demand that Loughlin be court-martialed, for American submariners were not supposed to torpedo vessels traveling under promise of safe passage.

Japanese authorities, by contrast, had compromised the ship's status by cramming her holds with contraband and using her (according to the admiral's clouded memory) to smuggle 25 million dollars in gold to Shanghai! Captain Hamada had hazarded his ship by not sounding her horn in the fog; had he done so, the misperception that culminated in the erroneous sinking of the *Awa maru* might not have occurred.

That tragedy, then, just like another in which his lads had sunk five then-neutral Soviet ships, was simply the result of error. The "foul-up factor"—enhanced by Japanese misbehavior—rather than brutality or moral insensitivity, had sent the *Awa maru* to the bottom. In Lockwood's view Loughlin and his crew deserved praise, for torpedoing the ship was simply a human error that, in the grand scheme of things, paled in comparison to their achievements.[36]

In July 1949 Lockwood presented his account of the Pacific submarine war to the public at large in a series of *Saturday Evening Post* articles entitled "We Gave the Japs a Licking Underseas."[37] These lavishly illustrated essays told a simply structured tale: the Japanese had legitimized unrestricted submarine warfare by putting men, munitions, and war supplies on every vessel that flew their flag. American "men of lonely heroism" had responded by fighting "sealed off beneath the sea in great steel hulls that sometimes became their tombs." When captured, they endured torture. They swallowed "the bitterest pill of all," bombing by friendly aircraft, when they tried to rescue downed American aviators. Nonetheless, they avenged Japan's early victories, demonstrated "submarine versatility," and put 6 million tons of ships— "the lifeblood of an island nation"—on the bottom of the Pacific well before atomic bombs fell on Hiroshima and Nagasaki.[38]

The men who did all these things were not gods but human heroes. They made mistakes, and for that reason the admiral felt compelled to write at length about what he termed "our greatest submarine error in World War II," the destruction of the *Awa maru*. Lockwood confessed that he had been "deeply distressed" at the time by the *Queenfish*'s deed. His thoughts had run first to others—to picking up more survivors and preventing reprisals against American submariners in Japanese hands. He did not lay exclusive blame for the error on Commander Loughlin; Captain Hamada was at fault for poor seamanship and failure to stick to the ship's prearranged course and schedule. Lockwood admitted that he himself was partially responsible for the sinking in that he had not directed a more specific message to American subs in the *Awa maru*'s area warning them of her expected movements.

But even "such a tragic mistake" had positive consequences. After the sinking, Lockwood issued more specific instructions about attacking enemy ships of "doubtful identity." Japan's violation of the safe-conduct agreement was revealed by the recovery of contraband from the sunken ship. And American submariners fought on, whether as prisoners standing up to "brutal beating by the bitter Japanese" or as raiders making daring forays into the Sea of Japan. America's undersea warriors were clearly men of character despite their commission of error.[39]

While Admiral Lockwood was transforming these articles into a much fuller, autobiographical account of the Pacific submarine war, two other versions of the *Awa maru* story were put before the public. The first appeared in December 1949 in *United States Submarine Operations in World War,* a massive, beautifully illustrated and crafted work that listed Theodore Roscoe as its author. Published by the Naval Institute Press with the ostensible purpose of informing the next generation of submariners about their predecessors' deeds, the volume was the public version of the work Admiral Lockwood had commissioned five years earlier. Roscoe, a professional writer of adventure stories, had revised the original text, and Voge had polished it during the last months prior to his death. The book was meant to reach and influence not just naval men but also the American public at large.[40]

Its opening words left no doubt that the volume was meant to be a weapon in the war over service roles, missions, and budgets. Fleet Admiral Nimitz began it by lauding the submarine as the *only* usable weapon at his disposal immediately after Pearl Harbor. Subs had saved the day until shipyards and factories could repair damaged vessels and produce new ships and planes.[41] Did that experience not demonstrate the folly of relying on a single weapon, the very policy navy partisans accused air power enthusiasts of trying to foist on the public?

Voge made an even blunter pitch for the submarine in his introduction to the book. In a democracy, the president's senior military advisers make policy recommendations to him, but Congress, which consists of representatives of the sovereign people, decides on the budget that transforms those proposals into reality. If weapons vital to the national defense were not to be discarded in error, the public must know what they had done, as well as what they might do. Thus, submariners, who had "too long been content to let the record speak for itself," were putting the full story of the submarine war of 1941–1945 before the people.[42] When ordinary citizens read that saga, they would surely grasp its implications for current and future national defense policy.

What followed was a detailed account of the submarine war, with strong moral and policy overtones. Shrewd and at times desperate adaptation to the demands of unanticipated war situations—not criminal intent—drove the submarine war against Japan. The Pearl Harbor attack had "deranged" the navy's preferred strategy as laid down in War Plan Orange, which had been planned and rehearsed for decades. American submariners had fought an unavoidable war of enemy commerce destruction, in which they had achieved retribution for what Japan had done. The policy-relevant message in this telling of the submarine war story was much blunter than anything Lockwood had written. "Those who lived by the Samurai sword," Roscoe and Voge said, "died by the air bomb and the submarine torpedo." By the time the former hit them, the latter had already assured their defeat. The fires ignited by atomic bombs at Hiroshima and Nagasaki were simply "the funeral pyre of an enemy who had been drowned."[43]

How did the sinking of the *Awa maru* fit into this saga? The incident had to be mentioned, for it had exacted a heavy price in lives lost, "seriously impugned" the international reputation of the U.S. government, and smudged the record of "one of the finest officers in the Submarine Service." It was "a tragedy of carelessness" that arose from miscommunication. Error of that sort, Roscoe and Voge argued, was an inevitable feature of war at sea. Indeed, the *Queenfish's* wolfpack mate *Spot* (SS 413) had barely escaped destruction from the guns of an American destroyer whose captain somehow "didn't get the word" not to enter the submarine's war patrol zone.[44]

The *Awa maru* had not been so lucky for several reasons. Those who drafted her safe-passage guarantee had not written into it a procedure for identification in fog of the sort that hung over the Taiwan Strait in the spring of the year. Captain Hamada had not maintained "rigid adherence" to the schedule and track promulgated to American submariners. Nor had he zigzagged to avoid torpedoes they might fire in error. But the preponderance of responsibility for the "embarrassment" caused by the *Queenfish's* sinking of the *Awa maru* lay upon the submarine's communications personnel. Their "dereliction of duty" explained why Loughlin had not seen *all* the messages about the *Awa maru's* protected status and probable positions.

Despite the harshness of that judgment, the authors of *United States Submarine Operations in World War II* did not damn the *Queenfish* and her crew. They portrayed the submariners as men caught in a tragic situation like those of which the ancient Greek dramatists had written; the *Queenfish* crew and those on board the *Awa maru* met in a manner that Fate decreed they could not avoid. No blame or moral stigma was attached to the men who sank the ship by mistake. The court-martial, in convicting Loughlin of but one of three charges and assigning him the lightest possible penalty, had rendered a just verdict.[45]

That treatment of the *Awa maru* story bothered someone of influence within the navy, perhaps Lockwood himself. That person obtained and secured posthumous publication of what appears to have been Voge's original formulation of the tale. The article appeared in the March 1950 issue of the U.S. Naval Institute *Proceedings*, the professional journal for American naval officers. Its title, "Too Much Accuracy," conveyed a double meaning.

The *Queenfish* skipper had been a crack shot—with basketballs as a member of the 1933 Naval Academy team, and with torpedoes on 1 April 1945. Heaped with praise for the first performance, he had been unfairly demeaned for the second. The naval justice system had been technically accurate but morally wrong in convicting a "most honorable, efficient, and outstanding officer" at the Guam court-martial.[46]

Voge developed that thesis in a most intriguing way. He did not diminish the significance of what Loughlin had done: destroying the *Awa maru* was not "a minor infraction of Navy Regulations." Some seventeen hundred (by Voge's mistaken count) "innocent but enemy persons" had perished, and "a ten million dollar" vessel had been destroyed. Nonetheless, he vigorously attacked the naval justice system. Capt. Chester Bruton, Loughlin's defense counsel, had not understood that the "fundamental issue" in the court-martial was "moral, not technical." Bruton, in Voge's view, had wrongly based Loughlin's defense on the premise that the *Awa maru* had surrendered her immunity from attack by carrying contraband. When the court rejected that argument, Bruton unwisely chose not to have the *Queenfish* skipper testify in his own defense.

Moreover, Bruton had declined to make the argument that was crucial to destroying the claim that Commander Loughlin had intentionally violated the terms of the safe-passage agreement. The fact that he had rescued Shimoda Kantarō and thus provided independent proof that the *Queenfish* had sunk the *Awa maru* attested to the sub skipper's honesty and innocence. Loughlin could have left Shimoda to drown and concealed the identity of the sunken ship with a plausible lie; but he did not. If, as Voge insisted was the case, the fundamental reason for the *Awa maru*'s destruction was Loughlin's ignorance of the Japanese ship's movements and his "inherent aggressiveness and skill in carrying the war to the enemy at every opportunity," he should have been completely exonerated rather than lightly punished.

The court-martial, Voge argued, had failed to give due weight to the multiple factors that brought about the sinking of the *Awa maru*. The Japanese had violated the spirit, if not the letter, of the safe-passage agreement. Commander Loughlin's subordinates bore some of the blame for the wrongful sinking because they had not forwarded all the critical warning messages about the *Awa maru*'s probable position to him. Captain Hamada had conspired in his own death by failing to sound fog signals that would otherwise have alerted Loughlin to the *Awa maru*'s presence and protected character. A good man, then, had been wrongly convicted. Lawyers arguing over technicalities had twisted lack of criminal intent into turpitude. Thus, Voge concluded, the aggressor on the night of 1 April 1945 became the victim—a victim of errors committed by subordinates and foes and of wrongdoing by those who judged him. Loughlin had destroyed the *Awa maru* by acting honorably and professionally in a good cause. But then he had fallen victim to superiors who "went by the book" and convicted him without giving due weight to mitigating circumstances.[47]

These arguments provided the most powerfully exculpatory explanation for the *Awa maru* incident yet to appear in print. They were, however, legally and logically flawed. Any shrewd "sea lawyer" could have retorted that the fundamental purpose of a court-martial is not to rule on the morality of an accused's actions but rather to determine whether or not he has violated military law. Voge's arguments also came close to endorsing the dubious proposition that in a good war those who are fighting evil can do no wrong.

Voge's article never reached the huge audiences that *United States Submarine Operations in World War II* and Admiral Lockwood's *Saturday Evening Post* articles and book commanded.[48] But it remains noteworthy for the development of the American *Awa maru* story for at least two reasons. First, Voge wrote what Lockwood said privately in 1945 but felt he could not say openly five years later. Second, the article expressed much more widely held notions about the nature of the Pacific submarine war, the justice of particular actions within it, and the responsibility of individuals for what occurred. Voge transformed Elliott Loughlin into an even purer hero than Lockwood had dared make him, and in so doing he gave voice to the deepest feelings of American submariners. For those who fought the good war as members of an extraordinarily dangerous and successful element within a proud navy, sinking an enemy vessel could never be a morally culpable, punishable act.

A year after Voge's article appeared, Lockwood published *Sink 'Em All*, his autobiographical account of the Pacific submarine war. The book drew high praise; the *New York Times* reviewer called it "the best handbook on submarining" he had ever read.[49] It sold well, even though the admiral simply elaborated in it on what he had said in earlier speeches and articles. The work was important less for the detail it provided than for the way it wove the *Awa maru* story into a broader triumphal and inspirational interpretation

of the Pacific submarine war. The admiral praised the "ordinary heroism" of
the Americans who fought it. He showed how individual initiative and persistence overcame bureaucratic blindness to defects in weaponry and to
other urgent needs of undersea warriors.[50]

What little he said about the mistakes they committed reaffirmed their
heroism. Their enemy was deceitful. The Japanese disguised warships as
merchantmen, crammed the *Awa maru*'s holds full of contraband, and falsely
charged Americans with deliberately sinking hospital ships. Americans, by
contrast, were honest and noble in adversity. In marked contrast to Voge,
who depicted Loughlin as a victim of the naval justice system, Lockwood
portrayed him and the superiors who tried and convicted him as victims of
circumstance. The *Queenfish* skipper "took the rap" for subordinates who
failed to show him all of the messages warning of the *Awa maru*'s presence
in his sub's operating area. Commander Loughlin's superiors recognized
that he had to be punished lest the Japanese "wreak barbarous reprisals"
on American POWs. All made difficult, but ultimately correct, decisions.
Although unintended, the errors that led to the destruction of the *Awa maru*
gave the Japanese just what they deserved.[51]

This ending of the book's *Awa maru* chapter pointed toward a positive
moral that Lockwood drew from the story of the Pacific submarine war as a
whole. What happened between 1941 and 1945 should serve as a beacon of
hope to those dispirited by the challenges that war in Korea and the Cold
War presented. Submarines and submariners had shown that "there is practically nothing they cannot do." If the American people maintained the
proper spirit and provided those who fought underseas with the appropriate
weaponry, then they would triumph in these latter struggles just as they had
in the Pacific War.[52]

The publication of *Sink 'Em All* in 1951 marked the end of the first phase
in the development of American public memory of the Pacific submarine
war and the sinking of the *Awa maru*. Admiral Lockwood, acting on behalf
of the U.S. Navy, dominated that process. He made common knowledge the
once secret and silent Pacific undersea war. He and his protégés used the
story of that struggle to build support for a strong, state-of-the-art submarine fleet. His books, and others whose production he supported, became the
definitive works about the undersea war against Japan, providing readers
with both a comprehensive interpretation of that campaign and a detailed

account of important incidents within it.[53] The admiral also put his gloss on the *Awa maru* story; the sinking was a true tragedy—something inevitable but not intentional, an act for which no American individual was to blame. It demonstrated that even heroes in the good war were only human.

But even as Lockwood wrote, the forces that would wrest away from him control over the shaping and substance of American public memory of the Pacific submarine war and the *Awa maru* tragedy appeared on the scene. By mid-century the printed word was but one of several media that contributed to the public's remembrance of the Pacific War. What people saw on huge screens in motion picture theaters or on tiny black-and-white television tubes at home had an ever-increasing effect on what they thought and felt about the past. Visual representation was every bit as important as verbal characterization in shaping public memory.

Although he had been born in the previous century, Admiral Lockwood grasped that truth. He helped others put the submarine war story before American audiences in the form of documentaries, docudramas, and feature films. But in so doing, the admiral lost control over that story. His very human submariners became "heroes rising from the sea";[54] the greatest of the errors that they committed, the *Queenfish*'s sinking of the *Awa maru*, disappeared from public view.

Lockwood was directly responsible for the creation of visual images that others used to tell and modify the story of the submarine war against Japan. A few weeks before the *Awa maru* left Moji on her mission of mercy, he had approved Lt. Cdr. Dwight Long's request to begin making a motion picture record of that war. One of many in the Hollywood community who obtained wartime reserve commissions, Lieutenant Commander Long had just completed *Fighting Lady*, the prize-winning story of the carrier USS *Enterprise* (CV 6). The admiral granted Long's request to fit as many cameras as could be found onto the eyepieces of periscopes so as to film enemy ships as Americans sank them. Long located a hundred cameras, trained nearly as many enlisted men to operate them, and persuaded submarine skippers to cooperate in the film-making project. He was such a good salesman that by the closing months of the war, Lockwood's lads were moving into unprecedentedly close ranges in order to get good images of their dying prey. By war's end this cooperation between the sub force commander, the filmmaker, and submarine crews had produced about eighty thousand feet of film.[55]

This film might have appeared on theater screens all over the country shortly after the war ended if Secretary of the Navy Forrestal had had his way. The secretary had a fine appreciation for how the media shaped popular feelings that could be translated into support for his policies.[56] He handed over the through-the-periscope films to Robert Montgomery, an actor turned wartime Naval Reserve officer turned producer. Montgomery commissioned a script for a feature film about the submarine war that would mix drama and combat footage.[57] Returning sailors, soldiers, and airmen had had enough of war, however, and those whom they had left back home were surfeited with what they had seen of it on the screen.[58] The opportunity to put "the real thing" before the public in theaters across the country thus slipped away.

Instead, the navy used the film to produce its own short subject for training and recruiting purposes. *Silent Service* tried to convey to its viewers the adventure, romance, and significance of the wartime submariner's experience. Admiral Lockwood had supported its production while on active duty. He appeared in the first few minutes of the film, standing alongside the skipper of the *Sealion* (SS 315), who had sunk the battleship *Kongo*. The film showed submarine crewmen firing torpedoes, surviving depth-charging, enjoying the pleasures of Waikiki, and going on to sink a Japanese aircraft carrier.[59]

Lockwood used the film, in what may have been its first West Coast screening, to enthrall an audience of Catholic youth near his home. Once these potential submarine sailors-to-be had seen it, he told them more about the heroic deeds his men had performed. Indeed, he pointed out that the *Queenfish* was one of four boats that had rescued more than 150 British and Australian prisoners of war from death in the depths of the Pacific.[60] But he said nothing about her having sunk the *Awa maru*. Navy recruiters put on similar performances across the nation.

The significance of this official documentary for the formation of American public memory of the Pacific submarine war paled, however, in comparison to that of the first documentary film series made for national television —*Victory at Sea*.[61] This program was the stepchild of official naval histories begotten during the war and grown large even before Admiral Lockwood's works reached the public. Its technical adviser was Capt. Walter Karig, a reserve officer whom Navy Secretary Frank Knox had commissioned to write and publish quickly a popular operational history. By the time Admiral Lockwood's *Saturday Evening Post* articles appeared in 1949, Captain Karig and his collaborators had put five volumes of stirring, heroic naval combat stories before the public.[62]

Victory at Sea's guiding genius was a protégé, of sorts, of Harvard historian Samuel Eliot Morison, whom President Roosevelt had authorized in 1942 to travel the globe and gather material for what was to be *the* operational history of naval actions against the Axis.[63] Henry "Pete" Saloman, the scion of a wealthy New England family, had gone, like so many of his class, to Harvard. His roommate there was the son of Gen. David Sarnoff, the broadcasting entrepreneur who built the NBC radio and television networks. When war came, Saloman enlisted as a navy yeoman, earned a commission, and began producing a navy-sponsored network radio series. His old Harvard professor, Morison, then recruited him as a member of his research team for the official naval history project, and in that capacity Saloman took part in major amphibious landings in the Pacific and in 1946 interviewed former adversaries in Tokyo. Too ambitious a man to understudy anyone for long, he left the Morison team the following year to begin work on *Victory at Sea*.[64]

Saloman mobilized all kinds of resources to make this series truly spectacular television. He got access to captured enemy films as well as those of the Allies and the U.S. Navy. He recruited a team of writers and film editors who shaped this material into twenty-six television episodes. He then persuaded composer Richard Rodgers, whose war-based musical *South Pacific* was a big hit on Broadway, to produce a score for the films. The music made the dramatic stories of naval warfare that Saloman and his team crafted even more mesmerizing to viewers.[65] "Navy Brass and other D.C. biggies," as one reviewer called them, were absolutely delighted when they previewed the series just before its television debut in October 1952.[66]

Viewers did not see "Full Fathom Five," the episode devoted to the submarine war against Japan, until the following spring.[67] It compressed the story of the Pacific submarine war into a twenty-six-minute account of the "anonymous adventures" of "killer fish" that ate at "the vitals of Japan." Viewers heard a solemn-voiced narrator tell how the attack on Pearl Harbor had created "an ocean of men welded together in common spirit and common purpose." They saw Admiral Lockwood and repeatedly heard his instruction to boats setting out in search of enemy ships: "Find 'em, chase 'em, sink 'em. . . . Sink 'em all!" Scenes of submariners being depth-charged attested to their courage, and shots of their pulling enemy survivors and Allied POWs out of the water gave proof of their humanity. Submariners, as the film's narrator told millions of viewers, were men "whose contribution to victory is second to none." They were the ones who had "sunk the Japanese Empire!"

"Full Fathom Five," like the rest of the *Victory at Sea* series, left no doubt as to the centrality of the navy's role in defeating the Axis. Unfortunately, though, the program compressed the Pacific submarine war story as Admiral Lockwood had presented it to the point of near-caricaturization. Submariners, none save Lockwood mentioned by name, became heroes of the first order. Nothing controversial flickered across the television screen. The narrator justified unrestricted submarine warfare simply by saying "If the Axis can do it, so can the Allies." Although viewers saw downed Japanese airmen or navymen pulled from the Pacific and led, blindfolded, down gangplanks to prisoner-of-war camps, none died on camera. Only Long's through-the-periscope footage of Japanese merchant ships exploding and vanishing beneath the waves hinted at the death of individual human beings. Neither the *Queenfish* nor the *Awa maru* nor anything suggesting that human error figured in submarine warfare appeared on the television screen. In "Full Fathom Five" the submariners Lockwood had portrayed as "ordinary heroes" mushroomed into men of superheroic stature.[68]

Despite its flaws, *Victory at Sea* proved so enormously popular as to pave the way for a second television series devoted entirely to the submarine war of 1941–1945. *The Silent Service* was the brainchild of retired Rear Adm. Thomas M. Dykers. The product of a Louisiana plantation-owning family and a 1927 graduate of the Naval Academy, Dykers had "command presence" in spades. He skippered the *Jack* (SS 259) on four highly successful war patrols in 1943–1944. In April 1945 he commanded the *Queenfish*'s squadron and wrote a laudatory endorsement of her actions, including the sinking of the *Awa maru*. Four years later he retired and moved to Hollywood where, in time, he formed Twin Dolphins Production Company.[69]

By June 1955 Dykers had pieced together sufficient Hollywood and Washington connections to make a pilot film for the projected series. The navy loaned Dykers two reserve boats, the *Steelhead* (SS 280) and *Sawfish* (SS 276), for use in filming off the southern California coast.[70] Admiral Lockwood liked the pilot film and may have helped his former subordinate get access to through-the-periscope combat footage.[71] The slight but energetic Dykers also persuaded his own former shipmates and a host of Lockwood's lads to appear on the projected program.

Dykers produced what viewers today would recognize as docudramas— programs that mixed documentary footage, dramatized scenes, and interviews with those who had actually fought the submarine war. Each opened with a submarine broaching the surface while an all-male chorus intoned, "Take her down, and watch them dive, to the deep blue hush beneath the ocean. . . ." Then Dykers, clean shaven, his hair in a crew cut, extended a "welcome aboard" to viewers and introduced the story of a particular boat that was to follow. He always mentioned the name and hometown of her captain and executive officer before letting the actors who played them introduce the principal theme of the show. What followed blended history drawn from war patrol reports with personal stories and information about other U.S. Navy and enemy surface ships in action. Dykers then reappeared to introduce someone, usually an officer, who had been on board the boat in the action just dramatized and who now vouched for the authenticity of the reenactment, praised his former shipmates, and provided an overarching moral for the tale. After Dykers invited viewers to return the following week for "another exciting true adventure," the orchestra and chorus reminded them that the nation would be safe "as long as our submarines are underneath the sea."[72] This television series, much like Admiral Lockwood's speeches, articles, and books, was clearly meant to build support for the current submarine service needs in the Cold War.

When *The Silent Service* premiered in New York City in April 1957, critics compared it unfavorably to *Victory at Sea*. They thought its combat footage was old and scratchy and found its format too formulaic.[73] The public loved it anyway, so much so that thirty-eight more episodes, each thanking the Defense and Navy Departments for their cooperation and the Navy League for its endorsement, appeared that season. Another thirty-nine films were televised the next year in more than 170 cities across the country.[74] Admiral Dykers clearly had a hit.

Rear Adm. Thomas M. Dykers, producer of the television series *The Silent Service*. *Cdr. Thomas M. Dykers, Jr., USN (Ret.)*

His programs told heroes' tales and made the heroes real in a way *Victory at Sea*'s "Full Fathom Five" could not. They were actual men with particular names and faces, who told their own and their boats' stories. Each program took time to develop human interest value. If actors who portrayed the submariners bent the truth by combining several discrete events into one, someone who had experienced the episode firsthand corrected that impression. The earnest, mostly young and handsome submariners that Dykers put before viewers brought Lockwood's ordinary heroes to life. They exuded patriotism, courage, self-sacrifice, and concern for others in ways that made them role models for the next generation.[75]

Accurate in their particulars, Dykers's television programs nonetheless helped perpetuate a distorted view of the submarine war against Japan. Because each focused on a particular boat's exploits, none raised questions about the ethics of the strategy of unrestricted submarine warfare that underlay them. The films told how some boats were lost, and they excelled in showing how men were forced to make and carry out momentous decisions under great pressure. But Dykers's heroes made judgments about technical or behavioral matters that would determine their own fates, not choices that spelled life or death for their foes. The consequences of American actions for individual Japanese were even less evident in these programs than in the *Victory at Sea* Pacific submarine war episode. No *Queenfish*, no *Awa maru*, and certainly no Shimoda Kantarō were to be seen in Dykers's docudramas.

The admiral appears to have deliberately excluded them. He could easily have put the *Awa maru* story before television viewers for, as the *Queenfish*'s division commander in April 1945, he certainly knew it. He had praised Elliott Loughlin and his crew at the time for sinking the ship. Dykers could have contacted the *Queenfish*'s skipper, prospective commanding officer, and executive officer, all of whom were on active duty and within reach of his cameras during the production period.[76] They might have presented their own gloss on Admiral Lockwood's version of what had happened—commission of a tragic error followed by heroic, if not redemptive, rescue of downed American aviators.

But for reasons that must remain speculative, Dykers chose not to do so. Perhaps he was inhibited by too many years spent in pursuit of professional perfection in a navy that frowned on error. Perhaps he worried that viewers might draw from the *Awa maru* story an analogy harmful to *The Silent Service*'s current policy message. If imprecise orders, lapses in their communication, and target misidentification had caused the *Queenfish* to do so much harm in 1945 with ordinary torpedoes, how much more damage might the captain of one of the atomic-powered boats then under construction that were armed with nuclear Polaris missiles inflict if he were plagued by similar errors? In any event, *The Silent Service* never told the story of how and why the *Queenfish* had sunk the *Awa maru*. The series simply projected into public memory an image of brave American submariners fighting and winning "the good war."

While Dykers was readying his docudramas for television screens, Lockwood was making his most direct contribution to Americans' visual memory of the submarine war against Japan, by collaborating in the production of the feature film, *Hellcats of the Navy*. The movie was one of several that appeared in the late 1950s to tap the popular interest in submarine warfare sparked by the USS *Nautilus* (SSN 571), the navy's first nuclear-powered submarine.[77] The film premiered in Hollywood just prior to her arrival on the West Coast for "exercises" that at times looked more like public relations cruises for VIPs than training for war.[78] The star of *Hellcats of the Navy* was none other than future president Ronald Reagan.[79]

The film was based on *Hellcats of the Sea*, a book Admiral Lockwood had coauthored in 1955 with his neighbor, retired air force colonel Hans Christian Adamson.[80] Adamson had compelling personal reasons to put yet another laudatory account of the submarine war against Japan before the public; he had drifted—helpless, with a broken back—on a raft in the Pacific for twenty-four days during the war before being rescued by submariners.[81] Lockwood saw another chance to remedy the American public's ignorance of what his men had done in the Pacific submarine war. By providing readers with "the intimate details of . . . their hopes, fears, and thoughts in moments of intense danger," he sought to secure their place in the pantheon of American heroes.

The book offered readers Lockwood's personal account of "one of the most difficult" operations of the Pacific submarine war—the penetration of the Sea of Japan.[82] He made the story of Operation Barney a tale of moral as well as technical triumph. It opened with tragedy, the loss in 1943 of the first American boat to enter the emperor's "private lake," the *Wahoo* (SS 238). It told of travails and triumphs on the road to avenging that loss. Lockwood chronicled his personal fight to have a frequency-modulated sonar device developed, distributed, and tested in order to protect his submariners from the mines guarding the entrances to the Sea of Japan. He then described their escapades inside "Hirohito's lake"—deeds meant to sink ships of all sorts and strike fear among the Japanese that the flow of food and energy resources from the Asian mainland to their homeland might soon be stopped. The admiral wrote forthrightly about the operation's cost—the loss of the *Bonefish* and all on board her. He also acknowledged error, alluding to the *Queenfish*'s sinking of the *Awa maru* and a Hellcat's destruction of a Soviet freighter. In addition, he and his collaborator left no doubt of the relative unimportance of such mistakes and the magnitude of the operational and moral triumph that Operation Barney achieved in June 1945. His men had destroyed twenty-eight Japanese vessels; demonstrated their ability to threaten Japan's lifelines to the Asian continent; and, not least, exacted revenge for the loss of the *Wahoo*.[83]

The book *Hellcats of the Sea* enthralled a Columbia Pictures producer, who commissioned a preliminary screen treatment of the book and invited Admiral Lockwood to help transform it into a major feature film. When the admiral saw the first rendition of his work in the summer of 1956, he felt "a little discouraged" because it differed from what he had written.[84] But that feeling soon metamorphosed into determination to make the film much better. Lockwood made two trips to Hollywood, dictating corrections to the proposed script to his wife as they drove down the Pacific Coast Highway from northern California. He chose not to serve as the film's technical director but secured an able alternative. The admiral also persuaded his old boss, Fleet Admiral Nimitz, to appear at the beginning of the film and read a paraphrase of the paean of praise to American submariners that he had written as the introduction to the book version of *Hellcats of the Sea*.[85]

Despite these efforts, however, the film bore only a slight resemblance to what the admiral and his collaborator had written. Their book had told the story of ordinary heroes who fought as part of a team. Their individual struggles—quarrels with distant bureaucrats loath to give them the newest technology needed to fight, or operational difficulties encountered while in the Sea of Japan—mattered only insofar as they contributed to overall victory. The film, on the other hand, focused on individual emotional concerns, almost to the exclusion of all else.

That was due in large part to its star, Ronald Reagan. He had wanted to make a "big" action film that would transform him from the television spokesman for General Electric into a second John Wayne.[86] He appeared as the skipper of the fictional *Starfish*, playing a man plagued by command and personal problems. He had to contend with psychological hang-ups arising from the loss of a fellow officer on a previous cruise; with a contentious and distrustful executive officer; and with a crew so fractious (and humorous) that Admiral Lockwood would have disowned it. Much of the film focused on his relationship with a woman played by his real-life spouse, Nancy Davis. The future first lady played the part of a navy nurse who helped skipper Reagan regain his mental composure and discover his capacity for true love. The distinguished character actor who portrayed an avuncular Admiral Lockwood had just a small part in the film's story.[87] Ronald Reagan got the heroic role he coveted.

Given these departures from what he had written, the admiral, not surprisingly, declined to attend the Hollywood premiere of *Hellcats of the Navy* in April 1957.[88] That gesture of protest was appropriate, for Lockwood had lost control over his own story as it moved from the printed page to the sil-

Ronald Reagan starred in the film version of *Hellcats of the Navy. Columbia Pictures/ Sony Corporation*

ver screen. The man who wanted to tell the American public the story of the submarine war against Japan—to get it right and to be sure that it served what he perceived as the navy's interest in the maintenance of sound national defense capabilities—saw others modify that story in accordance with their own desires and the demands of the media they used. Pete Saloman had compressed and depersonalized the story of the Pacific submarine war in the "Full Fathom Five" episode of *Victory at Sea*. Admiral Dykers had restored its humanity but eschewed any mention of error, such as the sinking of the *Awa maru*. The star and producer of the film *Hellcats of the Navy* added ingredients to it that produced a box office hit that bore too little resemblance to the truth of undersea warfare as Admiral Lockwood and those under his command had known it.[89]

Yet despite these departures from that truth, neither the admiral nor his onetime subordinates had good reason, as the fifteenth anniversary of the sinking of the *Awa maru* and of the end of the war against Japan approached, to be dissatisfied. Their quintessential point about the Pacific submarine war had become the cornerstone of American public memory about that conflict. They were good men who had fought and triumphed in a good and necessary war. The significance of their heroic deeds far overshadowed that of the errors they may have committed. A grateful Congress had recognized that point in 1955, when it chartered their special veterans organization, the Submarine Veterans of World War II.[90] They were certain to have an honored place in the nation's history.

Four years later, when he spoke before those submarine veterans for the last time, at their national meeting in Denver, Admiral Lockwood reaffirmed that quintessential point about them and the war they had fought. "The lads I had the honor to command in World War Two," he intoned, were "skillful, resourceful and courageous." Neither supermen nor creatures endowed with "supernatural qualities of heroism," they were merely "top-notch" American men—"well trained, well treated, well armed, and [well] provided with superb ships"—who had fought their way to victory. *That* was what deserved remembrance and what would inspire those who sailed nuclear submarines to defend America against whatever threat from the sea the new Soviet enemy might present.[91]

That hymn of praise sealed in American public memory an imperfect image of the Pacific submarine war. That conflict had not been simply an ad hoc response to the immediate post–Pearl Harbor situation. On the contrary, as a long-suppressed study by Yale historian Samuel Flagg Bemis suggested as early as 1961, the undersea war was the logical outgrowth of plans and policies put in place well before the first Japanese bombs hit Hawaii.[92] Admiral Lockwood was correct in his basic estimation of the qualities of his subordinates; they were heroes whose skill, bravery, and endurance contributed mightily to the victory won in 1945. But they were human, men who erred even as they succeeded. And their commander, no less than the producers of television programs and feature films who gave way to the demands of compression and dramatization in their media, found it difficult to deal with their greatest mistake, the sinking of the *Awa maru*.

Although Lockwood admitted the error and accepted some share of the blame for it, he never considered it apart from a morally judgmental framework in which the Japanese bore the ultimate responsibility for all of the evils that flowed from war in the Pacific. Thus a "past imperfect" became the past fixed in the public's mind.[93]

That fact was obvious as the twentieth anniversary of the sinking of the *Awa maru* and the end of the Pacific War approached. By the early 1960s those Americans most directly involved in the former event had all but forgotten about it. Elliott Loughlin had harbored misgivings about going to Japan during the Korean War, but Japanese naval officers' polite silence about the tragedy dispelled them.[94] When he came up for promotion to flag rank, he feared that those on the selection board might remember that he had committed "the greatest submarine error of World War II" and deny him a rear admiral's stars. Instead, when one senior admiral brought up the incident, another dismissed it by snapping, "Hell, he sank a lot of Japanese ships, didn't he?"[95] The navy was more than willing to forget the biggest mistake of his career.

An amnesia of sorts also healed Admiral Lockwood's bitterness about the sinking and about the maltreatment of Americans that had given rise to the voyage of the *Awa maru*. When he and his wife made a last visit to Japan in the sunset of his retirement, they traveled up and down the island of Honshū, visiting temples and shrines, marveling at the reconstruction of Tokyo, and talking to the Japanese with a youthful enthusiasm that covered over the wounds of war.[96] Similar experiences softened the memories of *Queenfish* crew members who served in postwar Japan or on ships homeported at American bases there. They did not come away from that experience hating the Japanese or haunted by the memory of having mistakenly caused the deaths of so many of them.[97]

Instead, the warm afterglow of the positive achievements of the Pacific submarine war glazed over Americans' individual and public memories of that campaign. Nothing better illustrated that fact than the events surrounding the end of the *Queenfish*. When she was decommissioned in March 1963 and her name was given to a new, nuclear submarine, only one of the plankowners who had witnessed the raising of her commissioning pennant nearly twenty years earlier was present to see it hauled down. On that day, now-Capt. John Bennett recalled for reporters great moments in the sub's World War II career: first ships sunk; prisoners of war and downed aviators rescued; and wolfpack campaigns with sister subs. He also misremembered (if the journalist who interviewed him is to be believed) the sinking of the *Awa maru*. Her sole survivor was described as "a Japanese prisoner of war" captured by the *Queenfish* crew—proof of their prowess rather than witness to their commission of "the greatest submarine error of World War II."[98]

A few months later, after a stripped-down *Queenfish* was sunk after being used for target practice off the coast of Hawaii, Captain Bennett carried a relic from her, a portion of a pressure gauge from the forward bank of torpedo tubes, to Perth, Australia. There, on the new *Queenfish* (SSN 661), he presented it to one of the prisoners of war that his shipmates had pulled from the sea on her very first war patrol. The gift brought tears to the Australian's eyes and marked a fitting end to the career of the *Queenfish*, to her story, and to the story of the Pacific submarine war as Bennett, his shipmates, and his generation—indeed all of the American people—had come to understand it.[99] Good deeds done in the good war simply eradicated or altered recollections of tragedies such as the sinking of the *Awa maru*.

Looking back on that result more than three decades later, it would be easy to conclude that "victor's history" had prevailed in America. Those who won the Pacific submarine war chose to remember what was best about it and suppressed all memory of its gravest error. The story of the *Awa maru* in postwar America points to a different conclusion, however. What became American public memory of the undersea war in the Pacific and its gravest error was neither an artifact of the event nor an artifice of those who would conceal the truth. It was, on the contrary, the residue of the efforts of one man, Admiral Lockwood, to tell the truth as he perceived it about what had been a secret war. He made that truth the handmaiden of postwar naval and national needs, serving up portraits of human heroes in hopes of inspiring coming generations to similar deeds of valor in defense of their country. He revealed error, such as the sinking of the *Awa maru*, even as he wrestled, unsuccessfully, with its incongruence with his professional values and his moralistic view of the war in which it occurred.

Those who followed him in presenting visual images of the Pacific submarine war to the American public chose not to grapple with such error. The demands of their media—compression, personalization, and overdramatization of the events of war—rather than deliberate intent to conceal the truth led them to leave the *Awa maru* out of what they put on television and movie screens. The tragedy of 1 April 1945 vanished from American public memory.

In that memory, as in real life, the *Awa maru* was an accidental, not a deliberate, victim. She never became a ghost of war that haunted her destroyers. In time, and without malice aforethought, they simply forgot her.

But those who see themselves as victims in war, especially those who regard themselves as victims of error in war, cannot forget.

9

Victims

I N JAPAN the most vivid expressions of public memory of the sinking of
the *Awa maru* and the Pacific submarine war are not to be found in books
or movies, but in monuments. Monuments proclaim and enshrine public
memory. They attempt to quiet the ghost of war by honoring those who died
in it. One generation uses them to pass along to the next a proper understanding of the war it fought and to remind those that follow of how the past
has shaped their present. But the memories such monuments enshrine—
especially for those who lose a war—are often conflicted.

The Japanese erected two monuments to those who died in the *Awa maru*
tragedy. One is at Renjōji, a tiny, obscure temple built six hundred years
ago on the southern side of Japan's ancient capital, Nara.[1] On 1 June 1966,
priests, local notables, and bereaved family members crowded into its jewel-
like garden to dedicate a simple memorial to the *Awa maru* victims. They
bowed in prayer before a large statue of Buddha in the manifestation of
Kannon, the goddess of mercy, that rested on a gray, marble-faced block.
Only three characters, which signify *Awa maru*, are carved into its face, hint-
ing of the tragedy the monument commemorates. That was what Renjōji's

chief priest and his daughter-in-law, who had raised the money to honor the son and husband they had lost, wanted.[2] A masterpiece of understatement, the Renjōji *Awa maru* monument embodies their resigned acceptance of what for them and other bereaved families was the most terrible event in a disastrous war.

The other *Awa maru* monument is at Zōjōji, the temple burial grounds in Tokyo of the Tokugawa shoguns who ruled Japan for more than three centuries. The monument nestles against the huge red gate of this rich and famous temple.[3] On 1 April 1977 a throng of politicians, diplomats, corporate executives, and bereaved family members from all over Japan surged through that massive portal, wheeled to the right through cherry trees in full bloom, and witnessed the ground breaking of this second tribute.[4]

When they returned six months later for ceremonies marking its completion, they saw a large gray cenotaph, bracketed by polished black granite walls. After the formalities they crowded forward, looking for their loved ones' names among the more than two thousand carved into the face of those walls. They also paused to admire the cenotaph that told the *Awa maru* story. On its face they saw a green marble cross that replicated the symbol of safety that had failed to protect the ship on the night of 1 April 1945. On its obverse side they read the essence of the victims' story: that the *Queenfish* sank them in violation of international law; their government betrayed them by abandoning the right of indemnification; and their bones lay in the depth of the Taiwan Strait, with the cause of their deaths still not fully explained. That was no understatement.[5]

The two *Awa maru* monuments commemorate the same tragedy in dramatically different ways. One exudes an aura of resigned acceptance of what had been lost in war and of release for the spirits of the dead, precisely as Buddhist teaching directs. The other breathes a spirit of defiant, unresolved anger and grief. It cries out for justice unachieved and peace for the "hungry ghosts" whose remains have yet to be returned to their homeland.[6] Each in its own way marks a stopping point along the way to defining Japan's public memory of the *Awa maru* sinking. Nonetheless, both express the Japanese sense of victimization in the war in which that tragedy occurred. In memorializing particular individuals who died on a single ship, the two monuments proclaim that the Japanese people as a whole were the ultimate victims of a terrible, lost war.

How and why did that view of the event and of the war come to prevail in Japanese public memory? By what alchemy were the *Awa maru* victims transformed into symbols for the entire nation's victimization in war? What clues does the Japanese story of the *Awa maru* story provide for understanding how and why the Japanese public memory of the tragedy and the war in which it occurred came to be so very different from the American one?

Three persons who witnessed the dedication of the Zōjōji *Awa maru* monument on that April 1977 day—a former naval officer, a novelist, and a widow —hold the keys to answering those questions. They told a tale that neither Tokyo nor Washington officials wanted the Japanese people to hear. Yet, ironically, the two governments had fostered the notion that Japan was the ultimate victim of the Pacific War—a concept that provided the framework within which all three major Japanese interpreters told the *Awa maru* story. Before considering how and why each person told that tale, the origins of that broader understanding of the Pacific War must be explained.

The notion that the Japanese people were victims rather than victimizers in that conflict had its roots in America. During the fighting, President Franklin D. Roosevelt had been careful to distinguish between Axis governments and enemy peoples; the former had to be destroyed before the latter could be saved.[7] Thus, when American occupation troops landed on Japanese soil, they carried with them a commitment to the "democratization" of Japan that required rewriting Japanese history. Barely ninety days after their arrival, Gen. Douglas MacArthur issued orders for the excision of "militaristic" ideas from textbooks—a task that impoverished students accomplished simply by tearing or scratching out the offending portions of their books.[8] Radio programs broadcast a second form of revisionist history: they suggested that Japan started and lost the war because militarist leaders had dragged unknowing ordinary people into it.[9] War crimes trials that stretched over the first three postwar years hammered home the same notion: past leaders and those who had acquiesced in their leadership were responsible for the disasters of war and destruction of the prosperity that Japan had once known.[10] And if that message, drawn from the victor's history, was too blunt to be fully credible, early postwar movies (which had passed occupation censorship) presented it in a more subtle form.[11]

During the early postwar years, various sorts of Japanese helped spread this theory of victimization that their conquerors had originated. Prime Minister Yoshida Shigeru, for example, harbored strong feelings against military leaders and found it convenient to present himself as one who had resisted them and their civilian collaborators during the war.[12] Liberal intellectuals eager to promote democratization found congenial what would later be called the "war crimes" interpretation of the recent past.[13] Hordes of returning soldiers, in the misery of their persons, affirmed the notion of Japan's victimization by the military. Those with literary talents produced novels and short stories that mocked military leaders and chronicled ordinary soldiers' sufferings.[14] These native figures helped implant the foreign-born notion that ordinary Japanese citizens were the preeminent victims of the war that had just ended.

This victor's history sidestepped or ignored the question of American responsibility for actions that had brought very real harm to the Japanese people. It implied what Admiral Lockwood had made explicit in his treatment of the submarine war: Japanese actions justified American counteractions that killed ordinary Japanese. It also relied on the power of occupation officials to ban publication and public discussion of Japanese victimization at American hands. The atomic bombing of Hiroshima and Nagasaki were taboo subjects in occupied Japan.[15] The deaths of tens of thousands of Japanese merchant marine sailors at the hands of American submariners were treated as private tragedies rather than subjects for public debate and acknowledgment.[16] When the occupation ended in April 1952, rehabilitated nationalistic politicians who might have raised questions about particularly harmful American acts during the war did not do so. They, like Prime Minister Yoshida, had no desire to speak harshly about what the United States— once enemy, now powerful ally and protector—had done in the past.

It took another accident—a thermonuclear accident—to root in Japanese consciousness the notion that Americans as well as their own former leaders had been victimizers in the Pacific War. That traumatic event occurred almost nine years to the day after the *Awa maru* incident, when fallout from hydrogen bomb testing near Bikini in the Marshall Islands irradiated the Japanese fishing boat *Lucky Dragon*. Media stories about what her crew had seen, contamination of the tuna they brought back, and the strange illness that led to the death of one of them triggered waves of public protest. American diplomats responded by pledging to indemnify the victims, and this time Washington kept that promise. But Japanese politicians of all sorts could not resist the groundswell of popular feeling triggered by this accident. The *Lucky Dragon* incident gave rise to the antinuclear movement in Japan, provided the occasion for the first major commemorative ceremonies at Hiroshima and Nagasaki, and helped transform 6 and 15 August of each year into days for remembering the sacrifices made by Japanese victims of the Pacific War.[17]

Those rituals did not, however, address the question of responsibility for what had occurred. That problem tormented the first man to present the *Awa maru* story to the postwar Japanese public: Chihaya Masataka, who himself was a war victim. Until the end of 1945, the Imperial Japanese Navy defined his place in society and purpose in life. Born the eldest son of a colonial official in Taiwan, Chihaya had graduated, at age twenty, from the naval academy at Etajima. As a junior officer he became a gunnery expert, and when Pearl Harbor came he was serving on the battleship *Musashi,* known within the navy as "the hope of Japan," preparing her for service as flagship for the commander in chief, Combined Fleet. Eleven months later Chihaya got his first taste of sea battle in the third round of fighting around Guadalcanal.[18] Called back to Tokyo for duty on the Naval General Staff and for study at the Naval Staff College, he demonstrated a strength of character that matched his obvious intellectual and operational skills. He refused to accept his instructors' premise that any American fleet attacking Japan would be defeated. That independence of mind served him well when, in 1945, he helped plan the naval aerial defenses of Luzon, Okinawa, and the Japanese home islands. Determined to the end, Chihaya was drilling sailors and marines at Naval General Headquarters on the day the emperor announced Japan's surrender.[19]

Chihaya had ample opportunity during the first few months of peace to ponder the defeat of his navy and nation. Working under Rear Adm. Tomioka Sadatoshi in a naval historical group that provided documents and reports to the American conquerors, Chihaya accepted an intellectualized but somewhat watered-down version of their war crimes interpretation of the Pacific War. Commander Chihaya felt "full of shame" because, as a former naval officer, he was "not quite free" of responsibility for "utter, bottomless defeat" and the misery it inflicted on the Japanese people.[20] The more he studied the

Imperial Japanese Navy's conduct of the war, the more convinced he became that defeat was, in substantial measure, self-inflicted. As Chihaya saw it, the U.S. Navy had had a strategy, while Japan's navy had had only battle plans.[21]

The former commander harbored ambivalent feelings toward Americans. He had to admire them intellectually for their success in war, but he could not forget what they had done to him personally. In 1944 they had shot down and killed his younger brother, a crack navy pilot who had bombed Pearl Harbor.[22] Fires ignited by American bombs had ravaged the Tokyo neighborhood where Chihaya's wife and family lived in the spring of 1945.[23] By December of that year the victors had abolished the Imperial Japanese Navy, destroying at a stroke Chihaya's chance to achieve flag rank.[24] Thus, rather than working within an elite of highly respected senior naval officers, he now had to eke out a living—first by serving Japan's conquerors, then by working as a translator and journalist for the uneducated, self-made publisher of a news service for foreigners.[25]

Despite his loss of profession and status at their hands, however, Chihaya did not hate Americans. He became life-long friends with Dr. Gordon Prange, chief historian for the U.S. Army Forces Far East Command in the early postwar years and later a prolific producer of books on the Pacific War.[26] Chihaya also sensed Americans' commitment to fairness and justice firsthand when, in 1949, they allowed him to go to Rabaul to help defend former colleagues accused of war crimes.[27]

Strong feelings about war, responsibility, and justice figured in Commander Chihaya's telling of the *Awa maru* story, but just why he revived it when he did remains unclear. He may have read and taken exception to what Admiral Lockwood and then-rear admiral Richard Voge had written. He may have been shocked by the *Lucky Dragon* accident into writing about another American wrong, so as to help restore wounded personal, professional, and national pride. Perhaps he was spurred to write by lingering connections with strong nationalists who had championed the old Imperial Japanese Navy and who now dreamt of salvaging the *Awa maru* to harvest her supposedly precious cargo. He may simply have hoped to make some money and gain a little fame by publishing the unfortunate ship's story. In any event, his account intrigued the editor of the prestigious *Bungei Shunju,* who published it in August 1956, just when the annual ceremonies at Hiroshima were calling attention to Japan's victimization in war.[28]

Cdr. Chihaya Masataka, Imperial Japanese Navy (Ret.). *Author's photograph*

Chihaya told the *Awa maru* story very differently from Lockwood and Voge. They defined it narrowly, explaining the sinking and either defending or damning the court-martial that followed it. Chihaya made it a much broader, open-ended tale. His article encompassed the sinking and court-martial, the proposed indemnification and its undoing, and the possibility of salvaging the *Awa maru*. While the Americans treated the sinking as an anomalous, accidental incident for which no one was morally culpable, Chihaya hinted that it might have been a deliberate, or perhaps even a typical, act—one that betrayed patterns of illegality and injustice that would reappear in American postwar bargaining behavior.[29] While the Americans wanted to achieve closure about a painful incident, Chihaya left the story unresolved in a manner that challenged the prevailing war crimes interpretation of the Pacific War.

Commander Chihaya opened his article by attacking head-on Admiral Lockwood's claim that the *Awa maru*'s carriage of contraband justified her being sunk. That wrong did not justify another—the Americans' "act of madness" in torpedoing the ship.[30] International law, as Chihaya interpreted it, provided viable alternatives to that action—boarding and inspecting her;

escorting her to the nearest port if contraband were discovered; or at the very least, providing warning before sinking her. Elliott Loughlin and his crew had simply ignored all of that. Their sinking of the *Awa maru* without warning was a criminal act.[31]

But why had the American submariners behaved as they did on the night of 1 April 1945? Chihaya found their behavior bizarre and their account of what had happened problematic. Why, when the third warning message about the *Awa maru*'s probable presence was received, did they not search radio files for copies of the two earlier messages about her? They claimed fog had obscured the illuminated, telltale crosses that identified the *Awa maru* as a protected vessel. However, neither Japanese weather bureau records nor the sole survivor, Shimoda Kantarō, indicated the presence of fog that night in the Taiwan Strait. The Americans said seas were too rough to save more than a single victim and insisted that others who might have been rescued had refused assistance. But if, as the *Queenfish* submariners claimed, surface fog hid the *Awa maru* from their eyes, it was highly unlikely that winds would have raised waves big enough to preclude saving more Japanese lives. Moreover, most of the *Awa maru*'s passengers were civilians, not military personnel trained to prefer death rather than captivity. Chihaya also wondered if the full truth about the sinking had come out in the court-martial. If it had, why did Washington officials keep the trial record secret, and why did American naval officers who claimed knowledge of the tragedy refuse to discuss it?[32]

Chihaya found the postwar behavior of the American and Japanese governments almost as outrageous as that of Commander Loughlin and his crew. If Shimoda received the special treatment he said he had—a flight home and a meeting with General MacArthur—and then disappeared into a void of obscurity, then perhaps the Americans had purchased his silence about some terrible, and still unknown, truth about the sinking.[33] The diplomats who negotiated the claims-abandonment agreement were, in Chihaya's view, utterly despicable. A Japanese government made up of "yes-men" had submissively accepted the morally indefensible and "completely outrageous" proposal that William Sebald put before them.[34] Yoshida Shigeru's craven sacrifice of victims' rights of indemnification suggested that his government was every bit as willing to victimize its own citizens as the "militarist" cabinets that had plunged Japan into an unwinnable war.

Chihaya closed the article with a disclaimer, a plea, and a proposal. He did not want to stir up harsh feelings toward the Americans, for hating them would not bring the war dead back to life. Simple justice, though, demanded that the Japanese know the full truth about how and why more than two thousand of their countrymen had been plunged to death in the depths of the Taiwan Strait. The Japanese had been doubly victimized by their own and the American government, Chihaya insisted. But they might redeem that humiliation by making a serious effort to locate and salvage the *Awa maru*, the remains of their dead, and the wealth known to have been crammed into her holds.[35]

Although that proposal was premature, what Chihaya wrote defined the parameters and character of the *Awa maru* story as the Japanese would know it. He presented it as a challenge to the American version of events. It quickly became just that, for the soon-to-be editor of the *Japan Times* read the article, and he translated and published a paraphrased version that transformed Chihaya's often oblique suggestions into explicit statements bluntly critical of the Americans.[36] Neither Japanese Foreign Ministry officials nor American diplomats liked that, and the commander suddenly stopped receiving invitations to American embassy functions.[37]

He also made the *Awa maru* story a mystery, an account so filled with riddles and unresolved questions as to attract Japanese readers of all sorts. Over the next twenty-three years, he would write or inspire four more articles about the ill-fated ship, produce a volume of essays that bore her name, and become one of Japan's most distinguished naval historians.[38] None of the additional detail he provided in these works altered his basic line of argument or resolved fully the questions he posed in this first essay. Still, the notion of unresolved mysteries surrounding the hulk lying on the bottom of the Taiwan Strait became a critical element of virtually every other Japanese rendering of the *Awa maru* story. That tantalizing thought gave the tale a life in Japan that no government, however displeased or disgruntled by it, could snuff out.

Commander Chihaya performed one other function vital to the development of the *Awa maru* story in Japan: he brought Shimoda Kantarō out of the shadows of obscurity into the limelight of national attention. When he first located and interviewed him, the former navy commander had doubts about the accuracy of at least some of the sole survivor's memories of the

Shimoda Kantarō, the sole
survivor, was interviewed
on Tokyo television. He is
remembered here by his
widow, Shimoda Mitsuko.
Author's photograph

events surrounding the sinking of the *Awa maru*.[39] But when he revised his
first essay for republication in 1961, Chihaya used Shimoda's words to provide verisimilitude and color to his account of events on board the doomed
ship on the night she was sunk.[40] That the man expressed emotional, if not
literal, truth may have prompted Chihaya to introduce Shimoda to the publisher of *Bungei shunju*. As a result, in 1963 his account of his *Awa maru* experiences appeared in that prestigious and widely read journal.[41] And when the
twentieth anniversary of the sinking approached two years later, Chihaya
interviewed Shimoda on Tokyo television.[42]

In two ways, Shimoda reinforced what Chihaya had said. First, he made
victimization real. Readers and viewers learned how he had been hurled,
unconscious, from the deck of the *Awa maru* into the pitch-black waters of
the Taiwan Strait. He remembered being hauled aboard the *Queenfish*, having his stomach pumped, and being shackled to a large barrel—a weight
he thought would be tossed overboard to drag him to the depths of the sea.
Shimoda recounted how he had watched in horror as Elliott Loughlin pulled

a photograph of the *Awa maru* from his desk drawer; its very existence convinced him that the American had known of the ship's protected character before torpedoing her. Shimoda implied that her destroyers were indeed demons when he described the *Queenfish* crew dancing and embracing one another after sinking two Japanese transports on the voyage back to Guam.[43]

The sole survivor also lent strength to Chihaya's allegations of American disingenuousness after the sinking. In his version of events, a besotted Admiral Nimitz, his arm in a sling and his ears flush with the telltale redness of the alcoholic, had presided over a three-week-long court-martial of Elliott Loughlin. When Shimoda told the court about the birth of a child on the doomed ship, Nimitz and another member of the court had gasped in horror and blessed themselves with the sign of the cross. The sole survivor also said he had spurned American efforts to suborn him into permanent silence. Although he had gotten red-carpet treatment when he returned to Japan in February 1946, he felt humiliated by General MacArthur and intimidated by the tall guards at the supreme commander's headquarters. The Americans had offered him a house to replace the one their bombs had destroyed; but he could never have endured the pain of living in a home provided by Japan's conquerors.[44]

Much, if not most, of what Shimoda said was false. He misremembered improbable details and may have fashioned fables that exaggerated his suffering to lessen the shame he felt at being the sole survivor.[45] At least insofar as the development of the Japanese version of the *Awa maru* story was concerned, however, those inaccuracies did not matter. What counted was the ending to the story that Shimoda provided. He was the quintessential Japanese war victim, but when, in the spring of 1965, he appeared on television, he became the quintessential survivor. Although he suffered persistent digestive disorders that may have originated in the seawater, oil, and sludge he had swallowed on the night of 1 April 1945, Shimoda had survived and prospered. Dressed in a dark business suit, he presented the image of an independent, self-sustaining, and industrious citizen—a well-to-do grandfather—to television viewers. In him, they saw the victim who had transcended his victimization.[46]

That end to the *Awa maru* story resonated powerfully with what by the mid-1960s had become essential elements of Japan's public memory of the recent past. The Pacific War had been a disaster in which ordinary Japanese were victimized, but their postwar sweat and sacrifice had produced miracles —Tokyo rebuilt into a city capable of hosting the 1964 Olympics; unprecedented economic growth; and a level of well-being for the average citizen unimaginable before Pearl Harbor. Shimoda, and millions of other war victims, had survived. He had overcome his sufferings in the *Awa maru* tragedy, and his countrymen had transcended defeat and loss in the war in which that tragedy had occurred. Thus, the ending of the *Awa maru* story—and, with it, that of the Pacific War—was not death and disaster but triumph and transcendence. The ghost of war, so it appeared, had been exorcised.

That was not the conclusion that Arima Yorichika, the second major teller of the *Awa maru* tale, gave to *The Silence of a Survivor,* his novel about the tragedy.[47] Arima was no ordinary Japanese; he was a vanquished aristocrat who tried to find meaning in the war that had destroyed his class and its empire. Born in 1918, the third son of a count whose family had ruled the Kurume domain during the Tokugawa era, Arima enjoyed all the pleasures and privileges that wealth and social position could buy in prewar Japan. He attended the Peers Preparatory School, then shifted to Narimichi High School, where he excelled in tennis and baseball. After leaving school for a time, he entered Waseda University Preparatory Academy. But his passion for baseball (evident in the photograph below) exceeded his devotion to study, and he refused to behave like the son of a cabinet minister that he was. He published short stories for money in a businessmen's magazine scorned by his family and teachers. Eventually expelled from school, he drifted for a time, lost his exemption from conscription, and in January 1940 entered the Imperial Japanese Army.[48]

By that time his father headed the Imperial Rule Assistance Association, which had been established to assure political support for Japan's war in China. Arima enjoyed fighting that war. Posted to the northwest frontier of empire, along the borders of Manchukuo, the Soviet Union, and Chinese Inner Mongolia, he rose through the ranks to become a lieutenant colonel. For him and for many of his countrymen, the battles they fought were part of a crusade against the triple perils of Soviet Bolshevism, Chiang Kai-shek's corrupt Chinese nationalism, and Mao Tse Tung's Chinese Communism.

Forced to quick maturity by combat, Arima became a genuine patriot—so much so that he refused a first offer to leave the front for a less dangerous job in Tokyo.[49]

In April 1943, however, he quit the army and became a journalist for Dōmei, Japan's official news agency.[50] For a time he dallied with private affairs, grieving over the death of a favorite geisha, becoming special patron to a second, and then dismissing a third. In 1944 he married a woman others considered far beneath his social status.[51] Arima then turned back to public service and became chief of his local neighborhood association in Tokyo. The position, once meant to drum up support for the war against the United States, had become that of organizer of defenses against American firebombs. By the time the *Queenfish* sank the *Awa maru*, Arima was struggling to prevent the destruction of his beloved Tokyo.[52]

The novelist had good reason, twenty years after the fact, to be bitter about the war, the sinking of the *Awa maru*, and the defeat that led to American occupation of Japan. He and his family were victimized by all three. A beloved cousin—a young diplomat and sometime tennis partner—perished with the *Awa maru* in April 1945.[53] After Japan's surrender, the Americans arrested Arima's father as a war criminal and took him away to Sugamo Prison. While he languished there, occupation authorities seized his properties, and runaway inflation devoured the Arima family's wealth. In 1947, the year the novelist considered the worst in his life, the Americans humiliated his father even as they released him without ever having brought him to trial: they simply dumped the old man, in ragged clothes without a yen in his pocket, at a train station far from home.[54] By that time American-inspired Japanese "reformers" had abolished the peerage, and the cloud of suspicion hanging over Count Arima's head precluded his returning to an active political career.[55] In October 1947 Arima lost a favorite uncle, his death hastened, so it was said, by the death of his son on board the *Awa maru*.[56] Arima also suffered the shock and humiliation of having his watch stolen by an American GI.[57] So it was that the once-proud warrior and scion of the aristocracy was reduced to having to earn a living as a sports journalist.[58]

Arima eventually turned these war-born experiences to his advantage. Money, social position, and privilege had deserted him, but he could still write. During the first twenty postwar years, Arima published forty-one novels or collections of short stories and poetry, many of which appeared

Arima Yorichika. *Mrs. Arima
Chiyoko*

first in mass-circulation magazines and newspapers. He tried in his fiction to
recapture what the Japanese had suffered during and immediately after the
war. He wrote about baseball—*the* game of the occupation era—and eventually became a baseball coach at Narimichi High School. He wrote about
his tangled wartime love life, his memories of battle, and about the ways in
which American occupiers struck terror in the hearts of ordinary Japanese.
By the early 1960s he had become a famous, prosperous, prize-winning
author.[59]

   But the ghost of war continued to haunt him. It emerged from the shadows of the past in a new way in 1961, when Arima read Commander Chihaya's essay about the sinking of the *Awa maru*.[60] That rekindled the anger
he still felt over his cousin's death on board her and reawakened memories of
the injustices he and his family had suffered in the early postwar years.
Arima contacted and befriended Commander Chihaya, spent an afternoon
with the widow of the second-ranking diplomat on board the *Awa maru*, and
found an army officer who had witnessed the loading of contraband aboard
the luckless vessel.[61] What he heard from these sources convinced Arima

that the *Awa maru* story had all the makings of a good novel. Its mystery, psychological complexity, and emotional power might be used to awaken a new generation of Japanese to the ways in which war had victimized their parents and their nation. Arima began writing what emerged in 1963 as serialized magazine articles and metamorphosed, three years later, into a novel about the *Awa maru*.[62]

The book blended fact and fiction, much as Admiral Dykers had done in *The Silent Service* television programs.[63] Although he called his story *The Silence of a Survivor*, Arima made its protagonists a journalist (a composite of himself and Commander Chihaya) and a young widow (a mix of his aunt and the wife of the second-ranking diplomat on board the ship).[64] They first met while waiting in vain at Moji for the return of the *Awa maru*, then reconnected in the rubble of Tokyo during the last days of the war. Once the fighting stopped, they set out to find Shimoda Kantarō in hopes of learning the full truth about what had befallen the *Awa maru*. Although the characters failed in that quest, Arima used them to give the ship's story new, wider, and more powerful meaning for his readers.[65]

In his hands, it became the ultimate tale of victimization in and by war. The victimizers, in Arima's view, were as much Japanese as American. Relying on the testimony of a Third Transport Command officer who claimed that contraband had been loaded aboard the passenger-cargo vessel at Singapore and attested to the presence of self-destructive devices on board, he held the Japanese government partly responsible for the thousands of deaths that had occurred.[66] Then he pointed an accusatory finger at the Americans —not just for sinking the ship but also for silencing Shimoda.[67] But Arima saved his greatest wrath for postwar Japanese politicians. He quoted approvingly the speeches of Diet members who had opposed what he regarded as Yoshida Shigeru's capitulation to the Americans in abandoning Japan's indemnification rights. To hammer home the point of ordinary citizens' victimization at official hands, he had the fictional legislator who was supposedly helping his protagonists in their search for the truth about the *Awa maru* betray them by using the information they had provided to launch a potentially self-enriching scheme to salvage the ship.[68]

Arima etched into public memory an unforgettable image of the victims of the sunken *Awa maru* and of the Pacific War. They were the survivors, not those who had perished. His journalist hero barely escaped death from American bombs near the Tokyo railroad station. The young widow whom he met and moved in with just when the fighting stopped lived in a half-ruined house surrounded not by the garden and tennis court her dead husband had planned but by rubble and devastation. The two found so little to eat on the black market, their only source, that they hallucinated, imagining that brown-skinned potatoes were khaki-clad soldiers. The man whose knowledge of the *Awa maru*'s fate they craved turned out to be an even greater victim: he had to become the pawn of heartless officials in order to get money to survive.[69]

These physical sufferings paled, however, in comparison to the intangible losses that Arima's protagonists endured. The *Awa maru* tragedy and other disasters of war made them emotional cripples. Although the journalist and the widow fell in love and lived together, they were unable to consummate their relationship sexually. The Shimoda Kantarō they eventually found was a loathsome person—a bigamist, a man who had sold out to officials, and a person who, having lost his moral compass, could not speak truthfully about the *Awa maru*. When the journalist and the widow realized they would never resolve the riddles surrounding the loss of the ship, he turned to drink and she buried herself in grief. Their relationship fell apart, and their sense of purpose in life vanished. Arima left no doubt that their future would be emotionally bleak, despite politicians' promises that economic recovery would bring happiness.[70] The victims he portrayed could never exorcise the ghost of war.

That was Arima Yorichika's essential point in telling the *Awa maru* story as he did. He wanted his readers to see that the generation of Japanese who fought and lived through the Pacific War were its ultimate victims. They lost much more than friends and relatives on ships like the *Awa maru,* or the property destroyed by bombing, or their leaders wrongfully executed as war criminals.[71] They had embraced war as he had, as patriots; but many, far too many, had ended it as corpses. Those who were left were alienated forever from governments, which claimed to be defending the national interest. Capable of the most intense emotional commitment when the fighting began, the survivor-victims emerged from its ashes as emotional cripples unable to escape the past and incapable of enjoying a material plenty that could never compensate them for what they had lost.[72] The protagonists of Arima Yorichika's *Awa maru* story were permanent victims, not triumphant survivors.

But neither they, nor their creator, nor the people who inspired them were helpless. By properly commemorating the war dead, they could assure the lost a place in public memory. They might even, Arima hinted in his afterword to *The Silence of a Survivor*, quiet the ghost of war that haunted them by participating in the activities of the recently created *Awa maru* Bereaved Families Association.[73]

The formation of that group in October 1964 came at a time when national circumstance and government policy had shifted so as to prompt reexamination of Pacific War–related issues. The Japanese government had long since taken steps to compensate families of the war dead and to recognize a national organization for those bereaved by war.[74] Health and Welfare Ministry officials had begun planning to recover the remains of millions who had perished overseas. Early in 1962, between publication of Chihaya Masataka's *The Accursed Awa maru* and the appearance of Arima Yorichika's serialized version of *The Silence of a Survivor*, NHK presented a moving series of programs about "people who did not return" from the war. On 15 August 1963 the Shōwa emperor recognized their sacrifices by attending the first official national war memorial service to be held in more than a decade. A year later, two Japanese soldiers emerged from nineteen years of hiding on a U.S. Marine Corps base on Guam. The reappearance of men so long faithful to a lost cause electrified the Japanese nation, stimulating public memory by alerting those too young to have known the Pacific War firsthand to the sacrifices that their parents' generation had made.[75]

This revival of public interest in the war gave fresh hope to a group of widows of diplomats who had perished on board the *Awa maru*. They felt the time had come to mark the twentieth anniversary of their spouses' deaths and to get official recognition and proper compensation for their loss. One woman placed a full-page notice in the conservative daily newspaper *Sankei shimbun* asking others bereaved by the *Awa maru* sinking to contact her. Within six months she had responses from more than three hundred people from all over Japan. On 3 October 1964, fifty of them gathered in Tokyo to found what became the *Awa maru* Bereaved Families Association. The occasion must have been a very moving one, for many of these spouses, brothers and sisters, sons and daughters had never met or had the chance to share their grief with others whose lives had been so dramatically changed by that event.[76]

The group decided to establish a permanent organization that would properly memorialize the dead—especially on the upcoming twentieth anniversary of the *Awa maru* tragedy. In addition, it would work to erect a memorial, recover the remains of the victims, and document the event that had taken their lives. Following prewar norms that recognized social-class distinctions and professional rank, the group chose as its president and vice-president the sons of the senior diplomat who died on the *Awa maru* and of her captain, respectively. In a decision that hinted at their determination to press the Japanese government to remedy the injustice and hardship created by its abandonment of indemnification rights and refusal to pay more than paltry consolation sums, the group chose as its senior adviser a sitting member of the upper house of the Diet. He was Aoki Kazuo, a prewar minister of finance and wartime head of the Ministry of Greater East Asia, who had lost a younger brother on board the *Awa maru*.[77]

The group readily achieved its first goal. On 1 April 1965, six hundred people gathered at Zōjōji Temple in Tokyo for a memorial service that honored the *Awa maru* dead. An assembly of former ambassadors, politicians, and, most notably, a junior diplomat dispatched by American ambassador Edwin O. Reischauer (who had been born in Japan and understood the importance of such a gesture of sympathy) joined the mourners. When reporters questioned those present about what the association planned to do next, they were told that the families were thinking of building a memorial to the victims and pressing the Japanese government for more compensation for the losses they had suffered.[78] Within a year, however, it became clear that there was no consensus within the association over how best to pursue those goals. By January 1966 the new organization had split in a manner that echoed the centuries-old rivalry between the Kansai (Ōsaka-Kyōto) and Kantō (Tokyo-Yokohama) regions of the country. Each group was spearheaded by a determined widow who thought her sense of what was proper should determine what was to be done.[79] In the Kansai area, Mrs. Arai Keiko mounted a fund-raising campaign to build what barely six months later became the Renjōji *Awa maru* memorial in Nara. She clearly felt that the

The *Awa maru* memorial in Renjōji Temple, Nara. *Shimotsuma Kazuho*

association's purpose should be more spiritual than political.[80] To mark the twenty-first anniversary of the tragedy, members of her group participated in another ceremony to console the spirits of the *Awa maru* victims. They chartered a Japan Airlines plane, flew to the presumed site of the sinking, and dropped cherry blossoms and paper thousand-year cranes into the waters of the Taiwan Strait.[81]

Back in Tokyo, that gesture struck Mrs. Tōkō Takeko as poetic but futile.[82] She was the widow of the second-ranking diplomat who died on the ship and the model for the heroine of Arima Yorichika's novel. By 1966 she had become the driving force within the national *Awa maru* Bereaved Families Association. Her political savvy, social status, and persistent sense of injustice made her the group's natural leader and one of Japan's most remarkable war widows.

Mrs. Tōkō had been born in 1915 as Okajima Takeko, daughter of a wealthy and politically well-connected Ōsaka newspaper publisher. Her family, which claimed descent from one of the famous forty-seven masterless samurai of the Tokugawa era who had preferred death to dishonor, raised her in accordance with the strict social norms observed by upper-class

Japanese families early in the twentieth century. After finishing high school, she was sent to study English literature at Ōsaka Special School for Girls (later Ōsaka Women's University). Following graduation, and as befitted a young woman of her wealth and social position, she married a fellow Ōsaka native, the young diplomat Tōkō Takezō. This real Takeko, unlike Arima's fictional heroine, bore her husband two daughters before he embarked on the *Awa maru* for Southeast Asia in February 1945.[83] She could not travel to Moji to await his return, as her fictional counterpart did, but she was as grief stricken by his death as any imagined heroine could be.[84]

That loss, together with the economic and social upheavals that followed Japan's defeat, set Tōkō Takeko on a course she could not have imagined before Pearl Harbor. No longer a wife and mother comfortably situated near the top of the Japanese social hierarchy, the young widow had to go out and find a job. She became private secretary to the power-and-money broker Tsuji Karoku. His funds, squeezed from peasants and workers during the war for the manufacture of Imperial Japanese Army uniforms, allegedly fed Liberal Party coffers and were used to try to make the nationalistic Hatoyama Ichirō prime minister. Mrs. Tōkō learned the art of political fund-raising so well that Tsuji said she could easily win election to the Diet, but she spurned that possibility as something unseemly for a woman of her class. Instead, after Tsuji died in 1948, she went to work for a semi-governmental political and public opinion research organization that fed data to the occupation bureaucrats of General MacArthur's Supreme Commander Allied Powers.[85]

In that job and in her family life, Mrs. Tōkō found it impossible to avoid contact with Americans—the people whose submariners had taken her husband's life. Her daughters played with the children of an American neighbor, Herbert Passin—then a minor occupation official, later a distinguished professor of sociology at Columbia University.[86] After the occupation ended, she moved back into the diplomatic world as general manager of the Japan-Canada Society. There she cemented ties with such members of the prewar nobility as the society's chairman (and former first Japanese ambassador to Canada), Marquis Tokugawa Iemasa.[87]

Despite this partial recovery of her prewar social and economic status, Mrs. Tōkō remained deeply troubled by her husband's death on board the *Awa maru*. She told her daughters about a recurring dream in which her

Mrs. Tōkō Takeko.
Author's photograph

young bridegroom, who had been a championship swimmer at Tokyo Commercial College (later Hitotsubashi University), appeared at the entrance to their home, dripping wet as if he had just stepped out of the ocean's depths. That, she explained, meant his soul would not be at rest until his bodily remains were reclaimed from the sea.[88] She nagged his former Foreign Ministry entering-class members to undo the "unfair" indemnity abandonment bargain Tokyo had struck with Washington.[89] After it had become clear they would do nothing, she read Commander Chihaya's first *Awa maru* article and praised him for exposing the supine and craven behavior of Japanese diplomats.[90] Well aware of the value of publicity for her cause, she also gladly granted Arima Yorichika the long interview that gave birth to his fictional heroine.[91]

For most of the first eight years of the *Awa maru* Bereaved Families Association's existence, Mrs. Tōkō worked behind the scenes to get more compensation from the Japanese government for its members' losses. She helped arrange meetings of its president with successive ministers of foreign affairs and of health and welfare.[92] She used her political skills to lobby Diet members. Substantial majorities in both houses of the legislature agreed—in private—that the mere seventy thousand yen in consolation monies previously paid to the family of each *Awa maru* victim was inadequate. But despite their approval of payments to other sorts of war victims, the legislators declined to vote additional consolation compensation for families whose lives had been shattered by the deaths of loved ones on board the ill-starred ship. In public, cabinet members simply told questioners that it would be "difficult" to authorize supplementary payments.[93]

When, in February 1972, the *Awa maru* Bereaved Families Association turned to Prime Minister Satō Eisaku, a Yoshida Shigeru protégé, for help, it fared no better. Mrs. Tōkō helped craft fine words that praised his negotiation of an Okinawa reversion accord with the Americans. She suggested that the time had passed when Washington might take offense at anything that cast doubt on the fairness of the claims-abandonment agreement. Satō turned a deaf ear to these pleas, however; he simply was not willing to overrule his subordinates' objections to any legislative action regarding the *Awa maru* tragedy.[94]

Given this failure, Mrs. Tōkō pointed the *Awa maru* Bereaved Families Association in other directions in the early 1970s. The bereaved expressed support for efforts to salvage the ship (efforts that are best reserved for the next chapter). But most of their energy went into a fund-raising campaign that Mrs. Tōkō hoped would guarantee the *Awa maru* victims a permanent place in public memory. With the association's permission, she set out to raise 60 million yen for the building of an *Awa maru* monument. That project became for her a means of proclaiming Japan's victimization in the Pacific War, and she left her Japan-Canada Society position to work on it full time. By early 1977 she had induced scattered and far-from-wealthy bereaved family members to begin contributing what would amount to 2 million yen —for a memorial that was expected to cost at least thirty times that amount.[95]

Anticipating that gap between necessity and reality, Mrs. Tōkō turned to other probable sources of money for the monument. First she contacted the money-men of conservative politics, Prime Minister Tanaka Kakuei's secretary first among them, asking for contributions. Then she reached out to corporations whose employees had died on the ship; the Furukawa Mining Corporation, based in Niigata, capital of Tanaka's mountain fiefdom, stood at the top of her list. By the time construction work began on the monument, she had raised half of its cost from such corporate donors. The remainder of the monies not donated by family members came from classmates, other relatives, and political acquaintances of the *Awa maru* victims.[96] Their diversity testified not only to her fund-raising skills but also to the depth and breadth of the tragedy's impact upon Japanese society. Conservative and communist politicians, powerful bureaucrats and long-since-powerless Imperial Japanese Navy Staff College graduates, elite literary and social clubs, and even a department store chain made contributions.[97] This Tokyo monument—not the stone Buddha in Renjōji's garden in Nara—would be the embodiment of Japanese public memory of the *Awa maru* disaster.

Mrs. Tōkō was responsible for its siting and design as well as its financing. Her association with Marquis Tokugawa, together with the religious affiliation of other, more senior diplomats' widows, secured its favorable location within the precincts of Zōjōji Temple.[98] The monument's basic design—a simple but somber gray cenotaph bracketed by black granite walls—sprang from the mind of one of her daughters' boyfriends, an architect. She brought back from a trip to the United States that included a visit to the USS *Arizona* (BB 39) memorial at Pearl Harbor the idea of listing the name of every victim who had died on the *Awa maru*. The irony of borrowing an American technique to memorialize those who she and her countrymen believed had been wrongly deprived of life by American submariners apparently did not strike Mrs. Tōkō.[99] She simply wanted to guarantee the *Awa maru* victims a permanent place in Japan's public memory of the Pacific War.

When she and other bereaved family members, together with a host of political, religious, and corporate luminaries, gathered on 1 October 1977 to dedicate the completed memorial, that goal appeared to have been achieved. The stonemason had carved on the cenotaph the essence of the *Awa maru* story as the Japanese had come to understand it from Chihaya Masataka, Arima Yorichika, and Tōkō Takeko. That tale proclaimed the injustice of war, the irresponsibility of governments, and the need to resolve the mysteries and unfinished business that surrounded the ship. The Americans had illegally attacked and destroyed her. The Japanese government had betrayed her victims and their families by abandoning the right of indemnification. The bones of the hungry ghosts who had perished on board her awaited

The *Awa maru* memorial in Zōjōji Temple, Tokyo. *Author's photograph*

recovery and proper interment in their homeland. The victims of a long-ago tragedy continued to be victimized.[100]

More than two years after that day of dedication, on another auspicious date, 7 December 1979, NHK televised a ninety-minute documentary about the sinking of the *Awa maru*. The program differed from all previous Japanese television presentations about the tragedy in one fundamental respect: viewers heard from the former *Queenfish* skipper, now-retired Rear Adm. Charles Elliott Loughlin, an authoritative American account of what had happened on the night of 1 April 1945. Sitting in his Annapolis home, the white-haired, soft-spoken North Carolinian told his Japanese visitors the same story he had told Admiral Lockwood and his defense counsel in April 1945 and interviewers ever since: namely, that the sinking had been an error, caused by mishandling of warning messages and by fog that prevented closer inspection of the target. He had sunk the *Awa maru* believing that she was a warship. Further, if he had it to do all over again, under the same circumstances and conditions that he had faced on that fateful April night so long ago, he would do exactly what he had done then.

The old submariner's challenge to what by then had long since become a totally different Japanese understanding of how and why the *Awa maru* was sunk, fell on deaf ears. Public memory about the tragedy had crystallized, and the program's producers were unwilling to refute it. They retained the conceptual framework that all previous Japanese tellers of the *Awa maru* tale had used; the story remained one of unjust and still incompletely explained American actions and victimization of the Japanese. To give it emotional force, they filmed Mrs. Tōkō telling her own story. To heighten its mystery, they presented both Commander Chihaya's challenges to the American version of events and evidence that raised questions about his findings. Nonetheless, the program ended the *Awa maru* story with a moral that echoed the mantra chanted on so many previous occasions of war remembrance in Japan: "Never again!" Never again should the Japanese people let themselves be victimized in war.[101]

That was the essence of the *Awa maru* story as it existed in Japanese public memory. That it survived diplomatic efforts to extinguish it was due to the efforts of individuals who in various ways were victims of the Pacific War. Without Commander Chihaya, Arima Yorichika, and Mrs. Tōkō, the tale would have vanished or shrunk to the point of insignificance in Japan's collective memory of the past. That they succeeded in keeping it alive and making it relevant to the nation's experience as a whole, however, resulted from forces at work in postwar Japan that they did not control. The particulars of the *Awa maru* story resonated with overtones of a larger account of national victimization in the Pacific War, a version of the past that both Washington and Tokyo had fostered. In time, particularly when told by Shimoda Kantarō, it became an account of victims who transcended that tragedy—precisely as the Japanese people as a whole recovered from defeat. Still later, Mrs. Tōkō transformed it into a tale of ordinary citizens combining to protest their own government's unjustness and to honor the war dead. Those larger themes, so congruent with those of Japan's recent history, were what made the Japanese version of the *Awa maru* story so different from, and impenetrable by, its American counterpart.

Fixed though it was, the tale of the *Awa maru* tragedy in Japan was not yet over. Those who gathered to dedicate the *Awa maru* memorial on that October 1977 day in Tokyo knew that. Just as the autumn leaves on nearby trees reminded them of life's fleeting character, so too were their feelings of joy at seeing the monument completed tempered by sadness at its emptiness. The bones of their dead had not come home for interment. Many, if not most, of those present doubted that they ever would. Nonetheless, one man in that crowd thought he could transform what seemed vain hope into reality. He would find the *Awa maru*, salvage the ship, bring home the remains of her hungry ghosts, and so set their spirits free. That man believed that he could fashion a triumphant last chapter to the *Awa maru* story.

But on that solemn autumn day, neither he nor anyone else present at the dedication of the *Awa maru* memorial could imagine just how stunning the end to the tale would be.

10

Salvage: "No More Than a Pipe Dream"

MINORU FUKUMITSU was an anomaly in the crowd that gathered to dedicate the *Awa maru* memorial. A Japanese-American in a sea of Japanese, a non-victim surrounded by those victimized by the sinking of the ship, he, unlike almost everyone else present, believed that the bones of the *Awa maru* dead might soon be repatriated. Only a few days before the ceremony he had written the first of what would become many letters to Chinese Vice Premier Deng Xiaoping seeking permission to salvage the *Awa maru*.[1] That had been an act so direct, so bold that most Japanese would have thought it rude; but it was characteristic of this enigmatic "man of many dreams."[2] One of those dreams was to find and salvage the *Awa maru*. By October 1977 Fukumitsu had begun to suspect that the only way it could come true was to act in collaboration with the Americans—indeed with some of the very men who had sunk the ship.

That was not a plan of action that most of those who gathered to dedicate the memorial at Zōjōji would have embraced, nor was it a scheme destined to yield success. In fact, just as the Japanese mourners completed their monument, Chinese salvagers ended their first season of searching for the hulk of the *Awa maru*. Less than two years later, the Chinese would proclaim to the world that they had found the ship and the remains of her hungry ghosts.[3]

The Chinese discovery made Fukumitsu's vision of the future "no more than a pipe dream."[4] It shattered the hopes of Americans who had hoped to find and profit greatly from the hulk of the *Awa maru*. Also, it precluded what might have been a very different ending to the *Awa maru* story: Japanese-American collaboration in raising the ship from the bottom of the sea and returning the remains of those killed in error to their proper resting place.

Who or what frustrated the Japanese-American joint salvage of the *Awa maru*, which could have exorcised her hungry ghosts and helped heal the wounds of war?

Twenty-eight years before the dedication of the *Awa maru* monument in Tokyo, a bitter exchange took place in a Yokohama military courtroom. Hundreds of designated class B and C war criminals were on trial there for having committed or sanctioned atrocities against American and Allied prisoners during the Pacific War.[5] As the proceedings began, the defense objected: American occupation authorities had no moral right to try Japanese for allegedly illegal actions during the war. How could they, when Americans had committed one of history's most egregious violations of international law—sinking the *Awa maru?*

That question touched off a debate over whether or not the ship had lost her guarantee of safe passage by carrying contraband cargo. In an effort to sustain that argument, the prosecution tried to obtain a copy of the *Awa maru*'s manifest. Former Imperial Japanese Navy sources claimed to be unable to find one, but Imperial Japanese Army officers who had been in Singapore in March 1945 eventually produced a four-page list that included thousands of tons of valuable minerals and industrial raw materials.[6]

When the proceedings resumed, former Capt. Hidaka Shinsaku, who had headed the navy's Chō [Tides] intelligence organization in Malaya and Singapore in 1945, laid the immediate issue to rest. Once a politically well-connected rising star in the naval intelligence establishment, he, like his brother-in-law, the purged veteran politician Kōno Ichirō, was now a man without a profession. Hidaka confirmed that raw rubber, tin ingots, and tungsten had been loaded aboard the *Awa maru*. The trial proceeded without further challenge to the moral authority of those who had convened it.[7]

But Hidaka, perhaps to counterbalance testimony that helped seal the fate of his countrymen on trial, also planted one of the most important seeds of discord among Japanese and Americans who would later try to find and salvage the *Awa maru*. He said that three additional safes had been installed on the ship to carry valuables taken from Imperial Military Headquarters in Singapore—British and American currency, industrial diamonds, and gold and other precious metals—back to Japan.[8] The *Awa maru* was thus a treasure ship as well as the embodiment of tragic error in the Pacific submarine war. He who found her would become a hero—and a very wealthy man.

Minoru Fukumitsu heard Hidaka's story firsthand, and what the former navy captain said changed his life. War had long since dramatically disrupted it. Fukumitsu had been born in Utah in 1913 as one of two sons of an immigrant railroad worker. Like many Japanese-Americans of his generation, he had returned to Japan for education, completing a course of study at the Tottori Higher Agricultural School. The life of a farmer held little appeal for him, however, and he recrossed the Pacific and went to Salt Lake City, where he entered the University of Utah. Fukumitsu graduated there in June 1941, only a few months before the outbreak of war forced a choice upon him that he could not have imagined before Pearl Harbor. His parents had returned to their ancestral home in Hiroshima—but Fukumitsu "fought" for America. Fukumitsu began teaching Japanese to American soldiers at Fort Layton, near Salt Lake City, and went on to become an instructor at the Navy Japanese Language School at the University of Colorado.[9]

But as the fighting continued, Fukumitsu apparently came to feel more and more ambivalent about the choice he had made. He never suffered the hardships of internment, but (if his later testimony is to be believed) he did see himself as a member of an ethnic group that had suffered monumental injustice at U.S. government hands.[10] In 1944 Fukumitsu left Boulder for New York City, where he took courses in international law at New York University. As the war neared its end, he must have feared more and more for the lives of his parents. They managed somehow to survive the atomic bombing of Hiroshima, but concern for them, anger over that attack, or perhaps just the realization that his language skills were highly marketable prompted Fukumitsu to return to Japan. There he took a most unusual job. The Japanese-American became a staff researcher for the defense in the Yokohama War Crimes Tribunal.[11]

What Fukumitsu heard from Captain Hidaka while serving in that capacity inspired his search for the wreck of the *Awa maru*. When the Yokohama war crimes trials ended he decided to stay on in Japan, ostensibly as an international businessman. Probably as a consequence of his involvement in the defense of former Japanese military men, Fukumitsu fell in with strong nationalists who sought to undo at least part of the humiliation of defeat and occupation by recovering "treasures" lost during the war. In 1953 Fukumitsu left Japan for the Philippines to become president of the Kirin Beer subsidiary there. In fact, however, he devoted his energies to searching for the valuables that Gen. Yamashita Tomoyuki, the last Imperial Japanese Army occupation force commander, had supposedly buried there.[12] In 1955 he participated for the first time in a Japanese effort to find and salvage the *Awa maru*.[13] Twenty-one years and five such attempts later, Fukumitsu was recognized as the most persistent pursuer and would-be salvager of the hapless ship.[14]

That was ironic for, in reality, he participated only occasionally in Japan-based efforts to find the *Awa maru*. He had nothing to do with the first such attempt, a tiny operation mounted from Chiba, on the eastern shore of Tokyo Bay. It ran on again, off again, for a year and half, beginning in 1950. Its organizers found nothing because they presumed that the *Awa maru* had been sunk off the coast of Taiwan rather than near the Chinese mainland.[15]

The second effort was spearheaded by Kataoka Kyūhachi, vice president of the Chūgai Metals Corporation. He wanted to recover the tin and other industrial metals listed on the *Awa maru*'s manifest. Kataoka correctly assumed that the sinking had occurred off the Chinese coast; in 1955 he engaged Fukumitsu to go to Hong Kong to talk with someone who claimed to have seen cargo boxes and raw rubber from the *Awa maru* wash ashore. In fact, however, the man had no real idea of where the ship had gone down, and so this second Japanese salvage attempt ended in failure.[16]

Fukumitsu did not play a role in the third such attempt, the principal figure of which was T'an Hsiang-po. T'an, of dual Japanese and Chinese nationality, was a prewar adventurer who had served as military and political adviser to Chinese warlords in the late 1920s and early 1930s. He had maintained ties to Chinese Nationalist generals after they and their master, Chiang Kai-shek, fled the mainland for Taiwan in 1949. In 1957, after negotiating a twenty-page salvage agreement that detailed how whatever might be found on board the *Awa maru* would be shared by the Chinese and Japanese, he brought a Chinese Nationalist general to Tokyo to see Yoshida Shigeru. T'an hoped the former prime minister would endorse the endeavor, but whether he did or not remains unknown.

In 1958 a small vessel with thirty-three divers on board headed for what T'an and his Chinese Nationalist collaborators presumed was the site of the sinking, a spot north and east of the Nationalist-held Quemoy Island. Unfortunately, they arrived just in time to get caught in the cross fire of Nationalist and Communist artillery barrages during the Taiwan Straits crisis of that year. Undeterred by that misfortune but cursed by misinformation as to just where the ship had gone down, T'an made two more unsuccessful attempts over the next three years to find the *Awa maru*.[17]

Minoru Fukumitsu almost certainly played a behind-the-scenes role in the next Japanese attempt to locate and salvage the ship, which took shape in 1960. During the first post-occupation years he became acquainted with, and may even have accepted employment from, the project's sponsor, Sasakawa Ryōichi. None of the would-be Japanese salvagers of the *Awa maru* were more forthright of purpose or elusive in action than this billionaire entrepreneur and political fixer. He had no need for the wealth that might be found on board the hulk. Born the heir to a brewery fortune, he had seen its value shrink during the war and shrivel still further during the rampant inflation of the early postwar years. By the late 1950s, when he began his quest for the *Awa maru*, however, Sasakawa had more than recovered from that loss; control over government-sanctioned gambling on motorboat racing brought him yen in the billions.[18]

Sasakawa wanted to salvage the doomed ship for patriotic and personal, not economic, reasons. He had always been an arch-patriot. In his youth he had trained as an Imperial Japanese Army pilot until an accident cut short his military career. Undaunted, he plunged into politics in the 1930s. He founded *Kokubō* [National Defense] magazine, formed the People's National Essence Party, and promoted the development of Japanese civil aviation. Sasakawa's passionately nationalistic political activities landed him in jail for two years during the middle of that decade, but by its end he had emerged as a "friend" of the renowned Adm. Yamamoto Isoroku. The admiral made him an unofficial emissary to Southeast Asia, and in 1941 he traveled on the pioneering flight of the *Yamato* aircraft to Rome, where he met Mussolini. Elected to the Diet in 1942, Sasakawa maintained his connections with Japanese naval intelligence. During the war he traveled to China and Korea, supposedly as a mining and drilling entrepreneur but probably in the service of the Imperial Japanese Navy.[19]

Japan's defeat made Sasakawa a defiant war victim and unrepentant patriot. American bombs destroyed his Tokyo home. Many of his friends perished in the war—some of them on board the *Awa maru*. He himself was arrested and charged as a class A war criminal in December 1945. Thumbing his nose at American occupation authorities, he marched to Sugamo Prison accompanied by a brass band. While there, he wrote General MacArthur to insist that Japan's war had been a defensive one. Three years later, just like Arima Yorichika's father, he was released without ever having been tried.[20]

Sasakawa returned to civilian life with two important goals. One, inspired by *Life* magazine pictures he had seen while imprisoned, was to recoup his fortune by making motorboat racing a government-sanctioned gambling industry. The other was to redeem the honor, recover the remains, and perpetuate the memory of his countrymen who had fought and died in the Pacific War. He pursued the two simultaneously. In 1949, while American Occupation authorities were still doing everything possible to discredit the Japanese military, Sasakawa formed the Shiragiku [White Chrysanthemum] Society, an association of families bereaved by the war; it derived its name from the flower that appeared on the imperial family's crest.[21] Over the next decade he amassed funds to build a huge globe capped with a pagoda-like spire at Ibaraki, his family's ancestral home near Ōsaka. While it purported to be a monument to all who had lost their lives in World War II, this was actually a memorial to Japan's war dead.[22] That was where Sasakawa intended to inter the remains of his friends who had perished along with the *Awa maru*.[23]

In May 1960, at a moment of great crisis in Japanese-American relations, Sasakawa flew to Taipei. A debate was heating up over ratification of a revised U.S.–Japan Security Treaty; it would culminate in riots, cancellation of President Dwight D. Eisenhower's planned visit to Japan, and Prime Minister Kishi Nobusuke's resignation.[24] But Sasakawa, now the head of his own marine enterprises firm, had his eyes fixed on a past wrong rather than the present danger. He hoped to learn from Chinese Nationalist would-be *Awa maru* salvagers and co-opt them into his own effort to find the ship.

Sasakawa spoke with two men in Taipei who claimed to own salvage rights to the *Awa maru*. They insisted she lay on the sea bottom about twenty-five nautical miles northeast of Amoy Bay. The Japanese entrepreneur, who apparently relied upon Commander Chihaya's previously published work, doubted that that was the site of the sinking. He also questioned his Chinese hosts' technological capabilities, even as he insisted that, with his expertise, the ship could be found within six months to a year. When he returned home, Sasakawa confidently proclaimed to reporters, "The *Awa maru* is being salvaged!"[25] For reasons that remain unclear, however, the ebullient patriot-entrepreneur did nothing.

While he was quiescent, the Itō Chū Trading Corporation launched a fourth Japanese effort to find and salvage the *Awa maru*. The firm's leader, Seshima Ryūzō, had personal and patriotic reasons for doing so. He was the archetypical former Imperial Japanese Army officer turned entrepreneur. A brilliant staff officer, he had fought at Guadalcanal and had planned the withdrawal of army troops from that island. Transferred to Manchuria, he was captured there in the closing days of the war. Seshima then endured more than a decade of imprisonment and hard labor in Siberia before being repatriated when Tokyo and Moscow restored diplomatic relations in 1956. Over the next ten years, he devoted his intellect, leadership skills, and personal drive to reviving the fortunes of Itō Chū.[26] The achievements of this war victim triumphant were so great as to make him the hero of a novel and a nationally broadcast television series.[27]

Seshima deputized another military man-turned-corporate-bureaucrat, Kobayashi Ichizō, to find answers to three key questions about the *Awa maru*. Where, exactly, did the ship lie? What had really been loaded aboard her? Would salvaging her be technologically and economically feasible?[28] Kobayashi, not Fukumitsu, became the first Japan-based salvager to seek American help. In 1965 he had Itō Chū's New York City representative contact now-retired Ambassador William Sebald. Sebald, who had served as ambassador to Burma and Australia after leaving Japan, was then living in Washington, D.C. Visiting Sebald at his home, the Itō Chū agent said his Tokyo superiors hoped to salvage the *Awa maru*. Might the ambassador be able to help them in determining just where the ship had been sunk? Suspecting that the Japanese firm simply wanted to profit from her purportedly valuable cargo, Sebald asked the visitor his employer's reasons. The man replied that Itō Chū was simply trying to recover remains of the dead.

That drew an understanding nod from Ambassador Sebald. He picked up the telephone, called the Naval Historical Center at the Washington Navy Yard, and asked experts there to confirm where the *Queenfish* had sunk the *Awa maru*. About three hours later, much to his surprise, someone from the center called back with the coordinates for the site of the tragedy as recorded in the *Queenfish*'s deck log. Sebald then passed that information on to Itō Chū's man in New York City.[29]

Sebald thought that would be the end of the matter, for the reported sinking site was within waters that China, then anything but friendly toward Japan, claimed as its own.[30] Still, Kobayashi Ichizō was not deterred. He mounted a massive investigation of the engineering aspects, costs and possible benefits, and international legal ramifications of a salvage attempt. He dispatched interviewers to quiz thirty-six former military men who had been in Singapore in March 1945 about what had been loaded onto the *Awa maru*. He may have sought out Minoru Fukumitsu, and he definitely contacted leaders of the recently formed *Awa maru* Bereaved Families Association, among them Mrs. Tōkō. She pleaded for recovery of the human remains still on the ship as a matter of national honor, arguing that the prospective value of the cargo recovered would more than cover the costs of the salvage endeavor.[31]

What Kobayashi learned from these sources and from his own subordinates convinced him that salvaging the *Awa maru* was physically possible and commercially feasible. Divers reported that if the ship lay at a depth of no more than fifty meters (approximately 170 feet), she could readily be salvaged. Economists estimated that the current value of the tin ingots known to be in her holds would, quite apart from the other booty military informants claimed had been carried on board her, make salvaging the *Awa maru* profitable.[32]

Notwithstanding these encouraging reports, however, Seshima Ryūzō concluded that the political and diplomatic obstacles attending any salvage attempt were too great to be overcome. Tokyo as yet had neither a peace treaty nor formal diplomatic relations with Beijing; even if both had been in place, the Cultural Revolution was beginning its devastating sweep across the Chinese political landscape. What chance was there that Chairman Mao Tse-tung, whose xenophobic minions were attacking everything foreign, would allow a Japanese corporation—especially one that was helping Japan make billions of dollars annually by supporting the American war effort against China's ally in Vietnam—conduct salvage operations on China's doorstep? Itō Chū thus shelved its *Awa maru* salvage project.[33]

That left the field open for Sasakawa Ryōichi, working through Fukumitsu, to revive Japanese efforts to find the ship. By the early 1970s the entrepreneur had a new motive for doing so. While he still wanted to recover the remains of the dead and scoop up the wealth allegedly stowed away on the ship, he was also determined to demonstrate Japan's maritime technological prowess. Sasakawa had already called attention to the possibilities of underwater resource development by donning, at age seventy-one, a wet suit and Aqua-Lung, swimming down to an underwater habitat, and posing for photographers while telephoning Prime Minister Satō Eisaku.[34] Also, as president of the Japan Shipbuilding Industry Foundation, he had committed millions of dollars to the construction of a ship-shaped marine science museum in Tokyo Bay.[35] Using new underwater technologies to recover the remains of the hungry ghosts and the purported treasure trove on board the *Awa maru* would be one more way of demonstrating Japan's remarkable recovery from defeat in the Pacific War.

Sasakawa's money probably financed Fukumitsu's 1972 journey to the United States. The Japanese-American, who by that time had formed his own consulting firm, had induced the *Awa maru* Bereaved Families Association to sanction his effort to learn from American sources precisely where the ship had been sunk—information vital for any salvage endeavor.[36] Fukumitsu obtained access to only some of the documents he wanted. While in Washington, D.C., he read the diplomatic correspondence concerning the voyage of the *Awa maru*, poured over the *Queenfish*'s deck log and war patrol reports, and copied the submariners' official report on the sinking; he did not, however, gain access to Elliott Loughlin's court-martial record.[37] In an effort to compensate for that failure, he traveled to nearby Annapolis, Maryland, where he met the former skipper of the *Queenfish*, now director of the U.S. Naval Academy Foundation, at his home.[38]

Their interview, according to Loughlin, went quite well. The Japanese-American came presupposing that the *Queenfish* had deliberately sunk a ship her officers knew was the *Awa maru*. After hearing Loughlin's account of the sinking, which portrayed the tragedy as a product of accidental error rather than deliberate policy, Fukumitsu softened his views. He enlisted Loughlin's sympathy for the bereaved families, eliciting expressions of surprise that they had received so little and of hope for their appropriate indemnification. By the time their conversation drew to a close, the former *Queenfish* skipper "really became pretty good friends" with the man who had come to investigate the biggest blunder of his naval career.[39]

Fukumitsu then traveled to Sacramento, California, where he looked up retired Capt. John E. Bennett. The *Queenfish* navigator of 1945 had by that time become Governor Ronald Reagan's director of the California State Office of Navigation and Ocean Development. Bennett provided graphic details of the sinking of the *Awa maru* and the rescue of Shimoda Kantarō. He held the safe-passage agreement's drafters partially responsible for the sinking because they had not specified that the Japanese ship must sound her horn when traveling through heavy fog. He cast doubt on the sole survivor's account of the sinking and rescue. Further, like his former skipper, Bennett condemned the Japanese government for paying so little to those bereaved by the events of 1 April 1945.[40]

But the former navigator of the *Queenfish* suspected that his visitor was after much more than historical truth or endorsement of a cause; the Japanese-American was, in Bennett's view, first and foremost a treasure hunter. So he declined to tell him that he now believed the officially recorded sinking site was in error, based as it had been on a series of dead-reckoning plots rather than more accurate daily sun shots taken with a sextant.[41]

Fukumitsu, however, returned to Japan convinced that he had the information needed to find and salvage the *Awa maru* and to achieve a reconciliation of sorts between her victims and their victimizers. He sold his version of the ship's story to the Yomiuri shimbunsha, a firm that published Japan's largest circulating newspaper and was a prime investor in deep-sea research and development technology.[42] In August 1973 the firm published *The Awa maru Incident* and promoted Fukumitsu's book through an article in its popular weekly magazine.[43]

The book advanced three basic arguments for trying to find and salvage the ill-fated ship. The first was simple: profit. Fukumitsu repeated what Hidaka Shinsaku had said at the Yokohama war crimes trials about the secret loading of valuables aboard the ship. Former Gen. Inada Seijun, who had had direct responsibility for loading her, confirmed for him that the navy officer had used "pirates" to put secret cargo in her special safes. Fukumitsu suggested that if in fact the *Awa maru* lay on the bottom of the Taiwan Strait in international waters, her precious cargo, if recovered by the Japanese, would belong to Japan.[44]

Fukumitsu's second reason for finding and salvaging the *Awa maru* was to discover the truth about how she had been sunk. The evidence he brought back from America convinced him that Commander Chihaya had erred in implying that the sinking was deliberate. He also doubted the theory that self-destructive devices installed by the Japanese army had destroyed the ship, for they had been removed before she began her voyage home. The Americans, he argued, had much more to lose (international prestige and continued provision of relief to the prisoners) than whatever they might gain (destruction of an insignificant amount of contraband) by deliberately sinking the *Awa maru*. They could have tried to cover up the disaster by hiding away the sole survivor, Shimoda Kantarō, but instead they had admitted what had occurred and offered Japan a replacement vessel. America's behavior, in short, was not consistent with that of a nation determined to destroy the *Awa maru*. Salvaging the ship would prove that American torpedoes had sunk her by mistake.[45]

Fukumitsu's third argument for finding and raising the ship was the most compelling: justice could, at long last, be done. He held the Japanese government partly responsible for the heavy loss of life on the night of 1 April 1945. Their awareness of the Japanese submarine force commander's earlier order not to make heroic efforts to save enemy personnel had reduced the willingness of the *Queenfish* crewmen to brave darkness and rising seas in an effort to rescue more *Awa maru* victims. Fukumitsu also blamed the Japanese government, far more than the American, for the shabby treatment of bereaved families. The enormity of their loss was undeniable, as he demonstrated by publishing, for the first time, a list of those known to have perished with the *Awa maru*. Nonetheless, while Americans provided at least some solace and clues as to their fate by opening documents pertinent to the sinking, Tokyo officials had spurned his (and the bereaved families') requests for access to information in Japanese archives about the tragedy. Japanese politicians and bureaucrats had also turned a deaf ear to the bereaved's request for additional compensation, even though those spearheading their efforts to obtain it were themselves former high-ranking diplomats and members of the House of Peers. Fukumitsu concluded that salvaging the *Awa maru* so as to bring home the remains of her hungry ghosts would at least provide spiritual comfort to families long mistreated by their own government.[46]

Despite the clarity of its arguments, Fukumitsu's book failed in its immediate purposes. What the Japanese-American wrote in defense of the *Queenfish* and her crew made no impression upon his Japanese readers. No document or testimony from the far side of the Pacific, coming long after the *Awa maru* story had crystallized in Japan into a tale of sheer victimization, was likely to alter public memory of the sinking. Fukumitsu's dream of being at the center of any Japanese expedition to recover the remains of the *Awa maru* dead was also unrealistic. No Japanese government of the early 1970s would have entrusted to a Japanese-American the sensitive task of retrieving and returning the remains of war dead from Chinese waters. Even though Prime Minister Tanaka Kakuei made a pilgrimage to Beijing just after President Richard Nixon's visit there in 1972, Japan lacked the formal diplomatic relations and broad informal contacts needed to gain China's approval for salvage operations in, or very near, Chinese waters.[47]

Nevertheless, Fukumitsu kept on trying to salvage the *Awa maru*. Still an American citizen, he went to Honolulu, incorporated the (American) International Salvage Corporation, and peppered government officials with requests for recognition and assistance. In April 1976, for example, Fukumitsu informed the Chinese ambassador in Washington that his firm would soon be commencing salvage operations in the Taiwan Strait near the China coast. At the same time he wrote Secretary of State Henry Kissinger expressing hope that "necessary arrangements" for the security of his salvage expedition operating in the "troubled international waters" of the Taiwan Strait could be made.[48] No evidence exists to indicate that Kissinger did anything in response to that vague request for American naval protection. Minoru Fukumitsu had not been a complete failure, however. He gave the *Awa maru* story new life when it might otherwise have faded in Japanese public memory; he may also have prompted (or possibly even have helped) the man who headed the sixth Japanese salvage effort—the only one to search at or near the right place—to seek American help in locating the hulk of the unlucky ship.

That individual was Funada Naka, one of the most durable and respected figures on the postwar Japanese political scene. Like Sasakawa Ryōichi, he had led a riches-to-rags-to-riches life. In his youth he did all the right things to arrive in the corridors of political power. He graduated from Tokyo Imperial University, married the daughter of a cabinet minister and privy councilor, and acquired a brother-in-law who became a lieutenant general. Before his election to the Diet in 1930 he served as secretary to a cabinet, deputy mayor of Tokyo, and personal secretary to a prime minister. Funada went on to become parliamentary councilor to the Foreign Ministry and chief of the Cabinet Legislation Bureau in the first Konoye cabinet (1937–1939). During the war he served on the Central Cooperative Council of the Imperial Rule Assistance Association.[49]

That work guaranteed that he would be purged from political life during the first years of American military occupation. Nonetheless, Funada, like so many other politicians of his generation, arose phoenix-like from that humiliation to positions of power and honor. By 1955 he had become a leading figure in the newly formed Liberal Democratic Party. Over the next twenty-two years he moved up from service as chief of the fledgling Defense Agency through chairmanship of his party's Foreign Affairs Committee and the speakership of the lower house of the Diet to the vice presidency of the party.[50] As he regained power, Funada shed whatever bitterness he may once have felt toward the United States. By the early 1970s, when he began his search for the *Awa maru*, Funada was regarded as a friend of America, a staunch supporter of the U.S.–Japan Security Treaty, and a promoter of cooperation between the U.S. Navy and the Japanese Maritime Self-Defense Force.[51]

Funada thus had a strong interest in laying to rest the ghost of a war that had once made Japanese and Americans bitter enemies. That may be why, in

Funada Naka. *Funada Hajime*

1971, he became president of the *Kaiyō senbotsusha shūyō kai* (Association for the Recovery of Those Who Died in the War at Sea). That organization was one of many veterans and patriotic groups that sprang up in the late 1960s and early 1970s to support and supplement official efforts to recover the remains of the war dead. Funada's group eventually acquired an experienced salvager as its director and purchased a three-hundred-ton salvage vessel, the *Aotaka maru*. During the early 1970s, that ship secretly shuttled high-ranking Japanese political and military figures to Taiwan. The association's managing director, who was also Funada's private secretary, insisted that these voyages were simply "scholarly exchanges"; they may in fact have provided the occasion for discussing a joint effort by Tokyo and Taipei to find and salvage the *Awa maru*.[52]

The fierce internecine struggles after 1972 within the Liberal Democratic Party over Sino-Japanese relations, however, made it unwise for Funada to tilt too openly toward Taipei.[53] He publicly denied any involvement with the association for the recovery of war dead, its finances, or with the *Awa maru*

Bereaved Families Association.[54] Nonetheless, as the 1970s unfolded, Funada was drawn, perhaps by the argument implicit in Fukumitsu's book, to a strategy of cooperation with the Americans in trying to find and salvage the ship. Funada may well have been the ultimate source of a request for information about her reported sinking site that was received by the Naval Historical Center in Washington on 26 June 1975. Officials there recorded receiving an inquiry "from the Japanese government." Just as they had ten years earlier for William Sebald, so now they gave that official requester the coordinates for the spot where the *Queenfish* had reported sinking the *Awa maru*.[55]

That information provided Funada's group with the information needed to commence salvage operations. More than a year passed, however, before the *Aotaka maru*, on 30 July 1976, slipped out of Mito harbor in Shizuoka Prefecture. Laden with divers and salvage equipment, she was bound for Keelung, the Taiwanese port closest to the purported *Awa maru* sinking site. The secrecy that enshrouded her on this and two subsequent voyages later in 1976 was highly unusual for vessels seeking to find and return the remains of Japanese war dead from the sea. Efforts made to preserve that secrecy prompted speculation in Tokyo that Funada and his associates were in fact searching for the *Awa maru*. Indeed, they were, and they nearly succeeded in the attempt. The *Aotaka maru* approached the site of the star-crossed ship's sinking as reported by the Americans, only to be driven away by the Chinese.[56]

Had he been thinking of the broader terms of the U.S.–Japan security relationship, Funada might, like Fukumitsu, have sought some form of American naval protection for his *Awa maru* salvage endeavor; but other developments in 1976 made him and all of the other Japan-based pursuers of the ship and her gold mine reject genuine collaboration with the Americans. The United States and Japan were beginning to look at each other as competitors as well as allies. Both nations were bidding for access to China's resources and markets as they sought to restore full diplomatic relations with Beijing.[57] In November 1976, wire services reported that an American group based in San Diego, California, was trying to obtain permission from China to salvage the *Awa maru*.[58] That news shattered whatever immediate prospects there may have been for Japanese-American collaboration in finding the ship and recovering what remained on board her.

It also sent the Japanese media scurrying for more information about those suddenly unmasked as competitors in what now looked like a race to reach the *Awa maru*. In an effort to learn more, the *Tokyo shimbun* offered the American group's leader a free ticket to Japan—only to have him decline.[59] *Yomiuri shimbun* editors ordered their Los Angeles bureau chief to contact the men mentioned in the initial report; when he did so, they represented themselves as private entrepreneurs sensitive to Japanese concerns about recovering the remains of the dead.[60] A *Yomiuri* reporter contacted Chihaya Masataka, however, and found he doubted that story. The former navy commander thought the San Diego group might be a front for an official U.S. government attempt to find and salvage the *Awa maru*.

Chihaya's surmise was almost, but not quite, true.[61] The American group, while private in form, was indeed a stepchild of the U.S. Navy. Its leader was a former navy civilian employee, and its most prominent members were all navy veterans. They would be using navy-developed technologies in their search for the *Awa maru*. Whether or not they could begin it depended upon the success of Washington's efforts to reestablish full diplomatic and commercial relations with the People's Republic of China.

The man who spearheaded the American group was William J. Bunton, a seasoned professional diver who had devoted the best years of his career to working for the U.S. Navy. Thirty-two years old in 1976, this imaginative, technically skilled, and ambitious individual had come a long way from his working-class childhood in Detroit. As he grew into a lithe young man, Bunton had developed a passion for aquatic sports. In 1950, at age seventeen, he left home to join the army. That took him to Korea, where, as a member of the 187th Regimental Combat Team, he thrived on the dangerous job of landing behind enemy lines. Discharged in 1952, Bunton then went to California, where he became a professional deep-sea diver. There he married and fathered five children, which gave him a strong economic incentive to excel in his chosen field.[62]

Bunton's connection with the navy began in 1960, when he became a support diver for the bathyscaph *Trieste* during its exploration of the deep-sea trench off Guam. Exploiting that connection, he had posed in full wet suit and scuba-diving gear as an "underwater research specialist" in a 1963 Camel cigarette advertisement. Drawn into the navy's Deep Sea Submergence Project, in 1965 he became a civilian supervisor at the Naval Undersea

Warfare Center in San Diego—the position from which he volunteered to participate in the navy's SEALAB II "man-in-the-sea" experiment. Bunton remained fully committed to that program until 1969, when he left naval employment and became a consulting master diver for offshore oil development firms.[63]

Bunton's *Awa maru* salvage group originated in the SEALAB II project. SEALAB, the navy's deep-sea underwater experimental program, was itself a by-product of "history's worst submarine disaster," the loss of the nuclear submarine *Thresher* (SSN 593) with all hands in April 1963. To explain that tragedy and prevent more like it, navy officials created what became the Deep Submergence Systems Project within the office of the CNO. Championed by Rear Adm. Hyman Rickover, the controversial father of the nuclear navy, this effort commanded millions of dollars for the creation of a nuclear-powered deep-sea submarine recovery vehicle, the study of the ocean floor, the development of instruments to recover from the depths small items of high intelligence value (such as Soviet missile nose cones), and the creation of a deep-sea habitat (SEALAB) from which divers could work.[64]

SEALAB II, established off the southern California coast near San Diego in the early fall of 1965, tested what came to be known as saturation-diving techniques, in which men worked out of an underwater habitat that was pressurized to the depth at which it was situated. That enabled them to work at great depths and later return to the surface after a relatively brief decompression based on depth, rather than length of time underwater.[65] The experiment brought Bill Bunton into close contact with the men who, eleven years later, emerged as his principal collaborators in the American *Awa maru* salvage effort. Captain Bennett served as a sub-project director in the Deep Sea Systems Project in Washington; in 1968 he became commander, Submarine Squadron 3, based in San Diego, with responsibility for the SEALAB submersible.[66] Astronaut-turned-aquanaut M. Scott Carpenter, later political liaison man for Bunton's salvage group, garnered publicity for SEALAB II by remaining in the submersible longer than anyone else and speaking from it to an astronaut then circling the globe.[67]

SEALAB II also introduced Bunton to Dr. George W. Bond, father of the saturation-diving techniques he wanted to use in salvaging the *Awa maru*, and his sometime deputy, the project's physiological control officer, Capt.

William J. Bunton, would-
be salvager of the *Awa
maru. R.J.R. Nabisco*

Walter F. Mazzone.[68] It was through SEALAB as well that Bunton met Bob
Barth, a navy master diver who became a valuable consultant in developing
plans to recover the riches supposedly housed on the sunken Japanese ship.[69]

How did Bill Bunton find out about that treasure? Some of his associates
believe he first heard of the *Awa maru* in the SEALAB II underwater habitat. He and others would while away their long hours of confinement by discussing the future of deep-sea exploration. They speculated that ships sunk
at depths previously thought too great to be reached might now be located
and salvaged. Someone, perhaps Captain Mazzone, who as a lieutenant on
board the *Crevalle* (SS 291) had shadowed her on the night before she was
destroyed, mentioned the *Awa maru*.[70] He and Scott Carpenter, in "Mickey
Mouse" voices made high by prolonged breathing of saturated oxygen, had
a vigorous conversation about the Japanese ship.[71] Words failed to produce
action, however; Bunton and the others were too busy with their SEALAB
duties to follow up on what had been said.

Bunton himself remembers San Diego businessman Robert Briggs as the source of the "*Awa maru* bug" that bit him so hard. His hydroproducts firm had built and marketed an underwater camera that Bunton had designed. The business relationship blossomed into friendship, and one evening over dinner Briggs sought Bunton's help in assessing a proposition put to him during a recent trip to Taiwan. There, men associated with the same group of would-be *Awa maru* salvagers that Sasakawa Ryōichi had met wanted to use Briggs's underwater searching equipment. They offered to pay him 20 percent of their third of the profits from a joint venture between business and the Chinese Nationalist government to salvage the Japanese ship. They estimated her cargo was worth 5 billion dollars and believed she had been sunk about thirty to fifty nautical miles west of Taichung, a port city roughly halfway down the west coast of Taiwan.[72]

Briggs asked Bunton for help in verifying what the Chinese said about the sinking of the *Awa maru*; the diver, who often traveled to Washington, D.C., in connection with the man-in-the-sea project, said he would do what he could. In 1966 Bunton went to the Classified Operational Archives at the Washington Navy Yard, where he calculated the sinking site coordinates from the *Queenfish*'s deck log. His estimate put the site barely ten miles away from Communist territory—far north of where the Taiwan-based would-be salvagers claimed the ship lay. When Bunton told Briggs what he had found, what might have become a Taiwanese-American joint effort to salvage the *Awa maru* died.[73]

Seven years later, however, Bunton stood ready to lead an exclusively American attempt. In 1971, while working for a firm run by fellow diver and former navy frogman Jon Lindbergh (the son of aviation pioneer Charles and author Anne Morrow Lindbergh), Bunton went to Japan. There he worked for two months on an Inland Sea drilling rig owned by a subsidiary of the Yomiuri shimbunsha.[74] It was probably at this time that he acquired an original copy of the *Awa maru*'s plans. Those drawings indicated just where divers might find her reportedly laden holds and special safes.[75]

In 1972 and 1973 the prospective value of that information rose sharply. The value of the tin known to have been loaded aboard the *Awa maru* began to climb sharply in international commodity markets;[76] in addition, Richard Nixon and Henry Kissinger were poking holes in the wall of Sino-American hostility that would have to be breached before any salvage operation could

begin. A year after Nixon went to China, Kissinger negotiated the truce that
ended America's war with China's client and ally, Vietnam. Shortly after that
he proposed, and Chinese Premier Chou En-lai agreed to, the opening of
official liaison offices in Beijing and Washington.[77] These developments
made Bill Bunton think the time had come to try to strike it rich by salvaging
the *Awa maru*.

To do so he needed cash, knowledgeable collaborators, and Chinese cooperation. Money remained a constant problem for Bunton because, unlike
Fukumitsu, he had no wealthy patrons. In January 1974 he retained an attorney, Donald Freeman, who became his first partner-investor in the salvage
venture.[78] He then looked east to Texas, home of the burgeoning offshore oil
drilling industry, where he tried unsuccessfully to interest a Houston bank in
the project. Undaunted, Bunton then approached Oceaneering Corporation,
a subsidiary of the prestigious and politically influential Brown and Root
construction firm. Oceaneering officials expressed interest in his plan to salvage the *Awa maru* but declined to fund it.[79] That meant Bunton had to
scrape together what he could from small investors in and around San
Diego; by August 1975 they had provided enough for him to incorporate
Salvage and Diving, Inc., the firm in whose name his efforts to salvage the
Awa maru would go forward.[80]

Bunton had much better luck in bringing together expert collaborators.
His sometime employer, Jon Lindbergh, who had helped develop the technology used to locate and recover Soviet missile nose cones from the depths
of the Pacific, was seeking a change of pace.[81] Former SEALAB colleagues
were open to new adventure. Scott Carpenter, retired from the navy and
serving as director of a pioneering waste recycling project in Los Angeles,
was willing to put his name and political skills to work on Bunton's behalf.[82]
Retired navy master diver Bob Barth, whose Florida Hydroquip Corporation served the needs of the growing gulf offshore drilling industry, signed
on, giving Bunton the benefit of his business connections and technological
know-how.[83]

Bunton's biggest coup, however, was drawing the retired captain Jack
Bennett to his side. The two men met through Robert Briggs.[84] Bunton knew
that Bennett, who was then liaison to private industry for the Scripps Institute of Oceanography in nearby La Jolla, could help pinpoint the site where

the *Awa maru* had been sunk. He also believed that Fukumitsu had tried to enlist Bennett's services for a Japanese attempt to salvage the ship. The former navy captain, who had become a shrewd businessman, contracted in June 1975 to serve as Bunton's technical adviser, but only for eighteen months.[85]

Bennett brought three strengths to the San Diego group's salvage efforts. One was his memory. He recalled that overcast skies on the days preceding the sinking had forced him as the navigator of the *Queenfish* to rely on dead-reckoning rather than celestial observations to determine the noon positions recorded in the submarine's deck log. He also remembered having had difficulties with the sub's gyrocompass. Those recollections cautioned against relying solely on official reports to determine where the *Awa maru* had been sunk.[86] Bennett also brought valuable official contacts that might be used to further the search for the ship. His friends in the Department of Defense Hydrographic Office had extremely sophisticated undersea mapping capabilities that might provide a more accurate indication than old official reports as to where the *Awa maru* lay on the bottom of the Taiwan Strait.[87] Bennett's third contribution was his friendship with other *Queenfish* officers and crewmen, among them Capt. Frank N. Shamer, the sub's prospective commanding officer in April 1945. Shamer, who had become a San Diego parochial school teacher after retirement, could provide a valuable double-check against the ebullient Bennett's memory.[88]

Getting Chinese approval to salvage the *Awa maru* proved a much more frustrating, expensive, and protracted task than Bill Bunton imagined. His early indirect attempts to gain a hearing in Beijing failed. A front organization that he set up in Hong Kong in 1974, the International Salvage and Diving Corporation, proved useless.[89] Efforts on his behalf by Sidney Weintraub, a second-level official in the American Liaison Office in Beijing, were no more effective.[90] So Bunton turned to Scott Carpenter, still a political operator of sorts. The former astronaut briefed George Bush, who had just been named to open the American Liaison Office in Beijing, on the diplomatic and commercial benefits that might flow from Sino-American cooperation in salvaging the *Awa maru*.[91] Carpenter also introduced Bunton to retired Ambassador Christopher Phillips, president of the newly formed National Council for U.S.–China Trade.[92] Salvage and Diving became one of its constituent firms, and Phillips set an aide to work lobbying the first Chinese diplomats resident in Washington on behalf of Bunton's scheme.[93]

For a brief time in the fall of 1974 this quasi-official approach showed signs of yielding success. Chinese diplomats in Washington were persuaded to come west to the Brentwood neighborhood of Los Angeles, since made famous by the O.J. Simpson case. There they met secretly with Bunton and a representative of the National Council for U.S.–China Trade at a secluded mansion that had once been home to Greta Garbo.[94] Bunton expounded on the merits of his salvage plan, and his listeners arranged for the idea to go before the China Council for Promotion of International Trade. Barely sixty days later, however, word filtered back from Beijing to the effect that because his scheme was not really a trade project, it would require "proper government authority" before it could go forward.[95]

That rejection pushed Bunton into the arms of a man whom he later regarded as betrayer but who then seemed a savior. Harned Pettus Hoose was a professional go-between for Americans seeking to do business in China. In the fall of 1974 he seemed to Bunton to have all the qualifications needed to win Beijing's approval for the *Awa maru* salvage project. His ties to China ran deep, going back beyond the bitter civil war, through the years of Sino-American cooperation in the war against Japan, to the missionary endeavor earlier in the century. The scion of missionaries famous for their relief work in central China, Hoose had grown up in Beijing. In 1938, fluent in Chinese and already the author of a treatise on Chinese pigeons and pigeon-flutes, he returned to Los Angeles to attend the University of Southern California. Graduating just as World War II began, he joined the Naval Reserve and went back to China where, in time, he came to command a special naval intelligence unit behind Japanese lines. After the war ended, he returned to his alma mater for law school, joined a prestigious Los Angeles law firm, and dabbled in Republican politics.[96]

Hoose also had political connections, a growing professional reputation, and a personal flair that made him attractive to Bunton. He had established his own international trade and legal consulting firm but never completely dropped his ties to the American intelligence establishment. He claimed to have helped the National Security Council staff prepare for President Nixon's 1972 visit to Beijing. Hoose traveled with the first groups of American businessmen to go to China; revived contacts with old acquaintances there; and by late 1974 was advocating Sino-American collaboration in Southeast Asian development and aid programs. Hoose also sported a carefully waxed mustache that called attention to himself—the very thing Bunton needed someone to do on his behalf in Beijing.[97]

It took the former diver six months to make the old China hand his "man in Beijing." They first met in September 1974. Ninety days later, on a dark and rainy December night, Bunton drove to Tijuana, Mexico, with Hoose's agent, George H. White, who had experience in the oil business in Southeast Asia before the Pacific War and had been a prisoner of the Japanese during it, initialed an agreement that promised Hoose twenty-five thousand dollars for his help in securing Chinese approval for American *Awa maru* salvage operations. The two men then climbed into Bunton's father's car, borrowed for the evening, only to wreck it on their way back across the border. Ninety days later Bunton finalized with Hoose the terms of a consulting contract.[98]

The accident and the delay proved omens of difficult times to come in the Bunton-Hoose relationship. Over the course of the next year Hoose shuttled back and forth across the Pacific to and from China. He gained recognition as an expert on China's undeveloped energy resources; by the spring of 1976 he had become a policy gadfly, advocating Sino-American leadership in Pacific Asia.[99] Fleshing out his salvage scheme, Bunton put "A Confidential Report to the People's Republic of China: The Sinking and Proposed Salvage of the *Awa maru*" in Hoose's hands in June 1976 for delivery to Chinese leaders in Beijing.[100] The go-between looked it over but declined to press just then for its approval. With an eye to the political instability expected to follow Mao Tse-tung's impending death, he advised Bunton to be patient, revise the salvage proposal, and keep it secret.[101]

Although it galled him to wait, the diver accepted Hoose's advice. Delay, however, proved fatal, at least insofar as keeping his group's effort secret was concerned. For a time Bunton had managed it by pledging each of his collaborators to secrecy and taping his telephone conversations with them.[102] In November 1975 he stanched a leak by buying off Meinhard J. Lagies, an investigative reporter for the *San Diego Tribune* who had gotten wind of his activities and was preparing a news story about them. Bunton promised to make Lagies the official chronicler of what he hoped would be a salvage saga worthy of lucrative film, television, and book coverage. The journalist agreed to sit on the story.[103] However, in November 1976 Lagies's managing editor, for a mix of personal and professional reasons, forced the reporter to print what he knew about Bunton and his plans to salvage the *Awa maru*.[104] That shattered the secrecy Harned Hoose thought essential for the success of salvage negotiations in Beijing.

Angry and alarmed, Bunton tried to put a positive spin on the disclosure, which threatened to spell disaster for his efforts. He talked with reporters, gave them photographs of himself and his collaborators, and appeared on CBS television news.[105] In these interviews Bunton spoke expansively about the *Awa maru* fortune. Her manifests, he said, indicated that definitely 25 million dollars', and probably 241 million dollars', worth of minerals rested in her holds. The total value of what could be recovered from her might reach 5 billion dollars.[106] Schooled in circumspection by Harned Hoose, Bunton disclaimed responsibility for the disclosure of his efforts to secure Beijing's permission for a salvage expedition. He said he was willing to tell the Chinese what he knew so that they could act alone or jointly with his group.[107] The diver-turned-salvage entrepreneur also tried to assuage what he felt might be wounded Japanese sensibilities. Saying he was "very interested" in recovering the remains of the *Awa maru* dead, he offered to perform whatever religious rites the Japanese thought necessary when they were found.[108]

Despite Bunton's honeyed words, however, disclosure had fundamentally changed the situation. From November 1976 onward, Japanese and Americans regarded one another as competitors as well as potential collaborators in the search for the *Awa maru*. More importantly, Chinese leaders now had good reason to try to find her. As soon as weather and sea conditions in the spring of 1977 permitted, they mounted their own secret salvage effort.[109] Thus, something happened that neither Bill Bunton nor Fukumitsu could have imagined: America, Japan, and China became competitors in a race to reach the *Awa maru*.

That race proved to be a very odd contest. Americans ran it with a blithe self-confidence that blinded them to their own weaknesses and the probable behavior of their competitors; the Japanese behaved like schizophrenics, unable to decide whether the Americans were rivals or collaborators; the Chinese ran as stealth runners. The dragon's cunning made possible its defeat of the American hare and the Japanese tortoise.

Bunton entered that race convinced that the advantages he held—precise knowledge of where the *Awa maru* lay and what she contained, plus wisdom drawn from his long experience as a professional diver—would guarantee victory. He hoped those strengths would commend him to the Chinese authorities whose permission he needed to conduct salvage operations. In fact, however, Bunton was a crippled competitor. In December 1976, only weeks after his endeavors became public knowledge, he suffered the loss of his most knowledgeable and best-connected collaborator, Jack Bennett. The former *Queenfish* navigator, who now sought to become an independent operator in the highly competitive underwater resource development industry, declined to renew his contract with Bunton.[110]

The diver, consequently, had to rely more and more upon Harned Hoose, who first delayed in, and then diverted him from, the pursuit of the *Awa maru*. In February 1977 Hoose got Bunton to revise his contract so as to add a Chinese to his lobbying team.[111] Six months later he offered encouraging but ultimately distracting advice. The leadership faction in Beijing then headed by the "more moderate" Hua Guo-feng and "soon to be . . . led in substantial measure" by Deng Xiaoping, Hoose reported, was "strongly in favor" of using foreign technological aid to develop China's offshore oil resources. However, that element, which included Defense Minister Yeh Chien-ying, did not command the unanimous support of the leadership group in Beijing. Moderates needed something less explicitly profit-oriented than salvaging the *Awa maru* to win the agreement of Communist hard-liners to opening the door to foreign involvement in offshore resource development. Hoose suggested that offering to build and staff a diving school to teach Chinese how to exploit their presumably rich seabed resources should precede requesting permission to salvage the Japanese ship.[112]

Bunton reluctantly followed that advice, and over the next two years he watched what was meant as a tactical shift turn into a strategic disaster. In August 1977 he traveled to Panama City, Florida, to get his old SEALAB colleagues Bob Barth and Dr. Bond to help with the diving school project. Bond estimated that building an advanced diver training facility would cost nearly 20 million dollars.[113] Lacking access to that kind of money, Bunton persuaded Barth to approach another onetime navy master diver and SEALAB veteran, Ken Wallace, who headed Taylor Diving and Salvage, a firm that specialized in providing diving and underwater construction services to the offshore oil industry. He asked retired Lt. Cdr. John V. Harter, who had been a member of the U.S. Navy Experimental Diving Unit (in Washington, D.C.), to review the proposal. The lieutenant commander saw "action and not just dreaming" in it and recommended investing twenty-five thousand dollars in the project.[114]

Bunton took the cash but soon learned just how much money could talk. Taylor Diving and Salvage abjured any interest in salvaging the *Awa maru*, and Hoose urged Bunton to drop that project from what was to be proposed to the Chinese.[115] Grudgingly accepting that advice, the diver then worked with Barth to transform what was dubbed the "Red Book" (in imitation of Mao Tse-tung's famous pamphlet of that color) from a thin sketch filled with "industrial chickenshit" into a thick tome crammed with technological detail, equipment photographs, individual and corporate biographies, and specific plans for the diving school project.[116] Hoose reportedly presented that volume to China's most senior leaders in December 1977.[117]

That apparent success, however, proved simply a precursor of more troubles for Bill Bunton. He became more and more dependent upon his collaborators, each of whom had their own ideas about what should be done next. In March 1978 Ken Wallace took steps to bring Brown and Root, one of America's biggest and, supposedly, most politically influential construction and engineering companies, into the diving school project; that firm's officials asked Texas Sen. Lloyd Bentsen to use his "usual finesse" to smooth its way into the project. Two months later Brown and Root became the principal agent in the proposal.[118] Harned Hoose objected to that, saying that Bunton's modest firm was more likely than a massive corporation to be welcomed as a joint venture partner by the Chinese. Overruled, he demanded a sizable advance to continue lobbying in Beijing for the much-modified proposal.[119]

By the fall of 1978 Bunton feared his dream of salvaging the *Awa maru* was about to die. He did what little he could to keep it alive. Nearly broke, he staved off Hoose's demand for money by promising to pay him from his own share of the diving school's expected profits.[120] He also did what he could politically to make his altered proposal look like a winner. Bunton renewed contacts with George Bush, who had returned from China and announced his candidacy for the 1980 Republican presidential nomination.[121] He sent the owner-editor of a Republican news sheet to Houston to do interviews about the China diving school project, interviews that would be published just before the anticipated 1 January 1979 restoration of full diplomatic relations between the United States and China.[122] Four months later he pressed John Harter, who was going to China with a group of New Orleans businessmen, to take along a copy of the Red Book diving school proposal to present to appropriate officials.[123]

By the spring of 1979, though, whatever Harter did was too little, too late. The Chinese were already preparing for their third season of diving on or near the *Awa maru*. Within days of Harter's arrival they announced their independent discovery of the sunken ship[124]—without benefit of Bunton's knowledge or of the training he and his partners had presumed they needed. Worse still, when Harter stopped in Tokyo en route to Shanghai, he found the Japanese poised to muscle in on what Bunton and his collaborators envisaged as an exclusively Sino-American joint venture; a representative of the Mitsui conglomerate approached him and expressed interest in collaborating in building a hyperbaric diving training complex in China.[125] Thus, in the final moments of a race they were about to lose, Bill Bunton and his associates woke up to the fact that there were Japanese competitors in it.

But those competitors had no agreed-upon strategy for winning the race to salvage the *Awa maru*. When the Bunton group's existence was disclosed, Fukumitsu had apparently decided to ignore the Americans and woo the Chinese. Considering himself the sole possessor of the secret of the ship's whereabouts, in September 1977 he forwarded that claim, and a copy of his book to support it, to Chinese Prime Minister Huang Hua and Vice Premier Deng Xiaoping. Every month thereafter for the next twenty months he sent the two Chinese officials a letter in which he presented himself as an advocate for families bereaved by the sinking of the *Awa maru*. Fukumitsu repeated what had been told to official Chinese visitors to Japan years earlier: the Japanese wanted to recover the remains of their dead. He then asked permission to confirm the present location of the ship and commence salvaging operations. In an appeal to Chinese generosity, he asked Beijing's leaders to share with the bereaved family members some of the treasure certain to be found on the *Awa maru*.[126] Writing such letters may have satisfied Fukumitsu's ego, but he received only silence in reply.

To Funada, in the wake of the disclosures from America, silence about the *Awa maru* seemed the best policy. For two years after November 1976 he appears to have neither said nor done anything about salvaging her. Shrewd politician that he was, Funada probably wanted to wait until the politics and diplomacy of restoring relations with the People's Republic of China sorted themselves out. That process, however, proved more complicated and protracted than he or anyone else in the Japanese political establishment imagined; Japan and China did not sign a peace treaty that fully restored diplomatic relations until August 1978.[127] It was October of that year before Vice Premier Deng Xiaoping came to Tokyo to exchange ratifications of the treaty and form his own impression of Japan's remarkable economic success.[128]

In the warm afterglow of that triumphal visit, Funada decided that the time was ripe to renew efforts to find and salvage the *Awa maru*. On 7 November 1978 he invited Foreign Minister Sonoda Sunao to his office. After chatting about the upcoming election for president of the Liberal Democratic party, which would determine who the next prime minister would be, Funada expressed support for Sonoda's continuation as foreign minister.[129] Then the older man sought the younger's help in bringing home the hungry ghosts still on board the *Awa maru*. He knew Sonoda would be receptive, for the foreign minister had commanded an Imperial Japanese Navy suicide torpedo (*kaiten*) unit in 1945 and had remained a strong nationalist. Also, as Minister of Health and Welfare in the late 1960s, Sonoda had overseen efforts to recover the remains of war dead from overseas.[130]

Funada gave the foreign minister a sheaf of papers and a navigational chart wrapped in newspaper. Sonoda scanned them, said he would do what he could, and rose to leave. As he walked out of Funada's office, he thrust these materials into his private secretary's hands, whispering that they were "extremely confidential—top secret!" When the aide opened the packet later that evening, he spotted on the navigational chart an *X* marked "*Awa maru.*" He immediately recognized the name for, years earlier, when he had been a political journalist for NHK, he had read Arima Yorichika's *The Silence of a Survivor* with great interest. The other papers in the packet outlined an extraordinary proposal: Funada wanted Sonoda to get Chinese permission for, or acquiescence in, a Japanese-American attempt to salvage the *Awa maru*.

Whoever was behind this scheme proposed paying the Global Marine Development Corporation between 200 and 300 million yen for the use of a most unusual American vessel, the *Glomar Explorer.*[131] The ship had a successful but murky past. Built a decade earlier at the request of the CIA, in 1968 she had become the centerpiece in Project Jennifer, a secret operation in which the U.S. Navy attempted to recover a sunken Soviet nuclear submarine from the depths of the Pacific.[132] Her existence became common knowledge when she became the object of a bizarre battle between her one-time owner, the Hughes Summa Corporation, and the Los Angeles County tax assessor. By 1978 that storm had passed, and the U.S. Navy had become her owner. The navy in turn leased the *Glomar Explorer* to Global Marine Development, ostensibly for use in deep-sea mining ventures.[133]

The vessel was ready for service in pursuit of the *Awa maru*. She had a 324-foot submersible barge, which could be used to haul up both human and material remains from the hulk. She had already gone from the American West Coast to Hawaii.[134] Once appropriate clearances—precisely what Funada sought through Sonoda from the Chinese—were in hand, the *Glomar Explorer* was to go to the Taiwan Strait to commence salvaging the *Awa maru*. The *Glomar Explorer*'s notoriety and doubts about the real originators of this proposal made Foreign Minister Sonoda's secretary leery of it. Was Funada, as he claimed, simply passing on a request from the Americans? Or was he, despite his earlier disclaimers of involvement in *Awa maru* salvage efforts, the real sponsor of the plan? Should the foreign minister, in the wake of former Prime Minister Tanaka's arrest for taking bribes from the Lockheed Corporation, run the risk of exposure as a collaborator with another American firm whose vessel reeked of ties to the CIA? How, indeed, would the press and public regard the foreign minister if he were shown to have participated in a highly speculative but potentially very profitable salvage scheme?[135]

These troublesome questions prompted the private secretary to devise an ingenious way for Sonoda to respond to Funada's request. He drafted a personal letter from the foreign minister to his Chinese counterpart that asked permission for the *Glomar Explorer* to commence operations in Chinese territorial waters. A few weeks later, on 29 November 1978, Sonoda sent Funada a personal reply to his original request. It implied that Beijing had responded favorably; an American-flag vessel would be permitted to move into Chinese waters to locate the *Awa maru* and remove human remains. Nonetheless, Sonoda had taken his secretary's worries about possible negative publicity to heart. Reaffirming his own intention to keep the salvage effort secret, he sought reassurances from Funada that the Americans involved would keep their ship's activities out of the public eye.[136]

As matters turned out, neither Funada nor Sonoda had anything to worry about. The Chinese who had granted permission for what might have been a collaborative Japanese-American effort to salvage the *Awa maru* knew full well that nothing much could be done until spring calmed the Taiwan Strait. By the time the *Glomar Explorer* could have moved into position over the hulk, they themselves would have announced to the world their success in retrieving human and material remains from it.[137] The stealth runner had simply thrown sand in the eyes of two competitors who, had they combined their strengths, might have beaten him.

Ironically, Minoru Fukumitsu proposed Japanese-American collaboration to Jack Bennett in December 1978, barely a month after Sonoda sent his confirming but cautionary reply to Funada. The Japanese-American by that time suspected that the Chinese might themselves be searching for the *Awa maru*. Hoping to reach her before they did, Fukumitsu wrote Bennett in hopes of transforming their on-again, off-again acquaintance into a business relationship. Might the former *Queenfish* navigator be willing, he asked, to join *his* team in locating and salvaging the *Awa maru?*[138]

In that inquiry, Fukumitsu sent mixed signals about the Chinese. On the one hand, he suggested they would acquiesce in foreign recovery of the *Awa maru*'s wreckage. He claimed that the Chinese were using Sen. Masayuki "Spark" Matsunaga of Hawaii as their liaison to the U.S. government on *Awa maru*–related matters. He also said that the *Awa maru* Salvage Committee, which he headed, was "very sure" to "get an understanding" from Beijing by April 1979; salvage operations could begin shortly thereafter. On the other hand, Fukumitsu asked Bennett, "Is it true that the Chinese are search[ing for the *Awa maru*]?"—a hint that the Chinese might be competitors rather than facilitators.[139]

Two months later, apparently convinced that Beijing would look favorably upon a Japanese-American salvage venture, Fukumitsu visited Bennett's Solana Beach, California, home. He was accompanied by Tamanai Katsumi, president of Nippon Marine Development Co., Ltd. The two men wanted to talk about just how the *Awa maru* might be salvaged. Bennett, who by this time had become vice president of Gulf Maritime Explorations, Inc., a firm that controlled the oceanographic submarine *Auguste Piccard*, spoke to them about that vessel's possible employment. It could be used as an underwater habitat from which divers could be dispatched to remove valuable industrial materials, the presumed bonanza, and human remains from the hulk of the *Awa maru*. Impressed by what Bennett said, Fukumitsu and Tamanai initialed an agreement that authorized him to "assume charge of the search for, location, and verification of the *Awa maru*." The former navy captain would sign the agreement and be paid ten thousand dollars once Beijing granted permission for salvage work to go forward.[140]

The most persistent of all Japan-based searchers for the *Awa maru*, the man who claimed that he alone knew just where she had been sunk had at long last openly sought the help of the most knowledgeable would-be American salvager. He was prepared to forget the wounds of the past in order to reap an enormous profit. Lest Bennett cool to the idea of collaborating with the Japanese, Fukumitsu telephoned him a few days later, on the eve of his return to Tokyo. He hinted that his project had political support, mentioning Inoue Takeshi, the Japanese ambassador in Beijing, and Leonard Woodcock, who headed the American Liaison Office there. Fukumitsu implied that Foreign Minister Sonoda and former Prime Minister Tanaka had endorsed his efforts. With support of that sort, Fukumitsu confidently predicted, the Chinese would approve it soon. Bennett would have the promised ten thousand dollars "next month."[141]

When Fukumitsu returned to Tokyo, however, he apparently became worried that he might be displaced as the preeminent *Awa maru* pursuer. Just why that happened remains unclear. The Japanese-American may have gotten wind of what Funada Naka was up to. He had almost certainly spoken with his longtime patron, Sasakawa Ryōichi, about his conversations with Jack Bennett, and the old man may not have been as enthusiastic as he had once been about Fukumitsu's endeavors. Japanese maritime industrial firms (which fell within Sasakawa's purview as president of the Japan Shipping Industry Foundation) had received lucrative contracts from the Chinese to build floating cranes that could be (and in fact were) used to salvage wrecks like the *Awa maru*.[142]

Perhaps Sasakawa felt it would be better to let the Chinese get to the ship first. That would preclude a messy quarrel over who owned whatever might be found on board her. The preceding August, Tokyo and Beijing had made no mention of war-related claims in their treaty restoring formal diplomatic relations. Their silence constituted an implicit deal: China would not seek indemnification for deaths and atrocities Japan had inflicted on its people in that theater of the 1931–1945 Greater East Asia War. Japan, in turn, dropped its right to recover property abandoned or lost in China—a right that would apply to what was on a Japanese ship resting in Chinese territorial waters.[143] Abandoning the *Awa maru* may have seemed to Sasakawa a small price to pay to preserve that tacit bargain.

Whatever the reason, Fukumitsu realized that he needed Bennett all the more. He wrote the American reaffirming that the "things" in six *Awa maru* safes were worth "many million dollars" beyond the value of the tin known to be in her holds. He urged Bennett to prepare the way for selling the *Awa maru* story, which presumably would climax with the discovery of lost treasure and the return home of hungry ghosts, to "someone in Hollywood" who could turn it into a blockbuster, money-making movie. Fukumitsu closed by asking that their agreement to cooperate be finalized; the former *Queenfish* navigator was to cable him urging his return to California by mid-March 1979.[144] The Japanese-American was, at long last, reaching back to the land of his birth for genuine collaboration in salvaging the *Awa maru*.

His plea, like Funada's request for Foreign Minister Sonoda's intercession with the Chinese for approval of *his* version of Japanese-American collaboration, was the cry of an already defeated man, for the Chinese had won the race to the *Awa maru*. On Saturday morning, 24 March 1979, Chinese Vice Minister of Transportation, Peng Teh-ch'ing, came to Sonoda Sunao's reception room on the fourth floor of the squat, glass-and-concrete Foreign Ministry building. Ushered into the minister's office, he presented a model of the hulk of the *Awa maru* as she had been found on the floor of the Taiwan Strait. "The Chinese Government has located and begun to salvage the *Awa maru*," he said quietly.[145] Barely a month later, the *Peoples' Daily* proclaimed that triumph to the world.[146]

The Chinese dragon had indeed beaten the American hare and the Japanese tortoise in the race to find the *Awa maru*.

That news stunned Minoru Fukumitsu and Bill Bunton. Both men struggled to explain their defeat. The Japanese-American did so with grace and resignation; perhaps fear of doing or saying something that might prevent the return of the remains of the *Awa maru* dead for interment in the monument at Zōjōji Temple softened his words.[147] The American, on the other hand, exploded in paranoid anger. Defeat had not come naturally; someone must have betrayed him. Perhaps it was Jack Bennett, who, Bunton suspected, had revealed the innermost secrets of his quest for the *Awa maru* to Texas competitors in the underwater resource development business. More likely it was Harned Hoose, who professed to be as surprised as Bunton by news of the Chinese discovery. That, the diver insisted, was just another lie; the go-between who had strung him along for so long must have been the source that pointed the Chinese stealth salvagers to the right spot.[148]

Once the anger that prompted such outrageous speculations died down, Bunton and Fukumitsu faced up to the fact that they were beaten men. They confronted some difficult questions. Why had the Chinese defeated them in the race to reach the *Awa maru?* Why had their supposedly superior knowledge, more advanced technology, and presumed wisdom not brought them victory, either singly or together, in that contest?

Neither man could answer the first question. A full response to it remains beyond reach even as these words are written. The People's Republic of China was, two decades ago, and remains now, a dictatorship whose decisions and actions are anything but transparent. The Chinese who actually salvaged the *Awa maru* eventually met with some of Bunton's associates and told them when and how they had struggled to bring to the surface what lay on board her. Their story was one of determination, skill, and even death for their own men over three seasons of diving on the hulk.[149] However, neither they, the Chinese experts who have written about their effort, nor the Americans and Japanese who were in Beijing as official rapporteurs have revealed anything of the top-level political events and decisions that, as Harned Hoose correctly surmised, set the pace of China's quest for the *Awa maru.*[150]

Thus, only tentative conclusions as to why the Chinese triumphed can be drawn. First, geography was on their side. The *Awa maru* lay in less than two hundred feet of water barely ten miles off one of their many islands in a region frequented by fishermen. Sooner or later a sonar-equipped boat would stumble upon her hulk, which, like a reef, drew fish and fishermen to where it lay. That was the explanation, embellished by an account of preliminary clashes between Communist and Nationalist fishermen, that the Chinese subsequently gave for how they had found the *Awa maru*.[151]

It was at best half true. What seems more likely is that Japanese searchers tipped off their Chinese rivals to the probable presence of something of great value on the sea bottom at or very near where the *Awa maru* lay. The voyages of Funada's *Aotaka maru* may well have confirmed what Minoru Fukumitsu had suggested in his book and Bill Bunton had disclosed through Harned Hoose's informal entreaties: the ship was to be found at, or not far from, the place where the Americans said they had sunk her. While trying to gain permission to salvage the *Awa maru*, Japanese and Americans thus gave the Chinese valuable clues as to why and where they should look for her themselves.

Beijing officials were also shrewd enough to cover their own tracks. Their differences with one another were not so strong, as Hoose hypothesized, to prevent one or more of them from making a command decision to proceed with the salvage endeavor. Their ability to keep non-Chinese away from the relatively remote, island-filled region was unchallenged. No foreign spy, agent provocateur, or even errant businessman was likely to go there.

Finally, Chinese skill in confusing competitors was unmatched. They agreed to let the *Glomar Explorer* enter their waters at a time when weather conditions would delay her arrival until their own salvaging was far advanced. They let Bunton and his corporate collaborators think they needed foreign expertise when in fact they already had the trained men and technology necessary to reach the *Awa maru* on the floor of the Taiwan Strait. They exploited Japanese maritime technology firms' desire to penetrate their market, without ever revealing that their purchases would be used to salvage the Japanese ship.

But that supposed difference of intelligence cannot explain why Japanese and Americans failed to join in a manner that would have enabled them to beat the Chinese in the race to find and salvage the *Awa maru*. None of those defeated in 1979 have said anything about that aspect of their failure, but in retrospect four obstacles to their effective collaboration loom large.[152]

Profit was first among them. Japanese and Americans were rivals from first to last in this race because they were each tantalized by dreams of reaping great wealth from salvaging the ship. Hidaka Shinsaku's tale of secret loot lingered on long after his death thirteen years later, thanks to what Chihaya Masataka and Arima Yorichika wrote and published.[153] The spectacular rise in the 1970s of commodity prices for the tin and other industrial materials known to be in the *Awa maru*'s holds[154] made Jack Bennett leery of working with Minoru Fukumitsu, and it made Bill Bunton determined to keep his salvage project secret. The prospect of profit kept Japanese and Americans from pooling their knowledge and resources, just as it would have separated competitors in any potentially lucrative endeavor.

Pride created a second barrier to effective Japanese-American cooperation in pursuit of the *Awa maru*. Salvagers cannot afford to be humble; they must project self-confidence if they are to lure others into providing the financial, technological, and governmental support they need to pursue their dreams. All the Japanese and American would-be *Awa maru* salvagers had such pride—in ample measure—but it was tinged with nationalism that ruled out cooperation with each other. Bill Bunton was so convinced of the superiority of American technology that he failed to take the Japanese seriously as either potential collaborators or competitors. Still smarting from defeat in war, Sasakawa Ryōichi and the other early Japanese pursuers of the *Awa maru* looked to Taiwan rather than America for assistance. Six years passed between Minoru Fukumitsu's first meeting with Jack Bennett and his acknowledgment that the former *Queenfish* navigator was the best man to supervise a joint *Awa maru* salvage operation. Nationalistic pride kept Funada Naka and Sonoda Sunao from openly acknowledging that Japan needed the American-built *Glomar Explorer* to complete the recovery of the *Awa maru* and whatever remained on board her. Japanese and Americans were Cold War allies, but, at least in this endeavor, nationalistic pride kept them from treating one another as partners.

Lack of government support constituted a third impediment to Japanese-American cooperation in salvaging the *Awa maru*. Diplomats are paid to try to prevent war or, that failing, to do their best to heal its wounds. While they wanted to forget the *Awa maru* in the late 1940s, three decades later they might have facilitated cooperation in her joint recovery. A multinational operation that gave first priority to finding and repatriating the remains of her victims might have garnered Chinese support in a way that separate trea-

the Pacific War)[157] until far too late for that change to have any practical effect on the salvaging of the *Awa maru*.

The ghost of war also kept Americans who might otherwise have done so from working closely with Japanese to find the ship. In 1972 and again in 1979, Elliott Loughlin readily told the Japanese who came to his door how she had been destroyed. Nonetheless, his sympathy for the *Awa maru* victims never deepened to the point of proposing or endorsing joint action to recover their remains. For his part, Jack Bennett remained a Pearl Harbor survivor; he found it impossible to shed feelings of distrust toward the Japanese, whether in 1972 as seekers of information, in 1979 as prospective business partners, or later as collaborators in another less emotionally charged salvage project.[158] Heroes and victims could not work together to salvage the *Awa maru* because neither could exorcise fully the ghost of war.

What might have been a joint triumph—locating the *Awa maru*, recovering the remains of her victims and whatever precious goods she carried, and reconciling conflicting national public memories of the Pacific War and what had befallen her in it—therefore ended in joint chagrin. The Japanese and Americans who wanted to salvage her were defeated by the Chinese.

Once that defeat became public knowledge, only one question remained to be answered: How were the *Awa maru* and her hungry ghosts to be laid to rest, once and for all?

sure hunts could not. Beijing had, after all, allowed repatriation of the remains of Japanese war dead even before China and Japan signed a treaty normalizing their relations.[155] Leaders anxious to strengthen relations with Washington and Tokyo (in order to check what they perceived as a threat emanating from Moscow) might have welcomed joint recovery of the *Awa maru* as a means of furthering that goal. Even if the Chinese had insisted on participating in a joint salvage venture, shared victory would have been better for the Japanese and American competitors than separate defeat.

In fact, none of the Japanese or Americans who wanted to salvage the *Awa maru*, save perhaps Funada, made meaningful efforts to get the diplomatic assistance that might have enabled them to do so. In America, Bill Bunton gave priority to obtaining corporate rather than American governmental assistance, and he turned to an unofficial go-between, Harned Hoose, for help in getting Chinese permission for his proposal. His claims of Republican support for it were just that—mere claims. In Japan, neither Seshima Ryūzō nor Sasakawa Ryōichi pressed the conservative cabinets of the 1960s for help in overcoming expected Chinese resistance to a salvage attempt. By the early 1970s, when Minoru Fukumitsu and the *Awa maru* Bereaved Families Association stepped into the spotlight as would-be salvagers, they presented themselves as adversaries and victims of the Japanese government rather than suppliants for its aid.[156] Funada's eleventh-hour covert request for diplomatic assistance was simply of no use.

The ghost of war posed the fourth and most formidable obstacle to Japanese-American collaboration in salvaging the *Awa maru*. It hovered over would-be salvagers, dividing them more deeply and for a longer time than they would have cared to admit. Because they regarded themselves as victims and heroes, respectively, and because they had very different public memories of the sinking of the *Awa maru* and of the war in which it occurred, Japanese and Americans could not readily collaborate in salvaging her. Commander Chihaya had worked with Americans to reconstruct the naval history of the Pacific War; he could, quite logically, have called in his 1956 article for Japanese-American collaboration to resolve the riddles surrounding the *Awa maru*'s destruction. Because he remained, physically and emotionally, a victim of the lost war, however, he could not end her story that way. Similarly, the scars of war slowed Sasakawa Ryōichi's transformation into an advocate of Japanese-American cooperation (on issues not related to

11

The Ghost of War Returns

WHEN PENG TEH-CH'ING came to Sonoda Sunao's office on Saturday morning, 24 March 1979, it seemed for a moment that the answer to that question was simple. The Chinese vice-minister of transportation showed the Japanese foreign minister a model of the *Awa maru* as she had been found, along with photographs of items retrieved from the wreck and of portions of its interior.[1] By telling the truth—revealing all that was now known and returning all that could be recovered from the *Awa maru*—the Chinese seemed to be saying that the ghost of war could be laid to rest.

But in diplomacy truth is often in short supply. Only moments after he revealed China's secret, Peng began asking questions about the *Awa maru*'s cargo: Had she been loaded with anything other than industrial materials? If she had, where had the treasure that had tantalized the Americans, Japanese, and Chinese been placed? Could the foreign minister provide the Chinese government with a copy of the ship's cargo manifest, and as soon as possible? Sonoda paused for a moment, then put off his Chinese visitor with a polite reply; he said he would look into the matter. Peng then left quietly.[2]

That exchange marked the beginning of Sino-Japanese efforts to craft a new ending for the *Awa maru* story. Just as William Sebald and Yoshida Shigeru had done thirty years earlier, so now Chinese and Japanese officials tried to bend the truth so as to make that ending politically correct. They did not press one another for the full truth about where the *Awa maru* had been found, what was on board her, or how she had been destroyed. Instead, Chinese and Japanese officials stage-managed the return of the remains of her hungry ghosts to Japan so as to emphasize harmony and cooperation between their two nations. In so doing they widened the gap between Japanese and American public memories of the ship's sinking and of the war in which that tragedy occurred. The return of the *Awa maru* thus guaranteed that the ghost of war would continue to haunt relations between America and Japan.

Peng's March 1979 disclosure that the *Awa maru* had been found presented the Chinese and Japanese governments with potentially embarrassing problems. China had beaten competitors from its most important trade and investment partner, Japan, as well as those from its newfound strategic partner in the struggle against the Soviet Union, the United States.[3] Communist bureaucrats had won the race to find the *Awa maru* by deceiving their capitalist adversaries. Japan, as Foreign Minister Sonoda's aides quickly realized, was in danger of being caught collaborating with the Chinese after Funada Naka had told his American associates that Tokyo would intercede on their behalf with Beijing.[4] Beyond that, there was the real danger that the *Awa maru* salvagers might dredge up disquieting evidence of official misbehavior —contraband or loot taken from Southeast Asian colonies—that would validate American claims of mitigating circumstances surrounding the sinking, and the suspicions of bereaved families that their loved ones had been used as human shields against American torpedoes. The *Awa maru* may well have looked to Japanese and Chinese diplomats like an old naval mine that had floated up from the depths and threatened to sink any ship of state that touched it.

As a result, Tokyo and Beijing dealt in a gingerly way with the *Awa maru*. They first agreed not to ask one another potentially vexing questions about her. About a week after Peng Teh-ch'ing's revelation of her discovery, Sonoda Sunao summoned the Chinese official back to his office and showed him a copy of the ship's manifest that had been retrieved from the archives. No gold, diamonds, or other valuables were listed on it. That piece of evidence appeared to satisfy Peng. He did not raise the next, obvious point: the manifest might not have listed everything that Japanese military officials in Singapore had secreted aboard the ship. Both he and Sonoda got what they wanted from that exchange—plausible deniability. If the Chinese had in fact recovered war booty from the *Awa maru,* they need not say anything about that discovery. The Japanese, in turn, could rest assured that no discomfiting evidence of wartime looting was about to be made public knowledge.

Sonoda, in turn, did not press Peng for precise information as to where and how the *Awa maru* had been found. His silence signaled Japan's willingness to abide by the terms of the bargain implicit in the Sino-Japanese peace treaty, which he had taken such pride in concluding only a few months earlier. It said nothing about claims; Tokyo would not now press claims of ownership to anything found on board the *Awa maru,* regardless of its official character or the location, in international or Chinese territorial waters, of the ship. That reassurance enabled the two men to part company having agreed to say nothing for the time being about her discovery.[5]

Three weeks later, however, Beijing and Tokyo collaborated in announcing to the world that the *Awa maru* had been found. In a brief statement on 27 April 1979, Chinese officials revealed that she had been discovered in their territorial waters, off Fukien Province. The ship had broken into two pieces and lay on the seabed at a depth of sixty meters (approximately 203 feet). Divers had recovered thirty items from her hulk. The Chinese said they were prepared to return them and deliver an unstated number of human remains to Japan. A spokesman for the Japanese Ministry of Health and Welfare rebroadcast the message, adding to it a brief account of the sinking, postwar claims-abandonment negotiations, and the payment of compensatory monies to bereaved families and the ship's owner. He also added a diplomatic flourish: the Chinese were returning what had been found, as a humanitarian gesture in the interests of promoting good relations between their country and Japan. The spokesman closed his press briefing by saying that an official emissary would soon depart for China to learn more about what had been found and work out details for its return to Japan.[6]

That news triggered first joy, then bravado, and then doubt that Chinese and Japanese officials were telling the whole truth. Bereaved families greeted the news with great hope for the future. Mrs. Tōkō implored the Chinese, "Please return the remains [of the victims] as soon as possible!" She urged them to allow family members to visit the exact spot where the *Awa maru* had been found.[7] Minoru Fukumitsu and Bill Bunton brazenly claimed partial credit for the discovery. Fukumitsu said he had gone to Beijing in 1977 and met with Deng Xiaoping in hopes of getting permission to salvage the ship.[8] Bunton sent the Chinese leader a telegram in which he volunteered his services "as described in my salvage proposal to your government over the past six years via . . . Dr. Harned Pettus Hoose."[9] He told the press he had revealed the existence of the *Awa maru*'s treasure trove to the Chinese in 1973 and had sent Hoose across the Pacific eighteen times in the ensuing five years in an effort to conclude a joint salvage agreement.[10]

But doubts as to the truth of official statements proved much more important than the defeated competitors' public relations puffery. Only five days after the discovery was announced, the *Yomiuri shimbun* printed interviews with two veterans who claimed to have loaded forty-six truckloads of gold and other valuables on board the *Awa maru* in March 1945.[11] Mrs. Tōkō and Fukumitsu insisted that the ship was indeed carrying priceless goods.[12] The Japanese official sent to Beijing to ascertain what had been found, and whether more might be recovered from her hulk, returned home with nothing to say on that subject.[13] The Chinese were slow to reveal precisely what they had discovered. It was late May before the Japanese learned that 168 sets of human remains and 384 (not thirty, as originally claimed) personal items belonging to *Awa maru* passengers had been recovered.[14] Discrepancies between what the Chinese disclosed and what seemingly knowledgeable Japanese believed fueled speculation in Japan that an official cover-up was under way. It was said that the *Awa maru* actually lay in international waters; if that were so, it was asserted, Japan might have some claim to the riches allegedly on board her. Kasumigaseki diplomats had supposedly chosen to drop that claim in the interest of promoting Sino-Japanese relations.[15]

Foreign Minister Sonoda realized that the rumors and doubts swirling around the *Awa maru* had to be quashed. The best way to do so was to shift public attention away from her supposed booty to her victims. Sonoda sympathized with war victims. As minister of health and welfare a decade earlier, he had implemented legislation that provided special compensation for the parents of war dead. He also may have helped transform into state-supported endeavors what had been private efforts to recover remains from Central Pacific islands.[16] Nonetheless, Sonoda did not want to be the principal player in what he hoped would be the last act of the *Awa maru* drama.

He turned, instead, to his junior cabinet colleague, Hashimoto Ryūtarō, for help. Hashimoto, who as these words are written is Japan's prime minister, was then a forty-year-old political *wunderkind*. A Liberal Democratic Party stalwart and staunch supporter of former Prime Minister Tanaka Kakuei, he had already sat in the Diet for fifteen years.[17] Now he occupied the cabinet position his father had held twice and had once given up to protest the Japanese government's miserly treatment of veterans and war-bereaved families.[18] Sonoda was confident that Hashimoto understood the politics and diplomacy of the return of remains in general and of the *Awa maru* matter in particular. Nine years earlier, as vice-minister of health and welfare, he had gone to Guam and other Pacific islands for ceremonies honoring Japan's war dead.[19] As neighbor to Mrs. Tōkō, moreover, Hashimoto knew all about her efforts to memorialize properly those who had perished on the *Awa maru*.[20]

When Sonoda asked Hashimoto to take primary responsibility for returning the remains of her dead from China, he knew the younger man would agree. From that point onward Hashimoto became the principal figure in what amounted to be a state funeral. He contacted the *Awa maru* Bereaved Families Association to assure its cooperation in what was being planned.[21] His subordinates chose ten of its members—a group that included the spiritually minded builders of the memorial at Renjōji in Nara but not the more worldly and outspoken Mrs. Tōkō—to accompany him to China.[22]

That Hashimoto headed such a group was unusual because second-level officials customarily accompanied relatives who traveled abroad to recover the remains of their war dead. Sonoda rewarded his colleague for taking on this assignment by giving him an additional task that broadened the significance of his mission. When Hashimoto met China's foreign minister on the morning of 3 July 1979, he thanked the minister for returning human remains from the *Awa maru* and asked for assistance in recovering those of fifty thousand Japanese war dead left behind in northeastern China.[23] That was sure to endear Hashimoto to conservatives within the ruling Liberal Democratic Party.

While Hashimoto met the foreign minister in Beijing, Peng Teh-ch'ing, the vice-minister of transportation, whose agency was supervising the *Awa maru* salvage operation, held a long press conference. He hoped to slake the Japanese thirst for more information about her victims and put an end to the rumors floating around her. Peng said the ship had been found at a point approximately twenty kilometers off the coast of Fukien Province. That put her in Chinese territorial, not international, waters, which ruled out the need for any claims-abandonment deal. Her two pieces rested on their sides in the shape of a tee on the sandy bottom. Although that complicated salvaging operations, Prime Minister Hua Guo-feng had ordered seventy divers to join the more than six hundred workers and ten boats that already worked the site. They had recovered tin and rubber, clearly contraband commodities in 1945, but they had not found any riches. Because her badly corroded state precluded raising the *Awa maru* in her entirety, Chinese divers would cut her into sections in order to find still more human and material remains. Peng clearly wanted to emphasize that salvaging the *Awa maru* and returning the remains of her dead was an act of goodwill and not a looting of their resting place.[24]

Buoyed by that message of hope, Hashimoto and his group departed in 1979 for Shanghai, where, in ceremonies on 4 July managed by the Chinese Red Cross Society, they solemnly received the remains and personal belongings of 158 *Awa maru* victims. The Japanese neither sought, nor were they given, any additional information about the salvage site or what had been found there. Instead, after thanking the Chinese government a second time for its help, Hashimoto and his party flew directly back to Tokyo.[25]

The next day solemn ceremonies were held at the Ministry of Health and Welfare and at Zōjōji Temple. In the morning, some six hundred people flooded into the ministry's fifth-floor auditorium, where a temporary altar had been erected; on it lay thirteen white boxes containing the remains. Minister Hashimoto opened the ceremonies by solemnly intoning, "The victims have returned." Following his speech of thanks to the Chinese for facilitating their return, bereaved family members filed forward to place chrysanthemums on the altar. After viewing some of the personal items that had been recovered from the ship, they then went to Zōjōji Temple for a ceremonial banquet, a report from those who had gone to China to recover the

"阿波丸"沉船死难
者遗骨、私人遗物

(一九八〇年打捞部分)

The *Awa maru*'s hungry ghosts return to their homeland.*Mrs. Iwama Kazuko*

remains, and formal interment of the latter at the *Awa maru* memorial.[26] The hungry ghosts had, at long last, been brought home to rest.

These events served the immediate purposes for which they were intended. The Japanese renewed and deepened their sense of victimization in the Pacific War. The return of the *Awa maru* victims' remains from China generated a wave of media coverage that humanized them and heaped sympathy upon their relatives.[27] *Awa maru* bereaved families became guests of honor at the annual national memorial service for the war dead, held on 15 August at the Budokan Arena, in the shadow of the Imperial Palace.[28] Their presence provided a symbolic link between their particular loss and the many other tragedies that had attended Japan's defeat in the Pacific War.

The Chinese emerged, in Japanese eyes, as friendly neighbors, whose motives and actions in this matter were not to be questioned. By summer's end the flurry of questions about what they were doing had vanished, only incompletely answered, from the Japanese media. Beijing proceeded quietly, at its own pace and in its own way, with *Awa maru* salvage operations for nearly two years longer. The Chinese revealed only as much as they wanted, when they chose to do so. They kept the specific salvage site—in murky waters off Niu-shan Tao [Cow Mountain Island] southeast of Pingtan in Fukien Province (as shown in the insert on the map on page 32) secret until March 1980. They continued to deny Japanese access to it until the end of that year, by which time the work was nearly finished.[29] So long as they continued to hand over human remains, no one in Japan (except bereaved family members) seemed to care about how those relics and anything else from the ship had been found.

Instead, the Japanese ritualized the return of their war dead and praised the Chinese for assisting in it. In January 1980 and again in May 1981 they repeated the events of July 1979. Each time a delegation of the bereaved, accompanied by Health and Welfare ministry officials, traveled to China. There they photographed what had been found, and on each occasion they returned with small white boxes containing relatives' remains—but without further significant information as to how and why the Chinese had salvaged the *Awa maru*.[30] The absence of full truth did not bother either government officials or the media. In the eyes of the bereaved, all that counted was that more hungry ghosts had returned and been interred in Japanese soil. In time the bereaved added stones to both the Nara and Tokyo *Awa maru* memorials on which they inscribed their eternal gratitude to the Chinese for making that return possible.[31]

Success in this diplomacy of the dead came, however, at a cost the significance of which would not become clear until years later. Japanese public memory of the sinking of the *Awa maru* and the Pacific War now froze into a form even more incompatible with American understanding of the same events. Questions Tokyo and Beijing officials left unanswered in 1979 metamorphosed into standing doubts within the Japanese *Awa maru* story. Chihaya Masataka's allegations of deliberate American intent in sinking her and duplicity after the fact reappeared in the press in July 1979 and also on the NHK documentary about the ship (mentioned in chapter 9) that was televised five months later.[32] The program closed in a way that left the sinking of the *Awa maru* an open wound, without coming to any conclusion about the truth or falsity of his allegations. It ended by affirming the same message that the return and interment of the ship's victims was meant to convey: Japanese were the ultimate victims of the Pacific War.[33]

That same message permeated what the Japanese read and saw about the sinking of the *Awa maru* during the 1991–1995 commemorations of the Pacific War. In 1990, spurred by requests from bereaved families, *Asahi shimbun* reporter Matsui Kakushin published a series of articles about the *Awa maru* tragedy.[34] He transformed these into a book, published in April 1994 to mark the forty-ninth anniversary of her victims' deaths—the point at which their spirits, according to Buddhist tradition, were finally freed from their last ties to earth. Matsui titled his book *Why Was the* Awa maru *Sunk?* In fact, however, it told more about the victims' lives, the injustices suffered by the bereaved, and the efforts of would-be *Awa maru* salvagers than it concluded about the circumstances of her sinking.[35] Indeed, Matsui ended his version of the *Awa maru* story with a tantalizing bit of speculation: he reported a Chinese official's insistence that the ship's position on the seabed proved that the American account of her sinking was false.[36]

In 1995, however, as the fiftieth anniversary of that tragic event approached, knowledge of the circumstances surrounding it had all but disappeared from Japanese public memory. Those who had striven to keep it alive —Shimoda Kantarō, Arima Yorichika, and Mrs. Tōkō—were dead.[37] Commander Chihaya had put down his pen. The stones of the *Awa maru* monument at Zōjōji Temple now told only a simple story of illegal American action, death for thousands of Japanese, and Chinese generosity in returning their remains.[38] The *Awa maru* story as it unfolded on Tokyo television was devoid of historical facts. Viewers followed a bereaved woman on her sad journey to the presumed sinking site, where she, amidst flowing tears and cries of grief, cast flowers upon the waters to console the spirits of the dead. The scene then shifted to a television studio, where panelists quizzed the woman about her feelings and offered emotional support for her recovery from a half-century of grief. In the end all that mattered, this program seemed to say, was Japan's victimization in the sinking of the *Awa maru* and the war in which that tragedy occurred.[39]

Furthermore, by 1995 that public memory was utterly at odds with what Americans knew and believed about the Pacific War. The sinking of the *Awa maru* remained virtually unknown to them. Bill Bunton's defeat in the race to find her had not elicited the volume and depth of media coverage that recovery and return of her human remains produced in Japan.[40] His lawsuit against his erstwhile partners in the abortive American salvage attempt sputtered into defeat with only minimal local newspaper reportage.[41] His considerably fictionalized account of the sinking, published in 1981 in an effort to raise funds to cover his losses in the salvage attempt, went out of print without having awakened many Americans to what had taken place.[42] Bunton and his sometime collaborators simply slipped back into the comfortable obscurity of retirement.

But the story of the broader submarine war in which the *Awa maru* tragedy occurred took on new life in the United States when veterans of the Pacific submarine war built a museum and memorial at Pearl Harbor. Its principal artifact is the *Bowfin,* which operated in the same waters as the *Queenfish* in the spring of 1945. The museum's emotional centerpiece, however, is a semicircle of fifty-two tombstone-like markers, each bearing the names of a lost submarine and every member of her crew.[43]

Bowfin Park embodies submariners' understanding of their past in a way that powerfully reaffirms American public memory of the Pacific War as a whole. Situated immediately adjacent to the USS *Arizona* Memorial, it is the omega to that monument's alpha. Any visitor can see what American submariners know and feel in their hearts: what began in tragedy—the Japanese attack on Pearl Harbor—had ended in triumph, thanks to the bravery, professionalism, and sacrifice of those who fought under the seas.

Neither this shrine to what American submariners accomplished nor their own writings published since Admiral Lockwood's death, however, give the sinking of the *Awa maru* the prominence it deserves. Submariner authors looking back on their war recall their triumphs and escapes from disaster—not the errors they committed and the tragedies they caused. The so-called greatest submarine error of World War II is all but absent from their works.[44] Visitors to *Bowfin* Park see nothing of it; indeed, the *Queenfish* herself can hardly be found there. Only a wooden plaque bearing her name and a postwar photograph of her navigator, Jack Bennett, claiming his bride at the Pearl Harbor Submarine Base chapel, alert visitors to her onetime existence.[45]

Thousands of miles from Pearl Harbor, across the seemingly limitless expanse of the Pacific, another museum perches on the edge of Yokohama harbor. It tells the history of NYK, the shipping firm that owned and operated the *Awa maru* in 1945 and went on to become one of the giants of the maritime industrial world. With a small, ship-shaped metal plaque for every

The USS *Bowfin* Submarine Museum and Park in Honolulu, Hawaii. *Author's photograph*

NYK vessel that was sunk, the museum commemorates the Japanese merchant mariners who died during the Pacific War. Each bears its name in Japanese characters and English letters. There the *Awa maru* is all but lost in the crowd of victims. In an adjoining room, however, in a display that shows where each ship went down, she stands out prominently. Extraordinary in memory no less than in reality, she alone is labeled in English as well as in Japanese.[46]

Her distinctive presence attests to the depth of the Japanese feeling that clings, more than a half century after the fact, to the loss of the ship and the thousands of men, women, and children on board her. The prominence of the *Awa maru* in the NYK Museum makes her absence from the museum in *Bowfin* Park all the more striking. The different treatments of her sinking in museum displays in Japan and the United States suggest that a tremendous gap, as wide or wider than the ocean that separates the two nations, exists between their public memories of the Pacific War.

That cross-cultural gap is not insignificant. Time and again during the half-century commemorations of that war it spewed friction into already troubled relations between the United States and Japan. The ghost of war long past haunted those who led the two nations, making it more difficult for them to resolve trade disputes and adjust to life in a post–Cold War world. In 1991, for instance, Japanese and Americans failed utterly to reconcile their differences over the Pearl Harbor attack fifty years earlier. The U.S. Postal Service commemorated it with a stamp whose release the Japanese Foreign Ministry tried to block;[47] the Japanese Diet failed to find words to apologize for the attack; and President George Bush, a downed aviator whom submariners saved from death in the Pacific in 1944, refused to link the Pearl Harbor attack to, or apologize for, the dropping of atomic bombs on Hiroshima and Nagasaki.[48]

Four years later Bill Clinton, America's first president born after World War II, and Murayama Tomiichi, Japan's first Socialist prime minister in nearly a half-century, found themselves caught up in similar controversy. Debate within and between Japan and the United States over the ending of the Pacific War poisoned the atmosphere in which negotiators tried, without success, to find solutions to disputes over computer chips, auto parts, and airport landing rights.[49] In Washington, President Clinton bowed to Japanese complaints and ordered the Postal Service to drop plans for a commemorative stamp that would have proclaimed the atomic bomb's efficacy in ending the war.[50] That did not prevent the outbreak of an ugly Japanese-American quarrel over the Smithsonian's planned exhibition of the *Enola Gay*, the B-29 that dropped the atomic bomb on Hiroshima. In Washington a raucous domestic political debate exploded; it emasculated the exhibit and left historians fuming over their inability to shape public discourse over the Pacific War.[51] In Tokyo, Prime Minister Murayama's quest to have Japan apologize for its actions in that war ran into a wall of conservative opposition in the Diet;[52] Japanese historians who resigned over the Ministry of Health and Welfare's plans for a museum to honor the generation that fought the Pacific War found they had no more power to shape public memory than did their American counterparts.[53] In 1995, no less than in 1945, Americans and Japanese refused to see themselves as other than heroes and victims in that war.

These events pose obvious questions: Can the two peoples close the gap between their public memories of the Pacific War? Must the differences of feeling and understanding of particular events in it, like the sinking of the *Awa maru*, remain forever unresolved? Will interpretations shaped during the first postwar half-century make it more difficult for Americans and Japanese in the next one to resolve their differences and preserve the peace?

The answer to such questions is, "It depends." The generation of Americans and Japanese who fought the Pacific submarine war, experienced its exhilaration and suffered its consequences, and provided much of the information used in this book will never completely reconcile their differences over it. Their lives were too deeply touched, their passions too strongly engaged, by events like the sinking of the *Awa maru* to allow them to change or abandon their understanding of what occurred between 1941 and 1945. The real Japanese victims—Mrs. Tōkō, Commander Chihaya, and members of *Awa maru* bereaved families—have gone, or will go, to their graves with unresolved doubts about how and why the ship was sunk, and unfulfilled longings for just recompense for their loss. The real American heroes —surviving *Queenfish* crew members, from Captains Bennett and Shamer down to Radioman Goberville—will depart this world knowing they committed a terrible error but bearing no guilt for an unpremeditated and unavoidable act. For them, the Pacific submarine war will forever be the most challenging, terrifying, and morally satisfying experience of their lives.

But those born too late to have experienced the Pacific War, while grateful for their predecessors' sacrifices and achievements, need not be bound by the preceding generation's view of the past. History is not written in stone. Public memory is not unchangeable. Differences between conflicting national public memories can be reconciled if reason rather than past passions or present politics is allowed to inform current historical discourse. Reason, in the form of carefully constructed, not exclusively national, history, can narrow and perhaps even destroy the gap between conflicting American and Japanese understandings of the Pacific War. That is what this book has tried to do.

At its end, the essential facts about the sinking of the *Awa maru*, the Pacific submarine war, and the impact of both on Japanese-American relations stand out clearly. The story of the *Awa maru* is neither a simple tale of tragedy at sea nor an account of conspiracy and victimization in high places.

It is, on the contrary, a story of error in war—in a submarine war that was necessary but neither good nor error-free. It is a tale of the consequences of error: for victims and victimizers at war; for governments striving to make and preserve peace; for the shapers of public memory; and for those who sought to recover and profit from war by salvaging the ship.

The error that led to the sinking of the *Awa maru* was rooted in misjudgment, not malice. Washington and Tokyo created the problem that the ship's voyage was meant to alleviate by mishandling their respective prisoner and internee problems. Japanese leaders failed utterly to realize how seriously their treatment of captives would inflame American opinion against them. President Roosevelt and his State Department advisers refused, until it was almost too late, to admit that reciprocity governs behavior in war as well as in peace. They declined to recognize the linkage between their treatment of interned Japanese and Japanese-Americans and Tokyo's attitude toward providing relief to Americans in Japanese custody. Both sides misjudged the depth of the Soviet Union's reluctance to facilitate provision of aid to those prisoners.

These errors were compounded by overconfidence on the part of those who wrote and implemented the *Awa maru* safe-passage agreement. They wrongly assumed that prior confidence-building measures—the voyages of the *Hoshi maru* and *Hakusan maru*—and a "fail-safe" system for communicating changes in the ship's course and schedule would save her from submarine attack. That presumption reflected their misunderstanding of the nature of war in general and of man's ability to control what happens in it. Those who made and implemented the *Awa maru* safe-passage agreement could not see that the Pacific submarine war had grown into an endeavor beyond their control. They could not, as Commander Loughlin's court-martial demonstrated, anticipate every contingency, prevent misdrafting and mishandling of warning messages, or direct the judgments and actions of every captain at sea.

These errors of presumption, which led to the sinking, were followed by others in the management of its consequences. Some were immediate. The *Queenfish*, as Admiral Lockwood recognized then and some of her crew members acknowledged later, might have done more to rescue *Awa maru* passengers; there need not have been only one survivor. Other errors came later. Admiral King and the State Department officials who insisted upon an immediate court-martial inquiry and indemnification if it demonstrated American responsibility for the tragedy were right. Admiral Lockwood, however, went too far in defending Commander Loughlin, and he exaggerated the importance of Captain Hamada's alleged errors as causes of the sinking. Also, the State Department officials who declined, shortly after the fighting stopped, to follow through on their wartime promise of indemnification made a terrible mistake.

Their in-house critics then and bereaved *Awa maru* family members much later were correct in saying that the United States had a legal and moral obligation to compensate Japanese victims for what they had lost. Justice was not properly served by the 1949 claims-abandonment agreement and its implementing legislation, but wisdom was, at least insofar as the politicians and diplomats of the day perceived it. They correctly judged that putting the ghost of war, as it appeared in the *Awa maru* claims, behind them was essential. It had to be banished if they were to build peace and security in a Cold War world threatened by the specter of still more terrible conflict. The lesser evil had to be accepted to achieve the greater good.

That was an argument to which American and Japanese shapers of public memory of the *Awa maru*'s sinking responded differently. Admiral Lockwood acknowledged its force. As author and aide in the creation of written and visual forms of public memory, he at first tried to preserve the humanity of his submariner heroes by acknowledging the enormity of the error they committed on the night of 1 April 1945. Over time, however, he gave way to pressures—some political and professional, others technological, commercial, and artistic—that demanded downplaying and eventually forgetting their greatest mistake.

The shapers of Japanese public memory of the *Awa maru* tragedy could never do that. They saw themselves as victims first, last, and always. In their pursuit of the truth about what had befallen the ship and why they had been treated as they were, they exaggerated their own, and Japan's, victimization. In 1956 Commander Chihaya drew sweeping conclusions of conspiracy and deliberate deception from inconsistent and incomplete evidence. A decade later Arima Yorichika wove together fact and fiction to offer his readers solid emotional, but poor historical, truth. Mrs. Tōkō and the *Awa maru* bereaved families exaggerated their mistreatment at governments' hands. They forgot that they had been paid a sum considerable at the time, when other war victims got nothing. They took later Japanese government compensation of bereaved families of civilian passengers on a ship American submariners had sunk as evidence of their own maltreatment.[54] Most importantly, they lost sight of the fact that no amount of money, paid by any government, could ever compensate them for their loss.

Self-deception of a similar sort dogged those who searched for and those who eventually found the *Awa maru*. Minoru Fukumitsu and Bill Bunton were probably correct in arguing that much more than what was listed on her manifest lay in the ship's holds and safes; they were utterly wrong, however, in believing that purely private efforts could recover that fortune from the sea. As their behavior in 1979–1981 demonstrated, Japanese and Chinese government officials were determined to bend truths about the salvaging to suit their perceived international and domestic political needs. Just as the competitors in the race to find the ship erred in not collaborating sooner and more effectively, so too these officials concealed the full truth of her salvage and failed to make it an occasion for Japanese-American reconciliation as well as one of Sino-Japanese cooperation. Cloaking their activities in secrecy and ritual, they missed an opportunity to heal old war wounds.

That end to the *Awa maru* story points to its larger and continuing significance. Americans and Japanese—and indeed all who fought the Pacific War —must see it for what it was. They need to reexamine the greatest conflict in their shared past, without distortions introduced by self-serving and contradictory national public memories, and with the benefit of solid historical research. Americans and Japanese must narrow the gap between their respective understandings of that war long past, so as to keep it from poisoning their current and future relations with one another.

More than that, they must let tales like the *Awa maru* story deepen their understanding of war so as to render its recurrence less likely. If younger generations appreciate that war is the province of error as well as of achievement, if they recognize that it brings tragedies like the sinking of the *Awa maru* as well as victories in battle and triumphs of the human spirit, then perhaps they will not have to learn those truths from bitter experience, as the generation that fought the Pacific War did. Only by welcoming the ghost of war past and listening to the truths it teaches can we hope to drive away the specter of wars yet to come.

Notes

Chapter 1. The Greatest Submarine Error

1. *Queenfish* Fourth War Patrol Report, 14 April, p. 12, box 66, Record Group (RG) 38, U.S. National Archives (NA). (*Queenfish* war patrol reports will hereinafter be cited as QFWPR, with report and page numbers following). Charles Elliott Loughlin War Patrol Log, 1 April 1945, in John E. Bennett papers, Solana Beach, California (this source will be cited as LWPL, with appropriate date indications); U.S. Navy Navigational Publication 157, copy provided by Capt. Frank Nickols Shamer, USN (Ret.).

2. QFWPR 4: 12; Interview with Capt. Frank Nickols Shamer, USN (Ret.), San Diego, California, 15 July 1992; Director of Naval History, *Dictionary of American Naval Fighting Ships*, Volume 5 (Washington: Office of Naval History, 1970), 412. This source will hereinafter be cited as *DANFS*, with appropriate volume and page indications.

3. Ibid (used here and in subsequent notes to refer to the *last* source cited in the preceding note); Shamer interviews, 15 July 1992 and 25 June 1993.

4. Richard T. Speer, "Let Pass Safely the *Awa Maru*," U.S. Naval Institute *Proceedings*, 100 (April 1974), 73; *DANFS*, 5: 413.

5. Shamer interview, 15 July 1992; Interviews with Capt. John E. Bennett, USN (Ret.), Solana Beach, California, 14 May and 7 July 1993.

6. QFWPR 4: 2.

7. Shamer interview, 15 July 1992. I have also drawn on Rear Adm. Corwin Mendenhall, *Submarine Diary* (Chapel Hill, N.C.: Algonquin Books of Chapel Hill, 1991), 8, for physical description of life aboard an American submarine.

8. Shamer interviews, 15 July 1992, 25 June 1993; Bennett interview, 14 May 1993; Clay Blair, Jr., *Silent Victory: The U.S. Submarine War Against Japan* (Philadelphia: Lippincott, 1975), 991–992.

9. Mendenhall, xiv.

10. Loughlin officer biography, officer biographies series, box 400, Classified Operational Archives, Naval Historical Center, Washington Navy Yard, Washington, D.C. This archive will hereinafter be cited as COA, NHC.

11. Speer, 71.

12. QFWPR 1, first endorsement by Vice Adm. Charles A. Lockwood, Jr., 18 October 1944; QFWPR 2, first endorsement by Capt. G.L. Russell, 6 December 1944, box 66, RG 38, NA. I am grateful to Capt. John E. Bennett for loaning me copies of these reports in his possession.

13. QFWPR 3: 15–28; Blair, 965.

14. Blair, 984–987, lists commanders in terms of their "efficiency." Commander Loughlin ranked thirty-sixth out of seventy-seven; Shamer interview, 15 July 1992. For additional evidence of submariners' penchant for measuring performance in terms of "efficiency," see Mendenhall, 29, 50, 69, 91, 116, 133, 152, 190, 215, 250, 269.

15. QFWPR 4: 3–12.

16. QFWPR 4: 12.

17. USS *Sea Fox* (SS 402) Report of Third War Patrol, 6 May 1945, 11, submarine war patrol report copies file, COA, NHC. This source will hereinafter be cited as SFWPR, with appropriate number and page indications.

18. Shamer interview, 15 July 1992.

19. Record of Proceedings of a General Court-Martial convened at Headquarters, Commander Forward Area, Central Pacific, by order of Commander-in-Chief, U.S. Pacific Fleet and Pacific Ocean Areas: Case of Charles E. Loughlin, Commander, U.S. Navy, April 1945, transcript of proceedings, 19 April 1945, 3, 11, 18, 22, microfilm copy, Navy Department Library, Naval Historical Center, Washington Navy Yard, Washington, D.C. This source will hereinafter be cited as Loughlin court-martial, with appropriate date and page citations.

20. QFWPR 4: 12; Shamer interview, 15 July 1992; Loughlin court-martial, 19 April, 3, 25.

21. Loughlin court-martial, 19 April, 3.

22. QFWPR 4: 12, SFWPR3: 12 indicated the message was received at 2231 on 1 April 1945.

23. Loughlin court-martial, 19 April, 3–4, 15, 20, 36; Shamer interview, 25 June 1993.

24. Ibid.; QFWPR 4: 12; Loughlin court-martial, 19 April, 23–24; Bennett interview, 14 May 1993.

25. Shamer interviews, 15 July 1992 and 25 June 1993.

26. QFWPR 4: 12; Loughlin court-martial, 19 April, 23–24.

27. QFWPR 4: 12; Loughlin court-martial, 19 April, 17, 19.

28. QFWPR 4: 12.

29. Shamer interviews, 15 July 1992 and 25 June 1993.

30. Shamer interview, 15 July 15; QFWPR 4: 12, 22.

31. Shamer interview, 15 July 1992; Bennett interview, 14 May 1993; I am indebted to Commander Seno Sadao, JMSDF (Ret.) for providing information about the variable size of Japanese destroyer and destroyer escort crews.

32. Minoru Fukumitsu, *Awa Maru jiken* [The *Awa maru* incident] (Tokyo: Yomiuri shimbunsha, 1973), 185–201.

33. W. Joe Innis with Bill Bunton, *In Pursuit of the Awa Maru* (New York: Bantam Books, 1981), 154. Blair, 623, records that the *Jack* (SS 259) sent an entire Imperial Japanese Army regiment of three thousand men to their deaths by sinking the freighter *Yoshida maru I* in April 1944. The *Bowfin* (SS 287)'s sinking of the *Tsushima maru* on 24 August 1944, took 1,484 civilian lives, fewer than the total number of passengers on the *Awa maru*, but far more women and children—evacuees from Okinawa—were among them. See George Feifer, *Tennozan: The Battle of Okinawa and the Atomic Bomb* (New York: Ticknor and Fields, 1992), 92. While John D. Alden, *U.S. Submarine Attacks during World War II (Including Allied Submarine Attacks in the Pacific Theater)* (Annapolis, Md.: Naval Institute Press, 1989), 126, confirms an attack on that date, Blair, 698, mistakenly places it on 22 July 1944.

34. Rear Adm. Richard G. Voge, "Too Much Accuracy," U.S. Naval Institute *Proceedings,* 76 (March 1950), 258.

35. Vice Adm. Charles A. Lockwood and Percy Finch, "We Gave the Japs a Licking Underseas," *Saturday Evening Post,* 222 (30 July 1949), 30.

Chapter 2. *Relief to the Prisoners*

1. Ronald H. Spector, *Eagle against the Sun: The American War with Japan* (New York: Vintage Books, 1985), 480; Janet M. Manson, *Diplomatic Ramifications of Unrestricted Submarine Warfare, 1939–1941* (New York: Greenwood Press, 1990), 157–158.

2. For a particularly poignant account of the Pearl Harbor Day internment of an American teaching in Japan, see Robert Crowder, "An American's Life in Japan before and after the Pearl Harbor Attack," *Journal of American-East Asian Relations* 3 (Fall 1994), 262–263.

3. Department of State Press Release, 24 October 1944, /10-2444, file 711.94114 supplies, box 3421, Record Group 59, U.S. National Archives; this file will hereinafter be cited as *Awa maru* file, with appropriate document and date citations. Throughout this study I have used "safe passage" in place of "safe conduct," the technical term in international law for this type of agreement, because the phrase conveys a clearer meaning of what was intended in the type of agreement that was negotiated.

4. Manson, 150–158, describes the origins of this order.

5. Carl Boyd and Yoshida Akihiko, *The Japanese Submarine Force and World War II* (Annapolis, Md.: Naval Institute Press, 1995), 65–67; Manson, 160.

6. Manson, 44–45, analyzes the origins and subsequent interpretation of Article

22 of the 1930 London Naval Treaty. By applying cruiser rules to the conduct of submarine warfare, it clearly banned sinking merchantmen without prior warning. Pages 148–158 demonstrate the impact of German actions on the pre–Pearl Harbor American decision to wage unrestricted submarine warfare against Japan in the event of a conflict.

7. *New York Times,* 10, 14 January 1942; Samuel I. Rosenman, comp., *The Public Papers and Addresses of Franklin D. Roosevelt, 1942 Volume: Humanity on the Defensive* (New York: Harper and Brothers, 1950): 36.

8. William Renzi and Mark D. Roehrs, *Never Look Back: A History of World War II in the Pacific* (Armonk, N. Y.: M.E. Sharpe, 1991), 50; E. Bartlett Kerr, *Surrender and Survival: The Experience of American POWs in the Pacific 1941–1945* (New York: Morrow, 1985), 35–38.

9. John Toland, *The Rising Sun* (New York: Bantam, 1971), 316; Renzi, 51–52.

10. R. Ernest Dupuy and Trevor Dupuy, *Encyclopedia of Military History,* rev. ed. (New York: Harper & Row, 1977), 1140; Kerr, 51–63; Donald J. Young, *The Battle of Bataan* (Jefferson, N.C.: McFarland, 1992), 303–331; Lester I. Tenney, *My Hitch in Hell: The Bataan Death March* (Washington, D.C.: Brassey's, 1995), 35–64.

11. P. Scott Corbett, *Quiet Passages: The Exchange of Civilians between the United States and Japan during the Second World War* (Kent, Ohio: Kent State University Press, 1987), 31, 37, 51–52.

12. Corbett, 36–37, 116. Roger Daniels, *Prisoners without Trial* (New York: Hill and Wang, 1993), 22–48, describes the events leading up to the order to relocate Japanese nationals and Japanese-Americans.

13. Corbett, 116; Unofficial approximation of American POWs and internees presently held by Japan, 24 February 1945, file A, box 2, Captain Harry L. Pence, USN, collection, Mandeville Special Collections Department, University of California San Diego Library, La Jolla, California.

14. Corbett, 3–4; Red Cross, International Committee, Geneva, *The International Red Cross in Geneva 1863–1943* (Geneva: International Red Cross, 1943), 22, 60–62 (the International Red Cross organization will hereinafter be abbreviated as ICRC).

15. Eliot Wadsworth to Gwin, n.d., 1946, file A: POW Convention 1929 proposed changes, box 2, Pence papers. For text of the 1929 Geneva Convention on Treatment of Prisoners of War, see Leon Friedman, ed., *The Law of War: A Documentary History* (New York: Random House, 1972) 1: 488–522.

16. *The International Red Cross in Geneva, 1863–1943,* 22. At its 1938 meeting in London, ICRC delegates simply discussed protection of prisoners in a possible war.

17. Corbett, 3–4, 50.

18. *The International Red Cross in Geneva,* 22.

19. Arthur Goodfriend, *The Jap Soldier* (Washington, D.C.: *The Infantry Journal,* 1943), 52.

20. Corbett, 83.

21. The War Relocation Authority was established by executive order on 18 March 1942. See Daniels, 55; Hata Ikuhiko, "Taiheiyō sensō ki no Nihonjin furyo" [Japanese prisoners of war in the Pacific War period], *Seiji keizai shigaku* [Political and economic history] (February 1993), 78.

22. The Department of State had established its Special War Problems Division (SWPD) on 1 September 1939; Corbett, 1. By early 1945 SWPD consisted of three branches (Welfare and Whereabouts, Representation, and Internee) and one section (Relief), each headed by an assistant division chief. The Relief section had only four of the division's forty employees and was headed by Eldred D. Kuppinger; Special War Problems Division description and telephone directory, folder B, box 2, Pence papers. Ōta Ichirō, *Nihon gaikō shi dai nijūyonkan Dai TōA sensō senji gaikō* [A history of Japanese diplomacy, Volume 24, diplomacy during the Greater East Asia War] (Tokyo: Kajima kenkyūjo shuppan kai, 1971), 45–46; Marcel Junod, *Warriors without Weapons* (London: Jonathan Cape, 1951), 275–276, indicates that a Central Liaison Office for prisoner and internee matters was established in the Japanese Ministry of Foreign Affairs.

23. Corbett, 44–46, 123.

24. Junod, 236, 254, 274, demonstrates the slowness and weakness of the ICRC organization. It depended upon Swiss citizens resident in Japan to volunteer for prisoner and internee camp visits. Its official delegate resident in Tokyo died in 1944, and not until five days before war's end did a replacement reach the Japanese capital.

25. Corbett, 30–36.

26. Kerr, 39, 83. Tokinotani Masaru, *Nihon kindai shi jiten* [Dictionary of modern Japanese history] (Tokyo: Tōyō keizai shimbunsha, 1958), 694.

27. Hata, "Nihonjin furyo," 80–81. The Red Cross inquiry followed a previous U.S. government request that Japan provide quinine to American prisoners of war. See Swiss Minister, Tokyo, to Ministry of Foreign Affairs, 26 February 1942, frames 303–304, S. 1.7.0.0-38, Ippan oyobi shomondai: Tekkokujin kyūjutsu mondai [General and specific problems: the problem of providing relief to enemy aliens], reel S 579, Library of Congress microform 5039, Library of Congress (documents from this source will hereinafter be identified by reel and microform number only. The reels and subject designators are those provided in Cecil Uyehara and Edwin G. Beal, *Checklist of Archives of the Japanese Ministry of Foreign Affairs, Tokyo Japan, 1868–1945, Microfilmed by the Library of Congress* [Washington: Library of Congress Photoduplication Service, 1954]).

28. Shinobu Jumpei, "DaiTōA sensō to furyo toriatsukai mondai" [The Greater East Asia War and the problem of prisoner treatment], *Gaikō jiho* (15 May 1942), cited by Hata, "Nihonjin furyo," 80; Kamisaka Tsunesaburō, ed., *Who's Who in Japan, with Manchoukuo and China, 1939–1940* (Tokyo: Who's Who in Japan Publishing Company, 1939), 863. Charles B. Burdick and Ursula Moessner, *The German Prisoners-of-War in Japan, 1914–1920* (Lanham, Md.: University Press of America, 1984), demonstrates that being a prisoner of war in World War I Japan was no picnic.

29. Chronological Record of Efforts to Arrange for Shipment of Supplies to American Nationals in Far East, 17 January 1944, 1–1744, *Awa maru* file (this State Department document will hereinafter be referred to as Chronological Record, with appropriate citation of specific messages noted).

30. Corbett, 56–71, details events culminating in the first *Gripsholm* exchange.

31. Department of State to Bern, #2061, 29 August, Bern to Department of State, #4186, 13 September 1942, Chronological Record; San Francisco KWID 31 August 1942 broadcast transcript, frame 221, reel 579, S 1.7.0.0-38, Library of Congress Microform 5079.

32. Corbett, 10, paints an acid portrait of Long. Irvin F. Gellman, *Secret Affairs: Franklin Roosevelt, Cordell Hull, and Sumner Welles* (Baltimore: Johns Hopkins University Press, 1995), 231–232, presents a more balanced view of the assistant secretary of state.

33. Fred L. Israel, ed., *The War Diary of Breckinridge Long* (Lincoln: University of Nebraska Press, 1966), 27 August 1942 entry, 280.

34. Hata, "Nihonjin furyo," 81.

35. Corbett, 73–78.

36. Corbett, 89, 144–146, 163. John K. Emmerson, *The Japanese Thread: A Life in the U.S. Foreign Service* (New York: Holt, Rinehart and Winston, 1978), 125–149, details Peruvian-American cooperation in interning Japanese.

37. Corbett, 85.

38. "Americans Return from Jap Prison Camps," *Life* 13 (7 September 1942), 23. This same issue carried photographs of the American embassy staff during its captivity in Tokyo, and also a young American woman's account of her internment at the University of Santo Tomas in Manila and subsequent release to join the first *Gripsholm* exchange group. See "American Diplomats Held in Tokyo: Lives in a Virtual State of Suspension," and Frances Long, " 'Yankee Girl': Adventures of a Young American Who Spent Five Months in Japanese Internment Camp at Manila," 24–25, 82–91.

39. John B. Powell, "Prisoner of the Japanese: Experiences in Shanghai," *Nation* 155 (10 October 1942), 335–337; reprinted in abbreviated form, *Readers Digest* 41 (November 1942), 63–66. Other published tales of Japanese mistreatment of Americans in their custody included Robert Bellaire, "Tokyo Nightmare: Six Months of Terror and Starvation in Japan's Worst Concentration Camp," *Collier's* 110 (26 September 1942), 37 ff; Max Hill, "Tokio [*sic*] Christmas," *The New Yorker* 18 (December 1942), 42 ff; Max Hill and W. Brown, *Exchange Ship* (New York: Farrar, Rinehart, and Company, 1942); "Tell America What They Have Done to Us," *Saturday Review of Literature* 26 (9 January 1943), 5–7; Joseph Alsop, "City in Prison: Americans Interned in a Hongkong Brothel," and "Starvation Is Torture Too: Stanley Internment Camp in Hongkong," *Saturday Evening Post* 215 (9, 16 January 1943), 12–13 ff, 28–29 ff. Alsop was a distant cousin to President Roosevelt. See Joseph Alsop, *FDR, 1882–1945: A Centenary Remembrance* (New York: Viking Press, 1982), 14–15.

40. Corbett, 86–87.

41. Department of State to Kuibyshev, #41, 18 January 1943, Chronological Record.

42. George Alexander Lensen, *The Strange Neutrality: Soviet-Japanese Relations during the Second World War 1941–1945* (Tallahassee, Fla.: The Diplomatic Press, 1972), 1–34; Akira Iriye, *The Origins of the Second World War in Asia and the Pacific* (New York: Longman, 1987), 128–138.

43. Martha Gibbon, "Food from Home," *Woman's Home Companion*, 69 (November 1942), 68–69, details the earlier development of American Red Cross efforts to provide succor to those in Japanese custody; Department of State to Kuibyshev, #41, 18 January 1943, Chronological Record.

44. Waldo Heinrichs, *Threshold of War: Franklin D. Roosevelt and American Entry into World War II* (New York: Oxford University Press, 1988), 8.

45. Francis Brown, comp., *The War in Maps* (New York: Oxford University Press, 1946), 78–79, 134–135.

46. Lensen, 60–73; Rudy Abramson, *Spanning the Century: The Life of W. Averell Harriman, 1891–1986* (New York: Morrow, 1992), 377; 20 February 1943 memorandum of conversation with Lozovski, box 17, William H. Standley papers, Regional Cultural Historical Collection, University of Southern California Library, Los Angeles. The Japanese subsequently freed three Soviet ships and then captured another. That prompted Soviet Foreign Minister Molotov to remark that "the Japanese were always seizing something that did not belong to them." See Memorandum of Standley-Molotov conversation, 2 July 1943, box 17, Standley papers.

47. Robert M. Scovell to L. M. Mitchell, 20 February 1943, box 33, Standley papers. Scovell was the American Red Cross Special Representative in Moscow.

48. Polish Government [in Exile] Declaration on the Discovery of Massacred Officers, 17 April 1943, Moscow correspondence file, box 17, Standley papers; William H. Standley and Arthur A. Ageton, *Admiral Ambassador to Russia* (Chicago: Henry Regnery, 1955), 403–405. For recent treatments of the Katyn Forest tragedy, see Vladimir Abarinov, *The Murderers of Katyn* (New York: Hippocrene Books, 1993), and Maurice Shanberg, *The KGB Solution at Katyn* (Franklin Lakes, N.J.: Lincoln Springs Press, 1989).

49. Standley and Ageton, 12–14, 39, 192–194. John C. Walter, "William Harrison Standley," in Robert William Love, Jr., *The Chiefs of Naval Operations* (Annapolis, Md.: Naval Institute Press, 1980), 98, suggests that desire to escape a vacuous Navy public relations job in Washington may also have figured in Standley's acceptance of the ambassadorship.

50. Abramson, 344.

51. Standley and Ageton, 123–125, 138–139, 150. The admiral's letters to his wife during his service in the Soviet Union are in box 16, Standley papers.

52. Department of State to Kuibyshev, #41, 18 January 1943, Chronological Record.

53. Standley and Ageton, 140; memorandum of Standley-Molotov conversation, 5 February 1943, box 17, Standley papers.

54. Ibid.; memorandum of Standley-Lozovski conversation, 20 February 1943, box 17, Standley papers.

55. Memorandum of Standley-Molotov conversation, 20 March 1943, box 17, Standley papers; Lensen, 15.

56. Bern to Department of State, #2178,7 April 1943, Chronological Record; Memorandum of Standley-Molotov conversation, 10 April 1943, box 17, Standley papers.

57. Standley to Molotov, aide memoire, 28 April 1943, box 17 Standley papers.

58. Moscow to Department of State, #416, 8 May 1943, Chronological Record.

59. Moscow to Department of State, #256, 26 May, Department of State to Moscow, #531, 7 July, #578, 17 July, #835, 11 September 1943, Chronological Record.

60. Moscow to Department of State, #1024, 5 August 1943, Chronological Record.

61. Stimson to Hull, 3 August 1943, *Awa maru* file, box 2250, RG 59; Standley and Ageton, 381.

62. Standley to Mrs. Standley, 11 August 1943, box 16, Standley papers.

63. Department of State to Moscow, #702, 17 August 1943, /8-1743 *Awa maru* file, box 2250, RG 59.

64. Gaud to Dorsz, 28 August 1943, /8-2843, *Awa maru* file, box 2250.

65. Moscow to Department of State, #1264, 4 September 1943, Chronological Record.

66. Standley to Mrs. Evelyn Standley, 16 September 1943, box 16, Standley papers. Standley's bitterness over his experience in the wartime Soviet Union translated into ferocious anti-communism during the postwar years. In retirement he pilloried the city fathers of San Diego for keeping a red star atop their civic center. See Walter, in Love, 98.

67. N.d. 1945 memorandum, "lists," file F, box 2, Pence papers.

68. Moscow to Department of State, #1869, 7 November, #2035, 24 November 1943, Chronological Record.

69. Release kits, file F, box 2, Pence papers; Department of State press release, 24 October 1944, *Awa maru* file, box 2252, RG 59.

70. Kerr, 210.

71. Corbett, 169, 182.

72. *New York Times*, 27, 29 January 1944. Sometime in July 1943 Navy Cdr. Melvin H. McCoy, Lt. Col. Steven M. Mellnik, U.S. Army, and Capt. William E. Dyess of the Army Air Corps escaped from a POW camp on Mindanao, the southernmost Philippine island, and fled to Australia. When they reached Brisbane, Gen. Douglas MacArthur invited them to his headquarters, heard their account of Japanese mistreatment of prisoners, and decorated them with Distinguished Service Medals. Vowing that "the Japanese will pay for that humiliation and suffering," the general sought Army Chief of Staff George C. Marshall's permission to make public what the three

officers had told him. Marshall, however, at the State Department's request, denied MacArthur's request, telling him that publicizing the escapees' story might disrupt "delicate" indirect negotiations with Japan for additional exchanges of internees and delivery of Red Cross relief parcels to prisoners of war. That left MacArthur fuming, and either he or a senior member of his staff saw to it that the arch-conservative Republican *Chicago Tribune* learned of the escapees' story. But the War Department succeeded in keeping it out of print. That decision was reversed in January 1944, when the War Department, in response to a former Office of War Information official's threat to charge the Japanese with murdering fifty thousand war prisoners, decided to release the story. See D. Clayton James, *The Years of MacArthur* 2 (Boston: Houghton Mifflin, 1975), 512–513; William Dyess, *The Dyess Story: The Eye-Witness Account of the Death March from Bataan and the Narrative of Experiences in Japanese Prison Camps and of Eventual Escape* (New York: G.P. Putnam's Sons, 1944). Steven Mellnik eventually published his account of defeat, imprisonment, and escape as *Philippine Diary 1939–1945* (New York: Van Nostrand and Reinhold, 1969).

73. *New York Times,* 1 February 1944.

74. *New York Times,* 1–6, 16 February 1944.

75. SRS 1346, #824, 27 June 1944 MAGIC diplomatic summary, 1995 "new releases," box 14, Records of the National Security Agency, Record Group 457, U.S. National Archives, Washington, D.C.

76. Bern to Department of State, #246, 11 January 1944, Chronological Record. By July 1943 the question of Allied attacks against Japanese hospital ships and Japanese misuse of such ships to transport war matériel had become a matter of serious concern to the U.S. Navy. See R.E. Schuirmann Memorandum for F-1234, 21 July 1943, in COMINCH Combat Intelligence Division File on Hospital Ships, SRH-323, Part I, Box 57, RG 457; R.E. Schuirmann Memorandum for F-1234, 22 July 1943, in COMINCH Combat Intelligence Division File on Hospital Ships, SRH-323, Part III, RG 457. The latter listed six alleged attacks on Japanese hospital ships.

77. *New York Times,* 29 January 1944.

78. Japanese Ministry of Foreign Affairs to Swiss Minister, Tokyo, 28 April 1944, frames 787–859, reel 578, S1.0.0-37 Ippan oyobi sho mondai: TaiNichi kōgi kankei Kōgi kiso shiryō Shūren sakusei: Kōgi jiken shiryō [General and specific problems: protests to Japan, section 4, materials for incidents worthy of protest, compiled by the Central Liaison Office], Library of Congress microform 5039.

79. *New York Times,* 4, 16 February 1944; Department of State to Bern, #627, 24 February, Supplement to Memorandum of 17 January 1944, 6 June 1944, relief chronology (documents from this supplement to the earlier chronology will hereinafter be cited as Supplement, Chronological Record, with appropriate date citations).

80. *New York Times,* 22 February 1944; Representative Mike Mansfield (D–Mont) to Hull, 10 May 1944, item 192, Supplement, Chronological Record.

81. Mrs. H. W. Bigger to Roosevelt, 16 March 1944, /3-1644, Mrs. E. P. King, Jr. to Hull, 9 March 1944, /3-944 *Awa maru* file, box 2250, RG 59.

82. Hull to Roosevelt, 16 June 1944, box 2517, RG 59, cited by Corbett, 124–125.

83. Murata Kiyoaki, *Enemy among Friends* (New York: Kodansha International, 1991), 123–124.

84. Corbett, 134–135.

85. Soviet Government to Japanese Government, 8 April 1944, item 68, Supplement, Chronological Record.

86. Hull to Leahy, Stimson, Knox, and Biddell, 15 March 1944, enclosing Bern to Department of State, #1218, 29 February 1944; Leahy to Hull, 31 March 1944; memorandum on minutes of 18 April 1944 meeting of interdepartmental board [on prisoners of war], 20 April 1944, Jap atrocities folder, box 88, SWPD papers, RG 59. (In this and subsequent citations from this source, I have used the original language on the folder.)

87. Japanese Government to United States Government, 10 May 1944, item 70, Supplement, Chronological Record.

88. Bern to Department of State, #3076, 14 May 1944, Jap atrocities folder, box 88, SWPD papers, RG 59.

89. Department of State #1180 to Moscow, #1180, 12 May 1944, item 72; Department of State to Moscow, #1709, 15 May 1944; United States Government to Government of U.S.S.R., 15 May 1944, item 76;, Department of State aide memoire to Soviet Ambassador, Washington, 20 May 1944, item 80; Department of State to London, 15 May 1944, item 81, Supplement, Chronological Record.

90. Moscow to Department of State, 15 May 1944, 25 May 1944, item 86, Supplement, Chronological Record.

91. Memorandum of Hull-Gromyko conversation, 29 May 1944, item 89, Supplement, Chronological Record; Editors of *Life* and Rand McNally, *Life Pictorial Atlas of the World* (New York: Time, Inc., 1961), 329, 354. Nakhodka, appropriately enough, is situated on the northwest side of Amerika Bay. See map NK-53, Army Map Series, Corps of Engineers, 12-60, Scale 1:250,000, compiled in 1950 from Manchuria, Siberia, and Mongolia, 1:1,000,000 Japanese General Staff maps, in University of California Los Angeles Maps Collection. I am indebted to Ms. Portia Chambliss for calling my attention to this and other small-scale maps pertinent to the *Awa maru* story.

92. Department of State to Moscow, #90, 29 May 1944, item 89; Department of State Press release, 6 June 1944, item 97, Supplement, Chronological Record

93. Corbett, 162, 183. The Japanese expressed complete inability to understand why the United States was taking custody of its nationals from Bolivia. On 1 June 1944, the Navy Department released a grim report on navy personnel held by the Japanese. See *New York Times*, 2 June 1944.

94. Tokyo circular #1479, 23 December 1944, H-158570, SRDJ 83813, in Japanese Messages Concerning the *Hoshi maru* and the *Awa maru* December 1944 through August 1945, SRH–122, box 20, Records of the National Security Agency, SRH-122, RG 457, U.S. National Archives, Washington, D.C.

95. Matsui Kakushin, "Kūhaku e no chōsen" [Challenge to the void: the *Awa Maru*

tragedy] 7, *Asahi shimbun*, 10 September 1990. Articles from this newspaper series will hereinafter be cited as Matsui, with the article's number in the sequence preceding the place and date of publication.

96. *New York Times*, 10 May 1944. The number of Japanese prisoners of war taken from the Southwest Pacific Area to the United States was only 604 at the end of 1943; it had risen to 4,435 by the beginning of the Philippine campaign in October 1944. See George G. Lewis and John Mewha, *History of Prisoner of War Utilization by the United States Army 1776–1945* (Washington: Center of Military History, United States Army, 1955), 1982 ed., 247. Alison B. Gilmore, "'We Have Been Reborn': Japanese Prisoners and the Allied Propaganda War in the Southwest Pacific," *Pacific Historical Review* 64 (May 1995), 196, contends that only a fivefold increase in the number of Japanese prisoners taken by U. S. Army, Southwest Pacific forces, occurred in 1944.

97. Corbett, 106.

98. The Tōjō Cabinet left office on 22 July 1944. Tokinotani, 694.

99. Kerr, 191. The vice-director was Colonel Odashima Tadashi.

100. John Prados, *Combined Fleet Decoded: The Secret History of American Intelligence and the Japanese Navy in World War II* (New York: Random House, 1995), 59–64, 623–624, 734–735. Edward J. Drea, *MacArthur's Ultra: Codebreaking and the War against Japan, 1942–1945* (Lawrence: University Press of Kansas, 1992), 213–214; Leon V. Sigal, *Fighting to a Finish: The Politics of War Termination in the United States and Japan, 1945* (Ithaca, N.Y.: Cornell University Press, 1988), 37–38.

101. Kerr, 195–204, details the sufferings prisoners endured during their shipment from Southeast Asia to Japan. Those trials included attack by American pilots and submariners, both unaware of the prisoners' presence on the ships hit.

102. Feifer, 80–82, 92–93; Alden, 110, 126.

103. Parillo, 206.

104. Bern to Department of State, #246, 11 January 1944, Chronological Record.

105. Information regarding prisoner-of-war-ship sinkings [in the] latter part [of] 1944, 19 March 1945 memorandum, List of Japanese ships sunk while transporting allied prisoners of war and civilians, n.d., file C, box 2, Pence papers

106. SRS-1363, #841, 14 July 1944, "New" non-sanitized MAGIC Diplomatic Summaries, January 1993 release, box 9, Records of the National Security Agency, RG 457, U.S. National Archives, Washington, D.C.

107. 6 October 1944 Japanese Government to U. S. Government, cited in Matsui 7, *Asahi shimbun*, 10 September 1990. In making these demands, the Japanese government appears to have gone beyond the norms of two different types of international legal agreements that allowed for the safe passage of a vessel. One was a "safe conduct," which allowed an enemy person or ship to proceed to a particular place "for a defined object." The other was a "cartel," a convention between belligerents "permitting certain kinds of non-hostile intercourse between them which would otherwise be

prevented by war." A cartel agreement presumed singularity of purpose and forbade trade or the carriage of contraband goods. Tokyo obviously had multiple purposes in mind in shaping this accord and did, as will be shown in chapter three, use the *Awa maru* to carry contraband. See L[assa Francis Lawrence] Oppenheim, *International Law: A Treatise*, Volume 2, *Disputes, War and Neutrality*, H. Lauterpacht, ed. (6th ed., revised, London: Longmans, Green and Co., 1944), 423–424, 429. Green Haywood Hackworth, *Digest of International Law* (Washington: Department of State, 1943) 6: 542–551, reveals the paucity of international law precedents for safe-conduct [safe passage] agreements in comparison to those for cartel ships.

108. 6 October 1944 Japanese Government to U. S. Government, cited in Matsui 7, *Asahi shimbun*, 10 September 1990.

109. A Japanese message of 9 October 1944 about payment of Soviet port taxes was received in garbled form in Bern and taken on 18 October as evidence of a break-through in the negotiations. See Bern to Department of State, 18 October 1944, *Awa maru* file, box 2252.

110. In addition to the State-War-Navy Coordinating Committee for broad war and postwar policy matters, an interdepartmental committee on prisoner of war matters had been formed. See Pence career summary, Pence papers; and SWPD memorandum, Suggestion that an official publicity campaign be directed against Japan and Germany based on their treatment of American prisoners of war, 8 January 1945, folder January–March 1945, box 88, Records of the Special War Problems Division, RG 59.

111. 78 Congress, 2nd Session, House Document 393, Japanese Atrocities to Pris-oners of War Joint Press Release of the War and Navy Departments Containing Sto-ries of Japanese Atrocities and Brutalities to the American and Philippine Armed Forces Who Were Prisoners of War in the Philippine Islands (Washington: Govern-ment Printing Office, 1944), in folder D, box 2, Pence papers.

112. Department of State Press Release, 24 October 1944, *Awa maru* file, box 2252, RG 59.

113. Memorandum to Admiral William F. Leahy, Jap atrocities folder, box 88, Records of the Special War Problems Division, Record Group 59; Kerr, 210.

114. Department of State to American Embassy Moscow, #2093, 31 August 1944, /8-2644, *Awa maru* file.

Chapter 3. Mission of Mercy

1. Bern to Department of State, #C6981, 21 October 1944, /10-2144; Matsui 8, *Asahi shimbun*, 11 September 1990.

2. Kuppinger memorandum, 23 October 1944, /10-2344, *Awa maru* file.

3. Bern to Department of State, #7256, 1 November, /11-144; Department of State, #2615 to Moscow, 6 November 1944, /11-644, *Awa maru* file.

4. Moscow to Department of State, #4351, 12 November, forwarding Vladivostok to Department of State, #161, 11 November 1944, / 11-1244, *Awa maru* file.

5. *New York Times*, 7 November 1944; Bern #7407 to Department of State, 8 November 1944, / 11-844, *Awa maru* file.

6. Bern to Department of State, #C6891, 21 October, / 10-2144; Bern to Department of State, #7503, 13 November, / 11-1344; Department of State to Bern, #4131, 7 December 1944, / 12-744, *Awa maru* file.

7. Moscow (Kennan) to Department of State, #4351, 12 November 1944, / 11-1244, *Awa maru* file.

8. Bern to Department of State, #C6891, 21 October, / 10-2144; Bern to Department of State, #7756, 25 November 1944, 11-2544, *Awa maru* file.

9. *New York Times*, 7 November 1944; Bern to Department of State, 25 November 1944, / 11-2544, *Awa maru* file.

10. Kuppinger to Plitt, 21 November 1944, / 11-2144, *Awa maru* file.

11. Bern to Department of State, #7756, 25 November 1944, / 11-2544, *Awa maru* file.

12. Department of State to Moscow, #2286, 25 November, / 11-2544, Department of State to Bern, #4131, 7 December 1944, / 12-744, *Awa maru* file.

13. Matsui 9, *Asahi shimbun*, 12 September 1990; Department of State unnumbered to Bern, 1 January 1945, / 1-145, *Awa maru* file; *New York Times*, 29 December 1944.

14. Tokyo circular #1479, 23 December, H-158570, SRDJ 83813; Tokyo circular #1495, 28 December 1944, SRH-122.

15. Department of State to Bern, unnumbered, 1 January 1945, / 1-145 *Awa maru* file.

16. Tokyo circular #1479, 23 December 1944, H-158570, SRDJ 83813; Shanghai to Tokyo, #37, 8 January 1945, H-161982, SRDJ 86568, SRH-122.

17. Tokyo circular, #G-37, 9 January 1945, H-162000, SRDJ 86588, SRH-122.

18. Tokyo to Shanghai, #G-009, 13 January 1945, H-162172, SRDJ 86711, SRH-122.

19. Shanghai to Tokyo, #C-026, 17 January 1945, H-162653, SRDJ 87160, SRH-122.

20. Tsingtao to Tokyo, #27, 16 January 1945, H-163671, SRDJ 88036, SRH-122.

21. Shanghai to Tokyo, #H-017, 13 January 1945, H-162173, SRDJ 86772; Tsingtao to Tokyo, #27, 16 January 1945, H-163671 SRDJ 88036; Tokyo to Shanghai, #C-245, 16 January 1945, H-162490, SRDJ 87405, SRH-122.

22. Norman Polmar and Thomas B. Allen, *World War II: America at War* (New York: Random House, 1991), 42. When Tokyo said B-29 pilots would be held responsible for the loss of life in these raids, the announcement was interpreted as a threat to execute them. See *New York Times*, 7 December 1944.

23. Bern to Department of State, #746, 2 February 1945, / 2-245, *Awa maru* file.

24. Polmar and Allen, *World War II*, 43.

25. Kerr, 243–247; *New York Times*, 2, 4 February 1945.

26. Memorandum: Policy regarding official release of atrocities committed by Japanese, n.d. 1944, folder Jap atrocities; SWPD memorandum: Suggestion that an official publicity campaign be directed against Japan and Germany based on their treatment of American prisoners of war, 8 January 1945, folder Jap atrocities January–March 1945, SWPD papers, RG 59.

27. *New York Times*, 4 February 1945.

28. SWPD memorandum: Suggestion that an official publicity campaign be directed against Japan and Germany based on their treatment of American prisoners of war, 8 January; Stettinius to Plitt, 13 January 1945, folder Jap atrocities January–March 1945, SWPD papers; Stettinius to Roosevelt, 2 January 1945, / 1-245, *Awa maru* file.

29. Robert Dallek, *Franklin D. Roosevelt and American Foreign Policy* (New York: Oxford University Press, 1979), 508–510, 517, 520. Stettinius went on from Yalta to Italy, Brazil, and Mexico, and was thus out of Washington during most of February 1945. See *New York Times*, 4, 13–15, 23 February 1945.

30. *New York Times*, 8 February 1945.

31. Mendenhall, xiv.

32. Nippon Yūsen Kabushiki Kaisha senji sen shi hensan iinkai, ed., *Nippon Yūsen senji senshi* [Japan Mail Steamship Company wartime ships' history] (Tokyo: Nippon Yūsen Kabushiki Kaisha, 1971), 182. This source will hereinafter be cited as *NYK Wartime Ships' History*, with appropriate pagination; Bern to Department of State, #746, 2 February 1945 / 2-245, *Awa maru* file.

33. Ibid.

34. *NYK Wartime Ships' History*, 182; Nippon Yūsen Kabushiki Kaisha, ed., *Nippon Yūsen Kabushiki Kaisha senji senshi shiryō shū jōkan* [Japan Mail Steamship Company wartime ships' history documentary collection, Volume 2] (Tokyo: Nippon Yūsen Kabushiki Kaisha, 1971), 90. This source will hereinafter be cited as *NYK Wartime Ships' History Documents*, with appropriate pagination. I have taken this official statement of the ship's speed as correct. The original 1 February announcement gave it as sixteen knots; Tokyo to Bern, #349, 14 August 1945, SRDJ 108564, H-201511, SRH-122 listed the ship's speed as "20.845 nautical miles" [per hour].

35. *NYK Wartime Ships' History*, 182; *Japan Biographical Encyclopedia and Who's Who* (2nd ed.: Tokyo: Rengo Press, 1960), 1440, suggests Shōda's lineage. For an informative discussion of the larger wartime shipbuilding program of which the *Awa maru* was a product, see Parillo, 152–172.

36. *Kodansha Encyclopedia of Japan* (Tokyo: Kodansha, 1983) 8: 59. The Awa name has survived to designate the Awa odori, a variation of the traditional Bon festival dance performed each August in Tokushima City. See ibid., 1: 124

37. Frank Fujita, *Foo: A Japanese-American Prisoner of the Rising Sun: The Secret*

Prison Diary of Frank "Foo" Fujita (Denton, Tex.: University of North Texas Press, 1993), 125–147, describes his life and work as a slave laborer in shipyards while at Fukuoka POW Camp #2, on Koyagi shima in Nagasaki Harbor. From his diary it appears possible that early in 1943 he or other POWs were doing the type of work needed to complete the *Awa maru*.

38. *NYK Wartime Ships' History*, 180.

39. Commanding Officer, USS *Queenfish*, to Commander, Submarine Force, Pacific, serial 07, 8 April 1945, in *Queenfish* Action Reports file, Classified Operational Archives, Naval Historical Center, Washington Navy Yard, Washington, D.C. This archival site will hereinafter be cited as COA, NHC.

40. *NYK Wartime Ships' History*, 183; Fukumitsu, 81. By 1943, when the *Awa maru* was launched, the Imperial Japanese Army controlled more than one out of every four ships in the Japanese merchant marine. See Parillo, 239.

41. Matsui 29, *Asahi shimbun*, 31 October 1990; Captain Hamada is pictured in this article, and in "Shijō saidai no higeki '*Awa maru*' gekichin no nazo" [The greatest tragedy in history: the riddle of the sinking of the *Awa maru*], *Shūkan bunshū* (13 June 1960): 58, and in Nippon Yūsen Kabushiki Kaisha, *Shichijūnen shi* [Seventy-year history (of the Japan Mail Steamship Line)] (Tokyo: Nippon Yūsen Kabushiki Kaisha, 1956), 345.

42. *NYK Wartime Ships' History Documents*, 2: 102,105; *NYK Wartime Ships' History*, 183; Alden, 66; Blair, pp. 490–491.

43. *NYK Wartime Ships' History*, 183; Alden, 124; Blair, 703.

44. Matsui 12, *Asahi shimbun*, 19 September 1990.

45. Tokyo to Bangkok, #49, 2 February 1945, H-165379, SRDJ 89335, Tokyo to Circular, #183, 21 February 1945, H-168571, SRH-122; SRDJ 91743, Fukumitsu, 15.

46. Thomas R. Havens, *Valley of Darkness: The Japanese People and World War Two* (New York: Norton, 1978), 160.

47. Tsunogawa Nihon chimei daijiten hensan iinkai, ed., *Tsunogawa Nihon chimei daijiten 35: Yamaguchi ken* [The Tsunogawa dictionary of Japanese place-names, Volume 35, Yamaguchi Prefecture] (Tokyo: Tsunogawa shoten, 1978), 139.

48. Commanding Officer, USS *Queenfish*, to Commander, Submarine Force Pacific, serial 07, 8 April 1945, in *Queenfish* Action reports file, COA, NHC. Captain Hamada told the NYK office manager at Takao, Taiwan, and the head of the Homeward Marine Transport Office at Jakarta that explosive devices had been fitted to his ship. See Matsui 14, 17, *Asahi shimbun*, 14, 26 September 1990. The removal of the ship's defensive armaments suggests that Japanese military authorities may have confused and conflated a vessel traveling under safe conduct (safe passage) with a cartel ship. The former need not be disarmed, while the latter is not permitted to carry "instruments of war, except one gun for firing signals." See Oppenheim 2: 423–424, 429.

49. Fukumitsu, 14; Sultan to Bissell, 6 March 1945, /3-645 *Awa maru* file.

50. Tokyo to Taihoku [Taipei], #011, 17 February, SRDJ 97414, H-177754; Tokyo to Circular, #183, 21 February 1945, H-168571, SRDJ 91743, SRH-122.

51. Matsui 12, 19 September 1990. Four young diplomat student secretaries and at least one consul destined for posts in Indochina and Burma also boarded the ship at Moji. See Tokyo to Phnom Penh, #3, 14 February SRDJ 90968, H-167518; Tokyo to Saigon, #64, 14 February, SRDJ 90967, H-167517; Tokyo to Rangoon, #32, 14 February 1945, SRDH 90966, H-167516, SRH-122.

52. Matsui 12, *Asahi shimbun*, 19 September 1990.

53. Available records do not indicate the presence of any women passengers on the *Awa maru*'s outward voyage.

54. Matsui 12, *Asahi shimbun*, 19 September 1990.

55. Ibid. The engineer's ninety-four-year-old widow later recalled his having written a letter in which he termed the *Awa maru* "a dangerous ship." See Matsui 13, *Asahi shimbun*, 20 September 1990.

56. Fukumitsu, 37.

57. Central Liaison Office (CLO) to Supreme Commander Allied Powers (SCAP), 28 November 1945, box II, Pence papers; Japanese Chief of Foreign Affairs Section, Taihoku (Taipei) to Japanese Ambassador Bangkok #9, 27 February 1945, SRDJ 93909, H-172763, SRH-122.

58. Shigemitsu to Saigon, #16, 23 February, SRDJ 91958, H-168885, SRH-122, RG 457; Matsui 13, 20 September 1990; CLO to SCAP #657 20 November 1945, box II, Pence papers.

59. Matsui 15, *Asahi shimbun*, 22 September 1990.

60. If, as their removal of the *Awa maru*'s defensive weapons suggested, Japanese military authorities regarded the vessel as a cartel ship, the carrying of munitions of any sort was a clear violation of international law. See Oppenheim, 6: 429.

61. Sultan to Bissell, 6 March 6 / 3-645, *Awa maru* file.

62. Fukumitsu, 37.

63. Matsui Kakushin, *Awa maru naze shizunda ka* [Why was the *Awa maru* sunk?] (Tokyo: Asahi shimbunsha, 1994), 95–96, cites a document prepared by Ambassador to Burma Ishii Chotarō that details these discussions. The representative-designate to the government of India, Nationalist Chandra Bose, was also to take part in the talks. The ambassador to French Indochina was unable to participate, because preparations for the coup of 9 March 1945, in which the Imperial Japanese Army ousted the colonial administrators, demanded his attention.

64. I have inferred this mission from their actions, detailed below.

65. E. Bruce Reynolds, *Thailand and Japan's Southern Advance, 1940–1945* (New York: St. Martin's Press, 1994), offers a thorough analysis of wartime Thai-Japanese relations. Pages 175–177, 201–203 focus on the military loans and "earmarked" gold repayment issue. See also Nimnonda Thamsook, *Thailand and the Japanese Presence, 1941–45*, Research Notes and Discussions No. 6 (Singapore: Institute of Southeast

Asian Studies, 1977), 9, 27, 83–85, 89; Tokyo to Bangkok, #189, 7 March 1944, SRDJ 54994, H-117392, SRH-122.

66. Matsui 16, *Asahi shimbun*, 25 September 1990.

67. Ibid.; Bangkok to Tokyo, #202, 3 March 1945, SRDJ 93316, H-171984; Tokyo to Bangkok, #49, 2 February 1945, SRDJ 89191, H-165379, SRH-122.

68. Tokyo to Bangkok, #38 1 February, H-165149, SRDJ 89192; Tokyo to Bangkok, #49 2 February, H-165379, SRDJ 89335-A; Tokyo to Bangkok #53 4 February 1945, H-166431, SRDJ 90148, SRH-122.

69. Bangkok to Tokyo, #118 2 February, SRDJ 89485, 3 February, "MAGIC" intercept files, box 109, RG 457, U.S. National Archives. I am grateful to Professor E. Bruce Reynolds of San Jose State University for making available to me his copies of selected documents in these files.

70. Bangkok to Tokyo, #184, 23 February 1945, SRDJ 114391, ibid.

71. Bangkok to Tokyo, #224, 13 March 1945, H-172316, SRDJ 939600, SRH-122. This message begins, "The *Awa maru* arrived here with a load of paper currency." This sentence appears to be a mistranslation of "The *Awa maru*'s load of paper currency arrived here." The original Japanese-language transcripts from decrypts of these messages remain classified and unavailable to researchers.

72. Bangkok to Tokyo [Greater East Asia Minister], #254, 18 March 1945, H-177778, SRDJ 97441, SRH-122.

73. Bern #1260 to Department of State, 26 February 1945, /2-2645, *Awa maru* file.

74. Five POW camps of "location unknown," plus one at Jakarta (Batavia) and another at Bandung, appear on American Red Cross "Alternations to Far East Map," a publication distributed to POW families and other interested parties, folder C, CLO to SCAP, 20 November 1945, folder I, box 2, Pence papers.

75. Matsui 17, *Asahi shimbun*, 26 September 1990.

76. *NYK Wartime Ships' History Documents* 2: 105; Saigon Shipping Board Representative Matsumoto to Shipping Board, Tokyo, no number, 9 March 1945, SRDJ 92829, H-171308, Tokyo to Saigon #4, 4 February, SRDJ 89463, H-166033; Saigon #76 to Tokyo, 14 September 1945, SRDJ 111160, H-206127, SRH-122; Matsui 17, *Asahi shimbun*, 26 September 1990; Matsuzawa Naokichi, *FutsuIn no kaisōroku Awa maru no saiki* [Memories of French Indochina: the last days of the *Awa maru*] (Tokyo: Kaibundo, 1971), 119.

77. I have deduced this from the ship's manifest in the form presented to American officials in June 1947, reprinted in Matsui, 105.

78. Editors of *Life* and Rand McNally, *Life Pictorial Atlas of the World* (New York: Time, Inc., 1961), 358, 535.

79. Matsui 17, *Asahi shimbun*, 26 September 1990.

80. Fukumitsu, 40; Bern to Department of State, #1260 26 February 1945, /2-2645, *Awa maru* file.

81. Asakai Kōichirō to Office of Political Adviser, SCAP, 26 May 1947, enclosure,

Shūsen go ni okeru baishō hōki mondai [The problem of abandoning claims after the war], frames 397–402, microfilm reel B'-0084, Document locator B'5.1.0.J/U2, Gaikō shiryyō kan [Diplomatic Record Office], Ministry of Foreign Affairs, Tokyo. Documents from this source will hereinafter be cited by file and reel number only. Fukumitsu, 3; Matsui, 105.

82. Matsui 15, 17, 18, *Asahi shimbun*, 22, 26–27 September 1990.

83. Tokyo to Saigon, Bangkok, #171, 16 February 1945, SRDJ 91641, H-168433, Bangkok to Tokyo, #14, 13 March 1945, SRDJ 94664, H-173749, SRH-122; Matsui 16, 25 September 1990.

84. The official list of *Awa maru* victims, broken down according to rank and occupation, is included in Asakai to Political Adviser, SCAP, 26 May 1947, Shūsen go ni okeru baishō hōki mondai [The problem of abandoning claims after the war], frames 397, 405–409, reel B'-0084, Japanese Ministry of Foreign Affairs documents; Fukumitsu, 185–201, lists individual victims and places them in broad categories of affiliation with government agencies.

85. *NYK Wartime Ships' History Documents* 2: 105; Saigon Shipping Board Representative Matsumoto to Shipping Board, Tokyo, no number, 9 March 1945, SRDJ 92829, H-171308, SRH-122; Matsuzawa, 119.

86. Fukumitsu, 177.

87. Ibid.; Chishitsu chōsajo *Awa maru* junansha tsuitō roku kankōkai, ed., *Awa maru junansha tsuitō roku* [A mourning memorial to the victims of the *Awa maru* disaster] (Tanidabe, Ibaraki Prefecture: Chishitsu chōsajo *Awa maru* junansha tsuitō roku kankōkai, 1979), 13, 78. Pages 39–45 of this source, which will hereinafter be cited as *Mourning Memorial*, outline the history of this geological research survey corps dispatched to Southeast Asia. Photographs on pages 60 and 84 of this volume indicate that at least five women participated in this effort, though none appear to have been passengers on the *Awa maru*.

88. *Mourning Memorial*, 28, 34, 89, 158, 177–178.

89. Matsui 20, *Asahi shimbun*, 2 October 1990.

90. Arai Shigeru interview, 8 October 1994, Nara, Japan; Fukumitsu, 193.

91. Umemura Fumiko interview, 3 October 1994, Tokyo, Japan. I am indebted to Nonomura Masao, President of the *Awa maru* Bereaved Families Association, Tokyo, for arranging a meeting with family members bereaved by the sinking of the ship, which provided the occasion for this interview.

92. Motomura Michiyasu interview, 3 October, 1994, Tokyo, Japan; *Asahi shimbun* 7 May 1981, file 341.33 *Awa maru*, 1949–1983, Periodicals Division, National Diet Library, Tokyo. This source will hereinafter be cited as NDL clippings file 341.33; Fukumitsu, 192–193.

93. *Asahi shimbun*, 25 October 1983, NDL clippings file 341.33; Fukumitsu, 188. Abe had gone to the island of Bintan sixteen years earlier to work for the Furukawa Mining Company. He had stayed on, learned Dutch, and been taken prisoner in the early days of the war. Repatriated the first time, he had returned to the island near Sin-

gapore in 1942 to help speed the economic development of the newly conquered Southern Region.

94. Fukumitsu, 177.

95. Matsui 18, *Asahi shimbun*, 27 September 1990; Fukumitsu, 188. I am indebted to Professor Takahashi Hisashi, formerly of the Japan Defense Agency and currently at Sophia University in Tokyo, for providing details about Iwahashi's career.

96. Fukumitsu, 177, 189; Ōmae Yukiyo interview, 10 October 1994, Tokyo, Japan.

97. Bangkok to Tokyo, #14, 13 March, SRDJ 94664, H-173749, Rangoon to Tokyo, #12, 20 March, SRDJ 94494, H-173546, Rangoon to Saigon #8, 19 February 1945, SRDJ 91636, H-168420, SRH-122; 26 July 1979, *Sankei shimbun*, NDL clippings file 341.33; Fukumitsu, 177, 185–186.

98. 26 July 1979, *Sankei shimbun*, NDL clippings file 341.33. The Indians were not included on an earlier list of non-Japanese who died on the *Awa maru* that included eleven Koreans, seventy-two Taiwanese, and three Malayans. See Zasshū Sankō shiryō [Various materials reference documents], frame 258, reel B'-0084.

99. Ikuse Katsuaki interview, 14 October 1994, Tokyo. Ikuse on this occasion elaborated on the original claims, made in the fourth of his series of articles, "Kaitei no mitsuyaku" [Secret promise at the bottom of the sea], which appeared in *Jidai* [The age] (November 1979), 184–185 and in *Shūkan posto* [Weekly post] (18 April 1980), 212.

100. *Yomiuri shimbun*, 2 May 1979, NDL clippings file 341.33.

101. *NYK Wartime Ships' History*, 186.

102. Fukumitsu, 4, 13.

103. Matsui 18, *Asahi shimbun*, 27 September 1990; Fukumitsu, 40.

104. Shimoda Kantarō, "*Awa maru* bakuchin no iki shōnin" [A living witness to the sinking of the *Awa maru*], *Bungei shunj* 41 (November 1963), 266.

105. This estimate of the total tonnage of cargo carried for Japan's benefit has been derived by applying the *Awa maru*'s cargo (as listed on her manifest, excluding any goods secreted aboard) to the total tonnage ratio of the *Hakusan maru* and *Hoshi maru*. By that measure the three ships carried 13,863 tons of goods for Japan on their homeward-bound voyages. They could have carried as much as fifteen thousand tons more of goods, exclusive of what was destined for enemy nationals, on their outbound voyages, bringing the total of Japanese goods carried to nearly twenty-nine thousand tons. That was more than fourteen times the tonnage of relief supplies they transported to American and Allied prisoners and internees. See Matsui, 75, 105; Matsui 8, *Asahi shimbun*, 11 September 1990; *NYK Wartime Ships' History*, 182.

106. Fukumitsu, 40; Bern to Department of State, #598, 2 February 1945, /2-245, *Awa maru* file. Why the *Awa maru* was ordered to Mutsure remains unclear. The island has a small harbor, which could have provided an appropriate stopping place to await clearance of a berth at Moji. Although it currently has a tank farm from which ships are refueled, prewar and early postwar maps indicate only a lighthouse on the tiny island. See Jinbunsha, ed., *Nihon toshi chizu zenshū* [Atlas of Japan's cities] (Tokyo: Jinbunsha, 1958) 4: 257; *Tsunogawa Nihon chimei daijiten*, 35: 999.

107. Polmar and Allen, *World War II*, 46; Shimonoseki shi shi hensan iinkai, *Shimonoseki shi shi* [A history of Shimonoseki City] (Shimonoseki: Shimonoseki City Office, 1955), 854. Parillo, 197, terms this mining "perhaps the [single] most damaging blow to Japanese maritime commerce" in the war.

108. Tokyo to Bern, #169, 30 March 1945, SRDJ 96145, H-175930, SRH-122.

109. *Life Pictorial Atlas*, 354; Tokyo to Moscow #95, 6 April 1945, SRDJ 96920, H-177231, SRH-122.

Chapter 4. The Queenfish *Gets Her Kill*

1. Shimoda, 266.

2. Matsui, 87.

3. Oppenheim, 424.

4. Matsui, 87. Kuppinger may have put the question to his Pentagon opposites in hope of eliciting a "no" that would recommit the Army and Navy departments to honoring the safe-passage agreement.

5. Interviews with William R. Braisted, 18 June 1992, Washington, D.C.; telephone interview, Austin, Texas, 18 October 1996. After graduating from the Navy Language School at the University of Colorado, Boulder, Professor Braisted served in the Japanese empire and the political economic branches of the Military Intelligence Division; William Joseph Sebald, Naval Institute oral history, 439. This source will hereinafter be cited as Sebald oral history, with appropriate page indications.

6. Matsui, 87.

7. Lockwood to Phyllis Lockwood, 3 April 1945, box 7, Vice Adm. Charles Andrews Lockwood, Jr. papers, Manuscripts Division, Library of Congress, Washington, D.C.

8. This point of view is evident in Nimitz's postwar provision of an affidavit in defense of Admiral Karl Doenitz, who was being tried as a war criminal for having conducted unlimited submarine warfare in the Atlantic. See Elmer B. Potter, *Nimitz* (Annapolis, Md.: Naval Institute Press, 1976), 422, and Manson, 181–182.

9. Voge, 258.

10. Commander, Submarine Force, Pacific, to KU6H, KN6D, 300239, 30 March 1945, exhibit 1, Loughlin court-martial; Voge, 258, erroneously claimed the message had been sent two days earlier; he offered only a paraphrase of its text in his article. Speer, 72, relying on Voge, repeated that error.

11. QFWPR 4: 1.

12. Bennett interview, 7 July 1993. The *Queenfish* captain's principal obituaries would be headlined "Elliott Loughlin," in deference to his preferred form of address. See *Washington Post*, and *Annapolis (Md.) Capital*, 1 November 1989. I am indebted to Ms. Alice S. Creighton of the Special Collections Department, Nimitz Library, U.S.

Naval Academy, for providing me copies of these articles; Rear Adm. Charles Elliott Loughlin 1968 biography, box 400, officer biography files, COA, NHC. Hereinafter cited as Loughlin officer biography.

13. *DANFS* 5: 412; Dupuy and Dupuy, 1146; Blair, *Silent Victory,* 268.

14. *DANFS,* 5: 412.

15. QFWPR 1, 1; Commissioning photograph, 11 March 1944, Bennett papers.

16. Loughlin 1968 officer biography; Charles Elliott Loughlin oral history, 19 August 1980, 1–25, prepared for U.S. Naval Institute, U.S. Naval Institute, Annapolis, Maryland. This source will hereinafter be cited as Loughlin Naval Institute oral history, with appropriate page citations; Voge, 256.

17. Loughlin Naval Institute oral history, 25; Norman Polmar and Thomas B. Allen, *Rickover* (New York: Simon and Schuster, 1982), 83–84.

18. Loughlin 1968 officer biography; Loughlin Naval Institute oral history, 53–66; Gary E. Weir, *Building American Submarines 1914–1940* (Washington, D.C.: Naval Historical Center, 1991), 28–38, 125, details the designing—and flaws—of the S-class boats.

19. Loughlin Naval Institute oral history, 66–70. Loughlin later recalled that he had opted for submarine school on a whim, in response to a remark by a friend. See ibid., 32.

20. Ibid., 84.

21. Bennett interview, 14 May 1993.

22. QFWPR 4: 3.

23. QFWPR 1: 5–6.

24. Ibid., 6; Charles Elliott Loughlin War Patrol Log, 31 August 1944, copy in Capt. John E. Bennett, USN (Ret.), papers, Solana Beach, California. This source will hereinafter be cited as LWPL, with appropriate dates. Loughlin Naval Institute oral history, 78.

25. QFWPR 1: 6.

26. Bennett interview, 14 May 1993.

27. First and Second Endorsements to *Queenfish* First War Patrol Report, 4, 18 October 1944, QFWPR 4: Preface; also 37–47.

28. QFWPR 1: 21.

29. Bennett interview, 14 May 1993; Loughlin Naval Institute oral history, 98.

30. Bennett interview, 14 May 1993.

31. QFWPR 1: 21; "Desperate" Desmond was a popular cartoon-strip character of the day. Bennett interview, 7 July 1993.

32. Arthur G. Bancroft and R.G. Roberts, *The Mikado's Guests* (2nd ed., North Perth: Print Image Pty., Ltd., n.d., reprint of 1st ed., 1945), 129; QFWPR 1: 22; Commander Loughlin later recalled that of those pulled aboard only Bancroft was "rational." See Loughlin Naval Institute oral history, 98–99; Bennett interviews, 14 May, 7 July 1993.

33. Ibid.; Bancroft and Roberts, 130; Joan and Clay Blair, *Return from the River Kwai* (New York: Simon and Schuster, 1979), 261–264 provides a slightly different account of the rescue, saying that Commander Loughlin at first hesitated to stop the *Queenfish* immediately in order to bring survivors aboard, for fear of enemy attack. Oddly, the usually meticulous Loughlin made no entries in his war patrol log for 17 and 19 September 1944, when these dramatic events took place. See LWPL, September 1944.

34. QFWPR 1: 22; Bennett interview, 14 May 1993.

35. Bancroft and Roberts, 93–111. Blair, *Return from the River Kwai*, 15, 20–26, 34, 61, 72, 270; Alden, 133.

36. Bancroft and Roberts, 117.

37. QFWPR 1: 53.

38. First Endorsement to *Queenfish* First War Patrol Report, 4 October 1944, QFWPR 1; Loughlin 1968 officer's biography; *DANFS*, 5: 413; Brown-Bennett and *Queenfish* photographs, Bennett papers.

39. QFWPR 2, 1.

40. Dupuy and Dupuy, 1176; *DANFS*, 2: 457; Charles A. Lockwood, Jr., biography, box 400, officer biography files, COA, NHC.

41. QFWPR 2: 2.

42. *Register of Alumni Graduates and Former Naval Cadets and Midshipmen* (1993 ed., Annapolis, Md.: The United States Naval Academy Alumni Association, 1992), 178. This source will hereinafter be cited as U.S. Naval Academy *Register of Alumni*; Theodore Roscoe, *United States Submarine Operations in World War II* (Annapolis, Md.: Naval Institute Press, 1949), 144. This source will hereinafter be cited as *USSOPS*.

43. Weir, 143; Blair, 66–67, 126.

44. *USSOPS*, 144; Blair, 79.

45. *USSOPS*, 144.

46. Blair, 366–367.

47. Vice Adm. Charles A. Lockwood, Jr., *Sink 'Em All: Submarine Warfare in the Pacific* (New York: Dutton, 1951); Lockwood to Mrs. Phyllis Lockwood, 3 April 1945, box 7, Lockwood papers.

48. Keith Wheeler, *War under the Pacific* (New York: Time-Life Books, 1980), 48.

49. Blair, 561; *Sink 'Em All*, 196.

50. Lockwood and Finch, "We Gave the Japs a Licking Underseas," *Saturday Evening Post*, 222 (23 July 1949), 62; and *Sink 'Em All*, 87–88, 122–124.

51. Thomas B. Buell, *Master of Sea Power: A Biography of Fleet Admiral Ernest J. King* (Boston: Little Brown, 1980), 412–413.

52. *Sink 'Em All*, 15.

53. Wheeler, 43; Lockwood welcoming USS *Bowfin* (SS 287), 4 July 1945, photograph on display, USS *Bowfin* Museum and Park, Pearl Harbor, Hawaii. Elliott

Loughlin recalled that whenever Vice Admiral Lockwood rode the *Queenfish* he made a point of going around and talking with individual crew members. See Clay and Joan Blair, n.d., 1971 interview with Charles Elliott Loughlin, Jr., Annapolis, Maryland, item 8295, Clay Blair, Jr. papers, American Heritage Center, University of Wyoming, Laramie, Wyoming. This source will hereinafter be cited as Loughlin Blair oral history.

54. Lockwood and Finch, "We Gave the Japs a Licking Underseas," *Saturday Evening Post*, 222 (16 July 1949), 119; Century Club listing, in June 1945 *Submarine Bulletin*, Bennett papers.

55. QFWPR 2: 2–5, 13, 17; LWPL, 8–15 November 1944.

56. Alden, 153–157; Rear Adm. Eugene B. Fluckey, *Thunder Below! The U.S.S. Barb Revolutionizes Submarine Warfare in World War II* (Urbana: University of Illinois Press, 1992), 164–203, provides a parallel account of this war patrol from the *Barb*'s point of view.

57. QFWPR 2: 2–3; Alden, 153.

58. QFWPR 2: 5–6; Alden, 155.

59. QFWPR 2: 7, 11–18.

60. Commander, Submarine Force, Pacific, endorsement, 10 December 1944, QFWPR 2.

61. Indefinite Call (240139) to SubPac, *Queenfish*, et al., 24 December 1944, Bennett papers.

62. QFWPR 3: 1; Bennett interview, 14 May 1993; for details of the career of Sam Dealey, the submarine captain for whom the camp was named, see Blair, 719–720.

63. QFWPR 3: 1; Alden, 167–168; First Endorsement to *Queenfish* Third War Patrol Report, 31 January 1945.

64. QFWPR 3: 4–6; LWPL, 8 January 1945; John G. Goberville diary, 8 January 1945, in possession of John G. Goberville, Altoona, Wisconsin. I am grateful to then-Radioman Goberville for making available to me a copy of his diary, the existence of which was not disclosed until September 1993.

65. Fluckey, 241–244. Fluckey dubbed the *Picuda*, the other boat in the wolfpack, the "Peculiar."

66. QFWPR 3: 6.

67. QFWPR 3: 8–9, 25–27; Fluckey, 255, felt the lack of success was due to mechanical failure, either in the torpedoes or the torpedo fire-control system; LWPL, 16 January 1945.

68. Fluckey, 255.

69. QFWPR 3: 9–10.

70. QFWPR 4: 1.

71. Fluckey, 53; Beth Bailey and David Farber, *The First Strange Place: The Alchemy of Race and Sex in World War II Hawaii* (New York: Free Press, 1992), especially chapters 2 and 3, provides an evocative description of the life of the American serviceman

in Hawaii; Goberville diary, 29 January 1945, recorded how he spent two weeks at the Royal Hawaiian Hotel at Waikiki without once going to downtown Honolulu.

72. Bennett interview, 14 May 1992; Bennett photograph, 8 February 1945, Bennett papers.

73. QFWPR 4: 1, 22. Comparison of the attack report on the *Awa maru* and those for attacks during the third war patrol reveals that "fish" fired in the latter were indeed a hodgepodge of components of varying origin. See QFWPR 3: 15–27.

74. QFWPR 4: 1.

75. Ibid.; Shamer interview, 25 June 1993.

76. QFWPR 4: 2. Thirteen submarine-qualified men, including four chiefs, five first-class, and two second-class petty officers were detached from the *Queenfish* at this time; Evans photograph, Bennett papers.

77. QFWPR 4: 1; Dupuy and Dupuy, 1191–1192; Karal Ann Marling and John Wetenhall, *Iwo Jima Monuments, Memories, and the American Hero* (Cambridge: Harvard University Press, 1991), 40–56, 62–72, detail the seizure of Mt. Suribachi and the photographing of marines raising the flag atop it.

78. QFWPR 4: 2; Dupuy and Dupuy, 1190.

79. QFWPR 4: 3; Loughlin War Patrol Log, 9 March 1945.

80. Voge, 258.

81. Loughlin Naval Institute oral history, 121; Bennett interview, 14 May 1993; Shamer interview, 25 June 1993.

82. Bennett interview, 14 May 1993.

83. John Goberville interview, 8 September 1993, Anaheim, California.

84. Bennett interview, 14 May 1993.

85. Ibid.; Radioman John Goberville subsequently recalled being bothered later by "some feeling of responsibility" for the mishandling of the original unencrypted messages. Goberville interview, 8 September 1993.

86. ComSubPac to KU6H KN6D #PR2597, 300239, 30 March 1945, exhibit 1, Loughlin court-martial transcript.

87. Testimony of Cdr. Richard G. Voge, 20 April 1945, Loughlin court-martial transcript, 44.

88. ComSubPac to KU6H, KN6D, #PR2597, 300239, 30 March 1945, exhibit 1, Loughlin court-martial transcript.

89. Loughlin Naval Institute oral history, 124.

90. ComSubPac to KU6H, KN6D, #PR2597 300239, 30 March 1945, exhibit 1, Loughlin court-martial transcript.

91. QFWPR 4: 3–12, 20; Loughlin War Patrol Log, 12 March–1 April 1945.

92. Shamer interviews, 7 July 1992 and 25 June 1993.

93. *Life Pictorial Atlas*, 354; Commanding Officer, USS *Queenfish*, to Commander, Submarine Force, Pacific, serial 07, 8 April 1945, *Queenfish* file, Action Reports file, COA, NHC.

94. Ibid.

95. Goberville diary, 1 April 1945.

96. Remarks of Howard "Shorty" Evans, USS *Queenfish* reunion, 7–9 October 1993, Kings Point, Georgia. I am indebted to Harry E. Hall of Moberly, Missouri, who served on the *Queenfish* after the war, for videotaping interviews with the sub's wartime crew members on this occasion. This source will hereinafter be cited as *Queenfish* reunion video, with name citations.

97. QFWPR 4: 13; LWPL, 1 April 1945.

98. Howard Evans interview, *Queenfish* reunion video.

99. QFWPR 4: 13; LWPL, 1 April 1945.

100. Goberville diary, 1 April 1945.

101. Robert J. "Boats" Reed interview, *Queenfish* reunion video.

102. QFWPR 4: 13; LWPL; Loughlin Naval Institute oral history, 125.

103. Robert J. "Boats" Reed interview, *Queenfish* reunion video.

104. QFWPR 4: 13; Commanding Officer, USS *Queenfish*, to Commander Submarine Force, Pacific, serial 07, 8 April 1945. Bennett interview, 14 May 1993; Shamer interview, 7 July 1992.

105. Robert J. "Boats" Reed interview, *Queenfish* reunion video.

106. Shimoda Kantarō, *Awa maru* gekichin no iki shōnin," [A living witness to the sinking of the *Awa maru*] *Bungei shunjū* 41 (November 1963): 266–267.

107. QFWPR 4: 13.

108. Ibid.

109. Robert J. "Boats" Reed interview, *Queenfish* reunion video.

110. Bennett interview, 14 May 1993; Commanding Officer, USS *Queenfish*, to Commander, Submarine Force, Pacific, serial 07, 8 April 1945; Bennett-Shimoda interview notes, n.d. April 1945, Bennett papers.

111. Bennett-Shimoda interview notes, n.d. April 1945, Bennett papers; Bennett interview, 14 May 1993.

112. Loughlin Naval Institute oral history, 125; Bennett interview, 14 May 1993.

113. For elaboration on and analysis of these allegations, see chapter 9, below.

114. Carl Maria von Clausewitz, *On War,* Michael Howard and Peter Paret, ed. and trans. (Princeton: Princeton University Press, 1976), 119–121.

115. The lists are to be found in Alden, *U.S. Submarine Attacks during World War II.*

116. Loughlin Naval Institute oral history, 122.

117. Matsui 15, *Asahi shimbun,* 22 September 1990.

118. Capt. Walter F. Mazzone, USN (Ret.), interview, 18 July 1994, San Diego, California. Then-Lieutenant Mazzone was aboard the *Crevalle* when the *Awa maru* was sunk.

119. QFWPR 4: 7.

120. Lockwood deposition, Loughlin court-martial transcript.

121. Shimoda Kantarō testimony, 19 April 1945, Loughlin court-martial transcript, 29.

Chapter 5. Court-Martial: "A Damned Shame"

1. Charles Andrews Lockwood, Jr., to Phyllis Lockwood, 3 April 1945, box 7, Lockwood papers.

2. *Queenfish* 020030 April to ComSubPac, serial 2, cited in ComSubPac 020653 April, Graybook summary 1 January–1 July 1945, Chester W. Nimitz papers, Classified Operational Archives, Naval Historical Center, Washington Navy Yard, Washington, D.C.

3. CinCPac Adv HQ to COMINCH and CNO, Nimitz for King only, 020840 April, cited in CincPac Adv HQ to COMINCH and CNO 030818 April 1945, in Graybook summary 1 January–1 July 1945, Nimitz papers.

4. The reaction to the sinking within both the ComSubPac and CinCPac Advanced Headquarters staffs on Guam must have been quite confused. Nimitz's message to King claimed that the ship had gone down 180 miles off her announced course; this was subsequently corrected to say only that she had been two hours ahead of projected schedule when sunk. See CinCPac Adv HQ to COMINCH and CNO 030818 April 1945, Graybook summary 1 January–1 July 1945, Nimitz papers.

5. Buell, 347; Forrestal to Stettinius, 2 April 1945, /4-245 *Awa maru* file.

6. Duffield to MacLeish, 3 April, /4-345, *Awa maru* file, box 3421, RG 59; 021350 April COMINCH and CNO to CinCPac Adv HQ, information ComSubPac, Graybook summary 1 January–1 July 1945, Nimitz papers. Twenty-four hours intervened between the Navy Department's reporting of the sinking to the State Department and King's order to Nimitz to try Commander Loughlin.

7. CinCPac Adv HQ to COMINCH 030818 April, Graybook summary, 1 January–1 July 1945, Nimitz papers.

8. QFWPR 4: 13; *Queenfish* deck log, 1548 2 April 1945, RG 24, U.S. National Archives; *Sea Fox* WPR, 3: 12.

9. *Sea Fox* WPR, 3: 12–13, 2–4 April 1945. Ironically, after rendezvousing with the *Tench*, Cdr. Roy C. Klinker decided that the seas were too rough to transfer the wounded man, who remained on his own sub for the rest of the patrol.

10. Loughlin War Patrol Log, 2–5 April; QFWPR 4: 13–14; Bennett interview, 14 May 1993.

11. Goberville diary, 1 April 1945.

12. Remarks of Robert J. "Boats" Reed, John Lynch, and Howard "Shorty" Evans, 7–9 October 1993, *Queenfish* reunion video.

13. Bennett-Shimoda interview notes, John E. Bennett papers; Interrogation of Japanese Survivor from *Awa maru*, appended to Commanding Officer, *Queenfish*, to Commander, Submarine Force, Pacific Fleet, serial 07, 8 April 1945, *Queenfish* in Action Reports file, COA, NHC; Kerr, 158–159. Shimoda said that he had served aboard the *Asama maru*, which had carried American internees from Japan, China, and French Indochina to the *Gripsholm* in 1942. Kerr, 90. He had survived sinkings of

the *Heiyo maru* (sunk near Truk on 23 January 1943), the *Teiko maru* (in a passage between Singapore and Borneo on 22 February 1944), and the *Teia maru* (in the Bashi Channel on 18 August 1944). See Alden, 29, 85, 124.

14. Bennett-Shimoda interview notes, Bennett papers; Fukumitsu, 185–201. Lists of names, addresses, and occupations of *Awa maru* passengers and crew, as known in September 1945, are in A-700-9-37-1 Dai Tōa sensō kankei ikken: Kokusai hō ihan kōi; *Awa maru* sōnan kankei [Concerning the Greater East Asia War: actions against international law with reference to the *Awa maru* disaster], Diplomatic Documentation Center, Ministry of Foreign Affairs, Tokyo.

15. *Queenfish* deck log, Loughlin War Patrol Log, 7 April; QFWPR 4: 15.

16. Lockwood had waited five days—half the time he had originally proposed—before summoning the *Queenfish* back to Guam. By the time he issued the order, negotiations with the CinCPac staff had suggested the trial might begin the week of 16 April. See Lockwood to Cdr. J.F. Davidson, 6 April, and Lockwood to Como. Merrill Comstock, 6 April 1945, box 15, Lockwood papers.

17. QFWPR 4: 22. 7 April was the forty-first day of this war patrol and the twenty-ninth since the *Queenfish* had departed Saipan. On her first patrol, she had stayed at sea for fifty-nine days. QFWPR 4: 1, 15; QFWPR 1: 1, 24.

18. *Queenfish* serial 007 to ComSubPac, 8 April 1945, *Queenfish* action reports file, COA, NHC. It is not clear from available materials whether this report was delivered by radio or by hand to ComSubPac. While the surviving copy bears an appropriate serial number, no record of the dispatch of serial 007 is to be found in Commander Loughlin's personal log or the *Queenfish*'s war patrol report. The fact that serial message 006, recorded in the latter, was not sent until the morning of 9 April suggests that if the report was sent, it was delayed for some time after its completion.

Two other points about the report are noteworthy. First, it circumscribed very narrowly the explanation of what had occurred, addressing how, not why, the *Queenfish* had sunk the *Awa maru*; also, it made no mention whatsoever of any of the warning messages. Second, the report also exaggerated somewhat the factors that were in the *Queenfish*'s favor. It claimed that a diligent search for survivors had been undertaken, despite the fact that "it was considered highly improbable that anyone could survive in the open water, temperature 56 degrees F, with no protection" for the more than nineteen hours between the sinking and the commencement of search operations. In fact the sea temperature had been sixty-eight degrees at the time of the sinking, rose to seventy-two by nine o'clock the next morning, dropping only (to fifty-eight degrees) when the *Queenfish* and the *Sea Fox* began searching in earnest. Within an hour thereafter the sea temperature rose to sixty-two. See the *Queenfish* deck log, 1–2 April 1945.

Directing as it did a search for passengers as well as cargo, ComSubPac obviously did not rate the chances of survival as low as the *Queenfish* officers did. Hypothermia would have gripped the *Awa maru* victims within an hour if the water temperatures had been as low as Elliott Loughlin reported; but in water at sixty-eight to seventy-two degrees, survival for up to a day in the water without the killing effects of hypothermia was possible. Telephone interview with Gary Crum, Los Angeles County Lifeguard Service, Hermosa Beach, California, 20 March 1995.

19. *Queenfish* deck log, 11–12 April; QFWPR 4: 17–18; LWPL, 11 April 1945. For whatever reason, Commander Loughlin ceased writing in his personal log book on this date.

20. QFWPR 4: 18–19. Some of the men taken aboard had been alert and well enough to be standing watch as lookouts and lofting red flares just before *Queenfish* spotted their life rafts. Loughlin later recalled that the rescuees were "in good condition. No strain." Loughlin Naval Institute oral history, 126.

21. ComSubPac 112211 April 1945 to *Queenfish*, exhibit 15, Loughlin court-martial transcript. Goberville diary, 8 March 1945, recorded receipt of the news that the *Queenfish* would be awarded the Presidential Unit Citation. However, a message received by Admiral Lockwood on the eve of the court-martial indicated that the citation was still on the Secretary of the Navy's desk, awaiting signature. See ComSubPac Ad Cmd to ComSubPac, 162014 April 1945, exhibit 13 Loughlin court-martial transcript.

22. Lockwood to Phyllis Lockwood, 9 April 1945, box 7, Lockwood papers; Frederick S. Voss, *Reporting the War: The Journalistic Coverage of World War II* (Washington: Smithsonian Institution Press, 1994), 59, 64.

23. *Queenfish* deck log, 14 April 1945.

24. Keith Wheeler, *War under the Pacific* (New York: Time-Life Books, 1980), 43; Lockwood and Finch, "We Gave the Japs a Licking Underseas," *Saturday Evening Post*, 222 (16 July 1949), 119.

25. Voge, 259; Speer, 74.

26. E. W. Grenfell to Loughlin, 8 April, box 15, Loughlin to Phyllis Loughlin, 14 April 1945, box 7, Lockwood papers.

27. Loughlin Naval Institute oral history, 126.

28. Voge, 259. Loughlin recalled that it had been ComSubPac's communication officer, William D. Irvin (later a rear admiral), who had conducted the search for the incriminating messages. Loughlin Naval Institute oral history, 127; U.S. Naval Academy *Register of Alumni*, 215. Irvin may well have felt some sympathy with Loughlin at the time. As skipper of the *Nautilus* (SS 168) he had on 6 March 1944 sunk the *America maru*, which was evacuating 1,700 women, children, and elderly persons from Saipan. See Blair, 591, and Alden, 89.

29. *Queenfish* deck log, 14 April 1945; Voge, 259; Loughlin Naval Institute oral history, 133.

30. *Queenfish* deck log, 15–16 April 1945.

31. Lockwood to Phyllis Lockwood, 4 April 1945, box 7, and Lockwood to Rear Admiral James Fife, 17 April, box 15, Lockwood papers; Lockwood, *Sink 'Em All*, 314–316.

32. Lockwood to Comstock, 4 April 1945, box 15, Lockwood papers.

33. Lockwood to Cdr. J.F. Davidson, 6 April, Comstock to Lockwood, 6 April, 9 April, and Lockwood to Comstock, 12 April 1945, box 15, Lockwood papers; Rear Adm. Henry Chester Bruton biography, box 77, officer biography files, COA, NHC. The defense counsel Admiral Lockwood wanted but did not get was Rear Adm. Harold "Togo" Biesemeier. See U.S. Naval Academy, *Register of Alumni,* 184.

34. Lockwood to Comstock, 14 April 1945, box 7, Lockwood papers.

35. Interrogatories and Deposition of Charles A. Lockwood, Jr., 17 April 1945, *United States v. Commander Charles E. Loughlin, U.S. Navy,* Loughlin court-martial transcript.

36. ComSubPac to CinC U.S. Pacific Fleet, 17 April 1945, First Endorsement to SS393/A9 ser. 07, 8 April 1945, *Queenfish* action reports file, COA, NHC.

37. Lockwood to Rear Adm. John H. Brown, Jr., and Merrill Comstock, 16 April, and Lockwood to Rear Adm. James Fife, 17 April 1945, box 15, Lockwood papers.

41. U.S. Government to Government of Japan, 10 April 1945, CCS 560 (4-2645), box 504, Records of the Joint Chiefs of Staff, Record Group 218, U.S. National Archives.

39. *New York Times,* 12 April 1945.

40. Loughlin could have been tried for violating the rules of war, under article 22 of Articles for the Government of the Navy. That would have raised the question of whether or not he had violated the norms of international law as they pertained to the sinking of the *Awa maru.* Royden J. Dangerfield and Robert D. Pownes, Jr., memorandum for Vice Admiral [Thomas L.] Gatch, Judge Advocate General of the Navy, 10 May 1945, attached to Loughlin court-martial transcript.

41. Nimitz to Capt. John C. McCutchen, enclosing charges and specifications in the case of Charles. E. Loughlin, Commander, U.S. Navy, 15 April 1945, Loughlin court-martial record. The fact that Nimitz signed these instructions on a Sunday hints at the urgency with which the case against Loughlin was prepared.

42. Commander Loughlin, in his Naval Institute oral history, 129, claimed the court was the highest-ranking court in the history of the U.S. Navy.

43. Vice Adm. John H. Hoover biography, box 312, officer biography files, COA, NHC; Blair, 839.

44. Vice Adm. Jesse Oldendorf biography, box 482; Loughlin biography, box 400, officer biography files, COA, NHC.

45. Rear Admiral Ernest L. Gunther biography, box 267, Rear Admiral John H. Brown biography, box 74, officer biography files, COA, NHC.

46. Nimitz to Hoover, Precept for a general court-martial, 14 April 1945, Loughlin court-martial transcript.

47. Hoover, Oldendorf, Gunther, Brown, Parks, and Allen biographies, boxes 74, 267, 312, 482, 492, officer biography files, COA, NHC.

48. Oldendorf biography, box 482, officer biography files, COA, NHC.

49. Rear Adm. Lewis S. Parks biography, box 492, officer biography files, COA, NHC; Blair, 114,458, 680–681, 839.

50. McCutchen biography, box 431, officer biography files, COA, NHC; *Queenfish* deck log, 14 April 1945.

51. U.S. Naval Academy *Register of Alumni*, 199, 209.

52. The assistant judge advocate general was Cdr. Frank. E. Bollman, a naval reserve officer in the Supply Corps. Whether he was a trained attorney or not cannot be determined from the available records. Nimitz to Bollman, 18 April 1945, Loughlin court-martial transcript.

53. CinC U.S. Pacific Fleet and Pacific Ocean Areas to Capt. John C. McCutchen, 15 April 1945, enclosing charges and specifications; Loughlin court-martial transcript, 19 April 1945, 1–2.

54. Shamer interview, 15 July 1992.

55. Loughlin court-martial transcript, 19 April 1945, 3–4.

56. Ibid., 4.

57. Ibid., 5–6.

58. Ibid., 7.

59. Loughlin Naval Institute oral history, 127. Loughlin recalled that he had given Geer an unsatisfactory fitness report for mishandling the critical messages concerning the *Awa maru.*

60. Loughlin court-martial transcript, 19 April 1945, 8–10.

61. Ibid., 11–13

62. Ibid., 14–21, 24–25.

63. Ibid., 14, 21.

64. Ibid., 28.

65. George G. Lewis and John Mewha, *History of Prisoner of War Utilization by the United States Army 1776–1945* (2nd. [1982] ed.: Washington: Center of Military History, United States Army, 1955), 250.

66. Loughlin court-martial transcript, 28–30.

67. Ibid., 30.

68. Rear Adm. Henry C. Bruton biography, officer biography files, box 77, COA, NHC; Blair, 309–310.

69. Loughlin Naval Institute oral history, 128.

70. Ibid., 128.

71. Loughlin court-martial transcript, 32–35, 38–40. The *Holland*'s navigator was Lt. Cdr. Bernard J. Germershausen, a member of the 1939 U.S. Naval Academy class. See U. S. Naval Academy *Register of Alumni*, 249. His brother, William Germershausen, had as skipper of the *Tambor* (SS 198) mistakenly attacked a Russian ship the preceding August. See Blair, 697.

72. Loughlin court-martial transcript, 37–38.

73. Ibid., 41–42.

74. Ibid., 42–43.

75. Ibid., 45–46. Kefauver was a member of Loughlin's Naval Academy graduating class and the former skipper of the *Tambor.* See U. S. Naval Academy *Register of Alumni,* 231; Blair, 942, 945, 953.

76. Loughlin court-martial transcript, 48–49; *United States v. Commander Charles E. Loughlin, U.S. Navy,* Interrogatories and Deposition of Vice Adm. Charles A. Lockwood, Jr., 17 April 1945.

77. Loughlin court-martial transcript, 49–54; and exhibits 8–12.

78. Loughlin court-martial transcript, 54–58. Bruton and Lieutenant Colonel Coffman, the assistant defense counsel, alternated in summing up their case. It is not possible to determine from the record precisely at what point each man was speaking.

79. Loughlin court-martial transcript, 58–63.

80. Ibid., 63–64.

81. Ibid., 64.

82. Ibid., 7, 24, 26, 30. Perhaps the most telling hint of the court's disposition toward Loughlin was that it repeatedly allowed testimony as to his character and professional conduct—despite prosecution objections concerning the impropriety of accepting such information during the trial proper rather than in the mitigation and sentencing phase immediately following. See 51–53.

83. Ibid., 30, 34, 40, 44.

84. Ibid., 64. Lt. Adam Feller, USN, staff legal officer, Long Beach, California Naval Shipyard, telephone interview, 24 March 1995.

85. Clay and Joan Blair-Loughlin 1971 interview tape, Archive of Contemporary American History, University of Wyoming Library, Laramie, Wyoming.

86. Midori jūji no fune—*Awa maru* [The green cross ship—*Awa maru*], NHK television program, broadcast 7 December 1979. I am indebted to Kogo Eiichi of the NHK Broadcast Culture Institute for enabling me to view a videotape of this program at the NHK archives in Tokyo. The term "green cross" is a mistake; it properly refers to the symbol for safety used in contemporary Japan.

87. Loughlin biography, officer biography files, box 400, COA, NHC. The aura of error was in the very air that Loughlin breathed aboard the *Pogy.* She was returning to Pearl Harbor for repairs after having been strafed by an Army Air Corps Liberator bomber while on lifeguard duty. See Blair, 842.

88. Lt. Adam Zeller telephone interview, 24 March 1995.

89. Loughlin to Lockwood, 1 June 1945, box 15, Lockwood papers.

90. J.M. Will, Commander, Submarine Squadron 28, to CinC United States Fleet, 19 April, enhanced Loughlin's chances for yet another decoration by labeling the sunken ship an "AP" (naval supply ship) rather than a merchant vessel; in First Endorsement, *Queenfish* 4th War Patrol Report, 18 April 1945. Commander Submarine Division 282, Captain Thomas M. Dykers, called the *Queenfish* an "outstandingly effective submarine." See Second Endorsement, *Queenfish* 4th War Patrol Report, 19 April 1945.

91. Lockwood to Loughlin, 7 June 1945, box 15, Lockwood papers.

92. Lt. Adam Feller telephone interview, 24 March 1995; Commander-in-Chief Pacific Fleet (Nimitz) to COMINCH US Fleet (King), 29 April 1945, Loughlin court-martial transcript.

93. Loughlin Naval Institute oral history, 130–131; Shamer interview, 17 July 1992. Captain Shamer believed that Nimitz wanted the members of court to "hilt" (give a tougher punishment to) Commander Loughlin, so that the admiral could show clemency by reducing it; Voge, 261, took the position that Nimitz was angry with the members of the court because of the inconsistency between their mild sentence and the supposed seriousness of Loughlin's offense. Blair, 840; Rear Adm. Lewis S. Parks biography, officer biography files, box 492, COA, NHC.

94. Commander-in-Chief Pacific Fleet (Nimitz) to COMINCH US Fleet (King), 29 April 1945, Loughlin court-martial transcript.

95. Lockwood to Loughlin, 7 June 1945, box 15, Lockwood papers.

96. Gatch memorandum, Loughlin court-martial transcript; U.S. Naval Academy *Register of Alumni*, 177–178; Loughlin Naval Institute oral history, 137.

97. Forrestal to Stettinius, 22 May 1945, 5-2245, *Awa maru* file.

98. R.D. Longyer to Plitt, 4 June 1945, /6-445 *Awa maru* file, RG 59.

99. Frank H. Owen to Senator Homer K. Ferguson (R-Michigan), enclosure to /6-545, *Awa maru* file, RG 59.

100. Forrestal to Stettinius, 22 May 1945, /5-2245, *Awa maru* file; *New York Times,* 15 July 1945.

101. *New York Times,* 16 September 1945. The article described Commander Loughlin as "one of the outstanding heroes of the service."

102. Loughlin Naval Institute oral history, 134; Secretary of the Navy to Cdr. Charles Elliott Loughlin, USN, 15 June 1945, Loughlin court-martial transcript.

103. Loughlin Naval Institute oral history, 134–135. CincSubLant was Rear Adm. Freeland Daubin, who had been Vice Admiral Lockwood's boyhood friend in Lamar, Missouri. Lockwood, *Sink 'Em All,* 84.

104. QFWPR.

105. Lockwood to Phyllis Lockwood, 14 April 1945, box 7, Lockwood papers.

Chapter 6. Promises Made, Promises Unkept

1. Tokyo urgent message to Bern, 10 April 1945, in /4-2045, *Awa maru* file.

2. United States Government to Japanese Government, 10 April 1945, in Supreme Commander Allied Powers [SCAP] (H.A. Allen) to JCS AG 560, 14 December 1945, CCS 560 (4-26-45), box 504, RG 218.

3. Fukumitsu, 188; Iwahashi officer biography, Office of War History, National Institute of Defense Studies, Japan Defense Agency, Tokyo.

4. 26 July 1979 *Mainichi shimbun,* 341.33 *Awa maru* clippings file, National Diet Library.

5. Bangkok to Tokyo #345, 15 April 1945, H-178417, SRDJ 97766, SRH-122, RG 457.

6. Adm. Suzuki Kantarō became prime minister on 7 April 1945. Tokinotani, 695.

7. *Japan Biographical Encyclopedia and Who's Who*, 342–343. Iguchi later served as ambassador to the United States, 1954–1956; Corbett, 194–195. Iguchi, in his former post as counselor at the Japanese embassy in Washington, came to be regarded as one of those most responsible for the fateful delay of the final Japanese note prior to the bombing of Pearl Harbor. See Hata Ikuhiko, "Going to War: Who Delayed the Final Note?" *Journal of American-East Asian Relations* 3 (Fall 1994), 240, 246.

8. Dōmei press release, 25 April 1945, 4-2545, *Awa maru* file.

9. Government of Japan to United States Government, 26 April 1945, in SCAP to JCS, AG 560, 14 December 1945, CCS 560 (4-26-45), box 504, RG 218. A summary of this note, together with a bloodless review of the safe-passage agreement negotiations and a brief account of the *Awa maru*'s mission of mercy, appeared in the Japanese press two days later. See *Asahi shimbun*, 28 April 1945.

10. Gen. Jonathan M. Wainwright, U.S. Army, to Pence, 8 October 1945, file D, box 2, Pence papers.

11. Pence interview with Capt. Leo Cromwell Thyson, USN, 10 December 1945, file D, box 2, Pence papers.

12. Robert Mouravieff, International Red Cross to International Red Cross Delegate in Washington, 6 July 1945, file B, box 2, Pence papers.

13. Plitt to Holmes, 4 April 1945, /4-445 *Awa maru* file.

14. Kuppinger to Plitt, 5 April 1945, /4-545, ibid.

15. Japanese Government to U.S. Government, 16 May 1945, CCS 560 (4-26-45), box 504, RG 218.

16. Grew to Stimson, Grew to Forrestal, 5 May 1945, /5-545, *Awa maru* file.

17. Kuppinger to Legal Affairs, 17 May 1945, /5-1745, ibid.

18. Clattenberg to Donald Russell, et al., 4 January 1946, copy provided by Nonomura Masao, President, *Awa maru* Bereaved Families Association, Tokyo.

19. Department of State to Bern, #1841, 18 May 1945, /5-1845; Department of State Press Release 29 May 1945, /5-3045 *Awa maru* file.

20. "Ring Open Wide the Golden Gates and Let Victors In," *Liberation Bulletin of Philippine Internment Camp Number One at Santo Tomás University, Manila* (3 February 1945), file D, box 2, Pence papers.

21. John L. Stivers to Truman, 14 April 45, /4-1445 *Awa maru* file.

22. Mr. and Mrs. J. D. Frazier to Truman, 29 May 1945, forwarded by the president's secretary, William D. Hassett, to Department of State, /5-2945 *Awa maru* file.

23. Stettinius to Forrestal, 2 April 1945, /2-445, *Awa maru* file. Eldred Kuppinger was the author of this proposal.

24. Grew to Forrestal, 24 April 1945, /4-2445, *Awa maru* file.

25. Capt. Harry L. Pence, USN (Ret.), draft letter to secretary of state (not sent), n.d. May 1945, folder B, box 2, Pence papers.

26. Basil O'Connor, President, American Red Cross, to Stettinius, 5 May 1945, /5-545, *Awa maru* file; Anna Rothe, ed., *Current Biography Who's News and Why 1944.* (New York: H.W. Wilson, 1944), 505–507.

27. Joint Logistics Committee (JLC) 305/1, 16 May, 1945, CCS 560 (4-26-45), box 504, RG 218. An interdepartmental subcommittee—consisting of Capt. T.H. Tonseth, Op-13, for the navy; Colonel Archibald King of the Judge Advocate General's Office; Lt. Col. M.E. Sprague of the Transportation Corps; and lt. cols. C.E. Yudelson of G-1 and R.C. Lowe, G-2, for the army; and Mr. Richard M. Bissell of the War Shipping Authority Maritime Agency—had been established on 28 April 1945 to consider the *Awa maru* replacement proposal. See JCS 1359, 29 May, SM-1931, JCS to State War Navy Coordinating Committee (SWNCC), 29 May, SWNCC 140/1, 8 June 1945, ibid.

28. Grew to Truman, 15 June, Grew to Stimson, 23 June 1945, CCS 560 (4-26-45), box 504, RG 218.

29. Joint Military Transportation Committee (JMC) to JCS, 5 July, JCS 1359/1, 6 July, SWNCC 140/3, 20 July, 1940, CCS 560 (4-26-45), box 504, RG 218.

30. United States Government to Japanese Government, 5 July 1945, CCS 560 (4-26-45), box 504, RG 218.

31. Department of State Press Release 549, 13 July 1945, /13-745, *Awa maru* file, indicates that the message accepting responsibility for the sinking had been dispatched to Tokyo on 29 June 1945.

32. *New York Times,* 15 July 1945.

33. John S. Dickey to Archibald MacLeish, 9 July 1945, /7-945, *Awa maru* file.

34. Acting Director, Overseas Bureau, Office of War Information, to MacLeish, 26 July 1945, /7-2645 *Awa maru* file; Richard B. Finn, *Winners in Peace: MacArthur, Yoshida, and Postwar Japan* (Berkeley: University of California Press, 1992), 2.

35. Capt. Harry L. Pence , USN (Ret.), personal statement 16 July 1970, Pence papers. Pence, then aged sixty-three, had graduated from the U. S. Naval Academy in the class of 1906. See United States Naval Academy *Register of Alumni,* 170.

36. Ibid., p. 178; Ellis M. Zacharias, *Secret Missions: The Story of an Intelligence Officer* (New York: G. P. Putnam's Sons, 1946), 3–70, 83–86, 147. Pages 327–349 detail the background leading up to Zacharias's first broadcast, on 8 May 1945.

37. Draft broadcast script, folder B, box 2, Pence papers; Acting Director, Overseas Bureau, Office of War Information, to MacLeish, 26 July 1945, /7-2645, *Awa maru* file. For details of the 1939 *Astoria* episode, see my "Farewell to Friendship," *Diplomatic History* 10 (Spring 1986), 121–139.

38. The proposed broadcast was scheduled for 19 August 1945. Acting Director, Overseas Bureau, Office of War Information, to MacLeish, 26 July 1945, /7-2645, *Awa maru* file.

39. Camille Gorge, Swiss Minister to Japan, to Minister of Foreign Affairs Tōgō Shigenori, 6 August 1945, A-700-9-37-1, Dai TōA sensō kankei ikken: Kokusai hō

ihan kōi *Awa maru* sōnan kankei [Matters concerning the Greater East Asia War: actions against International Law: the *Awa maru* disaster], Gaimushō, Gaikō Shiryō shitsu [Diplomatic Record Office, Ministry of Foreign Affairs], Tokyo. Documents from this source will hereinafter be cited by numerical designation only.

40. *New York Times* 9–10 August 1945.

41. Gorge to Tōgō Shigenori, 6 August 1945, A-700-9-37-1.

42. Japanese Government to United States Government, 10 August in SCAP (Allen) to JCS, 14 December 1945, CCS 560 (4-26-45), box 504, RG 218.

43. SRH-090, Japan's Surrender Maneuvers, RG 457, cited in Christopher Andrew, *For the President's Eyes Only: Secret Intelligence and the American Presidency from Washington to Bush* (New York: HarperCollins, 1995), 154.

44. Andrews, 155. The marginal note–writer misidentified the *Awa maru* as "a hospital ship."

45. Lockwood to Phyllis Lockwood, 15 August, 2 September 1945, box 7, Lockwood papers.

46. Capt. Frank Shamer interview, 15 July 1992; Radioman Denny Rathbun interview, Poulsbo, Washington, 29 April 1994

47. Lockwood to Phyllis Lockwood, 2 September 1945, box 7, Lockwood papers.

48. Matsui 34, *Asahi shimbun*, 23 October 1990.

49. Michael M. Yoshitsu, *Japan and the San Francisco Peace Settlement* (New York: Columbia University Press, 1983), 1; Finn, 17–27.

50. Col. H.W. Allen memorandum for Imperial Japanese Government, through Central Liaison Office, Tokyo, 13 October 1945, file I, box 2, Pence papers.

51. Central Liaison to SCAP CLO 657 (5.1), 20 November 1945, folder I, Box 2, Pence papers.

52. Col. H.W. Allen, SCAP, to Joint Chiefs of Staff, 14 December 1945, CCS 560 (4-26-45), box 504, RG 218.

53. The request was forwarded to the Department of State via SM 4567 of 27 December 1945; James C. Dunn, Chairman State War Navy Committee to Secretary of State, 28 December 1945, CCS 560 (4-26-45), box 504, RG 218.

54. Russell to Maurice Pate, International Red Cross, 2 January 1946, file I, box 2, Pence papers; Dean Acheson, *Present at the Creation: My Years in the State Department* (New York: Norton, 1969), 170.

55. Albert Clattenburg to Donald Russell, et al., 4 January 1946, copy provided by Nonomura Masao, President, *Awa maru* Bereaved Families Association, November 1995. The document is summarized in Matsui, 195–197. Clattenburg reminded Russell of the intradepartmental debate the preceding May over whether the United States was under any obligation to indemnify for loss of life among the passengers, since the Japanese had so overloaded the ship; nonetheless, he argued that Washington did in fact bear legal responsibility. He referred to the Japanese use of the ship to return contraband to the home islands as "blackmail," but he asserted that because the United

States had "accepted the situation" at the time, it was liable for repayment of the value of the cargo. The original Japanese request for payment sought indemnification according to the rank of the deceased: Washington was asked to pay 200,000 yen each for eighteen persons, 150,000 for 689, 100,000 for 287, and 50,000 for each of the remaining 1,009 passengers known to have gone down with the *Awa maru*. Japanese Government to U.S. Government, 10 August 1945, CCS 560 (4-26-45), box 504, RG 218.

56. Kuppinger to Pate, 28 January 1946 / 1-2846 *Awa maru* file.

57. Finn, 70–71.

58. Memoranda on Boone and Pate presentations, 16 January 1946, file D, box 2, Pence papers.

59. George H. Gallup, *The Gallup Poll*, Volume 1, *1935–1948* (New York: Random House, 1972), 521–522, 533–534.

60. "Unregenerate Japan," *Nation* 161 (22 September 1945), 273–274; F.D. Morris, "Seventy Million Problem Children," *Collier's* 116 (1 December 1945), 22–23, ff.

61. *New York Times*, 6–11, 14, 16, 21–22 September; 4, 14–15 October; 8, 14 December 1945; 6 January 1946. Lt. Gen. Ishii Shirō's biological warfare experiments are detailed in Sheldon H. Harris, *Factories of Death: Japanese Biological Warfare* (London: Routledge, 1994), 41–82. Harris, 130–131 disputes early postwar reports and concludes that the Japanese probably did not perform biological warfare experiments on American prisoners of war.

62. Kuppinger memorandum for the files, 28 January 1946, / 1-2846, *Awa maru* file; Capt. Thomas Henry Tonseth officer biography, box 642, officer biographies file, COA, NHC.

63. Acheson to Forrestal, 8 February 1946, / 2-846 *Awa maru* file.

64. Shimoda Kantarō, "*Awa maru* gekichin no iki shōnin" [A living witness to the sinking of the *Awa maru*], *Bungei shunjū* 41 (November 1963), 270; Capt. R. W. Kenney, USNR (Ret.), "'Mr. Lucky'—Sole Survivor of the *Awa maru*," *The Retired Officer* (August 1974), 73. Captain Kenney recalled having escorted Shimoda back to Tokyo.

65. POLAD [political adviser] to Department of State, 23 February 1946, attached to / 3-446, *Awa maru* file.

66. Shimoda, "*Awa maru* gekichin no iki shōnin," 270.

67. Matsui, 192–193; Shimoda Mitsuko interview, Ikebukuro, Tokyo, 15 January 1993.

68. MacArthur's secretary kept meticulous records of the general's schedule, including all visitors. There is no such record of visitors for 22 February 1946, a Saturday, which was the Washington's Birthday holiday for occupation forces. See MacArthur schedules, 21–24 February 1946, Record Group 5, Douglas MacArthur papers, MacArthur Memorial, Norfolk, Virginia.

69. Shimoda Mitsuko interview, 15 January 1993.

70. United States Naval War College, *International Law Documents, 1944–1945* (Newport, R.I.: U.S. Naval War College, 1946), 125–134. This collection was prepared with the aid of Prof. Payson Sibley Wild of the Harvard Law School. I am indebted to Ms. Maggie Rauch of the Naval War College Library staff for locating and making available a copy of this document.

71. Maurice Pate to Richard F. Allen, 3 October 1945, Draft of articles 39 and 39-a, revised Geneva Convention, 11 February 1946, Red Cross Prisoner of War Relief, Prisoner of War Convention 1929 Proposed Changes, International Red Cross, file A, box 2, Pence papers. For changes between the 1929 and 1949 Geneva Conventions concerning prisoners of war, contrast the seven brief articles in the earlier document with nine extensive, detailed ones in the latter. See Leon Friedman, ed., *The Law of War: A Documentary History,* Volume 1 (New York: Random House, 1972), 502–503; 613–617.

72. Matsui, 105, relying upon a 1947 cargo list, indicates that *Awa maru* carried 2.5 tons of goods for the French and an additional ton for the Swiss.

73. Minister of Switzerland to Department of State, 22 June 1946, /6-2246, *Awa maru* file. A year earlier Under Secretary Grew had raised the possibility of indemnifying the Swiss for food that they had lost when the *Awa maru* was sunk. Grew to Forrestal, 26 June 1945, /6-2645, *Awa maru* file.

74. Acting Secretary of the Navy W. John Kenney to Secretary of State James M. Byrnes, 27 March 1946 /3-2746, *Awa maru* file; Arthur H. Vandenberg to George C. Marshall, 23 December 1946, /12-2346, ibid., provided a copy of Senate Bill 240, authorizing payment of $425.88 to the Swiss.

75. Director, Bureau of the Budget, to Secretary of State, 6 March 1947 /3-647, *Awa maru* file, forwarded a copy of House Resolution 1040, authorizing such payment. The legislation had been formally introduced in mid-January 1947; it was approved by the full House of Representatives on 3 March and the Senate on 5 March 1947. President Truman signed it five days later. See *Congressional Record*, Volume 93, 80th Congress, First Session, Parts 1 and 2, 334, 816, 1608, 1623, 1679, 1758, 1760, 1903, 2312.

76. CLO 6651 (RJ) to POLAD, 7 December 1946, /12-746, box 3422, *Awa maru* file. The official Japanese request anticipated a plea from NYK President Asao Shinsuke for early indemnification for loss of the *Awa maru*. See Asao to [Prime Minister] Yoshida Shigeru and [Finance Minister] Ishibasahi Tanzan, 20 December 1946, file A-700-9-37-1, Diplomatic Documentation Center, Ministry of Foreign Affairs, Tokyo. State Department officials "lost" their original copy of this document and had to request another from Tokyo. See Department of State to POLAD, 9 December 1946, /12-946 *Awa maru* file. Asao, who had studied at Oxford University after receiving his degree from Tokyo University, was subsequently recognized as the architect of NYK's postwar recovery. *Japan Biographical Encyclopedia and Who's Who*, 78.

77. 29 January 1947 memorandum on 24 January meeting of Brig. Gen. Conrad E.

Snow (Legal Affairs); Robert A. Fearey (Northeast Asian Affairs); Rufus Burr Smith (Japan-Korea Division); and William H. McCahon and Mrs. Alice B. Correll (SWPD), attached to /12-746, *Awa maru* file; Department of State to POLAD, 4 February 1947, attached to /6-447, ibid.

78. CLO to POLAD, 26 May 1947, attached to /6-1147, *Awa maru* file.

79. Cabell Phillips, *The Truman Presidency: The History of a Triumphant Succession* (New York: Macmillan, 1966; 2nd ed., Baltimore: Pelican, 1972), 160–161.

80. Robert L. Messer, *The End of an Alliance: James F. Byrnes, Roosevelt, Truman and the Origins of the Cold War* (Chapel Hill: University of North Carolina Press, 1982), 216; Acheson, *Present at the Creation*, 283.

81. Acheson, 285.

82. Ibid., 285–314.

83. Historical Office, Department of State, *Foreign Relations of the United States 1947*, Volume 6, *The Far East* (Washington: Government Printing Office, 1972): 449–456. Documents from this series will hereinafter be cited as *FRUS*, with appropriate year, volume, and page indicated; Finn, 156–158; Howard B. Schonberger, *Aftermath of War: Americans and the Remaking of Japan, 1945–1952* (Kent, Ohio: Kent State University Press, 1989), 71–72; *FRUS, 1947*, 6: 457–515. For accounts of American difficulties with the particularly troublesome British and Australians, see Roger Buckley, *Occupation Diplomacy: Britain, the United States, and Japan, 1945–1952* (Cambridge: Cambridge University Press, 1982), 142–158, and my "The View from Down Under: Australia and Japan, 1945–1952," in *The Occupation of Japan: The International Context*, Thomas Burkman, ed. (Norfolk, Va.: MacArthur Memorial, 1984), 98–122.

84. Gallup, 1: 676–677.

85. *FRUS, 1947*, 6: 557, 589–590.

86. Schonberger, 171.

87. *Who's Who in America, 1970–71* (Chicago: Marquis Who's Who, 1971), 699.

88. Emmerson, 123.

89. Schonberger, 25.

90. Finn, 78; POLAD to Department of State, 9 Feb. 46 /2-946, folder 800, box 10, Tokyo post files, RG 84, Washington National Records Center, Suitland, Maryland.

91. POLAD to Department of State, 23 April 1946, /4-2346, 740.00119 Control (Japan), RG 59, cited in Nishi Toshio, *Unconditional Democracy: Education and Politics in Occupied Japan 1945–1952* (Stanford, Calif.: Hoover Institution Press, 1982), 266.

92. *FRUS, 1947* 6: 561–564

93. Finn, 197; Schonberger, 170–171.

94. Steven L. Rearden, *History of the Office of the Secretary of Defense*, Volume 1, *The Formative Years* (Washington: Historical Office, Office of the Secretary of Defense, 1984), 312–317, 325, 329, 333.

95. Sebald oral history, 440–441.

96. Finn, 197–198; Schonberger, 163–170

97. Fearey to POLAD, 24, 28 January 1948, /1-2448, /1-2848, *Awa maru* file.

98. MacArthur schedule 17 January 1948; POLAD #22 to Department of State, 31 January 1948, /1-3148, as analyzed in Bond to Clearing Officers, 6 February 1948, attached to /1-348 *Awa maru* file.

99. Fearey to POLAD, 24 January 1948 /1-2448, *Awa maru* file

100. POLAD to Department of State, 31 January 1948, attached to 1-1748; Bond to clearing officers, 6 February 1948, attached to /1-348, *Awa maru* file. D. Clayton James, *Years of MacArthur*, Volume 3, *Triumph and Disaster, 1945–1964* (Boston: Houghton Mifflin, 1985), 193–217, and Michael Schaller, *Douglas MacArthur: The Far Eastern General* (New York: Oxford University Press, 1989), 146–154, detail MacArthur's aspirations and experience in the 1948 presidential contest.

101. POLAD to Department of State, 31 January 1948, attached to /1-1748; Bond to clearing officers, 6 February 1948, attached to /1-348, *Awa maru* file.

102. Fearey to POLAD, 17 February 1948, /2-1748, *Awa maru* file.

103. Saitō Kiyoko to author, n.d. July 1994, 6 October 1994.

104. Thucydides—*The Peloponnesian War*, Rex Warner, trans. (Baltimore: Penguin Books, 1975), 217–222—offers the classic statement of this view of international morality.

105. Robert L. Bledsoe and Bolesaw A. Boczek, *The International Law Dictionary* (Santa Barbara, Calif.: ABC-Clio Press, 1987), 246–248, notes the difference between "classical" interpretation of *rebus sic stantibus* and that arising after conclusion of the 1969 Vienna Convention on the Law of Treaties. The situation in early 1948 does appear to meet all conditions the latter agreement laid down as defining the "fundamental change" needed to invoke the *rebus sic stantibus* doctrine. For an earlier and more traditional interpretation of the doctrine, see Melquiades J. Gamboa, *A Dictionary of International Law and Diplomacy* (Manila: Central Lawbook Publishing Company, 1973), 37–38.

Chapter 7. Laying the Ghost of War to Rest

1. Sebald to Department of State, POLAD A-157, 27 July 1948, /7-2748, *Awa maru* file.

2. *Awa maru* Claim Agreement and Agreed Terms of Understanding between the United States of America and Japan, Signed at Tokyo April 14, 1949, Entered into force April 14, 1949, Treaties and Other International Agreements Series, Department of State Publication 3528 (Washington: Government Printing Office, 1949). This document will hereinafter be cited as *Awa maru* Claim Agreement and Agreed Terms of Understanding.

3. Fukumitsu, 172.

4. William J. Sebald with Russell Brines, *With MacArthur in Japan: A Personal History of the Occupation* (New York: Norton, 1965), 74.

5. William Joseph Sebald diary, 9 April 1948, box 48, William Joseph Sebald papers, Nimitz Library, United States Naval Academy, Annapolis, Maryland. This source will hereinafter be cited as Sebald diary, with appropriate date citations. Sebald's residence at the time has since become part of the Museum of Modern Japanese Literature.

6. Shimokawabe Motoharu and Shindo Eiichi, eds., *Ashida Hitoshi nikki* [The diary of Ashida Hitoshi] (Tokyo: Iwanami shoten, 1986) 2: 92–93. This work will hereinafter be cited as *Ashida diary*, with appropriate volume and page references.

7. Sebald to Department of State, 21 April 1948, /4-2148, *Awa maru* file.

8. Sebald to John M. Allison, 22 April 1948, /4-2248, *Awa maru* file.

9. Sebald, 78–79.

10. U.S. Naval Academy *Register of Alumni*, 194; William Joseph Sebald oral history, U.S. Naval Institute, 52, 139, 165. This source will hereinafter be cited as Sebald oral history.

11. FBI report WFO 77-42459, n.d. 1953, file 77-56615, Federal Bureau of Investigation, made available via Freedom of Information Act request, 27 March 1991; Sebald oral history, 167, 249, 271, 288, 352.

12. Sebald oral history, 77, 85–97, 115.

13. Sebald oral history, 106–115; FBI Report WFO 77-42459. For examples of Edith deBecker's strong temperament, see her letters to Sebald, 6 September, n.d. September 1926, n.d. 1927, folder 1, box 23, Sebald papers; Sebald, 28, details his in-laws' family background.

14. Sebald oral history, 118, 139–142, 153–158; Sebald, 30–31.

15. Edith deBecker to Sebald, n.d. September 1926, folder 1; 7 September, 28 October, 4 November 1929, 4, 28 February, 30 July 1930, folder 2, box 23, Sebald papers; Sebald oral history, 163–169.

16. Sebald oral history, 174, 183–185. Sebald's father-in-law had died, leaving his firm to a young son unwilling and untrained to continue the business. The brother-in-law urged Sebald to return and take it over. See ibid., 163–166, 187, and Sebald, 31.

17. Sebald oral history, 188–193, 205, 211–212, 220–225. Sebald's publications were *Civil Code of Japan, Annotated* (1934); *Criminal Code of Japan* (1936); *A Selection of Japan's Emergency Legislation* (1937); and *Principal Tax Laws of Japan* (1938). See *Who's Who in Japan, with Manchoukuo and China 1939–1940*, 830.

18. Sebald oral history, 225–233. Sebald, 34–35, by contrast, implied that he had had to leave because the Japanese regarded him as a spy. He had previously been admitted to the District of Columbia bar. See Sebald oral history, 222; FBI Report WFO(77-42459), 17 March 1953.

19. Sebald oral history, 306.

20. Sebald oral history, 346–347.

21. Sebald resume, Sebald papers; Sebald oral history, 352–353.

22. Sebald to Edith Sebald, 3 January 1946, box 24; Edith Sebald to Sebald, 2 January, 18, 24 February, 19 April 2, 29 May, 2 June, 6 August 1946, box 23, Sebald papers; *Washington Evening Star,* 5 August 1946 and *Washington Post,* 6 August 1946 report of Edith deBecker Sebald's attainment of citizenship; Sebald oral history, 355.

23. Sebald to Edith Sebald, January 11, 17, 1946; Edith Sebald to Sebald, February 13, 19, 1946; For examples of Sebald's dealings with these elites, see Sebald diary, 14, 23, 25 January, 19 February, 6,19–20, 23–29 March 1946, box 48; 2, 12,23, July, 19 August, 24–25 September, 21 October, 24 November, 13 December 1947, Sebald appointments diaries, box 44, Sebald papers; Sebald oral history, 526–528. These sources indicate that Sebald began systematic entertaining of high-ranking Japanese political figures far sooner than December 1948, the date he mentioned in his published memoir, 69.

24. Sebald, 103–120; Sebald oral history, 413, 545–546; for Sebald's clash with his naval superiors, see Sebald oral history, 166–167.

25. Sebald, 137–146.

26. Sebald did not become a Foreign Service officer until 27 July 1947; he was the counselor of mission in Tokyo when the *Awa maru* negotiations commenced; FBI Report WFO 77-42459, 17 March 1953.

27. POLAD to Department of State, #213, 22 April 1948, /4-2248, *Awa maru* file; Hayashi Shigeru and Tsuji Akira, eds., *Nihon naikaku shiroku 5* [The historical record of Japan's cabinets, Volume 5] (Tokyo: Daichi hōkan shuppan sha, 1981), 140.

28. Shindo Eiichi, Introduction to *Ashida nikki* 1: 1–3, 36 –37; *Who's Who in Japan, with Manchoukuo and China, 1930–1940,* 58; *Japan Biographical Encyclopedia and Who's Who,* 79

29. Shindo in *Ashida diary,* 1: 37.

30. Finn, 172.

31. Hayashi and Tsuji, 5: 31–32. Ashida also served briefly as Shidehara's chief cabinet secretary. Australian diplomat W. Macmahon Ball noted that Ashida spoke English "with a quite good English accent." See Alan Rix, ed., *Intermittent Diplomat: The Japan and Batavia Diaries of W. Macmahon Ball* (Melbourne: Melbourne University Press, 1988), 221.

32. Finn, 116.

33. Finn, 148; Hayashi and Tsuji, 5: 102

34. Yoshitsu, 8; for a much less favorable assessment of Ashida's efforts, see Rix, 215.

35. Gascoigne to Foreign Office, F5729/5729/23 FO 371/63798, cited in Roger Buckley, *Occupation Diplomacy: Britain, the United States, and Japan 1945–1952* (Cambridge: Cambridge University Press, 1982), 197; Finn, 172.

36. Sebald appointment diary, 25 July, 25 September, 21 October, 7 November, 27 December 1947, box 44, Sebald papers; Ashida notebooks, 25 July, 25 September, 7 November, 27 December 1947, *Ashida Diary,* 1: 279, 290, 297, 306.

37. *Who's Who in Japan, with Manchoukuo and China, 1930–1940* 1111; Career summary, Naisei shi kenkyūkai, *Yoshizawa Seijirō danwa sokkiroku: Naisei shi kenkyū shiryō dai hyaku rokugo shū* [A record of interviews with Yoshizawa Seijirō: domestic political history documentary collection 165] (Tokyo: Naisei shi kenkyūkai, 1983). This source will hereinafter be cited as Yoshizawa interviews.

38. *Who's Who in Japan, with Manchoukuo and China*, 1111; *Yoshizawa Seijirō danwa sokkiroku*, career summary. For detailed discussion of the *Panay* negotiations, see Roger Dingman, "Yangtze River Crisis: A Reconsideration of the *Panay* Incident, 1937," in Gunji shi gakkai, ed., *Dai Niji sekai taisen: hassei to kakudai* [The Second World War: origins and enlargement] (Tokyo: Kinsei sha, 1990), 95–124.

39. POLAD to Department of State, #43, 20 January 1948, file 800, box 33, Tokyo post files, Record Group 84, Washington National Records Center, Suitland, Maryland.

40. Sebald diary, 22 April 1948.

41. POLAD to Department of State, #23, 22 April 1948, /4-2248, *Awa maru* file.

42. *Ashida diary*, 2: 97–98.

43. Secretary of State to POLAD, 27 April 1948, /4-2748, *Awa maru* file.

44. POLAD to Secretary of State, #359, 15 June 1948, /6-1548, *Awa maru* file; Sebald diary, 11 June 1948; Ashida diary, 2: 127.

45. POLAD to Department of State, #359, 15 June 1948, /6-1548, *Awa maru* file.

46. *Asahi shimbun*, 9 June 1948.

47. SCAP Daily Appointments Schedule, 18 June; Sebald diary, 18 June 1948.

48. *Who's Who in Government, 1975–1976* (Chicago: Marquis Who's Who, 1975), 198; Gaimushō, ed., *Shōki taiNichi senryō seisaku (jō) Asakai Kōichirō hokoku sho* [Early Occupation policy towards Japan: the Asakai Kōichirō reports, Part 1] (Tokyo: Asahi shimbunsha, 1978), 261; Finn, 71, 134; Rix, *Intermittent Diplomat*, 161.

Finn may have been responsible for passing to the Japanese side a citation from Rene Wormser, *Collection of International War Damage Claims* (New York: Alexander Publishing, 1944), which made the case for the legality and practicality of Japan's abandoning the *Awa maru* claims. It argued (on pages 267–268) that "the payment of any substantial sums" on account of Axis claims against the United States was "extremely unlikely." Wormser predicted that Washington, relying on World War I precedents, would use the sale of enemy assets seized by the Alien Property Custodian to pay any claims against it arising from Axis nations. Zasshū Sankō shiryō [Various materials reference documents], frame 0200, reel B'-0084.

49. POLAD to Department of State, #A-157, 27 July 1948, /7-2748 *Awa maru* file; Sebald diary, 29 July 1948.

50. Hayashi and Tsuji, 141–153; Finn, 163.

51. *Ashida diary*, 2: 125–127

52. *Ashida diary*, 2: 156; Schonberger, 124–126; Finn, 173–175.

53. James, 3: 148, 240–241; Schonberger, 185–194; Finn, 197–198, 203–204.

54. Sebald to Edith Sebald, 3, 17 January 1946, box 24, Sebald papers.

55. Sebald diary, 4 August 1948.

56. SCAP Daily Appointments Schedule, 24 August 1948; Ashida diary, 24 August 1948; POLAD to Department of State, #553, 24 August 1948, /8-2448, *Awa maru* file.

57. Sebald diary, 24 September 1948; *Ashida diary,* 2: 199

58. *Ashida diary,* 2: 200–214;Hayashi and Tsuji, 158–161; Finn, 177–178.

59. Sebald diary, 2 October 1948.

60. POLAD to Department of State, #227, /4-1449 *Awa maru* file.

61. POLAD to Department of State, #122, #227, 14 April 1949, /4-1449, *Awa maru* file.

62. Sebald diary, 16 October 1948.

63. Sebald, 97; Finn, 21–22, 150.

64. Togawa Isamu, *Shōwa no shushō dai yonkan Yoshida Shigeru to fukkō e no sentaku* [Shōwa (era) prime ministers, Volume 4, Yoshida Shigeru and the choices for recovery] (Tokyo: Kodansha, 1983), 93–95; Inoki Masamichi, *Hyōden: Yoshida Shigeru* [Yoshida Shigeru: a critical biography] (Tokyo: Yomiuri shimbunsha, 1981), 1: 7–99. Yoshida's father-in-law, Count Makino Shinken, was the adopted son of Okubo Toshimichi, one of the leaders of the Meiji Restoration of 1868.

65. Togawa, 95–102: Inoki, 1: 165–238; 3: 7–112, 181–236; Sebald diary, 22–23 December 1948; Finn, 20, 79, 188; Sebald, 175.

66. Inoki, 3: 247–248; Hayashi and Tsuji, 5: 74–79; Finn, 144.

67. Finn, 23, 124.

68. Finn, 110, 124, 127; James, 3: 310, points out that Yoshida met MacArthur more frequently than did any other prime minister during the occupation period. Yoshida's letters to MacArthur can be found in VIP file, RG 10, MacArthur papers.

69. Hayashi and Tsuji, 5: 168–172; Finn, 210–212. In addition to Yamazaki Takeshi, Miki Takeo, then head of the People's Cooperative Party but many years later prime minister, also spurned SCAP's advances.

70. Sebald diary, 3–4, 8, November 1948.

71. Sebald diary, 11, 17 November 1948.

72. Sebald diary, 10 November 1948. Information about the proposed settlement reached International News Service reporter Howard Handelman from a Japanese source. Sebald apparently persuaded Handelman to keep it secret, for nothing about the proposed agreement appeared in the American or the Japanese press.

73. Finn, 213–215.

74. Sebald diary, 22–23 December 1948.

75. Hayashi and Tsuji, 5: 179–180; Togawa, 213–215.

76. Hayashi and Tsuji, 5: 180–183; Finn, 216.

77. Finn 216–218; Togawa, 224–229. For a particularly insightful analysis of the roots and bureaucratic character of Yoshida's leadership style, see John W. Dower, *Japan in War and Peace: Selected Essays* (New York: New Press, 1993), 214–217, 229.

78. Hayashi and Tsuji, 5: 192–194; Finn, 223; Schonberger, 206–211.

79. Matsui, 211. Yoshida's actions appear to have followed a script prepared the preceding November and coordinated at the time with Sebald's office. See English drafts of the Diet resolution, draft schedule for a conference on it of five party leaders, and draft schedule for Diet approval, n.d. November 1948, Yōkyū kenhō ni kansuru to kokkai to no kankei (Kokkai teishutsu made no ikisatsu) [Concerning relations with the Diet over the abandonment of rights and claims (details up to the presentation of a proposal)], frames 219, 278–279, 298, reel B'-0084.

80. Ashida diary, 3: 81; *New York Times*, 5, 17, 21 April 1949.

81. Ashida diary, 6 April 1949, 3: 79; POLAD to Department of State, #105, /4-649, *Awa maru* file; Finn, 217.

82. POLAD to Department of State, #105, 6 April 1949, /4-649, *Awa maru* file.

83. *Japan Biographical Encyclopedia*, 1164; Yoshitsu, 22–23.

84. Nishimura Kumao, *San furanshisuko kōwa jōyaku* [The San Francisco peace treaty], Volume 27 of Kajima heiwa kenkyūjo, ed., *Nihon gaikō shi* [A history of Japanese diplomacy] (Tokyo: Kajima heiwa kenkyū jo shuppan kai, 1971), 27–47.

85. Matsui, 211.

86. *Kampo* [Official gazette], 7 April 1949, cited in Arima Yorichika, *Seizonsha no dammoku* [The silence of a survivor], in *Arima Yorichika heitai shosetsu denki sen 3* [Volume 3 of the selected military novels and diaries of Arima Yorichika] (Tokyo: Kojinsha, 1983), 193.

87. Arima, 192; Matsui, 211–212.

88. POLAD to Department of State, #105, 6 April 1949, /4-649 *Awa maru* file.

89. *Asahi shimbun, Mainichi shimbun, Yomiuri shimbun, Sekai keizai shimbun,* 7 April; *Akahata,* 8 April; *Asahi shimbun,* 9 April 1949, clippings in file 341.33, *Awa maru* National Diet Library clippings collection. This source will hereinafter be cited as NDL clippings collection.

90. *Asahi shimbun,* 23 April 1949; POLAD to Department of State, #137, 26 April 1949, /4-2649, *Awa maru* file.

91. Hayashi and Tsuji, 5: 193; *Ashida diary,* 3: 90.

92. POLAD to Department of State, #136, 26 April 1949, /4-2649, *Awa maru* file.

93. *Awa maru* Claim Agreement and Agreed Terms of Understanding.

94. POLAD to Department of State, #A-309, 15 November 1949, /11-1549, *Awa maru* file.

95. Japanese Government to United States Government, 10 August, in SCAP (Allen) to Joint Chiefs of Staff, 14 December 1945, CCS 560 (4-26-45), box 504, RG 218; POLAD to Department of State, #A-309, 15 November, /11-1549, #820, 26 November 1949, /11-2649 *Awa maru* file.

96. Fukumitsu, 174.

97. Ibid., 173–174; POLAD to Department of State, #A-309, 15 November 1949, /11-1549, *Awa maru* file.

98. POLAD to Department of State, #820, 26 November 1949, / 11-2649, *Awa maru* file.

99. Fukumitsu, 174.

100. Hayashi and Tsuji, 5: 203–205; Finn, 233–235.

101. Hayashi and Tsuji 5: 201–202; Finn, 249; John M. Allison, *Ambassador from the Prairie or Allison Wonderland* (Tokyo: Charles E. Tuttle Co., 1975), 145–149.

102. Roger Dingman, "The Dagger and the Gift: The Impact of the Korean War on Japan," *Journal of American-East Asian Relations* 2 (Spring 1991), 29–55; Hayashi and Tsuji, 5: 205–207; Finn, 263–268.

103. Fukumitsu, 172–173.

104. Ibid., 175. Nishimura, 151, 161–162, and Department of State, Historical Office, *Foreign Relations of the United States 1951,* Volume 6, *Asia and the Pacific, Part 1* (Washington, D.C.: Government Printing Office, 1977), 796, 852–854, 908–909, 915, 948–949, 987, 1014–1015, 1031–1033, 1093–1096, 1125–1230, detail the negotiation of the claims provisions of the Japanese Peace Treaty. They reveal that while John Foster Dulles on behalf of the United States originally proposed mutual abandonment of all claims arising from the war, Australia and Britain refused to do so.

105. The Socialist Diet member who claimed that the 1949 agreement had not committed Japan to repay the United States for early postwar aid was technically correct, for the GARIOA (Government and Relief in Occupied Areas) repayment provision was embodied, at Japan's request, in a supplementary "Agreed terms of understanding" signed by Yoshida, Sebald, and MacArthur. See *Awa maru* Claim Agreement and Agreed Terms of Understanding; *Asahi shimbun,* 25 March 1962, file 341.33, *Awa maru,* NDL clippings collection. The GARIOA debt was eventually set at $1.8 billion; in 1962, after years of negotiations, the Japanese government agreed to pay the principal sum of $490 million over a fifteen-year period. See Sebald, 74.

Chapter 8. Heroes

1. *Asahi shimbun,* 28 April 1979; *Los Angeles Times,* 4 May 1979.

2. The "good war" epithet was coined and popularized by Studs Terkel, *The Good War: An Oral History of World War Two* (New York: Pantheon, 1984).

3. My understanding of the differences between individual and public memories draws upon the arguments presented in Gerald Linderman, *Embattled Courage* (New York: Free Press, 1988); John Bodnar, *Remaking America: Public Memory, Commemoration and Patriotism in Twentieth Century America* (Princeton: Princeton University Press, 1992), especially 13–20; Karen Marling and John Wetenhall, *Iwo Jima: Monuments, Memories, and the American Hero* (Cambridge: Harvard University Press, 1991); and Kurt Piehler, *Remembering War the American Way* (Washington: Smithsonian Institution Press, 1995), particularly ix–x.

4. Charles A. Lockwood, Jr., with Percy Finch, "We Gave the Japs a Licking Underseas," *Saturday Evening Post* 222 (16 July 1949), 117; Charles A. Lockwood, *Sink 'Em All: Submarine Warfare in the Pacific* (New York: E. P. Dutton, 1951), 43.

5. I have inferred this point from Lockwood's character and later writings.

6. Lockwood to Phyllis Lockwood correspondence, 1941–1945, box 7, Lockwood papers.

7. *New York Times*, 3 May 1945.

8. Lockwood, *Sink 'Em All*, 333; *New York Times*, 5 July 1945.

9. Robert Trumbull, *Silversides* (New York: Henry Holt, 1945), xi–xii; *New York Times*, 19 August 1945.

10. Lockwood talk to Y.M. Institute, Catholic Church, 18 November 1949, box 19, Lockwood papers.

11. Theodore Roscoe et al., *United States Submarine Operations in World War II* (Annapolis, Md.: Naval Institute Press, 1949), xviii–xix. This work will hereinafter be cited as *USSOPS*, with appropriate page references.

12. *U.S. Submarine Losses World War II*, NavPers 15,784 (Washington: Government Publications Office, 1949), front cover interior.

13. Lockwood biography, box 400, officer biography files, COA, NHC; Lockwood biographical summary, Guide to Vice Adm. Charles A. Lockwood, Jr., Papers, Lockwood papers; Steven T. Ross, "Chester William Nimitz," in Robert A. Love, ed., *The Chiefs of Naval Operations* (Annapolis, Md.: Naval Institute Press, 1980), 184–185; Elmer B. Potter, *Nimitz* (Annapolis, Md.: Naval Institute Press, 1976), 407–410.

14. Lockwood, *Sink 'Em All*, 261.

15. Blair, 879–880.

16. Potter, 410.

17. Potter, 413–414. Nimitz retained Loughlin's defense counsel, Captain H.C. Bruton (who had been an aide to Admiral King) and took on Cdr. Eugene B. Fluckey, skipper of the *Queenfish*'s wolfpack mate, the *Barb* (SS 220).

18. Potter, 413.

19. *New York Times*, 28 October 1945; Norman Polmar and Thomas B. Allen, *Rickover* (New York: Simon and Schuster, 1982), 115–116; *Queenfish* November 1945 homecoming party photograph, Bennett papers.

20. Martin V. Melosi, *The Shadow of Pearl Harbor: Political Controversy over the Surprise Attack, 1941–1946* (College Station: Texas A&M University Press, 1977), 122–160; Jeffrey G. Barlow, *Revolt of the Admirals: The Fight for Naval Aviation, 1945–1950* (Washington: Naval Historical Center, Department of the Navy, 1994), 32–44; Townsend Hoopes and Douglas Brinkley, *Driven Patriot: The Life and Times of James Forrestal* (New York: Knopf, 1992), 321–350.

21. *U.S. Submarine Losses World War II*.

22. Navy Department press releases, 2 February 1946, COA, NHC; *New York Times*, 3 February 1946.

23. *Newsweek* 27 (11 February 1946), 44–45.

24. *USSOPS*, xix.

25. The works in question were *Submarine Operation History World War II*, 4 volumes, and *United States Naval Administration in World War II Submarine Commands*, 2 volumes, copies in COA, NHC.

26. Lockwood to Chief of Naval Communications, 17 June 1947, SRH 235, Comint Contributions Submarine Warfare in World War II, Special Collections, Nimitz Library, U.S. Naval Academy, Annapolis, Maryland.

27. N.d. 1946 data for Senate statement, box 19, Lockwood papers; *Newsweek* 27 (11 February 1946), 44.

28. Lockwood speeches to American Legion, Orange, New Jersey, and to Orange, New Jersey, High School students, 21 March 1946, box 19, Lockwood papers.

29. Charles A. Lockwood, Jr., "U.S. Subs Out of Date," *Science Newsletter* 51 (19 April 1947), 246.

30. Lockwood officer biography, box 400, COA, NHC; Lockwood biographical summary, Lockwood papers; Hans Christian Adamson, *Keepers of the Lights* (New York: Greenberg, 1955), xviii.

31. Lockwood speech, 7 December 1948, box 19, Lockwood papers,

32. Notes and references for Lockwood speeches, box 19, Lockwood papers; Charles A. Lockwood, Jr., with Percy Finch, "We Gave the Japs a Licking Underseas," *Saturday Evening Post* 222 (16 July 1949), 22–23, 116–119; (23 July 1949), 32–33, 62–66; (30 July 1949), 30, 92–94; Lockwood, *Sink 'Em All*.

33. Blair, 880.

34. Cabell Phillips, *The Truman Presidency: The History of a Triumphant Succession* (Baltimore: Penguin Books, 1979), 247; Barlow, 160.

35. Paolo E. Coletta, "Louis Emil Denfeld," in Love, ed., *The Chiefs of Naval Operations*, 194–204; Barlow, 142–143, 247–277; Hoopes and Brinkley, 405–428.

36. 7 December 1948 Lockwood speech, box 19, Lockwood papers.

37. Lockwood and Finch, (16 July 1949), 22–23, 116–119; (23 July 1949), 32–33, 62–66; (30 July 1949), 30, 92–94.

38. Ibid. (16 July 1949), 22, 116.

39. Ibid. (30 July 1949), 30, 94.

40. *USSOPS*, xix. Roscoe had published several short stories during the war, in the *American Magazine*. See "Border Incident" 132 (September 1941), 128; "Don't Count Your Chickens" 134 (September 1942), 44; "Officer and a Gentleman" 134 (October 1942), 32; "Manhunt in Tunisia" 135 (April 1943), 25; "Birthday Letter" 137 (January 1944), 53; and "Right Answer" 137 (February 1944), 55. He would later produce a historical mystery, *The Web of Conspiracy: The Complete Story of the Men Who Murdered Abraham Lincoln* (Englewood Cliffs, N.J.: Prentice-Hall, 1959).

41. *USSOPS*, v.

42. Ibid., xvii–xviii.

43. Ibid., 495.

44. Ibid., 458–460.

45. Ibid., 459–460.

46. Richard G. Voge, "Too Much Accuracy," U.S. Naval Institute *Proceedings* 76 (March 1950), 256–257, 263. An inquiry to the Naval Institute in February 1994 failed to produce any information about the person or persons responsible for posthumous publication of Voge's article.

47. Voge, 259–263.

48. *United States Submarine Operations in World War II* went through three printings in little more than ninety days, and by 1984 it was in its twelfth printing. *USSOPS*, iv. It appeared in an abridged, mass paperback edition as *Pigboats* (New York: Bantam Books, 1982). *Sink 'Em All* went through two printings in as many months in 1951, iv.

49. *New York Times*, 25 March 1951.

50. Lockwood, *Sink 'Em All*, passim, especially 147–165, 393.

51. Ibid., 301–306.

52. Ibid., 371–393.

53. Lockwood subsequently coauthored, with Hans Christian Adamson, three other books that dealt with the Pacific submarine war: *Hellcats of the Sea* (New York: Greenberg, 1955), *Through Hell and High Water* (New York: Greenberg, 1956), and *Zoomies, Subs and Zeros* (New York: Greenberg, 1956). Other accounts of that conflict that echo his interpretation include Edward L. Beach, *Submarine!* (New York: Henry Holt, 1952); Samuel Eliot Morison, *Victory in the Pacific*, volume 14 of *History of United States Naval Operations in World War II* (Boston: Little, Brown, 1960), 285–297; and W. Jasper Holmes, *Undersea Victory: The Influence of Submarine Operations on the War in the Pacific* (Garden City, N.Y.: Doubleday, 1966). Interestingly, Morison and Holmes replicated the differences in nuance that divided Admirals Voge and Lockwood in their treatment of the sinking of the *Awa maru*. While Morison presented it in a single paragraph, as simply "a far more unfortunate incident" than the mistaken firing by the USS *Case* (DD 370) upon the *Spot* (SS 413), Holmes paraphrased Lockwood and termed it "the biggest blunder" of the submarine war. See Morison, 290–291; Holmes, 456–457.

54. Stan Hasrato coined this phrase, which became the title of his article in *Collier's* 116 (28 July 1945), 14–15, 50; (4 August 1945), 54–55, 73.

55. Lockwood talk to Y.M. Institute, Catholic Church, 18 November 1949, box 19, Lockwood papers.

56. Hoopes and Brinkley, 190–194.

57. James Robert Parish and Ronald L. Powers, *The MGM Stock Company: The Golden Era* (New Rochelle, N.Y.: Arlington House, 1973), 498–501; *Variety Obituaries, 1980–1983* (New York: Garland Press, 1988), 9: 30 September 1981.

58. Only one feature film, *Operation Disaster*, that focused on submarine warfare appeared on movie screens between 1945 and the onset of the Korean War. Richard B.

and Mary Williams Armstrong, *The Movie List Book: A Reference Guide to Film Themes, Settings, and Series* (Jefferson, N.C.: McFarland and Company, 1990), 319–320; Debra Handy, ed., *Variety Film Reviews, 1907–1980* (New York: Garland, 1985) 16: 173–174.

59. Because during my research *Silent Service* was being transferred from the Department of Defense Moving Picture Facility at March Air Force Base, California, to the Motion Picture, Sound, and Video Branch of the National Archives, I was unable to view it in its entirety. However, I have reconstructed the gist from index cards (used in the production, and now stored at the latter facility) describing portions of the original film. See Negative 1-478, index 3844; negative 2-9174, index 3905; negative 1-98755, index 11760; and indices 17475, 19595, 20430, 20432, RG 428, Motion Picture, Sound, and Video branch, U.S. National Archives, Capitol Heights, Maryland.

60. Lockwood talk to Y. M. Institute, Catholic Church, 18 November 1949. He also used it to commemorate Pearl Harbor Day 1950, in a speech to the San Jose (California) Shrine Luncheon Club. Box 19, Lockwood papers.

61. Eugene Lyons, *Sarnoff* (New York: Harper and Row, 1966), 202.

62. Walter Karig, Russell L. Harris, and Frank A. Manson, *Battle Report*, Volume 5, *Victory in the Pacific* (New York: Rinehart & Co., 1949), v–vii. Karig's coauthors in this series included two newspapermen, a radio broadcaster, a novelist, and a schoolteacher who was a veteran of naval battles off the Philippines and Okinawa. Walter Karig et al., *Battle Report*, Volume 1, *Pearl Harbor to Coral Sea* (New York: Farrar and Rinehart, 1944); *Battle Report*, Volume 2, *The Atlantic War* (New York: Farrar, Rinehart, 1946); *Battle Report*, Volume 3, *Pacific War: Middle Phase* (New York: Holt, Rinehart and Company, 1947); *Battle Report*, Volume 4, *The End of an Empire* (New York: Rinehart and Company, 1948).

63. Samuel Eliot Morison, *History of United States Naval Operations in World War II* (Boston: Little, Brown, 1947–1962), 1: preface. This work will hereinafter be cited as Morison, *Naval Operations*, with appropriate volume and page citations.

64. *New York Times,* 2 February 1958; Lyons, 241; Saloman to Morison, n.d. February 1946, box 9, Samuel Eliot Morison papers, Classified Operational Archives, Naval Historical Center, Washington, D.C.; Gregory M. Pfitzer, *Samuel Eliot Morison's Historical World: In Quest of a New Parkman* (Boston: Northeastern University Press, 1991), 179, 182; 238–239 details the subsequent controversy between Morison and Saloman, in which the former threatened to sue to get greater credit for *Victory at Sea,* and the latter paid five thousand dollars to quash his claim.

65. *Variety Television Reviews,* 29 October 1952; Richard Rodgers, *Musical States: An Autobiography* (New York: Random House, 1975), 101, 278–281. Rodgers's music, as orchestrated by Richard Russell Bennett, sold millions of records and tapes over the ensuing decades; Frederick Nolan, *The Sound of Their Music: The Story of Rodgers and Hammerstein* (New York: Walker and Company, 1977), 183–184.

66. *Variety Television Reviews,* 29 October 1952.

67. Ibid., 6 May 1953. For a full listing of the *Victory at Sea* series, see Howard B. Hitchens, ed., *America on Film and Tape* (Westport, Conn.: Greenwood Press, 1985), 143–144.

68. Leonard Graves's narrative text, "Full Fathom Five," episode 21, *Victory at Sea*, Embassy Home Entertainment Special Collectors Edition, 1986. All subsequent citations of this episode of *Victory at Sea* refer to this edition of the film.

69. Rear Adm. Thomas M. Dykers biography, officer biography files, box 174, COA, NHC; U. S. Naval Academy *Register of Alumni*, 214; Blair, *Silent Victory*, 443–444, 446, 512, 583–584, 622–624, 641, 931, 938, 942, 948; Vice Adm. James F. Calvert, *Silent Running: My Years on a World War II Attack Submarine* (New York: John Wiley and Sons, 1995), 1–2, 33.

70. *Navy Times*, 6 April 1957, in Dykers biography file, box 174, COA, NHC; *New York Times*, 19 October 1958. Dykers also served as technical adviser on such feature films as *The Caine Mutiny*, *20,000 Leagues Under the Sea*, *The Frogman*, *Hell and High Water*, and *Flat Top*.

71. Lockwood to Fred Hamilton, 21 June, Lockwood to Capt. John S. Coye, Jr., 6 July 1955, box 9, Lockwood papers.

72. Generalizations in this paragraph are based on my viewing of four *Silent Service* episodes: "Tang versus Truk," "The *Nautilus* Story," "The *Sculpin* Story," and "Cargo for *Crevalle*." I am grateful to Republic Pictures, the current rights holder of these films, for making the first three available to me for research purposes. Capt. F. Walter Mazzone, hero of "Cargo for *Crevalle*," showed me his tape copy of that episode at his San Diego home, 19 July 1994.

73. *Variety Television Reviews* 6: 10 April, 9 May, 12 June 1957.

74. *New York Times*, 19 October 1958; *The Silent Service* film series list, Republic Pictures, Los Angeles, California.

75. Generalizations in this paragraph and the one following are based on my viewing of the four *The Silent Service* episodes previously mentioned.

76. During the 1956–1957 production period for this series, Elliott Loughlin was director of athletics at the U.S. Naval Academy. Capt. Frank Shamer was operations and plans officer for Commander in Chief, Atlantic Fleet, based in Norfolk, Virginia. Cdr. John E. Bennett was assistant athletic director at the U.S. Naval Academy, serving under Loughlin. See Loughlin officer biography, Shamer officer biography, boxes 400, 568, COA, NHC; Bennett career summary, enclosed in Bennett to author, 15 May 1993.

77. Armstrong, *Movie List Book*, 319–320. These films included: *Hell and High Water*, 1954; *Above Us the Waves*, 1956; *The Deep Six*, *The Silent Enemy*, *Torpedo Run*, and *Run Silent, Run Deep*, 1958; and *Atomic Submarine*, *On the Beach*, *Operation Petticoat*, and *Up Periscope*, 1959.

78. *Los Angeles Times*, 18 April 1957; *Navy Times*, 6 April 1957; Polmar and Allen, *Rickover*, 167–168.

79. *Variety Film Reviews 1907–1980* (New York: Garland Press, 1983), 9: 1 May 1957.

80. Charles A. Lockwood, Jr., and Hans Christian Adamson, *Hellcats of the Sea* (New York: Greenberg, 1955).

81. Hans Christian Adamson, *Keepers of the Lights* (New York: Greenberg, 1955), xviii. I have inferred the submariners' role in Colonel Adamson's rescue from another of his works coauthored with Vice Admiral Lockwood—*Zoomies, Subs, and Zeroes* (New York: Greenberg, 1956), especially xii–xiii.

82. Lockwood and Adamson, *Hellcats*, x. The phrases appear in Fleet Admiral Nimitz's foreword to the book.

83. *Hellcats of the Sea*, 3–9, 22, 79–83, 240–244, 292–295, 314–316.

84. Lockwood diary, 15–16 August 1956, box 2, Lockwood papers. The producer was Charles H. Schneer. See *Variety Film Reviews 1907–1980* 9: 1 May 1957.

85. Lockwood diary, 3, 17, 24, 27–28 November, 24 December 1956. When Schneer, in a letter Lockwood had reviewed, asked Admiral Nimitz to appear in the film, the admiral at first refused. Vice Admiral Lockwood then approached Mrs. Nimitz and with her help persuaded his former commander to change his mind.

86. Anne Edwards, *Early Reagan* (New York: Morrow, 1987), 463.

87. This summary of the plot of *Hellcats of the Navy* is based on my viewing of the video edition and on Tony Thomas, *The Films of Ronald Reagan* (Secaucus, N.J.: Citadel Press, 1980), 218–221.

88. Lockwood diary, 17 April 1957; *Los Angeles Times*, 18 April 1957. This gesture by no means ended Lockwood's Hollywood career. The admiral was a consultant for other submarine feature films, rewriting scripts, providing liaison to the Navy Department, and training actors to speak like submariners. He went to Australia to supervise submarine filming in *On the Beach*, Nevil Shute's novel about survivors after a nuclear exchange between the United States and the Soviet Union. See Lockwood diary, August 1958–January 1959, box 2, Lockwood papers.

89. A docent at the Ronald Reagan Presidential Museum described *Hellcats of the Navy* as the future president's "most successful film," 13 February 1994. For less enthusiastic retrospective evaluations of the film, see Thomas, 221, and Edwards, 463.

90. Notes for address at Convention of U.S. Submarine Veterans of World War II, 15 August 1959, box 19, Lockwood papers.

91. Notes for address at Convention of U.S. Submarine Veterans of World War II, 15 August 1959, box 19, Lockwood papers. The admiral borrowed these words from the closing paragraph of *Sink 'Em All*, 393.

92. J.E. Talbot, "Weapons Development, War Planning and Policy: The U.S. Navy and the Submarine, 1917–1941," *Naval War College Review* 37 (May–June 1984), 54–55. Talbot points out that the Bemis study remained classified until 1978.

93. Ted Mico, John Miller Monzon, and David Rubel, eds., Mark C. Carnes, general ed., *Past Imperfect: History According to the Movies* (New York: Holt, 1995), analyzes history as depicted in feature films.

94. Loughlin Naval Institute oral history, 178.

95. Joan and Clay Blair, Jr., 1971 interview with Rear Adm. Elliott Loughlin, item 8295, Clay Blair, Jr., collection, American Heritage Center, University of Wyoming; Loughlin Naval Institute oral history, 271.

96. Notes for unpublished article, "Japan Revisited," box 23, Lockwood papers.

97. Joe S. Parks and Denny Rathbun interview, Poulsbo, Washington, 29 April 1994; Bennett interview, 14 May 1993; Shamer interview, 25 June 1993.

98. *San Diego Tribune*, 2 March 1963, in John E. Bennett papers.

99. Bennett interview, 14 May 1993.

Chapter 9. Victims

1. Renjōji is located in Nishi Kidera chō, Nara. It is presently affiliated with the Jodō [Pure Land] sect of Buddhism. Its major structure was rebuilt in the 1730s, and its principal image of Buddha dates from the late Kamakura period. Kokushi daijiten henshū iinkai, ed., *Kokushi daijiten* [Dictionary of national history] (Tokyo: Yoshikawa Kobunkan, 1993), 4: 746.

2. Matsui, 40; *Asahi shimbun*, 30 October 1990; Arai Shigeru and Shimotsuma Kazuho interview, 8 October 1994, Nara, Japan.. Mrs. Arai Keiko, the young widow principally responsible for erecting the monument, raised funds for it by selling temple visitors small ceramic images of the Buddha that would constitute the memorial-to-be. The full text inscribed on the base of the statue reads: "Kannon with hands folded in prayer. *Awa maru*. Respectfully written by Shū Tan, Great Archbishop, Master of the Tendai Sect." The Tendai sect has its headquarters at Enryakuji Temple in Nara. See *Kodansha Encyclopedia of Japan*, 8: 4–5. Kannon, an originally masculine bodhisattva who evolved into a feminine form, is regarded in Buddhist theology as the personification of divine mercy. See Ernest Dale Saunders, *Buddhism in Japan, with an Outline of Its Origins in India* (Philadelphia: University of Pennsylvania Press, 1964), 172–174.

3. Zōjōji Temple information leaflet; *Kodansha Encyclopedia of Japan* 8: 379.

4. Nonomura Masao interview, 3 October 1994, Tokyo; *Japan Times*, 1 April; *Asahi shimbun*, 2 April 1977; Takeuchi Kiyoko to *Awa maru* Bereaved Families Association members, 15 April 1977. Professor Takahashi Hisashi, then at the Office of War History, National Defense Institute, Tokyo, discovered this postcard in a copy of Chihaya Masataka, *Norowareta Awa maru* [The accursed *Awa maru*] (Tokyo: Bungei shunjū, 1961), owned by General Inada Seijun. I am grateful to him for giving me this and other *Awa maru*–related materials that General Inada saved. This source will hereinafter be cited as Inada Seijun materials.

5. *Awa maru* memorial cenotaph inscription.

6. In Buddhist theology "hungry ghosts" (*preta*) temporarily inhabit the world of the dead, one of three bad destinations for the deceased. They are sent there or reborn in miserable condition in retribution for their previous actions. See Saunders, 59.

7. Robert E. Sherwood, *Roosevelt and Hopkins: An Intimate History* (New York: Grosset and Dunlop, 1948), 696–697.

8. Nishi Toshio, *Unconditional Democracy: Education and Politics in Occupied Japan 1945–1952* (Stanford: Hoover Institution Press, 1982), 163–173. For a different perspective on educational reform by one of its principal practitioners, see Joseph C. Trainer, *Educational Reform in Occupied Japan* (Tokyo: Meisei University Press, 1983); Satō Hideo, in Haruko Taya Cook and Theodore F. Cook, *Japan at War: An Oral History* (New York: New Press, 1992), 239.

9. Nishi, 89; NHK hōsō bunka chōsa kenkyū jo, hōsō jōhō chōsa bu, *GHQ bunsho ni yoru senryō ki hōsō shi nenpyō (Shōwa nijūichi nen tsuitachi-jūnigatsu sanjūichi nichi)* [A chronology of the history of broadcasting in the Occupation period according to (Supreme Commander Allied Powers) G(eneral) H(ead) Q(uarters) documents (1 January–31 December 1946)] (Tokyo: NHK hōsō bunka chōsa kenkyū jo, hōsō jōhō chōsa bu, 1988), 2–129, passim.

10. Peter Duus, "Remembering the Empire: Postwar Interpretation of the Greater East Asia Coprosperity Sphere," Woodrow Wilson Center Asia Program Occasional Paper 54 (Washington: Woodrow Wilson Center, Smithsonian Institution, 1993), 1–2.

11. Hirano Kyoko, *Mr. Smith Goes to Tokyo: Japanese Cinema under the American Occupation, 1945–1952* (Washington: Smithsonian Institution Press, 1992), 4–6, 49–53, 179–194.

12. Dower, 217–218; Yoshida Shigeru, *The Yoshida Memoirs: The Story of Japan in Crisis,* Yoshida Kenichi, trans. (Boston: Houghton Mifflin, 1962), 26–29, 184.

13. Rikki Kersten, *Democracy in Postwar Japan: Maruyama Masao and the Search for Autonomy* (London: Routledge, 1996), 13–48, 262–268, analyzes the thought on this subject of one of Japan's most prominent intellectuals.

14. Ibuse Mabuchi, *Lieutenant Look East,* John Bester, trans. (Tokyo: Kodansha International, 1971), 23–65; Osaragi Jirō, *Homecoming,* Brewster Horwitz, trans. (New York: Knopf, 1955); Takeyama Michio, *Harp of Burma,* Howard Hibbett, trans. (Rutland, Vt.: Charles A. Tuttle, 1966); Ōka Shōhei, *Fires on the Plain,* Ivan Morris, trans. (New York: Knopf, 1957).

15. Hirano, 59–66; Monica Braw, *The Atomic Bomb Suppressed: American Censorship in Occupied Japan* (Armonk, N.Y.: M.E. Sharpe, 1991), 89–143.

16. Senshi kankō kai, *Senbotsusha izoku no tebiki (Shōwa rokujūnen pan* [Handbook for families of the war dead, 1985 edition], 5–6, details the banning of public memorial services for war dead in 1945–1946.

17. Roger Dingman, "Alliance in Crisis: The *Lucky Dragon* Incident and Japanese-American Relations," in Warren I. Cohen and Akira Iriye, eds., *The Great Powers in East Asia 1953–1960* (New York: Columbia University Press, 1990), 187–214.

18. Hata, *Rikkaigun,* 210; Chihaya, *Norowareta Awa maru,* 230; Donald M. Goldstein and Katherine V. Dillon, eds., *The Pearl Harbor Papers: Inside the Japanese Plans* (Washington, D.C.: Brassey's [US], 1993), 333. This source will hereinafter be cited as *Pearl Harbor Papers,* with appropriate page references.

19. Hata, *Rikkaigun*, 265; *Pearl Harbor Papers*, 316–317, 323, 339; Commander Chihaya Masataka, IJN (Ret.), interview, 2 October 1994, Tokyo, Japan.

20. Gordon W. Prange, *God's Samurai: Lead Pilot at Pearl Harbor* (Washington, D.C.: Brassey's [US], 1990), 179–180; Chihaya Masataka interviews, 10 January 1993, 2 October 1994; *Pearl Harbor Papers*, 314.

21. *Pearl Harbor Papers*, 314.

22. Hata, *Rikkaigun*, 210; Prange, *God's Samurai*, 25, 50, 76, 123–124; Chihaya interview, 2 October 1994. Commander Chihaya hinted after the war at the emotional impact of his brother's death, writing that after the battle in which it occurred everything was "down, down, all down!" See *Pearl Harbor Papers*, 339.

23. Chihaya interview, 2 October 1994.

24. James E. Auer, *The Postwar Rearmament of Japanese Maritime Forces, 1945–1971* (New York: Praeger, 1973), 42, 311–312.

25. Prange, *God's Samurai*, 179–180; *Pearl Harbor Papers*, 4, 13, 17; Chihaya interview, 2 October 1994. Chihaya's employer, Okuyama Seihei, had worked as a lowly staff member on the prewar *Japan Advertiser*. His father-in-law, a diplomat who wrote occasional pieces for that paper, became acquainted with Okuyama, and the casual prewar connection provided the key to a postwar job. Okuyama founded the Okuyama Service, which metamorphosed into the *Tokyo News* (later the *Japan Shipping and Trade News*. The news service provided English translations to foreign diplomats and businessmen in Japan. See item 5401, Korean War Japanese Attitude File 7/22/10/3, A 5104, Australian Archives, Canberra, A.C.T., Australia.

26. Chihaya interview, 2 October 1994; Prange, *God's Samurai*, 324. Prange said he regarded Commander Chihaya as a brother. Prange's major works, published posthumously, are *At Dawn We Slept: The Untold Story of Pearl Harbor* (New York: McGraw-Hill, 1981) and *Miracle at Midway* (New York: McGraw-Hill, 1982).

27. Prange, *God's Samurai*, 197; Chihaya interview, 2 October 1994.

28. Chihaya interviews, 10 January 1993, 2 October 1994; Commander Seno Sadao, JMSDF (Ret.), interview, 4 October 1994. The editor was Ikejima Shimpei, a prewar historian-turned-journalist who is generally credited with restoring *Bungei shunjū* to a position of preeminence among Japanese magazines. He worked under Sasaki Mosaku, president of the parent publishing firm of the same name. Sasaki had worked for the *Jiji shimpo*, a prewar national newspaper that consistently supported maintenance of a strong imperial navy. See Hata, *Rikkaigun*, 634; *Jimbutsu refurensu jiten III gendai hen jō* [A reference biographical dictionary, Volume 3, Part 2: contemporary] (Tokyo: Nichigai assoshiatsu, 1983), 116; Shimonaka Yasaburō, ed., *Gendai Nihon jinmei jiten* [Contemporary Japan biographical dictionary] (Tokyo: Heibonsha, 1955), 47; *Japan Biographical Encyclopedia and Who's Who*, 360, 1321.

29. Chihaya Masataka, "Sekai saidai no chikarabune: *Awa maru* chimbotsu no nazo" [World's greatest treasure ship: the riddle of the sinking of the *Awa maru*], *Bungei shunjū* 34 (August 1956), 128–146. This source will hereinafter be cited as Chihaya 1, with appropriate page references.

30. Ibid., 128–132.

31. Ibid., 132–134. Commander Chihaya apparently assumed that the provisions of the 1936 London Protocol extending the rules of cruiser warfare to submarines continued to apply in 1945; in fact, as discussed in chapter four, those norms had long since been abandoned by World War II belligerents. He also appears to have presumed that the *Awa maru* was a cartel ship rather than a vessel traveling under promise of safe conduct. That assumption mirrors the conflation of the two in Japan, as discussed in chapter three, and ignores Washington's contemporary view that the ship was a safe-conduct vessel. That he blurred the difference in international law between a cartel ship and one traveling under guarantee of safe passage is understandable; one international legal authority writing in the *U.S. Naval War College International Studies 1955*, published in 1957, noted—even as he explained the distinction between the two types of vessels—that it was "not entirely free from obscurity." See Marjorie Whiteman, *Digest of International Law* (Washington: Department of State, 1968), 10: 624; Oppenheim 2: 423–424, 429; Hackworth, 6: 543–551.

32. Chihaya 1, 133–136, 139–140.

33. Ibid., 137–138.

34. Ibid., 142–145.

35. Ibid., 145–146.

36. Murata Kiyoaki telephone interview, 4 October 1994, Tokyo, Japan; *Japan Times*, 24 July 1956; *Gendai Nihon jinmei roku jō* [Who's who in contemporary Japan], 1: 1183–1184; Murata's *An Enemy among Friends* (New York: Kodansha International, 1991) describes his wartime experiences in America.

37. *Honolulu Bulletin*, 28 July 1956, Bennett papers; Chihaya interview, 2 October 1994.

38. Chihaya, *Norowareta Awa maru*, 5–55, 225–229; "*Awa maru* gekichin no fuhō o tsuku" [Attack the illegality of the torpedoing of the *Awa maru*], *Jinbutsu ōrai* (8 August 1965), 148–163. Commander Chihaya was also the probable author of the anonymously published "Shijō saidai no higeki *Awa maru* chimbotsu no nazo Taiwan oki de hikiagerareru hyaku oku no takarabune" [History's greatest disaster: the riddle of the sinking of the *Awa maru*, the one-hundred-million-yen treasure ship that can be salvaged off Taiwan], *Shūkan bunjū* (13 June 1960), 54–58.

Commander Chihaya's major historical publications include *Nihon kaigun no ogori sho kogun* [The pride of the Japanese navy: her forlorn forays] (Tokyo: Namiki shobo, 1980; *Nihon kaigun no senryaku hassō* [The origins of Japanese naval strategy] (Tokyo: Puresidentosha, 1982); *Middowei no ketsudan* [Decision at Midway] (Tokyo: Puresidentosha, 1985); *Nihon kaigun no meishō to meisanbō* [Famous admirals and staff officers of the Japanese navy] (Tokyo: Puresidentosha, 1986); *Nihon kaigun no ogori no hajimari* [The origins of the pride of the Japanese navy] (Tokyo: Namiki shobo, 1989); and *Nihon kaigun no kōzai: gonin no sakanga kataru rekishi no kyōkun* [The merits and faults of the Japanese navy: the lessons of history spoken by five commanders] (Tokyo: Puresidentosha, 1994). Commander Chihaya also translated *Fading Victory:*

The Diary of Admiral Ugaki Matome 1941–1945 (Pittsburgh: University of Pittsburgh Press, 1991).

39. Chihaya 1, 141; These doubts intensified later on. Chihaya interview, 10 January 1993.

40. Chihaya, *Norowareta Awa maru*, 5–10.

41. Commander Chihaya denied having ghostwritten the article, but given his status as the preeminent Japanese expert on the *Awa maru* tragedy and his continued association with the editor and publisher of Shimoda's article, it is difficult to believe he had not played any part in its appearance. Chihaya interview, 2 October 1994; Shimoda Kantarō," *Awa maru* gekichin no iki shōnin" [A living witness to the sinking of the *Awa maru*], *Bungei shunjū* 41 (November 1963), 262–270.

42. April 1965 photographs, Shimoda Mitsuko scrapbook.

43. Shimoda, 266–269.

44. Ibid., 269–270.

45. As pointed out in chapter five, Admiral Nimitz did not deliberately delay the Loughlin court-martial: the trial lasted two days, not three weeks, and the *Queenfish* found no prey on her return voyage to Guam but simply helped rescue downed American aviators.

46. Shimoda, 266–267; April 1965 photographs, Shimoda Mitsuko scrapbook.

47. Arima Yorichika, *Seizonsha no dammoku* [The silence of a survivor] (Tokyo: Bungei shunjū, 1966), 229–232. This first edition of the novel will hereinafter be cited as *Seizaonsha 1*.

48. Asahi shimbun sha, ed., *Gendai jinbutsu jiten* [Contemporary biographical dictionary] (Tokyo: Asahi shimbun sha, 1977), 63–64; *Encyclopedia Japonica 2001* (Tokyo: Shogakukan, 1984), 1: 741; *Kodansha Encyclopedia of Japan* (Tokyo: Kodansha, 1983), 1: 84; *Asahi shimbun*, 21 September 1964; Arima Yorichika, *Heitai shosetsu denki hen 3 Seizonsha no dammoku* [Military novels and biography, Volume 3, the silence of a survivor] (Tokyo: Kōjin sha, 1983), dustjacket. This second edition of Arima's novel will hereinafter be cited as *Seizonsha 2*, with appropriate page references.

49. *Kodansha Encyclopedia of Japan*, 1: 84; *Mainichi shimbun*, 20 July 1969. For additional evidence of Arima's enjoyment of military life, see the 29 April 1943 photograph with his troops, item 27280, Arima Yorichika papers, Kindai Nihon bungaku kan [Museum of Modern Japanese Literature], Komaba, Tokyo.

50. *Seizonsha 2*, dustjacket; *Kodansha Encyclopedia of Japan*, 2: 130.

51. *Mainichi shimbun*, 20 July 1969; Hirano Ken, *Hirano Ken zenshū* [The collected works of Hirano Ken], 9: 363; Arima Yorichika, "Intabyū: nijū nenme ni: kekkon shiki o ageta jijō" [Interview: on the twenty-fifth anniversary: the circumstances of (my) wedding ceremony], *Fujin kōron* [Women's review] (January 1969), 262.

52. *Seizonsha 2*, dustjacket; Havens, *Valley of Darkness*, 156–161.

53. *Mainichi shimbun*, 20 July 1964.

54. *Kodansha Encyclopedia of Japan*, 1: 84; *Asahi shimbun*, 22 December 1960.

55. Ibid.; Arima Yorimasa *Shichijūnen no kaisō* [Memoirs of seventy years], cited by Arima Yorichika in *Saishō Konoe Fumimaro* [Prime Minister Konoye Fumimaro] (Tokyo: Kodansha, 1970), 315. Arima's father served as minister of agriculture and forestry in the first Konoye cabinet (1937–1939).

56. *Mainichi shimbun*, 20 July 1969. Takie Sugiyama Lebra, *Above the Clouds: Status Culture of the Modern Japanese Nobility* (Berkeley: University of California Press, 1993), describes the condition of postwar nobility like the Arima family.

57. Hirano Ken, 9: 354.

58. *Seizonsha 2*, dustjacket.

59. *Asahi shimbun*, 21 September 1964; *Gendai jinbutsu jiten* (1977 edition), 64; Odaka Toshio, comp., *Nihon shōsetsu zen jōho 27/90* [Complete information about Japanese novels 27/90] (Tokyo: Kinokuniya shoten, 1991), 1: 112–115; *Seizonsha 2*, 238; Hirano Ken, 9: 353–355. The baseball novels included *Kuroi pennanto* [Black pennant] (Tokyo: Kadokawa shoten, 1959); another, *Yamakawa aruki* [Walking along the banks of a mountain stream] (Tokyo: Chūō kōron sha, 1962), told of his war experiences; *Shosetsu yasukuni jinja* [Yasukuni Shrine: a novel] (Tokyo: Mikasa shobo, 1964) dealt with memories of those experiences; *Karareta densha chin* [Borrowed train fare] (Tokyo: Kadokawa shoten, 1959) depicted his father's release from prison; *Sanjūrokunin no jōkyaku* [Thirty-six passengers] (Tokyo: Kadokawa shoten, 1957) took his feelings about being robbed by an American GI as its starting point. His short story, "Risu to Amerikajin" [The squirrel and the American], published in a collection of the same name (Tokyo: Kodansha, 1959), is a widely reprinted account of relations between military occupiers and the occupied. *Encyclopedia Japonica 2001*, 1: 741.

60. Arima, *Seizonsha 1*, 229.

61. Arima, *Seizonsha 1*, 229–231; Chihaya interview, 10 January 1993; Tōkō Takaeko interview, 15 January 1993, Tokyo.

62. *Seizonsha 1*, 229. The novel first appeared in serial form, beginning with the June 1963 issue of *Shōsetsu Chūō Kōron*. See original draft and page proofs of this version of *Seizonsha no dammoku*, item 27239, Arima Yorichika papers.

63. In *Seizonsha 1*, 230, Arima made it clear that in the novel, in contrast to his earlier docu-dramatic works, the dramatic took precedence over the documentary.

64. Chihaya interview, 10 January 1993; Tōkō Takeko interview, 13 January 1993. The discussion in this and succeeding paragraphs of plot, character, and incidents in Arima's novel is based upon my reading of it as published in *Seizonsha 2*.

66. Arima thinly disguised the Singapore Third Transport Command officer, Onodera Nobuichi, as Kono Shinichi (whose given name was a variant reading of the real person's). *Seizonsha 2*, 150–153, 169–170.

67. Ibid., 148–149.

68. Ibid., 188–198. Arima depicted what he perceived as the hollowness of postwar "democracy" by making the treacherous legislator a member of a "progressive" party rather than one of the conservatives clustered around Yoshida Shigeru.

69. Ibid., 108–109.

70. Ibid., 116, 121–123, 132, 144–145, 166–168.

71. Ibid., 123–126, 166–169, 173–175, 203–205, 209–211, 2210–221, 229–230.

72. Ibid., 181–182.

73. *Seizonsha 1*, 232–234.

74. Nihon izoku kai, *Senbotsusha izoku no tebiki (Shōwa 60 nenpan* [Handbook for families of the war dead, 1985 edition] (Tokyo: Nihon izoku kai, 1984), 77; Nihon izoku kai jimukyoku, ed., *Nihon izokukai yonjū nen no ayumi* [A thirty-year history of the Japan Association of Bereaved Families] (Tokyo: Nihon izoku kai, 1987) details the efforts of this organization to promote proper commemoration of the war dead.

75. Kōsei shō engo kyoku, *Hikiage to engo sanjūnen no ayumi* [Salvage and relief: a thirty-year history] (Tokyo: Kyosei, 1978), 399–400, 751, 756. The emperor and the prime minister, Yoshida Shigeru, had joined with other dignitaries in a war dead commemorative ceremony on 2 May 1953; *New York Times*, 4, 19, September, 22 October 1964.

76. *Sankei shimbun*, 8 October 1964. The diplomatic widows may have been members of the Kaoru kai, a select society of Ministry of Foreign Affairs wives. Atsuko Tōkō Fish telephone interview, 26 September 1994, Brookline, Massachusetts.

77. *Awa maru* Bereaved Families Association report, 5 December 1964, item 27320, Arima Yorichika papers; Aoki Kazuo had been president of the Cabinet Planning Board, then minister of finance in the prewar Abe Nobuyuki cabinet; he served as minister for Greater East Asia in the Tōjō cabinet. Purged during the occupation, he was rehabilitated and ran successfully for election to the upper house as a member of the Liberal Party. See *Who's Who in Japan, with Manchoukuo and China, 1939–1940*, 34; *Gendai Nihon jinmei jiten*, 2–3; Fukumitsu, 187.

78. *Asahi shimbun*, evening edition, 1 April 1977; Edwin O. Reischauer, *My Life between Japan and America* (New York: Harper and Row, 1986), 172–173, 195–197, 203, demonstrates his sensitivity to cross-cultural understanding. Reischauer recognized the importance of acknowledging American responsibility for the most spectacular of Japanese war deaths, breaking with his predecessors' pattern and laying a wreath on the memorial to Hiroshima victims at a time when the action was sure to get full press coverage. See ibid., 208.

79. *Awa maru* Bereaved Families Association president to membership, February 1966, *Awa maru* Bereaved Families Association papers, in custody of current president, Nonomura Masao, Tokyo.

80. Arai Shigeru and Shimotsuma Kazuho interview, 8 October 1994, Nara, Japan.

81. *Asahi shimbun*, 31 March 1966. The flight was funded by billionaire Sasakawa Ryōichi, whose broader role in the *Awa maru* story is detailed in chapter ten.

82. "Jitsuryoku posto NiKa kyōkai o sute *Awa maru* hikiage netsu no gaimushō kōkan mibōjin: Tōkō Takeko" [Tōkō Takeko: widow of a high-ranking Ministry of Foreign Affairs official who, having given up a powerful position at the Japan-Canada

Society, is eager to salvage the *Awa maru*], *Shūkan taishū* (24 May 1979), 18. This source will hereinafter be cited as *Shūkan taishū*, with appropriate page indications.

83. *Shūkan taishū*, 17; Tōkō Takeko interview, 13 January 1993; Atsuko Tōkō Fish telephone interview, 7 March 1994; Tōkō Takezō career summary provided by Diplomatic Documentation Center, Ministry of Foreign Affairs, Tokyo.

84. Forty-eight years after the event, Mrs. Tōkō's emotions were still strong. She began her 13 January 1993 interview by remarking that she had become a widow at twenty-nine, precisely the age of the Crown Princess-to-be, whose engagement to the heir to the throne had just been announced.

85. *Shūkan taishū*, 17–18; Theodore Cohen, *Remaking Japan: The American Occupation as New Deal*, Herbert Passin, ed. (New York: Free Press, 1987), 343; *Shōwa bukko jinmei roku Shōwa gannen-gojūyonen* [Biographical register of the deceased in the Shōwa era, 1925–1979] (Tokyo: Nichigai assoshiatsu, 1983), 325. The organization for which Mrs. Tōkō worked was the Seiron chōsakai.

86. Tōkō Takeko interview, 13 January 1993. Herbert Passin, *Encounter with Japan* (New York: Kodansha International, 1982), 107–172, details his Japan experiences during the occupation years.

87. *Shūkan taishū*, 18; John Schultz and Miwa Kimitada, eds., *Canada and Japan in the Twentieth Century* (Toronto: Oxford University Press, 1991), 112. Marquis Tokugawa Iemasa was the eldest son of Prince Tokugawa Iesato, who had headed the Japanese delegation to the Washington Conference of 1921–1922. He rose to the rank of ambassador to Turkey before resigning, in 1937, from the Ministry of Foreign Affairs. See *Japan Biographical Encyclopedia and Who's Who*, 1702.

88. Atsuko Tōkō Fish telephone interview, 7 March 1994. Mrs. Fish also recalls her mother saying that she would dig a hole in the back garden of their home to give the souls of the *Awa maru* dead a place to rest; Tōkō Takezō career summary.

89. Tōkō Takeko interview, 13 January 1993.

90. Chihaya, *Norowaretara*, 226–227.

91. *Seizonsha 1*, 231.

92. *Asahi shimbun*, 11 March 1966; Fukumitsu, 207.

93. Fukumitsu, 208; Petition for aid to *Awa maru* bereaved families, 2 May 1967; Record of interrogations in Upper House Finance Committee, 18 July 1967, Record of Upper House Budget Committee interrogations, 22 March, 9 April 1968, *Awa maru* Bereaved Families Association papers.

94. Fukumitsu, 208–212. Satō Eisaku had been chief cabinet secretary in the second Yoshida cabinet in late 1948 and early 1949, when the *Awa maru* claims-abandonment negotiations were reaching their climax. See Hayashi and Tsuji, 5: 167. A second petition, submitted 1 July 1973, fared no better. The *Awa maru* Bereaved Families Association political adviser who facilitated the submission of these petitions was Diet lower house member Yamada Hisanari, a career diplomat who had served in the occupation as director of the Political Bureau of the Central Liaison Office, became chief

of the Public Liaison Division of the Tokyo Metropolitan Government, and then ambassador to Iran. See *Japan Biographical Encyclopedia and Who's Who*, 1850, and *Gendai jinmei jiten*, 711.

95. *Awa maru junansha*, 240. Mrs. Tōkō's departure from the Japan-Canada Society may have been hastened by the accession of Yoshizawa Seijirō to its presidency. Yoshizawa had been the principal Japanese negotiator of the *Awa maru* claims-abandonment agreement; Yoshizawa Seijirō oral history. He may not have wanted the society's manager to be so deeply and openly involved in reviving memories of the *Awa maru* tragedy and in trying to obtain additional compensation for the victims' families. Nevertheless, Mrs. Tōkō remained friends with Mrs. Yoshizawa, and he contributed funds for building the *Awa maru* monument at Zōjōji Temple. Tōkō Takeko interview, 13 January 1993.

96. Ibid.; Takeuchi Kiyoko to *Awa maru* kai members, n.d. November 1977, Inada Seijun materials; *Shūkan taishū*, 18, omitted the fact that family members donated a relatively small percentage of the total cost of the monument.

97. Tōkō Takeko interview, 13 January 1993; Atsuko Tōkō Fish telephone interviews, 7 March, 26 September 1994; *Awa maru junansha*, 243–244. The full list of non-individual donors included government offices (Ministry of Foreign Affairs, the prime minister's office); political parties (Liberal Democratic Party, Japan Communist Party); professional organizations (Kaoru kai [The Lavender Club], Kainenshigen kai [Underwater Thermal Resources Society], Kasumi kai [Japan Foreign Service Officers Association], Shirakaba kai [The White Birch (Literary) Society], Dōmei tsūshin kai [Dōmei Communications Society], Shōwa rokkai [1931 Society] (of Hitotsubashi University), and Shōwa yonkai [1929 Society], Tokyo branch); and businesses (Ishihara sangyō [Ishihara Industries], International Salvage Company, A & P Japan, Teikoku sekiyu [Imperial Oil], Teikoku seni [Imperial Textiles], Denki kagaku [Electro-Chemical Industries], Nishijima seikai [Nishijima Manufacturing], Gōdō shigen sangyō [Amalgamated Resource Production Industries], Shin Nippon seitetsu [New Japan Steel], Shiroishi kiso kōji [Shiroishi Foundation Construction], Takada Ishimura; Daimaru Department Stores, Tokyo Tanker, Nagamura Ren'ichi shoten, Nippon Yūsen [NYK Shipping Company], Nippon keikinzoku [Japan Light Metals], Nichi bōshi [Japan Trade Credit], Hanwa kyōgyō, Heiki shoten, Furukawa kōgyō [Furukawa Mining], and Hotel New Otani).

98. Tōkō Takeko interview, 13 January 1993. Mrs. Tōkō suggested that the fact that the senior professional diplomat in the Ministry of Foreign Affairs in 1945 was a member of the Jōdo [Pure Land] sect of Buddhism, to which Zōjōji belonged, figured in the decision to locate the *Awa maru* memorial there; 1 December 1976 announcement of *Awa maru* memorial planning meeting, Inada Seijun materials.

99. Tōkō Takeko interview, 13 January 1993.

100. Ibid.; Zōjōji *Awa maru* memorial inscription. The dedication was commemorated by a series of postcards enclosed in a folder which depicted Aoki Kazuo's callig-

raphy on a still-empty marble box reserved for the remains of the *Awa maru* dead. See Inada Seijun materials.

101. "Midori jūji no fune: *Awa maru*" [The green cross ship: *Awa maru*], NHK television program broadcast 7 December 1979, tape copy, NHK Archive, Shibuya, Tokyo. I am indebted to Mr. Kogo Eichi of the NHK Broadcast Culture Institute for helping me gain access to and view this documentary film. The green cross in the title referred, mistakenly, to the symbol for safety widely used in contemporary Japan, not the white crosses that signified the *Awa maru*'s protected character in 1945. Commander Chihaya vigorously objected to the program's open-ended treatment of the question of whether or not there had been fog on the night of 1 April 1945 and to its interpretation of the Loughlin court-martial data. See Chihaya Masataka, "Izen toshite tokenai *Awa maru* chimbotsu no nazo" [The riddles of the sinking of the *Awa maru* remain unresolved], *Sekai no kansen* [Ships and warships of the world] (June 1980), 156–163.

Chapter 10. Salvage: "No More Than a Pipe Dream"

1. Anonymous, "*Awa maru* hikiage o Chūgoku no 'yokodori' sareta otoko no nesshin Nikkeijin Minoru Fukumitsu" [The zeal of the man who was beaten by China in salvaging the *Awa maru*: the Japanese-American Minoru Fukumitsu], *Shūkan yomiuri* 38 (20 May 1979): 160. While T'eng Hsaio-ping is the Wade-Giles rendering of the Chinese leader's name, I have used the more familiar (pinyin) Deng Xiaoping.

2. Matsui, 39, *Asahi shimbun*, 29 October 1990

3. Chang Chih-k'uei, "*A-po-wan* mi-chung chih mi" [The *Awa maru*: Riddles Inside of Riddles], *Hai-yang shih-chieh* [Ocean world] (May–June 1993), 32; Innis and Bunton, 267; *Asahi shimbun*, 28 April 1979.

4. *Asahi Evening News*, 20 November 1976.

5. Philip R. Piccigallo, *The Japanese on Trial: Allied War Crimes Operations in the East, 1945–1951* (Austin: University of Texas Press, 1979), 82, 226.

6. Capt. W. A. Doust with Peter Black, *The Ocean on a Plank* (London: Seeley, Service and Co., 1976), 126.

7. Matsui 39, *Asahi shimbun* 29 October 1990; Matsui, 222. Hidaka Shinsaku had graduated on 20 May 1933, as a mere lieutenant, in the thirty-first class of the prestigious Naval Staff College. He then served on the Naval General Staff. See Hata, *Rikkaigun*, 625–626; Hidaka Shigekatsu telephone interview, 10 October 1994, Tokyo. *Japan Biographical Encyclopedia and Who's Who*, 692; and Hayashi and Tsuji, 5: 278, 306, 336, provide biographical information on Kōno Ichirō.

8. Fukumitsu, 14–15; Matsui, 222.

9. Fukumitsu, 215; telephone interview, University of Utah Student Records and Transcripts Office, 24 May 1994. The University's documents mistakenly indicate that

Fukumitsu was born in Japan; Kay Fukumitsu telephone interview, 6 May 1996, Oak Harbor, Washington. Mrs. Fukumitsu is Minoru Fukumitsu's sister-in-law. She recalls that his brother George served in the U.S. Army Counter-Intelligence Corps. Navy Japanese Language School, University of Colorado, Boulder *sensei* [instructors] list, folder 12, box 3, Capt. Roger Pineau papers, Archives Department, Norlin Library, University of Colorado, Boulder, confirms Fukumitsu's status as a Japanese language instructor. I am indebted to archivist Marty Covey for locating this information.

10. *Shūkan yomiuri*, (20 May 1979), 162.

11. Kay Fukumitsu telephone interview, 6 May 1996; Fukumitsu, 215; New York University Law School records indicate that Fukumitsu attended from 25 September 1944 through 24 January 1945, probably taking the first half of "International Society: Its Reconstruction in the Postwar World." Telephone interviews, Ms. Kristina Edinger and Susan April, New York University Archives, 9, 13 June 1994, New York, N.Y.

12. Fukumitsu, 183; *Shūkan yomiuri* 38 (20 May 1979), 162; Matsui 39, *Asahi shimbun* 29 October 1990. Kay Fukumitsu, telephone interview, 6 May 1996, recalls that Fukumitsu published a book about his treasure-hunting in the Philippines, but neither she nor I have been able to locate a copy of it.

13. Fukumitsu, 184; Matsui, 222.

14. Anonymous, "Amerika no ippatsuya ga 'norowareta *Awa maru*' zaiho no shingan [Truth or falsehood of the treasure of the 'accursed' *Awa maru*: America's one-shots [have an] eye on the main chance], *Shūkan shinchō* 21 (2 December 1976), 142–143.

15. Fukumitsu, 183. This first salvage effort may have interfered with the plans of another group, which in April 1951 sent two representatives to the foreign ministry to claim that their firm, Asia Kōgyō, had exclusive salvage rights to the *Awa maru*. A firm of the same name had also requested permission to salvage the ship in December 1947; nine months later, in September 1948, the Central Liaison Office had asked SCAP to clarify the legal status of the ship's cargo as a first step in determining whether salvage was financially feasible or not. The request mistakenly estimated that the hulk lay near 119.12 east, 24.41 north at a depth of about five hundred feet. It predicted that determining the precise site of the wreck and salvaging it could take about six months and cost more than sixty-one million yen.

This first Japanese feasibility study of salvaging the *Awa maru* presumed a need for American naval protection from pirates—something that SCAP was not about to seek from Washington. See *Awa maru* hikiage mondai [The *Awa maru* salvage problem], frames 287–300, reel B'-0084.

16. Yamazaki Toshihisa, "Ōzeki repoto: Nittai ryōkai ni nemuro yonsen gohaku oku en no zaihō" (Treasure Report: The Four-Hundred-Fifty-Million-Yen Treasure That Sleeps in Japan–Republic of China Territorial Waters), *Ozeki* 3 (January 1973 special issue), 318–321; Fukumitsu, 183; Kataoka Kyūhachi was vice president of Chū-

gai Metals Corporation at the time of his death on 2 October 1958. See *Shōwa bukko jinmei roku,* 131.

17. Yamazaki, 320–322.

18. Andrew Marshall and Michiko Toyama, "In the Name of the Godfather," *Tokyo Journal* (October 1994), 29–31.

19. Paula Daventry, ed., *Sasakawa: The Warrior for Peace, the Global Philanthropist* (Oxford: Pergamon Press, 1981), 2, 10, 82–84; *New York Times,* 2 July 1974; Anonymous, *Sasakawa Ryōichi no hito to nari* [Becoming the man Sasakawa Ryōichi] (Tokyo: Nihon kaiji shimbunsha, n.d., c. 1975), n.p.; Yamaoka Sohachi, *Hatenko ningen Sasakawa Ryōichi* [Unprecedented: Sasakawa Ryōichi, the human being] (Tokyo: Yuho sha, 1988), 329.

20. Marshall and Toyama, 30–31; Daventry, 44–50; Sasakawa Ryōichi, *Kono keishō wa nariyamaẓu* [This fire alarm doesn't stop ringing] (Tokyo: Tokyo Shirakawa shoin, 1981), 244.

21. Daventry, 51. Sasakawa also funded the Nihon shōi gunjin kai [Japan Association of Wounded Veterans].

22. *Sasakawa Ryōichi hito to nari,* n.p. The organization Sasakawa created to build and maintain this monument was the Zen sensō junanshi irei kyōkai [Association for the Memorialization of Victims of All Wars].

23. Anonymous, "Shijō saidai no higeki *Awa maru* gekichin no nazo" [The greatest tragedy in history: the riddle of the sinking of the *Awa maru*], *Shūkan bunjū* (31 May 1960), 55.

24. George R. Packard, *Protest in Tokyo* (Princeton: Princeton University Press, 1966), details the Security Treaty crisis of 1960; *Shūkan bunjū* (31 May 1960), 55.

25. Ibid. Sasakawa's visit to Taiwan produced an interesting diplomatic exchange between Tokyo and Taipei. While he was there, Ambassador Iguchi Sadao put out feelers to the Chinese Nationalist Ministry of Foreign Affairs about a Sino-Japanese joint venture to salvage the *Awa maru.* Chinese diplomats responded coolly, saying that such a thing was impossible, because the ship was presumed to lie in the Quemoy-Matsu offshore island danger zone. They cited "international legal complications"— and, they hinted, their government might itself want to sponsor a salvage attempt. Nonetheless, they left the door ajar for "informal" Sino-Japanese cooperation, such as had occurred previously in the salvage of Japanese ships sunk in the Taiwan Strait.

Three weeks later, a report that the Chinese Nationalists had found the *Awa maru* sent Iguchi back to the Chinese foreign ministry. He learned that despite eight attempts to get help from Japanese and U.S. naval sources, the Chinese Nationalist navy had been unable to locate the ship. Taipei diplomats assured Iguchi that their government had no intention of salvaging the ship without taking account of Japan's claims to whatever might be found aboard.

See *Awa maru* hikiage mondai [The *Awa maru* salvage problem], frames 325–349, reel B'-0084.

26. Asahi shimbunsha, ed., *Asahi jinbutsu jiten* [Asahi biographical dictionary] (Tokyo: Asahi shimbunsha, 1990), 897–898; *Gendai Nihon jinmei roku* [Biographical directory of contemporary Japan] (Tokyo: Nichigai Associates, 1987), 881. Eliot P. Feldstein, "The Appeal of Sejima Ryūzō: Patriotism in the Historical Context," unpublished Harvard University B.A. honors thesis in East Asian studies, 1988, and Hosaka Masayasu, *Seshima Ryūzō* (Tokyo: Bungei shinjū, 1987) detail Seshima's career. I have used "Seshima," the romanization of his surname provided in P.G. O'Neill, *Japanese Names: A Comprehensive Index by Characters and Readings* (New York: John Weatherhill, 1972), 297.

27. Yamazaki Toyoko, *Fumō chitai* [The barren zone] (Tokyo, 1976), published as *The Barren Zone*, James T. Araki, trans. (Honolulu: University of Hawaii Press, 1985).

28. Matsui 38, *Asahi shimbun*, 16 October 1990.

29. Matsui 38, *Asahi shimbun*, 16 October 1990. The Itō Chū representative in New York City was Suzuki Noboru. Sebald career summary, box 1, Sebald papers; Sebald oral history, 1: 445–446. No record of the telephone exchange is to be found in the Classified Operational Archives' *Queenfish* inquiry log, which began in 1966. See *Queenfish*, World War II command files, box 1167, COA, NHC.

30. Sebald oral history, 1: 446. The reported sinking site of the *Awa maru* was 9.95 miles east-southeast of tiny Niu Shan Tao (Cow Mountain Island), which was in turn about half that distance from the much larger Hai-T'an Island. *Awa maru* sinking site chart, East China Sea Reference #94140, John E. Bennett papers. In 1965 the question of whether that site was within or outside of China's territorial waters remained a matter of international legal dispute. In contrast to most other nations, who claimed territorial rights out to twelve miles, the United States insisted that the jurisdiction of littoral nations was limited to three miles. That had assured the failure of United Nations conferences convened in 1958 and 1960 to redefine the law of the sea as to territorial waters; the issue was not resolved until 1982. See Edward Duncan Brown, *The International Law of the Sea*, Volume 1, *Introductory Manual* (Aldershot, England: Dartmouth, 1994), 43.

31. Matsui 39, *Asahi shimbun*, 29 October 1990

32. Matsui, 220–221.

33. Matsui 39, *Asahi shimbun*, 29 October 1990; Matsui, 221. Thomas R. Havens, *Fire Across the Sea* (Princeton: Princeton University Press, 1987), 92–106, details Japan's profit-taking from the Vietnam conflict.

34. Daventry, 6, 59–60; *Sasakawa Ryōichi no hito to nari*, n.p.

35. Daventry, 58; *Sasakawa Ryōichi no hito to nari*, n.p. The museum opened in May 1974.

36. Matsui, 222, names Fukumitsu's firm the International Salvage Company. Fukumitsu, however, also styled himself as chairman of the *Awa maru Salvage Committee* and, more simply, as "international consultant." See Fukumitsu to Bennett, 19 December 1978, 19 February 1979, Bennett papers.

37. Fukumitsu, 77–86; H.T. Wooley, Office of the Judge Advocate General, to Fukumitsu, 8 August 1972, cited in Fukumitsu, 148.

38. Fukumitsu, 138–144; *Annapolis (Maryland) Capital,* 1 November 1989. The U.S. Naval Academy Foundation was created to recruit prospective Academy athletes and raise money to support them in preparatory studies needed to assure their acceptance into the brigade of midshipmen.

39. Loughlin Naval Institute oral history, 138. Whether Fukumitsu solicited Rear Admiral Loughlin's active cooperation in his effort to salvage the *Awa maru* remains unclear. Mrs. Lynn Elliott Duval to author, 15 November 1996.

40. Fukumitsu, 150–153; Bennett to author, 15 May 1993.

41. Bennett interview, 14 May 1993

42. *Kodansha Encyclopedia of Japan,* 8: 336–337; James B. Sweeney, *A Pictorial History of Oceanographic Submersibles* (New York: Crown, 1970), 224.

43. Minoru Fukumitsu, *Awa maru jiken* [The *Awa maru* incident] (Tokyo: Yomiuri shimbunsha, 1973); Anonymous, "Kaimei no hitoguchi hagureru kōi ka guzen ka *Awa maru* gekichin no nazo" [Unraveling the threads of an explanation: deliberate or accidental: the riddles of the sinking of the *Awa maru*], *Shūkan yomiuri* (25 August 1973), 140–143. The book was published on 30 August 1973.

44. Ibid., 3–4, 13–15, 181.

45. Ibid., 125–129.

46. Ibid., 155–156, 185–201, 205–212.

47. Ogata Sadao, *Normalization with China: A Comparative Study of US and Japanese Processes* (Berkeley: Institute of East Asian Studies, University of California, 1988), 55.

48. Fukumitsu to Han Hsu, Fukumitsu to Henry Kissinger, 14 April 1976, copies in possession of Mrs. Lynn Elliott Duval.

49. *Who's Who in Japan, with Manchoukuo and China, 1930–1940,* 150; *Japan Biographical Encyclopedia and Who's Who,* 193; Shimonaka Yasaburō, ed., *Gendai Nihon jinmei jiten* [Contemporary Japanese biographical dictionary] (Tokyo: Heibonsha, 1955), 599. Funada's brother-in-law was Lieutenant General Ōbata Toshishirō, an anti-Soviet hawk who before the war had served as chief of the strategic planning section, Imperial Army General Staff, and as president of the military academy; in the first postwar cabinet, headed by Prince Higashikuni, he was a minister without portfolio. He died 10 January 1947. *Nihon jinmei dai jiten gendai dai nanakan* [Biographical dictionary of Japan, contemporary: Volume 7] (Tokyo: Heibonsha, 1955), 188–189.

50. *Nihon jinmei dai jiten gendai dai nanakan* [Biographical dictionary of Japan, contemporary: Volume 7], 188–189; *Jimbutsu jōhō jiten '82,* 114.

51. Madelaine Chi and Louis J. Smith, eds., *Foreign Relations of the United States, 1958–1960,* Volume 18, *Japan, Korea* (Washington: Government Printing Office, 1994), 204, 288–289, 294, 297–299, 327, documents Funada's close cooperation with Ambassador Douglas MacArthur III during the 1960 crisis over ratification of the revised United States–Japan Security Treaty. I am indebted to Cdr. James Auer, USN (Ret.),

who served as political advisor to the commander, Naval Forces Japan, 1971–1973, for information about Funada's relations with and attitudes toward the U.S. Navy.

52. Anonymous, "Mo hitotsu no *Awa maru* jōhō" [Additional intelligence on the *Awa maru*], *Shūkan shinchō* 21 (23/30 December 1976), 24. Kōseishō engokyoku, ed., *Hikiage to engo sanjūnen no ayumi* [A thirty-year history of recovery and relief] (Tokyo: Kosei, 1978), 311–314, 389–393, describes the origins of an official recovery-of-remains program and notes that governmental efforts to salvage remains from Japanese ships sunk in foreign waters did not begin formally until 1973.

53. Ogata, 37–83.

54. *Shūkan shinchō* (23/30 December 1976), 24.

55. *Queenfish* inquiry log, *Queenfish*, World War II command files, box 1167, COA, NHC. The inquiry came through a Lieutenant Colonel Barrett of the Office of International Security Affairs, Office of the Secretary of Defense.

56. *Shūkan shinchō* (23/30 December 1976), 24; Watanabe Ryōjirō, "Moto Gaishō hisshokan no kataru hitsuwa 13: Kodai *Awa maru* Toshohei chōnan" [Secret revelations of a former private secretary to the foreign minister: Number 13, Orphans, the *Awa maru* (and) Deng Xiaopeng's eldest son], *Jiyū* (October 1994), 140. The source for this claim of discovery was one of Funada Naka's two private secretaries.

57. Dwight H. Perkins, "Is There a China Market?" in William W. Whitson, *Doing Business with China* (New York: Praeger, 1974), 41–42, 72–76; Ogata, 14, 37–55, 83–85; Harry Harding, *A Fragile Relationship: The United States and China since 1972* (Washington: Brookings Institution, 1992), 42–67.

58. *Yomiuri shimbun, Mainichi shimbun*, 24 November 1976.

59. William J. Bunton interview, San Diego, California, 29 March 1996.

60. Uchida Tadao to Bill Bunton, 6 December 1976, enclosing translation of 24 November 1976 *Yomiuri shimbun* article, Bennett papers.

61. *Yomiuri shimbun*, 24 November 1976. Nearly five years earlier, according to a source which must remain confidential, a plan to salvage the *Awa maru* did float up from navy and CIA officials to the White House. The National Security Adviser, Henry Kissinger, vetoed the scheme, because he thought it would anger the Chinese and disrupt his secret efforts to arrange President Richard Nixon's 1972 visit to Beijing. This proposal became the factual kernel around which Thomas B. Allen and Normal Polmar shaped their fictional account of a failed *Awa maru* salvage endeavor, in *Ship of Gold* (New York: Macmillan, 1987).

62. W. Joe Innis with Bill Bunton, *In Pursuit of the Awa maru* (New York: Bantam Books, 1981), inside cover; Bunton interview, *The Republican*, November–December 1976, item 187, Materials filed 15 June 1987, Plaintiff exhibit 10, box 14, Case 84-301-G, Federal Records Center, Pacific Southwest Regional Archives, Laguna Niguel, California. Materials from this source are extremely disorganized; they will hereinafter be cited the identifying numbers or letters on the original, and by the case number.

63. Bunton interview, 29 March 1996; *Look* 27 (30 July 1963), 87. The San Diego

Naval Undersea Warfare Center, which changed its name to the Naval Undersea Research and Development Center during Burton's employment there, should not be confused with the more recently established Naval Undersea Warfare Center at Newport, Rhode Island. I am indebted to Mr. Thomas LaPuzza, Naval Command, Control, and Ocean Surveillance Research and Development Division, San Diego, California, for information about the organization's history.

64. Polmar and Allen, *Rickover,* 428–430, 435; Sweeney, 203, 208; Robert D. Ballard with Malcolm McConnell, *Explorations: My Quest for Adventure and Discovery under the Sea* (New York: Hyperion, 1995), 232, notes that the loss of the *Scorpion* (SSN 589) in 1968 created a special bond among those engaged in submersible and submarine recovery work, a bond that helped sustain the program.

65. Sweeney, 251–264, details the development of saturation diving techniques and the SEALAB experimental program.

66. Captain John E. Bennett officer biography, box 42, officer biography files, COA, NHC; Bennett biographical summary, enclosed in Bennett to author, 15 May 1993; Bennett interview, 19 July 1994.

67. *Who's Who in America, 1991–1992 Supplement* (Wilmette, Ill.: Marquis Who's Who, 1992), 160; Sweeney, 263; M. Scott Carpenter telephone interview, 18 August 1993, Vail, Colorado.

68. Robert Barth telephone interview, 29 October 1992, Panama City, Florida; Capt. Walter Mazzone interview, 19 July 1994, San Diego, California; Sweeney, 252–253, 257.

69. Robert Barth telephone interview, 29 October 1992.

70. Ibid.; Captain Mazzone, who was present in the SEALAB II underwater habitat, doubts that such a conversation took place. Mazzone interview, 19 July 1994.

71. Bennett interview, 14 May 1993.

72. Bunton interview, 29 March 1996; Emerson Company, Ltd., memorandum, n.d., c. 1966–1968, Bennett papers.

73. Bunton interview, 29 March 1996. The submarine deck logs were subsequently moved to Record Group 24 in the National Archives. Briggs also apparently contacted Capt. John Bennett seeking confirmation or denial of the Nationalist Chinese group's claims. Bennett drew independently the same conclusion as Bunton. Bennett interview, 14 May 1993.

74. Bunton interview, 29 March 1996; *The Republican,* November–December 1976, Materials filed 15 June 1987, Plaintiff exhibit 10, file 187, box 14, Case 84-301-G; *Seattle Post-Intelligencer,* 18 November 1976, copy in Bennett papers; Joyce Milton, *Loss of Eden: A Biography of Charles and Anne Morrow Lindbergh* (New York: Harper-Collins, 1993), 425–426.

75. Bunton interview, 29 March 1996. Bunton, who is preparing his own book on his attempt to salvage the *Awa maru,* was understandably reluctant to provide full details of his endeavor in this interview. He did indicate that he had been employed by

Ocean Systems (Japan), which was controlled by Ocean Systems, Inc., based in Santa Barbara, California. The name of the latter firm suggests that it might have been a subsidiary of Washington State–based Ocean Systems, which had been founded by Jon Lindbergh and Emory Land. Bennett interview, 14 May 1993.

76. Knight-Ridder Financial/Commodity Research Bureau, *The CRB Commodity Yearbook 1994* (New York: Wiley, 1994), 279. Tin prices increased fivefold between 1972, the year of Nixon's visit to China, and 1979, when the Chinese announced their discovery of the *Awa maru*.

77. Harding, 43–45.

78. 6 January 1974 Bunton-Freeman agreement, defense exhibit 04, item 149, volume 7, box 13; item 104, volume 4, box 13, Case CV 84-301-G. Donald Freeman was—and is, at this writing—Bunton's attorney.

79. Miscellaneous materials 18021.17, 1 April 1983 memorandum, item 184, Case CV 84-301-G.

80. Defense exhibit OM, 20 August 1975, volume 7, box 13, Case CV 84-301-G.

81. *Seattle Post-Intelligencer*, 18 November 1976, clipping in Bennett papers; *The Republican*, November–December 1976, item NN, Case CV 84-301-G; Anne Morrow Lindbergh, *North to the Orient* (New York: Harcourt, Brace & Company, 1935), describes Lindbergh's parents' pioneering flight to, and experiences in, China.

82. *Los Angeles Times*, 18 November 1973, 10 March 1974; *The Republican*, November–December 1976. Carpenter had married film producer Hal Roach's youngest daughter. Bunton interview, 29 March 1996.

83. Barth telephone interview, 29 October 1992.

84. Bennett interview, 14 May 1993

85. Bunton interview, 29 March 1996; Bennett interview, 14 March 1993; Bennett career summary, in Bennett to author, 15 May 1993.

86. Bennett interview, 14 May 1993.

87. Ibid. Bennett, as markings on the chart cited in footnote 30 above indicate, did in fact get this specialized data from Pentagon sources.

88. Shamer officer biography, box 568, COA, NHC; Shamer interview, 25 June 1993, San Diego, California; Bunton inscription to Shamer, in Shamer's copy of Innis and Bunton, *The Pursuit of the Awa maru*.

89. Freeman deposition, item 104, volume 4, box 13; Bunton deposition, 2–4 December 1985, item 184, box 13, Case CV 84-301-G.

90. Bunton interview, 29 March 1996.

91. *The Republican*, November–December 1976; *New York Times*, 5 September 1974.

92. *The Republican*, November–December 1976; Donald Freeman to National Council for US–China Trade, 6 March 1974, box 13, volume 7, item 149, defense exhibit 194, Case CV 84-301-G.

93. *The Republican*, November–December 1976.

94. Ibid. Participants in the dinner meeting included Eugene Theroux of the US-China Trade Council; Chang Tsien-hua, commercial counselor of the China Liaison Office in Washington; Wang Tien-ming, third secretary; and Tsui Kao-pi and Tung Chuh-kuang, also of that office, along with Bunton and Harned Hoose. Bunton interview, 29 March 1996; Barry Paris, *Garbo: A Biography* (New York: Knopf, 1995), 262. The mansion was at that time occupied by Harned Hoose.

95. *The Republican,* November–December 1976.

96. *Who's Who, 1978–1979* (Chicago: Marquis Who's Who, 1979), 1: 1546; Harned P. Hoose, *Peking Pigeons and Pigeon-Flutes* (Peking: College of Chinese Studies, California College in China, 1938); Winston Hoose telephone interview, 27 April 1993, San Francisco, California. Randall E. Stross, *Bulls in the China Shop and Other Sino-American Business Encounters* (New York: Pantheon Books, 1990), 11, 120.

97. *Los Angeles Times,* 26 May 1972, 17 December 1973, 13 October 1974; Winston Hoose telephone interview, 27 April 1993.

98. Bunton interview, 29 March 1996; exhibit KV, item 184, volume 7, box 13; item 184, sub-item 2; item 184, box 13, Case CV 84-301-G; Mrs. Polly White Elarkosa telephone interview, 7 July 1994, Pasadena, California. Mrs. Elarkosa is George White's daughter; Sub-item PX, item 184, box 13, Case CV 84-301-G.

99. Harned Pettus Hoose, "Petrochemicals," in Whitson, 312–333; *Los Angeles Times,* 21 March 1976, part iv: 1; part ii: d-4.

100. Plaintiff exhibit 12, item 149, volume 7, box 13, Case CV 84-301-G.

101. *New York Times,* 10 September 1976; 13 November 1976 plaintiff contentions, item 149, volume 7, box 13, Case CV 84-301-G.

102. Bunton interview, 29 March 1996; Bennett to author, 15 May 1993; Defense exhibit PI, 12 December 1975 Marie Carlile venture investment agreement, item 149, volume 7, box 13; San Diego County Superior Court case file 514620, Superior Court of California, County of San Diego Central Court, Old Records Division, San Diego, California.

103. Defense reservations, item 149, volume 7, box 13, Case CV 84-301-G.

104. Bunton interview, 29 March 1996; Bennett interview, 13 May 1993.

105. *San Diego Evening Tribune,* 17 November 1976; *Seattle Post-Intelligencer* 18 November 1976; *Tyler (Texas) Telegraph,* 22 November 1976; *Yomiuri shimbun, Mainichi shimbun,* 24 November 1976, file 331 *Awa maru,* National Diet Library; *Japan Times,* 18 November 1976; *Asahi Evening News,* 20 November 1976; *China News* (Taipei), 24 November 1976, Bennett papers. Bunton interview, 29 March 1996. Bunton recalled that CBS (Television) Evening News had broadcast a segment about his group and its activities.

106. *San Diego Evening Tribune,* 17 November 1976; *Asahi Evening News,* 20 November 1976.

107. *San Diego Evening Tribune,* 17 November 1976; *Asahi Evening News,* 20 November 1976.

108. *Yomiuri shimbun,* 24 November 1976.

109. Chang Chih-k'uei (May 1993): 32; Innis and Bunton, 267.

110. Bennett interview, 14 May 1993. The eighteen-month contract had been signed on 20 June 1975.

111. Salvage and Diving/Management Services International independent contractor services agreement, 13 February 1977; 20 February amendment to same; 20 February assignment of contingent fees and interest from George H. White (Management Services International) to Lee Pay-chu, Plaintiff exhibit 13, defense exhibits AJ and KY, item 149, volume 7, box 13, Case CV 84-301 G. I have been unable to determine the background of Lee Pay-chu, the Chinese whom Harned Hoose took on as an additional liaison person.

112. Hoose to George H. White, exhibit 1, item 237, volume 15, box 15; Bunton 1985 deposition, item 184, box 13; Bunton notes on meeting with Hoose and White, 27 July 1977, sub-item KZ, item 184, box 13, Case CV 84-301 G.

113. Robert Barth deposition, item 183, box 13; Bunton tape 16 August 1977, item 185, box 13; "Red Book" Proposal, item 130, volume 6, box 13, Case CV 84-301 G. Sweeney, 252–254, 257, details Bond's involvement in the GENESIS and SEALAB programs.

114. "Red Book" Proposal, item 130, volume 6, box 13, Case CV 84-301 G. Taylor Diving and Salvage had become a subsidiary of the Halliburton Company, which owned 80 percent of its stock, in 1968. Halliburton, in turn, had become a subsidiary of Brown and Root in 1962. See Gillian Wolf, "Halliburton Company," in Adele Hart, ed., *International Directory of Company Histories* (Chicago: St. James Press, 1991), 3: 498–499; John V. Harter 14 May 1987 deposition, item 183, box 13, Case CV 84-301 G; U.S. Naval Academy *Register of Alumni,* 330; Harter to Wallace, 31 August 1977, exhibit 1, item 130, volume 6, box 13, Case CV 84-301 G.

115. Bunton notes on meeting with Wallace and Harter, 6 October 1977, exhibit 4, item 130, volume 6, box 13; 2 November 1977 letter of intent to conclude Salvage and Diving/Taylor Diving and Salvage contract, exhibit 6, item 130, volume 6, box 13, Case CV 84-301 G; 14 October 1977 Salvage and Diving/Taylor Diving and Salvage Agreement, San Diego County Superior Court case file 514620.

116. Harter deposition, item 183, box 13; Robert A. Barth sworn statement, 5 July 1987, loose materials, Declarations in support of defense's motion for summary judgment, volume 2, box 13, , Case CV 84-301 G.

117. Barth to Bunton, 10 December 10 1976, loose documents, item 183, box 13, Case CV 84-301 G; "Red Book" proposal, December 1977, item 130, volume 6, box 13, ibid.; White to Bunton, 18 January 1979 [*sic*—1977], item 124, volume 5, box 13, Case CV 84-301 G. This presentation occurred just when the National Council for US-China Trade welcomed Chinese oil development officials for a three-week tour of the United States. See *Leasing Concession News,* 19 December 1977, item 75, volume 4, box 13, Case CV 84-301 G.

118. Taylor telex to Hugh Gordon of Brown and Root, 21 March 1978, item 149, volume 7, box 13; Wallace to Ben Power, 5 April 1978, item 130; 26 May 1978 document, item 129, volume 6, box 13, Case CV 84-301 G.

119. Harter deposition, item 183, box 13, Case CV 84-301 G.

120. Donald Freeman to George White, 25 September 1978, item 184, box 13, Case CV 84-301 G.

121. Bush to Bunton, 12 September 1978, copy in Bunton scrapbook; Bunton notes, 13–14 September 1978, Defense exhibits PZ, SQ, WF, item 149, volume 7, box 13, Case CV 84-301 G.

122. *The Republican*, December 1978; Plaintiff exhibit 149, item 149, volume 7, box 13, Case CV 84-301 G; Harding, 380–381.

123. Harter deposition, item 183, box 13; Harter-Bunton telephone conversation transcript, 11 April 1979, Defense exhibit TL, item 184, box 13, Case CV 84-301 G.

124. Chang Chih-k'uei (May 1993): 30–32; *Asahi shimbun*, 28 April 1979.

125. Harter diary excerpt, 19 April 1979, Defense exhibit CN, box 13, Case CV 84-301 G.

126. *Shūkan yomiuri* 38 (20 May 1979), 160–162; *Awa maru* Bereaved Families Association to Visiting Members of the Sino-Japanese Friendship Association, n.d. April 1973, *Awa maru* Bereaved Families Association papers.

127. *New York Times*, 13 August 1978; for text of the treaty, see J.A.S. Grenville and Bernard Wasserstein, *The Major International Treaties since 1945: A History and Guide with Texts* (London: Methuen, 1987), 306.

128. *Japan Times*, 23–26 October 1978.

129. Matsui, 225; *Japan Times*, 7–8 November 1978; Satō Seizaburō, Koyama Ken'ichi, and Kumon Shumpei, *Postwar Politician: The Life of Former Prime Minister Masayoshi Ohira* (Tokyo: Kodansha International, 1990), 425–437, details the intraparty struggle and election results.

130. *Jimbutsu jōhō jiten '82*, 71; Yokota Yutaka, *Aa kaiten tokkō tai: Kaerazaru seishun no kiroku* [On the navy's Suicide Torpedo Special Attack Corps: a record of youth gone forever] (Tokyo: Koinsha, 1971), 306–307; Carl Boyd and Yoshida Akihiko, *The Japanese Submarine Force and World War II* (Annapolis, Md.: Naval Institute Press, 1995), 167–175; Asahi shimbun sha, ed., *Asahi jinbutsu jiten* [Asahi biographical dictionary] (Tokyo: Asahi shimbun sha, 1990), 909; Kōsei shō, *Hikiage to engoku*, 763–765; Satō, Koyama, and Kumon, 121–232, 375, 379, 408, 443–444, provides an English-language summary of Sonoda's political career; Watanabe Ryojirō, "Moto Gaishō no hisshokan no kataru hitsuwa 13: Kodai *Awa maru* Toshohei chōnan" [Secret revelations of a former private secretary to the foreign minister, 13: Orphans, the *Awa maru*, and Deng Xiaoping's eldest son], *Jiyū* (October 1994), 131.

131. Matsui, 224–226. Matsui's account is based upon Watanabe Ryōjirō's handwritten notes concerning this affair, which he showed to the journalist in December 1989.

132. Matsui, 227; *New York Times*, 1, 21 March 1975; "Trying to 'Swipe' a Russian Sub Is Just Part of CIA Saga," *U.S. News and World Report* 78 (31 March 1975), 16; "Great Submarine Snatch," *Time* 105 (31 March 1975), 20; "Behind the Great Submarine Snatch," *Time* 108 (6 December 1976), 23.

133. *New York Times*, 27 April, 2, 10 May, 4 June 1975; 20 January, 23 May, 3 June, 7 September 1978.

134. At this time Global Marine Development gave out the story that it was involved in a $42.7 million U.S. Department of Energy project in Hawaii that contemplated generating electricity by exploiting the temperature differences between deep and surface levels of ocean water. See *New York Times*, 12 November 1978.

135. Satō, Koyama, Kumon, 362, 418; Watanabe, 129; Satō Yukio, then Foreign Minister Sonoda's official private secretary, put forward the view that this whole affair was redolent of CIA involvement. See Matsui, 232.

136. Matsui, 227–228; Watanabe, 141–142. Matsui suggests no reply had been received from Beijing; Watanabe wrote as if the opposite were true.

137. *Asahi shimbun*, 28 April 1979.

138. Fukumitsu to Bennett, 19 December 1978, Bennett papers; *Shūkan yomiuri* 38 (20 May 1979), 160; Bennett interview, 14 May 1993.

139. Fukumitsu to Bennett, 19 December 1978, Bennett papers. My attempt to find some trace of Senator Matsunaga's involvement in Fukumitsu's *Awa maru* salvage project in the senator's papers, housed in the Hawaii/Pacific Collection, Hamilton Library, University of Hawaii, yielded no results. Ms. Sherry Montano, a former member of the senator's Washington office staff who is currently involved in preparing the Matsunaga materials for researchers' use, could neither remember nor locate anything about Fukumitsu-Matsunaga contacts. Montano telephone interview, 16 March 1994, Honolulu, Hawaii.

140. 12 February 1979 Fukumitsu-Tamanai-Bennett agreement, Bennett to John Horton, 14 February 1979, Bennett papers. Horton, who had previously headed Chicago Bridge and Iron Co., purchased the Swiss submersible *Auguste Piccard*, brought it to Vancouver, and was engaged in converting it from tourist use to seabed oil exploration purposes. Bennett interview, 14 May 1993; Sweeney, 225.

141. Bennett-Fukumitsu telephone conversation notes, 16 February 1979, Bennett papers.

142. President, China National Salvage Company, to Stuart E.A. Bensley, attached to his declaration of 30 April 1987, loose materials, item 183, box 13, Case CV 84-301-G; Iwama Koichi interview, 3 October 1994, Tokyo.

143. Grenville and Wasserstein, 306.

144. Fukumitsu to Bennett, 19 February 1979, Bennett papers.

145. Watanabe, 142.

146. *Asahi shimbun*, 28 April 1979.

147. *Shūkan yomiuri* (20 May 1979), 160.

148. Transcript of taped Bunton-Harter telephone conversation, 11 May 1979; Bunton to Wallace, 23 May 1979, item 183, volume 7, box 13, Case CV 84-301 G; Captain Bennett vigorously denied these allegations of betrayal. Bennett interview, 14 May 1993.

149. Bob Barth telephone interview, 29 October 1992, Panama City, Florida; Robert Barth deposition, 8 May 1987; Stuart A. Bensley deposition, n.d. 1987; and Louis Crisler declaration, 5 May 1987 declaration on their July 1981 meeting with China National Salvage Company representatives, item 183, loose materials; John Harter to Zheng Jin Long, 7 July 1983, item 149, volume 7, box 13, Case CV 84-301 G; Watanabe, 142.

150. Chang Chih-k'uei (May 1993), 30–32, and (June 1993), 31–32. My 25 April 1994 fax message to J. Stapleton Ray, deputy chief of mission at the American embassy (in effect the ambassador) in Beijing when the Chinese announced their discovery of the *Awa maru*, drew no response.

151. Matsui, 228.

152. Funada Naka died within a month of the Chinese announcement of their discovery of the *Awa maru*. See *Jinbutsu jōhō jiten '82*, 114. His onetime private secretary, Masuoka Ichirō, declined to answer my 5 December 1994 inquiry about his efforts to salvage the ship.

153. Hidaka Shigekatsu telephone interview, 10 October 1994, Tokyo, Japan.

154. *The CRB Commodity Yearbook 1994*, 279; Bureau of the Census, United States Department of Commerce, *Statistical Abstract of the United States 1982–1983* (Washington: Department of Commerce, 1982), 734–737.

155. Kōseishō engo kyoku, *Hikiage to engo*, 315, 388.

156. N.d. April 1973 *Awa maru* Bereaved Families Association petition to visiting members of Sino-Japanese Friendship Association, *Awa maru* Bereaved Families Association papers; Loughlin Naval Institute oral history, 138; Bennett interview, 14 May 1993; *Shūkan yomiuri* 38 (20 May 1979), 161.

157. *Los Angeles Times*, 7 August 1981, 24 September 1982, 27 February 1983; *New York Times*, 17 April, 17 November 1979; Daventry, 62.

158. Bennett interview, 14 May 1993.

Chapter 11. The Ghost of War Returns

1. Matsui, 231; Watanabe, 142.

2. Matsui, *Awa maru*, 231.

3. Chung-kuo ching chi nien chien pien k'o wei yuan hui, ed., *Chung-kuo ching chi nien chien 1982* [Almanac of China's economy 1982] (Beijing: Pei-chin ching chi kuan li tsa chih she, 1982), VIII-34; Harding, 76, 89, 95, 105.

4. Matsui, 232; Watanabe, 140.

5. Watanabe, 142; Matsui, 232. The Sino-Japanese Treaty of Peace and Friendship of 1978, unlike the more general San Francisco Peace Treaty of 1951, made no mention of claims resolution. Grenville and Wasserstein, 306. Its silence on that issue could be interpreted to mean that Japan recognized China as an "Allied Power" under the terms of the 1951 treaty, which the Beijing government had not signed. In it the "Allied Powers" gained the right to seize and dispose of Japanese real property (article 14), and Japan waived all claims against them (article 19). See Fred L. Israel, ed., *Major Peace Treaties of Modern History 1648-1967* (New York: Chelsea House, 1967), 4: 649, 2653.

6. *Asahi shimbun*, *Yomiuri shimbun*, 28 April 1979; Kōseishō engo kyoku statement, 27 April 1979, Archives of the Health and Welfare Ministry, Tokyo. I am indebted to Mr. Shōji Yoshiki of the ministry's Assistance Bureau, Relief Planning Section, for locating and providing copies of this and other Health and Welfare Ministry documents to me.

7. *Yomiuri shimbun*, 28 April 1979.

8. *Asahi shimbun*, 28 April 1979.

9. Bunton-Harter 11 May 1979 telephone conversation transcript, Defense exhibit TP, item 184, loose materials, box 13, Case CV 84-301 G.

10. *Los Angeles Times*, 4 May 1979.

11. *Yomiuri shimbun*, 2 May 1979.

12. *Asahi shimbun*, 28 April 1979; *Yomiuri shimbun*, 28 April, 2 May 1979; *Shūkan yomiuri* (20 May 1979): 60; *Shūkan taishū* (24 May 1979): 16.

13. The man was Maruyama Kazuo of the Repatriation Bureau in the Ministry of Health and Welfare. *Japan Times*, 24 May 1979. He was accompanied by Hara Toyoaki and Ikeguchi Hayami of the ministry. Izumi Koide to author, forwarding information telephoned from Ministry of Health and Welfare, 6 September 1994. Just prior to his departure, the *Awa maru* Bereaved Families Association presented Minister Hashimoto with a petition that detailed its origin and purposes, sought permission to send as many members as possible to China, and invited his participation in privately funded interment ceremonies at Zōjōji Temple. See *Awa maru* Bereaved Families Association to Hashimoto Ryūtarō, 11 May 1979, *Awa maru* Bereaved Families Association papers.

14. *Japan Times*, 24 May 1979; *Yomiuri shimbun* 28 April 1979.

15. Anonymous, "Sanjūnen buri ni Chūgoku no te de hikiagerareta *Awa maru* no misuteri no chosen [Challenge to the void: mystery of the *Awa maru*, salvaged by the Chinese thirty years later], *Pureiboi* [Playboy weekly] (12 June 1979): 65.

16. Kōseishō, ed., *Hikiage to engo*, 312-313, 763.

17. *New York Times*, 7 January 1996; *Jimbutsu jōhō '82*, 106; *Gendai Nihon jinmei roku*, 3: 96.

18. Ibid.; Tsuji and Hayashi, 5: 186. Hashimoto's father, Hashimoto Ryōgo, served as Minister of Health and Welfare in the third Yoshida Shigeru cabinet and, in the second Kishi Nobusuke cabinet, both in that post and as Minister of Education. See *Japan*

Biographical Encyclopedia and Who's Who, 251; Shimonaka, ed., *Gendai Nihon jinmei jiten,* 541.

19. Kōseishō, *Hikiage to engo,* 768.

20. *Gendai Nihon jinmei roku,* 3: 196; Tōkō Takeko interview, 13 January 1993.

21. *Yomiuri shimbun,* 28 April 1979.

22. Minute, Kōseishō no hōChū ni tsuite [Concerning the Ministry of Health and Welfare visit to China], 18 June 1979, Ministry of Health and Welfare Archive; Arai Shigeru and Shimotsuma Kazuho interview, 8 October 1994, Nara, Japan; *Asahi shimbun,* 2 July 1979.

23. Foreign Broadcast Information Service China 79-130 5, 6 July 1979, 1: d2–d3.

24. *Japan Times, Mainichi shimbun, Asahi shimbun,* 4 July 1979.

25. *Asahi shimbun,* 5 July 1979; Arai Shigeru and Shimotsuma Kazuho interview, 8 October 1994, Nara, Japan.

26. *Asahi shimbun,* 5 July 1979; 5 July schedule, Kōsei daijin no hōChū ni tsuite, 18 June 1979, Ministry of Health and Welfare documents; *Tsuitō roku,* 241.

27. *Japan Times, Mainichi shimbun, Asahi shimbun,* 4 July 1979. *Asahi shimbun, Yomiuri shimbun, Mainichi shimbun,* 5 July; *Sankei shimbun,* 6 July, 1979; *Pureboi* (12 June 1979): 60–65.

28. *Sankei shimbun,* 16 August 1979.

29. *Sankei shimbun,* 22 March 1980; *Nihon keizai shimbun,* 27 December 1980; *Mainichi shimbun,* 8 April 1981, *Asahi shimbun,* 7 May 1981. The last article described how the son, a television director and diver, of one of the victims, who accompanied the third group of bereaved families to China, was denied permission to film the remains of the hulk at the sinking site. (Shanghai) *Renmin jibao,* 26 December 1980, *Awa maru* Bereaved Families Association papers.

30. Matsui, 234. The second Japanese group traveled to China from 24 to 31 January 1980, and a third went 3–6 May 1981, to receive additional remains recovered from the *Awa maru.* Ministry of Health and Welfare memoranda, dated 11 January 1980, and 24 April and 6 May 1981, detail the planning and scheduling of these visits. Mrs. Tōkō made one of these pilgrimages; Atsuko Tōkō Fish telephone interview, 26 September 1994, Brookline, Massachusetts. To my knowledge Minoru Fukumitsu, who was not bereaved, never went on one of these trips.

31. Author's observation of Nara and Tokyo monuments, 12 January 1993 and 10 October 1994.

32. Murata Kiyoaki, former editor of the *Japan Times,* who had spent the war in the United States as a college student, wrote an article summarizing Chihaya's views, *Japan Times,* 6 July 1979; Murata Kiyoaki telephone interview, 3 October 1994, Tokyo.

33. "Midori jūji no fune: *Awa maru*" [The green cross ship *Awa maru*], NHK television broadcast 7 December 1979.

34. Matsui Kakushin interview, 1 October 1994, Tokyo; Matsui published forty-one articles between 3 September and 31 October 1990 in the *Asahi shimbun.* I

am indebted to him for making copies available to me prior to the appearance of his book.

35. Matsui, *Awa maru naze shizunda ka* [Why was the *Awa maru* sunk?] (Tokyo: Asahi shimbunsha, 1994).

36. Matsui, 233. The official who made that claim was Liao Cheng Zi, chairman of the Japan-China Friendship Association.

37. Shimoda Kantarō died in 1970, Shimoda Mitsuko interview, Tokyo, 15 January 1993; Arima died in April 1980; Arima, *Seizonsha* 2, dustjacket. Tōkō Takeko died in Boston, Massachusetts, 11 December 1993; *Yomiuri shimbun,* 22 December, *Asahi shimbun,* 24 December 1993.

38. Author's observation of Nara and Tokyo monuments, 12 January 1993 and 10 October 1994.

39. Tokyo Television *Awa maru* Fiftieth Anniversary program, n.d. March 1995. I am indebted to Nonomura Masao of the *Awa maru* Bereaved Families Association for making a taped copy of this broadcast available to me.

40. *Los Angeles Times,* 4 May 1979; *San Diego Tribune,* 4 December 1980, in Bennett papers; Bunton-Innes telephone conversation, 18 January 1980, transcript, defense exhibit ZJ, loose materials, item 184, box 13, Case CV 84-301-G; Bunton interview, 29 March 1996.

41. *Los Angeles Times,* San Diego County edition, 15 January 1984; Stipulated order dismissing action with prejudice, 17 May 1988, item 253, volume 17, box 15, Case CV 84-301-G.

42. W. Joe Innis with Bill Bunton, *In Pursuit of the Awa maru* (New York: Bantam Books, 1981). To the dismay of the navy men among his sometime collaborators, Bunton appended to his story the ruminations of a fictitious *Queenfish* sailor suggesting that the sinking of the *Awa maru* had been anything but accidental. He went on to suggest that navy higher-ups had directed a conspiracy, involving the captain of the *Queenfish*'s wolfpack mate *Seafox,* designed to put *Queenfish* on a collision course with the *Awa maru.* Once that happened, Bunton and his coauthor implied, the odds were better than fifty-fifty that the aggressive Elliott Loughlin would try to strike the target that appeared on the *Queenfish*'s radar. Ibid., 256–261. Bunton's book was not reviewed in the *New York Times, Los Angeles Times,* or *Washington Post*; it did prompt articles in the *San Diego Tribune,* 4 June, 17 December 1980. Only two works about the *Awa maru* other than the Innis and Bunton volume were published after her discovery. David D. Lowman, "The Treasure of the *Awa maru,*" U.S. Naval Institute *Proceedings,* 108 (August 1982): 4–48, reached only a narrowly focused professional audience. Thomas B. Allen and Norman Polmar published *Ship of Gold* (New York: Macmillan, 1987), a novel that conflated the *Awa maru* with another Japanese vessel and made her the subject of a Cold War treasure and espionage tale. Only specialists, or perhaps World War II submarine veterans, would recognize Elliott Loughlin in the murdered David Gordon Porter, skipper of the fictional *Tigerfish.*

43. Barely a month after the first remains of *Awa maru* victims were interred in Tokyo, the U.S. Navy transferred custody of the USS *Bowfin* to the Pacific Fleet Submarine Memorial Association in Honolulu. The boat was opened to visitors in April 1981. The preceding November the Association obtained a long-term lease on property adjacent to the USS *Arizona* memorial. Following receipt of authorization to exhibit materials from the then nearly inaccessible museum at the Pearl Harbor Submarine Base, the *Bowfin* museum was designated a National Historic Landmark in 1986. Its doors opened to the public two years later. Paul A. Nelson, "Bowfin Park: A Dream Becomes a Reality," *Fore 'n Aft, Official Publication of the Honolulu Council, U.S. Navy League* (April 1989): 4–7. I am indebted to Stanley K. Nicholls of Honolulu, Hawaii, for providing a copy of this article and mimeographed brief histories of the USS *Bowfin* (SS 287); Captain Harvey Gray, Jr., interview, Honolulu, Hawaii, 13 October 1994

44. Blair, 836–840 (barely five pages in a thousand-page book) is the lengthiest of these treatments; Fluckey, *Thunder Below!* 105–106, 116–117,126–183, 219, and passim, details the *Queenfish*'s wolfpack operations with his *Barb* without mentioning the sinking of the *Awa maru*. Adm. I. J. Galantin's *Submarine Admiral: From Battlewagons to Ballistic Missiles* (Urbana: University of Illinois Press, 1995), 113–114, is unusual among recent submariners' books in mentioning that the *Queenfish* sank the *Awa maru*.

45. Author's observations, Pearl Harbor, Hawaii, 17 January 1993, 13 October 1994. What appears in any museum is a hybrid product of the accidents of survival and preservation, of history itself, and of the creative designs of its builders and curators. I do not believe those responsible for the *Bowfin* museum consciously excluded particular errors such as the sinking of the *Awa maru*. The absence of error reflects the museum designers' unquestioning acceptance of the heroic view of the American Pacific submariners and the war they fought, a perspective whose genesis is explained in chapter eight.

46. Author's observation of NYK Marine Museum, Yokohama, Japan, 13 October 1994. This visit occurred on the same date, but not the same day, as that to the *Bowfin* museum, due to my crossing the international date line en route from Japan to Hawaii.

47. Clarinet Electronic News Service, 4 December 1994.

48. *New York Times*, 2 December; *Japan Times,* 3, 5–6 December; *Los Angeles Times,* 7 December 1991. Roger Dingman, "Reflections on Pearl Harbor Anniversaries Past," *Journal of American–East Asian Relations* 3 (Fall 1994): 290–292, focuses on the 1991 Pearl Harbor observances. George Bush was downed on 2 September 1944 and rescued by the USS *Finback* (SS 230). See Joe Hyams, *Flight of the Avenger* (San Diego: Harcourt, Brace, and Jovanovich, 1991), 104, 119.

49. *Los Angeles Times*, 12, 15, 26 April, 6–7, 12, 14, 17–18 May, 22, 28–29 June, 14–15, 21 July, 13 August 1995.

50. Asada Sadao, "The Flap over the A-Bomb Stamp," *Japan Echo* 22 (Summer 1995): 79; *Los Angeles Times*, 3, 8–9, 12 December 1994.

51. Edward T. Linenthal and Tom Engelhardt, eds., *History Wars: The Enola Gay and Other Battles for the American Past* (Princeton: Princeton University Press, 1996), summarizes the controversy and captures American historians' anger.

52. *New York Times,* 12 June, 2 July, 15–16 August 1995.

53. *Asahi shimbun,* 24 January 1995. Historians Hata Ikuhiko and Hosoya Chihiro resigned from the committee, the former at this point, the latter the preceding September. The critic Kamisaka Fuyuko, a close friend of Minoru Fukumitsu, also left the committee, in January 1995.

54. Kōseishō, *Hikiage to engo,* 772. The ship in question was the *Tsushima maru,* sunk by the USS *Bowfin* on 22 August 1944. See Alden, 126, Feiffer, 92.

Bibliography

Unpublished Sources

GOVERNMENT DOCUMENTS

AUSTRALIA

Australian Archives, Canberra, A.C.T.

A 5104, File 7/22/10/3, Item 5401, Korean War Japanese Attitude.

JAPAN

Bōeichō Bōei kenshūjo [National Institute for Defense Studies, National Defense Agency].

Awa maru file.

Inada Seijun materials

Officer biography files.

Gaimushō Gaikō shiryō kan [Diplomatic Documentation Center, Ministry of Foreign Affairs].

A 700-9-37-1 Dai TōA sensō kankei ikken: Kokusai hō ihan koi *Awa maru* sōnan kankei [Concerning the Greater East Asia War: actions against international law with reference to the *Awa maru* disaster].

A 700-9-11-1-8 Dai TōA sensō kankei ikken: Ippan oyobi shomondai: Zai tekkoku horyojin kyūjutsu mondai [Concerning the Greater East Asia War: general and various problems; emergency relief supplies to those held in enemy countries].

A 700-9-11-4, Part 3 Dai Tōa sensō kankei ikken: Kosen kokkan tekkokujin oyobi horyo zaikyō Suisu kotaishikan ōfuku bunsho [Concerning the Greater East Asia War: documents concerning enemy persons and prisoners of war exchanged between the ministry of foreign affairs and the Swiss embassy in Tokyo].

B'5.1.oJ/U2, Microfilm B'-oo84.

Awa maru mondai shuri ni kansuru ikisatsu (hottan kara kaiketsu made) [Details concerning the disposition of the *Awa maru* problem (from beginning to settlement)].

Shūsen kenhō ni kansuru sōshireikan bu gaikō kyoku to no sesshō kankei [Concerning negotiations with the Office of the Political Adviser, SCAP, about the abandonment of rights and claims].

Jumbi shiryō [Preparatory documents].

Yōkyū ni kansuru to kokkai to no kankei (Kokkai teishutsu made no ikisatsu) [Concerning relations with the Diet over the abandonment of rights and claims (details up to the preparation of a proposal)].

Kokkai ni okeru yōkyū hōki an seikyū kenhō ketsugi kankei [Concerning the decision in the Diet for abandonment of rights and claims].

Awa maru yōkyū hōki shuri no tame no NichiBei kyōtei chōin kōfu [The signature and announcement of the Japanese-American agreement for disposition and abandonment of *Awa maru* claims].

Kokkai e no hōkoku oyobi rinkyū shitsumon kankei [Concerning urgent interpellations and the report to the Diet].

Seiron shimbun ronchō [Newspaper editorials and commentary].

Zasshū sankō shiryō [Various materials reference documents].

Izokukai kaisoku [Governing articles of the *Awa maru* Bereaved Families Association].

Awa maru hikiage mondai [The *Awa maru* salvage problem].

Tōkō Takezō career summary.

Kōseishō [Ministry of Health and Welfare].

Miscellaneous documents pertaining to visit of Minister Hashimoto Ryūtarō to China and recovery of remains from the *Awa maru*.

Kōseishō engo kyoku statement, 27 April 1979.

UNITED STATES OF AMERICA

Department of the Navy

Major R.K. Stutzel, USMC, Navy–Marine Corps Appellate Review Activity, Office of the Judge Advocate General, U.S. Navy, to Dingman, serial 40.22/64515, 16 June 1992.

Federal Bureau of Investigation, Washington, D.C.

Miscellaneous Reports pertaining to William Joseph Sebald, file 77-56615, released as Freedom of Information–Privacy Act #322, 515, March 1991.

Federal Records Center–Los Angeles, Pacific Southwest Regional Archives, Laguna Niguel, California.

United States District Court, San Diego, California, Case file CV 84-301-G.

Library of Congress

S 1.7.0.0-28 General and Specific Problems: Documents Relating to Treaty Provisions Concerning the Treatment of Prisoners of War [Ippan oyobi sho-mondai: Furyo no taigu ni kansuru joyaku kankei]. July 1929–March 1946. Reels S572-573, Documents of the Japanese Ministry of Foreign Affairs, Tokyo, filmed by the Library of Congress.

S.1.7.0.0-38 General and Specific Problems: Problems of the Relief of Enemy Aliens [Ippan oyobi sho mondai: Tekkokujin kyūjutsu mondai]. Reels S 578-580, Documents of the Japanese Ministry of Foreign Affairs, Tokyo, filmed by the Library of Congress.

S.1.7.0.0-42 Documents relating to enemy aliens in areas under Japanese jurisdiction [Teikoku kenka tekkokujin kankei].

Separate volume: Public opinion and press treatments regarding treatment accorded by the Japanese [Bessatsu: Teikoku no toriatsukai-buri ni kansuru gaikoku no yoron narabi ni shimbun ronchō], March 1942–April 1943. Reels S581-583, Documents of the Japanese Ministry of Foreign Affairs, Tokyo, filmed by the Library of Congress. Library of Congress microform 5039.

Naval Historical Center, Washington, D.C.

Classified Operational Archives

Action Reports. USS *Queenfish Awa maru* file, World War II Command files.

Commander Submarine Force, U.S. Pacific Fleet. *Submarine Operational History World War II,* 4 vols. Washington, D.C.: Chief of Naval Operations (Coordinator of Undersea Warfare), 1946.

Director of Naval History. *United States Naval Administration in World War II: Submarine Commands.* First draft narrative.

Navy Department. Press releases file.

Queenfish file. World War II command files. Officer biography files.

Navy Department Library
Record of Proceedings of a General Court-Martial Convened at Headquarters, Commander Forward Area, Central Pacific by order of Commander-in-Chief, U.S. Pacific Fleet and Pacific Ocean Areas: Case of Charles E. Loughlin, Commander, U.S. Navy. Transcript of proceedings, 19 April 1945, microfilm copy, NRS 1970-36.

United States National Archives and Records Administration, Washington, D.C., and Suitland, Maryland

Record Group 24. United States Navy ship deck logs.
USS *Queenfish.*
USS *Sea Fox.*

Record Group 38. Records of the Office of the Chief of Naval Operations.
Chief of Naval Operations General Correspondence.
U.S. Submarine War Patrol Reports and Related Documents, 1941–1945.

Record Group 59. General Records of the Department of State.
Decimal files, file 711.94114 Supplies.
Records of the Special War Projects Division, 1939–1954, Lot file 58-D-47.

Record Group 84. Records of the Department of State, Post Files.
Tokyo, Japan, post file, 1945–1949.

Record Group 218. Records of the Joint Chiefs of Staff.
File CCS (4-26-45)

Record Group 457. Records of the National Security Agency/Central Security Service.
SRDJ. "MAGIC" Intercepts and "MAGIC" diplomatic summaries, non-sanitized versions, released January 1993.
SRH 122. Japanese messages concerning the *HOSHI maru* and the *AWA maru* December 1944 through August 1945.
SRH 232. U.S. Navy COMINCH Radio Intelligence Appreciations Concerning German U-boat Activity in the Far East, January–April 1945.
SRH 235. Communications Intelligence Contributions Submarine Warfare in WW II.
SRH 323. COMINCH Combat Intelligence Division file on Hospital Ships, 12 January 1943–30 April 1945.

State of California, San Diego County Superior Court, San Diego, California
File 514620 Salvage and Diving vs. Taylor Diving.

PERSONAL PAPERS

Arima Yorichika. Kindai bungaku kan [Museum of Modern Literature], Komaba, Tokyo, Japan.

Awa maru Bereaved Families Association. In custody of Nonomura Masao, Setagaya, Tokyo, Japan.

Bennett, Capt. John E., USN (Ret.). Solana Beach, California.

Forrestal, James A. Diary, copy in Classified Operational Archives, Naval Historical Center, Washington Navy Yard, Washington, D.C.

Goberville, Radioman John G. Diary, in possession of John G. Goberville, Altoona, Wisconsin.

Inada, Gen. Seijun. Miscellaneous papers collected by Professor Takahashi Hisashi, Bōei kenshu jo [National Institute for Defense Studies], Meguro, Tokyo, Japan.

King, Fleet Adm. Ernest J. Manuscripts Division, Library of Congress, Washington, D.C.

Leahy, Fleet Adm. William D. Manuscripts Division, Library of Congress, Washington, D.C.

Lockwood, Vice Adm. Charles Andrews, Jr. Manuscript Division, Library of Congress, Washington, D.C.

Loughlin, Rear Adm. Charles Elliott. War Patrol Log, copies in possession of Mrs. Lynn Elliott Duval, Yorktown, Virginia, and Capt. John E. Bennett, Solana Beach, California.

MacArthur, General of the Army Douglas (SCAP). Daily Appointment Schedule and Memoranda to CinC, Record Group 5, MacArthur Memorial, Norfolk, Virginia.

Morison, Rear Adm. Samuel Eliot. Classified Operational Archives, Naval Historical Center, Washington, D.C.

Nimitz, Fleet Adm. Chester W. Graybook summary January–July 1945, Classified Operational Archives, Naval Historical Center, Washington Navy Yard, Washington, D.C.

Pence, Capt. Harry L., USN. Mandeville Special Collections Department, University of California San Diego Library, La Jolla, California.

Roosevelt, Franklin D. Map Room Papers, file MR 493. Hospital, Relief, Exchange, and Refugee Ships, Franklin D. Roosevelt Presidential Library, Hyde Park, New York.

Sebald, Capt. William Joseph USNR (Ret.). Special Collections Department, Nimitz Library, U.S. Naval Academy, Annapolis, Maryland.

Shimoda Kantarō. Scrapbooks, in custody of Shimoda Mitsuko, Ikebukuro, Tokyo, Japan.

Standley, Adm. William H. Regional Cultural Historical Collection, University of Southern California Library, Los Angeles, California.

ORAL HISTORIES

Cutter, Capt. Slade, USN. U.S. Naval Institute, Annapolis, Maryland.

Loughlin, Rear Adm. Charles Elliot, USN. U.S. Naval Institute, Annapolis, Maryland.

————. Joan and Clay Blair 1971 oral history tape, item 8295, Clay Blair, Jr. collection, American Heritage Center, University of Wyoming, Laramie, Wyoming.

Sebald, Capt. William Joseph, USNR. U.S. Naval Institute, Annapolis, Maryland.

Naisei shi kenkyūkai. *Yoshizawa Seijirō danwa sokkiroku: Naissei shi kenkyū shiryō dai hyaku rokugo shū* [A record of interviews with Yoshizawa Seijirō: domestic political history documentary collection 165] (Tokyo: Naisei shi kenkyūkai, 1983).

INTERVIEWS

April, Susan (New York University archivist). Law School Records office, 9, 13 June 1994. New York City (telephone).

Arai Shigeru. 8 October 1994. Nara, Japan.

Barth, Robert. 29 October 1992. Panama City, Florida (telephone).

Bennett, Capt. John E. USN (Ret.). 14 May, 7 July 1993. Solana Beach, California.

Braisted, Professor William. 18 June 1992. Washington, D.C.; 18 October 1996. Austin, Texas (telephone).

Bunton, William. 29 March, 1996. San Diego, California; 15 March 1993 (telephone).

Carpenter, Cdr. M. Scott. 18 August 1993. Vail, Colorado (telephone).

Chihaya, Cdr. Masataka, IJN (Ret.). 10 January 1993, 2 October 1994, Tokyo, Japan.

Crum, Gary, Los Angeles County Lifeguard Service, 20 March 1995. Hermosa Beach, California (telephone).

Elarkosa, Mrs. Polly White. 7 July 1994. Pasadena, California (telephone).

Feller, Lt. Adam, USN. 24 March 1995. Long Beach, California (telephone).

Fish, Mrs. Atsuko Tōkō. 26 September 1994. Brookline, Masschusetts (telephone).

Goberville, Radioman John G. 8 September 1993. Anaheim, California.

Gray, Capt. Harvey, Jr., USN (Ret.). 12 October 1994. Honolulu, Hawaii.

Hidaka Shigekatsu. 10 October 1994. Tokyo, Japan (telephone).

Hoose, Winston. 23, 27 April 1993. San Francisco, California (telephone).

Ikuse Katsuaki. 14 October 1994. Tokyo, Japan.

Iwama Kazuko. 3 October 1994. Tokyo, Japan.

Kanegai, George. 10 June 1994. Los Angeles, California (telephone).

Kobayashi Michio. 11 October 1994. Tokyo, Japan (telephone).

Matsui, Kakushin. 1 October 1994. Tokyo, Japan.

Mazzone, Capt. Walter F. Mazzone, USN (Ret.). 19 July 1994. San Diego, California. McNaughton, James. 30 June 1994. Naval Postgraduate School, Monterey, California (telephone).

Motomura Michiyasu. 3 October 1994. Tokyo, Japan.

Murata Kiyoaki. 4 October 1994. Tokyo, Japan (telephone).

Nonomura Masao, 3 October, 1994. Tokyo, Japan.

Ōmae Yukiyo. 10 October 1994. Tokyo, Japan.

Parks, Chief Petty Officer Joe S. 29 April 1994. Poulsbo, Washington.

Rathbun, Radioman Denny. 29 April 1994. Poulsbo, Washington.

Sebald, Capt. William Joseph, USNR (Ret.). 31 October 1979. Naples, Florida.

Seno, Cdr. Sadao, JMSDF (Ret.). 4 October 1994. Tokyo, Japan.

Shamer, Capt. Frank Nickols, USN (Ret.), 15 July 1992, 25 June 1993. San Diego, California.

Shimoda Mitsuko. 15 January 1993. Ikebukuro, Tokyo.

Shimotsuma Kazuho. 8 October 1994. Nara, Japan.

Submarine Veterans of World War II, joint interview with Capt. John E. Bennett, Radioman John G. Goberville, and Torpedoman "Willy" Wilson. 8 September 1993. Anaheim, California.

Tōkō Takeko. 13 January 1993. Tokyo, Japan.

Umemura Fumiko. 3 October 1994. Tokyo, Japan.

University of Utah Student Records and Transcripts Office. 24 May 1994. Salt Lake City, Utah (telephone).

Wilcox, Robert. 2 June 1995. Sherman Oaks, California (telephone).

Yoshida Kenzō, Ambassador. 1 October 1994. Tokyo, Japan (telephone).

OTHER

USS *Bowfin* Submarine Museum and Park materials, in possession of Stanley K. Nicholls, Honolulu, Hawaii.

Eldred D. Kuppinger to Dingman. 24 May 1994.

USS *Queenfish* Reunion Video. 7–9 October 1993. Kings Point, Georgia.

Silent Service, outtakes. Negative 1-478, index 3844; negative 2-9174, index 3905; negative 1-98755, index 11760; and indices 17475, 19595, 20430, 20432, record group 428, Motion Picture, Sound, and Video Branch, U.S. National Archives, Capitol Heights, Maryland.

Zōjōji Temple visitors' information pamphlet.

Published Sources

GOVERNMENT DOCUMENTS

Awa maru Claim Agreement and Agreed Terms of Understanding between the United States of America and Japan, Signed at Tokyo April 14, 1949. Entered into Force April 14, 1949. Treaties and Other International Agreements Series, Department of State Publication 3528. Washington: Government Printing Office, 1949.

Chi, Madelaine, and Smith, Louis J., eds. *Foreign Relations of the United States, 1958–1960.* Volume 18, *Japan, Korea.* Washington, D.C.: Government Printing Office, 1994.

Congressional Record. 80th Cong., 1st Sess., 1948. Vol. 93.

Dai gojūhachi kai kokkai sangiin yosan iinkai kaigiroku dai yongō dai jūnanagō (Shōwa yonjūsan nen sangatsu nijūni nichi, Shōwa yonjūsan nen shigatsu kokonoka) [Record of proceedings of the upper house budget committee, 22 March, 7 April 1968]. Tokyo: Dai gojūhachi kokkai, 1968.

U.S. Department of State, Historical Office. *Foreign Relations of the United States 1946.* Vol. 7, *The Far East.* Washington, D.C.: Government Printing Office, 1971.

————. *Foreign Relations of the United States 1947.* Vol. 6, *The Far East.* Washington, D.C.: Government Printing Office, 1972.

————. *Foreign Relations of the United States 1948.* Vol. 6, *The Far East and Australasia.* Washington, D.C.: Government Printing Office, 1974.

————. *Foreign Relations of the United States 1949.* Vol. 7, *The Far East and Australasia, Part 2.* Washington, D.C.: Government Printing Office, 1976.

————. *Foreign Relations of the United States 1951.* Vol. 6, *Asia and the Pacific, Part 1.* Washington, D.C.: Government Printing Office, 1977.

Foreign Broadcast Information Service. *FBIS CHINA 79-131* 1, no. 131 (6 July 1979): D-2.

International Law Documents, 1944–1945. Newport, R.I.: U.S. Naval War College, 1946.

Kōseishō engo kyoku. *Hikiage to engo sanjūnen no ayumi* [Salvage and relief: a thirty-year history]. Tokyo: Kyosei, 1978.

BOOKS

Abarinov, Vladimir. *The Murderers of Katyn.* New York: Hippocrene Books, 1993.

Abramson, Rudy. *Spanning the Century: The Life of W. Averell Harriman, 1891–1986.* New York: Morrow, 1992.

Acheson, Dean G. *Present at the Creation.* New York: Norton, 1969. Bantam ed., 1970.

Adamson, Hans Christian. *Keepers of the Lights.* New York: Greenberg, 1955.

Agawa Hiroyuki. *The Reluctant Admiral: Yamamoto and the Imperial Navy.* John Bester, trans. Tokyo: Kodansha International, 1979.

Alden, John D. *U.S. Submarine Attacks during World War II (Including Allied Submarine Attacks in the Pacific Theater).* Annapolis, Md.: Naval Institute Press, 1989.

Allen, Thomas B., and Norman Polmar. *Ship of Gold.* New York: Macmillan, 1987.

Allison, John M. *Ambassador from the Prairie, or Allison Wonderland.* Tokyo: Charles E. Tuttle, 1975.

Alsop, Joseph. *FDR, 1882–1945: A Centenary Remembrance.* New York: Viking Press, 1982.

Andrew, Christopher. *For the President's Eyes Only: Secret Intelligence and the American Presidency from Washington to Bush.* New York: HarperCollins, 1995.

Anonymous. *Sasakawa Ryōichi no hito to nari* [Becoming the man Sasakawa Ryōichi]. Tokyo: Nihon kaiji shimbunsha, n.d., c. 1975.

Arima Yorichika. *Heitai shosetsu denki sen 3 Seizonsha no dammoku* [Military novels and biography, Volume 3, the silence of a survivor]. Tokyo: Kojinsha, 1983.

———. *Seizonsha no dammoku* [The silence of a survivor]. Tokyo: Bungei shunjū,1966.

———. *Saishō Konoye Fumimaro* [Prime Minister Konoye Fumimaro]. Tokyo: Kodansha, 1970.

Armstrong, Richard B., and Mary Williams Armstrong. *The Movie List Book: A Reference Guide to Film Themes, Settings, and Series.* Jefferson, N.C.: McFarland and Co., 1990.

Asahi shimbunsha, ed. *Asahi jinbutsu jiten* [Asahi biographical dictionary]. Tokyo: Asahi shimbunsha, 1990.

———. *Gendai jinbutsu jiten* [Contemporary biographical dictionary]. Tokyo: Asahi shimbunsha, 1977.

Auer, James E. *The Postwar Rearmament of Japanese Maritime Forces, 1945–1971.* New York: Praeger, 1973.

Bailey, Beth, and David Farber. *The First Strange Place: The Alchemy of Race and Sex in World War II Hawaii.* New York: Free Press, 1992.

Ballard, Robert D., with Malcolm McConnell. *Explorations: My Quest for Adventure and Discovery under the Sea.* New York: Hyperion, 1995.

Bancroft, Arthur G., and R.G. Roberts. *The Mikado's Guests.* 2nd ed. Reprint (of 1945 1st edition), North Perth: Print Image Pty, Ltd., n.d.

Barlow, Jeffrey G. *Revolt of the Admirals: The Fight for Naval Aviation, 1945–1950.* Washington, D.C.: Naval Historical Center, 1994.

Bartholomew, Capt. C.A. *Mud, Muscle, and Miracles: Marine Salvage in the United States Navy.* Washington, D.C.: Naval Historical Center and Naval Sea Systems Command, 1990.

Beach, Capt. Edward L. *Submarine!* New York: Henry Holt, 1952.

Blair, Clay, Jr. *Silent Victory: The U.S. Submarine War against Japan.* Philadelphia: Lippincott, 1975.

Blair, Joan, and Clay Blair. *Return from the River Kwai.* New York: Simon and Schuster, 1979.

Bledsoe, Robert L., and Bolesaw A. Boczek. *The International Law Dictionary.* Santa Barbara, Calif.: ABC-Clio Press, 1987.

Bodnar, John. *Remaking America: Public Memory, Commemoration and Patriotism in Twentieth Century America.* Princeton, N.J.: Princeton University Press, 1992.

Borgese, Elisabeth Mann, ed. *Ocean Frontiers: Explorations by Oceanographers on Five Continents.* New York: Harry N. Abrams, 1972.

Boyd, Carl, and Yoshida Akihiko. *The Japanese Submarine Force and World War II.* Annapolis, Md.: Naval Institute Press, 1995.

Braw, Monica. *The Atomic Bomb Suppressed: American Censorship in Occupied Japan.* Armonk, N.Y.: M.E. Sharpe, 1991.

Brown, Edward Duncan. *The International Law of the Sea.* Vol. 1, *Introductory Manual.* Aldershot, England: Dartmouth, 1994.

Brown, Francis, comp. *The War in Maps.* New York: Oxford University Press, 1945.

Buckley, Roger. *Occupation Diplomacy: Britain, the United States, and Japan, 1945–1952.* Cambridge: Cambridge University Press, 1982.

Buell, Thomas B. *Master of Sea Power: A Biography of Fleet Admiral Ernest J. King.* Boston: Little, Brown, 1980.

Burdick, Charles B., and Ursula Moessner. *The German Prisoners of War in Japan, 1914–1920.* Lanham: University Press of Maryland, 1984.

Bureau of the Census. *Statistical Abstract of the United States 1982–1983.* Washington, D.C.: U.S. Department of Commerce, 1982.

Buruma, Ian. *Wages of Guilt: Memories of War in Germany and Japan.* New York: Farrar, Straus, and Giroux, 1994.

Busby, R. Frank. *Manned Submersibles.* Washington, D.C.: Office of the Oceanographer of the Navy, 1976.

Butowsky, Harry A. *Warships Associated with World War II in the Pacific.* Washington, D.C.: National Park Service, 1985.

Calvert, James F. *Silent Running: My Years on a World War II Attack Submarine.* New York: John Wiley and Sons, 1995.

Chigaku jiten [Geographical dictionary].Tokyo: Heibonsha, 1970.

Chihaya Masataka. *Norowareta Awa maru* [The accursed *Awa maru*]. Tokyo: Bungei shunjū, 1961.

Chishitsu chōsajo *Awa maru* junansha tsuitō roku kankōkai, ed. *Awa maru junansha tsuitō roku* [A mourning memorial to the geological researchers (who were) victims of the *Awa maru* disaster]. Tsukuba, Ibaraki Prefecture: Chishitsu chōsajo *Awa maru* junansha tsuitō roku kankōkai, 1979.

Chung-kuo ching chi nien chien pien k'o wei yuan hui, ed. *Chung-kuo ching chi nien chien 1982* [Almanac of China's economy 1982]. Beijing: Pei-ching ching chi kuan li tsa chih she, 1982.

Clausewitz, Carl Maria von. *On War.* Michael Howard and Peter Paret, ed. and trans. Princeton, N.J.: Princeton University Press, 1976.

Cohen, Theodore. *Remaking Japan: The American Occupation as New Deal.* Herbert Passin, ed. New York: Free Press, 1987.

Condit, Doris M. *History of the Office of Secretary of Defense: The Test of War, 1950–1953.* Washington, D.C.: Office of the Secretary of Defense, 1988.

Cook, Haruko Taya, and Theodore F. Cook. *Japan at War: An Oral History.* New York: New Press, 1992.

Corbett, P. Scott. *Quiet Passages: The Exchange of Civilians between the United States and Japan during the Second World War.* Kent, Ohio: Kent State University Press, 1987.

Dallek, Robert. *Franklin D. Roosevelt and American Foreign Policy.* New York: Oxford University Press, 1979.

Daniels, Roger. *Prisoners without Trial.* New York: Hill and Wang, 1993.

Daventry, Paula, ed. *Sasakawa: The Warrior for Peace, the Global Philanthropist.* Oxford: Pergamon Press, 1981.

Daws, Gavan. *Prisoners of the Japanese: POWs of World War II in the Pacific.* New York: Morrow, 1994.

Director of Naval History. *Dictionary of American Naval Fighting Ships.* 6 vols. Washington, D.C.: Office of Naval History, 1963–1970.

Doust, Capt. W.A., with Peter Black. *The Ocean on a Plank.* London: Seeley, Service, and Co., 1976.

Dower, John W. *Japan in War and Peace: Selected Essays.* New York: New Press, 1993.

Drea, Edward J. *MacArthur's Ultra: Codebreaking and the War against Japan, 1942–1945.* Lawrence: University Press of Kansas, 1992.

Dupuy, R. Ernest, and Trevor Dupuy. *Encyclopedia of Military History.* New York: Harper and Row, 1970.

Dyess, William. *The Dyess Story: The Eye-Witness Account of the Death March from Bataan and the Narrative of Experiences in Japanese Prison Camps and of Eventual Escape*. New York: G.P. Putnam's Sons, 1944.

Edwards, Anne. *Early Reagan*. New York: Morrow, 1987.

Emmerson, John K. *The Japanese Thread: A Life in the U.S. Foreign Service*. New York: Holt, Rinehart, and Winston, 1979.

Encyclopedia Japonica 2001. Tokyo Shogakukan, 1984.

Feifer, George. *Tennozan: The Battle of Okinawa and the Atomic Bomb*. New York: Ticknor and Fields, 1992.

Finn, Richard B. *Winners in Peace: MacArthur, Yoshida, and Postwar Japan*. Berkeley: University of California Press, 1992.

Fluckey, Rear Adm. Eugene B[ennett]. *Thunder Below! The USS* Barb *Revolutionizes Submarine Warfare in World War II*. Urbana: University of Illinois Press, 1992.

Friedman, Leon, ed. *The Law of War: A Documentary History*. Vol. 1. New York: Random House, 1972.

Fujita, Frank. *Foo: A Japanese-American Prisoner of the Rising Sun: The Secret Prison Diary of Frank "Foo" Fujita*. Denton: University of North Texas Press, 1993.

Fukumitsu, Minoru. *Awa Maru jiken* [The *Awa maru* incident]. Tokyo: Yomiuri shimbunsha, 1973.

Gaimushō, ed. *Shōki taiNichi senryō seisaku Asakai Kōichirō hōkoku sho* [Early Occupation policy towards Japan: the Asakai Kōichirō reports]. 2 vols. Tokyo: Mainichi shimbunsha, 1978.

Galantin, Adm. I.J. *Submarine Admiral: From Battlewagons to Ballistic Missiles*. Urbana: University of Illinois Press, 1995.

Gallup, George H. *The Gallup Poll*. Vol. 1, *1935–1948*. New York: Random House, 1972.

Gamboa, Melquiades J. *A Dictionary of International Law and Diplomacy*. Manila: Central Lawbook Publishing Company, 1973.

Gellman, Irvin F. *Secret Affairs: Franklin Roosevelt, Cordell Hull, and Sumner Welles*. Baltimore: Johns Hopkins University Press, 1995.

Gendai Nihon jinmei roku [Contemporary Japan who's who]. Tokyo: Nichigai Associates, 1987.

Goldstein, Donald M., and Katherine V. Dillon, eds. *The Pearl Harbor Papers: Inside the Japanese Plans*. Washington: Brassey's [US], 1993.

Goodfriend, Arthur. *The Jap Soldier*. Washington, D.C.: *The Infantry Journal*, 1943.

Grenville, J.A.S., and Bernard Wasserstein. *The Major International Treaties since 1945: A History and Guide with Texts*. London: Methuen, 1987.

Grider, George, and Lydel Sims. *War Fish*. Boston: Little, Brown, 1958.

Gurando gendai hyakka jiten [Grand contemporary encyclopedia]. Tokyo: Gakushu kenkyūsha, 1971.

Hackworth, Green Haywood. *Digest of International Law*. 8 vols. Washington, D.C.: Department of State, 1940–1944.

Halloran, Richard. *Japan: Images and Realities*. New York: Knopf, 1969.

Handy, Debra, ed. *Variety Film Reviews, 1907–1980*. 16 vols. New York: Garland, 1985.

Harding, Harry. *A Fragile Relationship: The United States and China since 1972*. Washington: Brookings Institution, 1992.

Harris, Sheldon H. *Factories of Death: Japanese Biological Warfare 1932–1945 and the American Coverup*. London: Routledge, 1994.

Hata, Ikuhiko, comp. *Nihon Rikkaigun sōgō jiten* [Composite dictionary of the Japanese army and navy]. Tokyo: Tokyo daigaku shuppan kai, 1991.

Havens, Thomas R. H. *Fire across the Sea*. Princeton, N.J.: Princeton University Press, 1987.

———. *Valley of Darkness: The Japanese People and World War Two*. New York: Norton, 1978.

Hayashi Shige and Tsuji Akira, eds. *Nihon naikaku shiroku 5* [The historical record of Japan's cabinets, Volume 5]. Tokyo: Daichi hōkan shuppansha, 1981.

Heinrichs, Waldo. *Threshold of War: American Entry into World War II*. New York: Oxford University Press, 1988.

Herring, George C., Jr. *Aid to Russia 1941–1946: Strategy, Diplomacy, and the Origins of the Cold War*. New York: Columbia University Press, 1973.

Hill, Max, and William Brown. *Exchange Ship*. New York: Farrar, Rinehart, and Co., 1942.

Hirano Ken. *Hirano Ken ɀenshū* [The collected works of Hirano Ken], Vol. 9. Tokyo: Shinchosha, 1975.

Hirano Kyoko. *Mr. Smith Goes to Tokyo: Japanese Cinema under the American Occupation, 1945–1952*. Washington: Smithsonian Institution Press, 1992.

Hitchens, Howard B., ed. *America on Film and Tape*. Westport, Conn.: Greenwood Press, 1985.

Holmes, W[ilfred] J[ay]. *Undersea Victory: The Influence of Submarine Operations on the War in the Pacific*. New York: Doubleday, 1966.

Hoopes, Townsend, and Douglas Brinkley. *Driven Patriot: The Life and Times of James V. Forrestal*. New York: Knopf, 1992.

Hoose, Harned P. *Peking Pigeons and Pigeon-Flutes*. Peking: College of Chinese Studies, California College in China, 1938.

Hoyt, Edwin P. *Submarines at War: The History of the American Silent Service*. New York: Stein and Day, 1983.

Hudson, Alec. *"Rendezvous" and Other Long and Short Stories about Our Navy in Action*. New York: Press of the Readers Club, 1943.

Hyams, Joe. *Flight of the Avenger*. San Diego: Harcourt, Brace, and Jovanovich, 1991.

Ibuse Mabuchi. *Lieutenant Look East*. John Bester, trans. Tokyo: Kodansha International, 1971.

Innis, W. Joe, with Bill Bunton. *In Pursuit of the Awa Maru*. New York: Bantam Books, 1981.

Inoki Masamichi. *Hyōden: Yoshida Shigeru* [Yoshida Shigeru: a critical biography]. 4 vols. Tokyo: Yomiuri shimbunsha, 1981.

Iriye, Akira. *The Origins of the Second World War in Asia and the Pacific*. New York: Longman, 1987.

Israel, Fred L., ed. *Major Peace Treaties of Modern History 1948–1967*. 4 vols. New York: Chelsea House, 1967.

———. *The War Diary of Breckinridge Long*. Lincoln: University of Nebraska Press, 1966.

James, D. Clayton. *The Years of MacArthur*. 3 vols. Boston: Houghton Mifflin, 1970–1985.

Japan Biographical Encyclopedia and Who's Who. 2nd ed. Tokyo: Rengō Press, 1960.

Jentschura, Hansgeorg. *Warships of the Imperial Japanese Navy, 1869–1945*. Annapolis, Md.: Naval Institute Press, 1977.

Jinbunsha, ed. *Nihon toshi chizu zenshū* [Atlas of Japan's cities]. Tokyo: Jinbunsha, 1958.

Jinbutsu jōhō jiten '82 [A dictionary of personnel information, (19)82]. Tokyo: Nichigai Associates, 1982.

Jinbutsu refurensu jiten III gendai hen jō [A reference biographical dictionary, Volume 3, part 2: contemporary]. Tokyo: Nichigai assoshiatsu, 1983.

Junod, Marcel. *Warriors without Weapons*. London: Jonathan Cape, 1951.

Kamisaka Tsunesaburō, ed. *Who's Who in Japan, with Manchoukuo and China, 1939–1940*. Tokyo: Who's Who in Japan Publishing Co., 1939.

Karig, Walter, et al. *Battle Report*. Vol. 1, *Pearl Harbor to Coral Sea*. New York: Farrar and Rinehart, 1944.

———. *Battle Report*. Vol. 2, *The Atlantic War*. New York: Farrar and Rinehart, 1944.

———. *Battle Report*. Vol. 3, *Pacific War; Middle Phase*. New York: Holt, Rinehart and Co., 1947.

———. *Battle Report*. Vol. 4, *The End of an Empire*. New York: Rinehart and Co., 1948.

Karig, Walter, Russell L. Harris, and Frank A. Manson. *Battle Report*. Vol. 5, *Victory in the Pacific*. New York: Rinehart and Co., 1949.

Kerr, E. Bartlett. *Surrender and Survival: The Experience of American Prisoners of War in the Pacific 1941–1945.* New York: Morrow, 1985.

Kersten, Rikki. *Democracy in Postwar Japan: Maruyama Masao and the Search for Autonomy.* London: Routledge, 1996.

Knight-Ridder Financial / Commodity Research Bureau. *The CRB Commodity Yearbook 1994.* New York: Wiley, 1994.

Kodansha Encyclopedia of Japan. 9 vols. Tokyo: Kodansha, 1983.

Kokushi daijiten henshu iinkai, ed. *Kokushi daijiten* [Dictionary of national history]. Tokyo: Yoshikawa Kobunkan, 1993.

Kōsei shō engo kyoku. *Hikiage to engo sanjūnen no ayumi* [Salvage and relief: a thirty-year history]. Tokyo: Kyosei, 1978.

Lebra, Takie Sugiyama. *Above the Clouds: Status Culture of the Modern Japanese Nobility.* Berkeley: University of California Press, 1993.

Leich, Marian. *Digest of United States Practice in International Law.* Washington, D.C.: Office of Legal Adviser, U.S. Department of State, 1989.

Lensen, George Alexander. *The Strange Neutrality: Soviet-Japanese Relations during the Second World War 1941–1945.* Tallahassee, Fla.: Diplomatic Press, 1972.

Lewis, George G., and John Mewha. *History of Prisoner of War Utilization by the United States Army 1776–1945.* 1982 ed. Washington, D.C.: Center of Military History, U.S. Army, 1955.

Life and Rand McNally, eds. *Life Pictorial Atlas of the World.* New York: Time, Inc., 1961.

Lindbergh, Anne Morrow. *North to the Orient.* New York: Harcourt, Brace and Co., 1935.

Linderman, Gerald. *Embattled Courage.* New York: Free Press, 1988.

Linenthal, Edward T., and Tom Engelhardt, eds. *History Wars: The Enola Gay and Other Battles for the American Past.* Princeton, N.J.: Princeton University Press, 1996.

Lockwood, Vice Adm. Charles A., Jr. *Battles of the Philippine Sea.* New York: Crowell, 1967.

———. *Down to the Sea in Subs.* New York: Norton, 1967.

———. *Sink 'Em All! Submarine Warfare in the Pacific.* New York: E. P. Dutton, 1951.

Lockwood, Vice Adm. Charles A., Jr., and Hans Christian Adamson. *Hellcats of the Sea.* New York: Greenberg, 1955.

———. *Hell at Fifty Fathoms.* Philadelphia: Chilton Books, 1962.

———. *Through Hell and High Water.* New York: Greenberg, 1956.

———. *Zoomies, Subs and Zeros.* New York: Greenberg, 1956.

Love, Robert W., Jr., ed. *The Chiefs of Naval Operations*. Annapolis, Md.: Naval Institute Press, 1980.

Low, A. Lani, and James F. Muche, comps. *U.S. Submarines: A Bibliography*. San Marino, Calif.: Fathom Eight Publications, 1986.

Lyons, Eugene. *Sarnoff*. New York: Harper and Row, 1966.

Manson, Janet M. *Diplomatic Ramifications of Unrestricted Submarine Warfare, 1939–1945*. Westport, Conn.: Greenwood Press, 1990.

Marling, Karal Ann, and John Wetenhall. *Iwo Jima Monuments, Memories, and the American Hero*. Cambridge: Harvard University Press, 1991.

Matsui Kakushin. *Awa maru naze shizunda ka* [Why was the *Awa maru* sunk?]. Tokyo: Asahi shimbunsha, 1994.

Matsuzawa Naokichi. *Futsuln kaisō roku* [A French Indochina memoir]. Tokyo: Kaibundo, 1971.

McCoy, Cdr. Melvyn H., USN, and Lt. Col. S.M. Mellnik, U.S. Army, as told to Lt. Welbourn Kelley, USN. *Ten Escape from Tōjō*. New York: Farrar and Rinehart, 1944.

Mellnik, Steven. *Philippine Diary 1939–1945*. New York: Van Nostrand and Reinhold, 1969.

Melosi, Martin V. *The Shadow of Pearl Harbor: Political Controversy over the Surprise Attack, 1941–1946*. College Station: Texas A &M University Press, 1977.

Mendenhall, Rear Adm. Corwin. *Submarine Diary*. Chapel Hill, N.C.: Algonquin Books of Chapel Hill, 1991.

Messer, Robert L. *The End of an Alliance: James F. Byrnes, Roosevelt, Truman, and the Origins of the Cold War*. Chapel Hill: University of North Carolina Press, 1982.

Mico, Ted, John Miller Monzon, and David Rubel, eds. *Past Imperfect: History according to the Movies*. General ed. Mark C. Carnes. New York: Holt, 1995.

Miller, Edward S. *War Plan Orange: The U.S. Strategy to Defeat Japan, 1937–1945*. Annapolis, Md.: Naval Institute Press, 1991.

Milton, Joyce. *Loss of Eden: A Biography of Charles and Anne Morrow Lindbergh*. New York: HarperCollins, 1993.

Morison, Rear Adm. Samuel Eliot. *History of United States Naval Operations in World War II*. 15 vols. Boston: Little, Brown, 1947–1962.

Murata Kiyoaki. *An Enemy among Friends*. Tokyo: Kodansha International, 1991.

Naval History Division, Office of Chief of Naval Operations. *Dictionary of America Naval Fighting Ships*. 6 vols. Washington, D.C.: U.S. Navy Department, 1963–1970.

New York Times Index 1941–1995. New York: *New York Times*, 1942–1996.

NHK hōsō bunka chōsa kenkyū jo hōsō jōhō chōsa bu *GHQ bunsho ni yoru senryō ki hōsō shi nenpyō (Shōwa nijūichinen tsuitachi—jūnigatsu sanjūichi nichi)* [A chronology of the history of broadcasting in the Occupation period according to (Supreme Commander Allied Powers) G(eneral) H(ead)Q(uarters) documents (1 January–31 December 1946)]. Tokyo: NHK hōsō bunka chōsa kenkyū jo hōsō jōhō chōsa bu, 1988.

Nihon izoku kai. *Senbotsusha izoku no tebiki (Shōwa 60 nenpan)* [Handbook for families of the war dead, 1985 edition]. Tokyo: Nihon izoku kai, 1984.

Nihon izoku kai jimukyoku, ed. *Nihon izokukai yonjūnen no ayumi* [A forty-year history of the Japan Association of Bereaved Families]. Tokyo: Nihon izoku kai, 1987.

Nippon Yūsen Kabushiki Kaisha, ed. *Nippon Yūsen Kabushiki Kaisha senji sen shi shiryō shū jōkan* [Nippon Mail Steamship Company wartime ships' history documentary collection, Volume 2]. Tokyo: Nippon Yūsen Kabushiki Kaisha, 1971.

Nippon Yūsen Kabushiki Kaisha senji sen shi hensan iinkai, ed. *Nippon Yūsen senji sen shi* [Nippon Mail Steamship Company wartime ships' history]. Tokyo: Nippon Yusen Kabushiki Kaisha, 1971.

Nippon Yūsen Kabushiki Kaisha. *Shichijūnen shi* [Seventy-year history (of the Japan Mail Steamship Line)]. Tokyo: Nippon Yūsen Kabushiki Kaisha, 1956.

Nishi Toshio. *Unconditional Democracy: Education and Politics in Occupied Japan 1945–1952.* Stanford: Hoover Institution Press, 1982.

Nishimura Kumao. *San furanshisuko kōwa joyaku* [The San Francisco Peace Treaty], Vol. 27 of Kajima heiwa kenkyū jo, ed. *Nihon gaikō shi* [A history of Japanese diplomacy]. Tokyo: Kajima heiwa kenkyū jo shuppan kai, 1971.

Nolan, Frederick. *The Sound of Their Music: The Story of Rodgers and Hammerstein.* New York: Walker and Co., 1977.

Ōdaka Toshio, comp. *Nihon shosetsu zen jōhō 27/90* [Complete Information about Japanese novels 27/90]. Tokyo: Kinokuniya shoten, 1991.

Ogata Sadako. *Normalization with China: A Comparative Study of United States and Japanese Processes.* Berkeley: Institute of East Asian Studies, University of California, 1988.

Ōka Shōhei. *Fires on the Plain.* Ivan Morris, trans. New York: Knopf, 1957.

O'Kane, Rear Adm. Richard H. *Clear the Bridge! The War Patrols of the USS* Tang. Chicago: Rand McNally, 1977.

———. *Wahoo: The Patrols of America's Most Famous World War II Submarine.* Novato, Calif.: Presidio, 1987.

O'Neill, P. G. *Japanese Names: A Comprehensive Index by Characters and Readings.* New York: John Weatherhill, 1972.

Oppenheim, L[assa Francis Lawrence]. *International Law: A Treatise.* Vol. 2, *Disputes, War and Neutrality.* H. Lauterpacht, ed. 6th ed. revised. London: Longmans, Green and Co., 1944.

Osaragi Jirō. *Homecoming.* Brewster Horwitz, trans. New York: Knopf, 1955.

Ōta Ichirō. *Nihon gaikō shi dai nijūyonkan Dai TōA sensō senji gaikō* [A history of Japanese diplomacy, Volume 24, Diplomacy during the Greater East Asia War]. Tokyo: Kajima kenkyūjo shuppan kai, 1971.

Ōyama Keisa. *Sasakawa Ryōichi no hito to nari-sono ayumi to jinsei shinjō* [Becoming the man Sasakawa Ryōichi: his path and human principles]. Tokyo: Nihon kaiji shimbun sha, n.d. c. 1974.

Packard, George R. *Protest in Tokyo.* Princeton, N.J.: Princeton University Press, 1966.

Parillo, Mark P. *The Japanese Merchant Marine in World War II.* Annapolis, Md.: Naval Institute Press, 1993.

Paris, Barry. *Garbo: A Biography.* New York: Knopf, 1995.

Parish, James Robert, and Ronald L. Powers. *The MGM Stock Company: The Golden Era.* New Rochelle, N.Y.: Arlington House, 1973.

Passin, Herbert. *Encounter with Japan.* New York: Kodansha International, 1982.

Pfitzer, Gregory M. *Samuel Eliot Morison's Historical World: In Quest of a New Parkman.* Boston: Northeastern University Press, 1991.

Phillips, Cabell. *The Truman Presidency: The History of a Triumphant Succession.* 2nd ed. Baltimore: Pelican, 1972.

Piccigallo, Philip R. *The Japanese on Trial: Allied War Crimes Operations in the East, 1945–1951.* Austin: University of Texas Press, 1979.

Piehler, Kurt. *Remembering War the American Way.* Washington, D.C.: Smithsonian Institution Press, 1995.

Polmar, Norman, and Thomas B. Allen. *Rickover.* New York: Simon and Schuster, 1982.

———. *World War II: America at War 1941–1945.* New York: Random House, 1991.

Potter, Elmer B. *Nimitz.* Annapolis, Md.: Naval Institute Press, 1976.

Prados, John. *Combined Fleet Decoded.* New York: Random House, 1995.

Prange, Gordon W., with Donald M. Goldstein and Katherine V. Dillon. *God's Samurai: Lead Pilot at Pearl Harbor.* Washington, D.C.: Brassey's (US) Inc., 1990.

Reader's Guide to Periodical Literature. Vols. 13–20. New York: H.W. Wilson, 1943–1955.

Rearden, Stephen L. *History of the Office of Secretary of Defense: The Formative Years, 1947–1950.* Washington, D.C.: Office of the Secretary of Defense, 1984.

Red Cross, International Committee. *The International Red Cross in Geneva 1863–1943.* Geneva: International Red Cross, 1943.

Reischauer, Edwin O. *My Life between Japan and America.* New York: Harper and Row, 1986.

Renzi, William, and Mark D. Roehrs. *Never Look Back: A History of World War II in the Pacific.* Armonk, N.Y.: M.E. Sharpe, 1991.

Reynolds, E. Bruce. *Thailand and Japan's Southern Advance, 1940–1945*. New York: St. Martin's Press, 1994.

Rix, Alan, ed. *Intermittent Diplomat: The Japan and Batavia Diaries of W. Macmahon Ball*. Melbourne: Melbourne University Press, 1988.

Rodgers, Richard. *Musical States: An Autobiography*. New York: Random House, 1975.

Roscoe, Theodore. *United States Submarine Operations in World War II*. Annapolis, Md.: Naval Institute Press, 1949.

Rosenman, Samuel I., comp. *The Public Papers and Addresses of Franklin D. Roosevelt 1942*. Vol. 11, *Humanity on the Defensive*. New York: Harper and Brothers, 1950.

Rothe, Anna, ed. *Current Biography: Who's News and Why 1944*. New York: H.W. Wilson, 1944.

Sasakawa Ryōichi. *Kono keisho wa nariyamazu* [This fire alarm doesn't stop ringing]. Tokyo: Tokyo Shirakawa shoin, 1981.

Satō Seizaburō, Koyama Ken'ichi, and Kumon Shumpei. *Postwar Politician: The Life of Former Prime Minister Masayoshi Ohira*. William R. Carter, trans. Tokyo: Kodansha International, 1990.

Saunders, Ernest Dale. *Buddhism in Japan: With an Outline of Its Origins in India*. Philadelphia: University of Pennsylvania Press, 1964.

Schaller, Michael. *Douglas MacArthur: The Far Eastern General*. New York: Oxford University Press, 1989.

Schonberger, Howard B. *Aftermath of War: Americans and the Remaking of Japan, 1945–1952*. Kent, Ohio: Kent State University Press, 1989.

Schratz, Capt. Paul R. *Submarine Commander: A Story of World War War II and Korea*. Lexington: University Press of Kentucky, 1988.

Schultz, John, and Miwa Kimitada, eds. *Canada and Japan in the Twentieth Century*. Toronto: Oxford University Press, 1991.

Sebald, William Joseph. *With MacArthur in Japan: A Personal History of the Occupation*. New York: Norton, 1965.

Senshi kankō kai. *Senbotsusha izoku no tebiki (Shōwa rokujūnen pan)* [Handbook for families of the war dead, 1985 edition]. Tokyo: Nihon izoku kai, 1984.

Shanberg, Maurice. *The KGB Solution at Katyn*. Franklin Lakes, N.J.: Lincoln Springs Press, 1989.

Sherwood, Robert E. *Roosevelt and Hopkins: An Intimate History*. New York: Grosset and Dunlop, 1948.

Shimokawabe Motoharu and Shindo Eiichi, eds. *Ashida Hitoshi nikki* [The diary of Ashida Hitoshi]. 3 vols. Tokyo: Iwanami shoten, 1986.

Shimonaka Yasaburō, ed. *Gendai Nihon jinmei jiten* [Biographical dictionary of contemporary Japan]. Tokyo: Heibonsha, 1955.

Shimonoseki shi shi hensan iinkai. *Shimonoseki shi shi* [A history of Shimonoseki City]. Shimonoseki: Shimonoseki City Office, 1955.

Shōwa bukko jinmei roku Shōwa gannen–gojūyonen [Biographical register of deceased (persons in the) Shōwa era 1925–1979]. Tokyo: Nichigai assoshiatsu, 1983.

Sigal, Leon V. *Fighting to a Finish: The Politics of War Termination in the United States and Japan, 1945*. Ithaca: Cornell University Press, 1988.

Spector, Ronald H. *Eagle against the Sun: The American War with Japan*. New York: Vintage Books, 1985.

Standley, William H., and Arthur A. Ageton. *Admiral Ambassador to Russia*. Chicago: Henry Regnery, 1955.

Sterling, Forest J. *Wake of the* Wahoo. Philadelphia: Chilton, 1960.

Stross, Randall E. *Bulls in the China Shop and Other Sino-American Encounters*. New York: Pantheon, 1990.

Sweeney, James R. *A Pictorial History of Oceanographic Submersibles*. New York: Crow Publishers, 1970.

Takeyama Michio. *Harp of Burma*. Howard Hibbett, trans. Rutland, Vt.: Charles A. Tuttle, 1966.

Tenney, Lester I. *My Hitch in Hell: The Bataan Death March*. Washington, D.C.: Brassey's, 1995.

Terkel, Studs. *The Good War: An Oral History of World War Two*. New York: Pantheon, 1984.

Thamsook Nimnonda. *Thailand and the Japanese Presence, 1941–45*. Research Notes and Discussions No. 6. Singapore: Institute of Southeast Asian Studies, 1977.

Thomas, Tony. *The Films of Ronald Reagan*. Secaucus, N.J.: Citadel Press, 1980.

Thucydides. *The Peloponnesian War*. Rex Warner, trans. Baltimore: Penguin Books, 1975.

Togawa Isamu. *Shōwa no shushō dai yonkan Yoshida Shigeru to fukkō e no sentaku* [Shōwa (era) prime ministers, Volume 4, Yoshida Shigeru and the choices for recovery]. Tokyo: Kodansha, 1983.

Tokinotani Masaru. *Nihon kindai shi jiten* [Dictionary of modern Japanese history]. Tokyo: Tōyō keizai shimbunsha, 1958.

Toland, John. *The Rising Sun*. New York: Bantam, 1971.

Trainer, Joseph C. *Educational Reform in Occupied Japan*. Tokyo: Meisei University Press, 1983.

Trumbull, Robert. *Silversides*. New York: Henry Holt, 1945.

Tsunogawa Nihon chimei daijiten hensan iinkai, ed. *Tsunogawa Nihon chimei daijiten 35: Yamaguchi ken* [The Tsunogawa dictionary of place names, Volume 35, Yamaguchi Prefecture]. Tokyo: Tsunogawa shoten, 1978.

Ugaki Matome. *Fading Victory: The Diary of Admiral Matome Ugaki 1941–1945*. Chihaya Masataka, trans. Pittsburgh: University of Pittsburgh Press, 1991.

Uyehara, Cecil, and Edwin G. Beal. *Checklist of Archives of the Japanese Ministry of Foreign Affairs, Tokyo, Japan, 1860–1945, Microfilmed by the Library of Congress*. Washington: Library of Congress Photoduplication Service, 1954.

Variety Film Reviews. 16 vols. New York: Garland Press, 1983.

Variety Film Reviews 1907–1983. 18 vols. New York: Garland Press, 1983.

Variety Obituaries, 1905–1994. 15 vols. New York: Garland Press, 1988–1995.

Variety Television Reviews. 15 vols. New York: Garland, 1989.

Variety Television Reviews 1946–1959. 6 vols. New York: Garland Press, 1989.

Voss, Frederick S. *Reporting the War: The Journalistic Coverage of World War II*. Washington, D.C.: Smithsonian Institution Press, 1994.

Webster's New Geographical Dictionary. Springfield, Mass.: Webster-Merriam, 1984.

Weir, Gary E. *Building American Submarines 1914–1940*. Washington, D.C.: Naval Historical Center, 1991.

Wheeler, Keith. *War under the Pacific*. New York: Time-Life Books, 1980.

Whiteman, Marjorie. *Digest of International Law*. 15 vols. Washington: Department of State, 1963–1973.

Whitson, William W. *Doing Business with China*. New York: Praeger, 1974.

Who's Who in America, 1970–1971. Vol. 36. Chicago: Marquis Who's Who, 1971.

Who's Who in America, 1978–1979. Vol 40. Chicago: Marquis Who's Who, 1979.

Who's Who in America, 1986–1987. 2 vols. Chicago: Marquis Who's Who, 1986.

Who's Who in America, 1991–1992 Supplement. Wilmette, Ill.: Marquis Who's Who, 1992.

Who's Who in Goverment, 1975–1976. Chicago: Marquis Who's Who, 1975.

Yamaoka Sohachi. *Hatenko ningen Sasakawa Ryōichi* [Unprecedented: Sasakawa Ryōichi, the human being]. Tokyo: Yuhosha, 1988.

Yamazaki Toyoko. *The Barren Zone* [Fumō chitai]. James T. Araki, trans. Honolulu: University of Hawaii Press, 1985.

Yokota Yutaka. *Aa kaiten tokkō tai: Kaerazaru seishun no kiroku* [The navy's suicide Torpedo Special Attack Corps: a record of youth gone forever]. Tokyo: Koinsha, 1971.

Yoshida Shigeru. *The Yoshida Memoirs: The Story of Japan in Crisis*. Yoshida Kenichi, trans. Boston: Houghton Mifflin, 1962.

Yoshitsu, Michael M. *Japan and the San Francisco Peace Settlement*. New York: Columbia University Press, 1983.

Young, Donald J. *The Battle of Bataan*. Jefferson, N.C.: McFarland, 1992.

Zacharias, Ellis M. *Secret Missions: The Story of an Intelligence Officer.* New York: G. P. Putnam's Sons, 1946.

ESSAYS AND JOURNAL ARTICLES

Alsop, Joseph. "City in Prison: Americans Interned in a Hongkong Brothel." *Saturday Evening Post* 215 (9 January 1943): 12 ff.

———. "Starvation Is Torture Too: Stanley Internment Camp in Hongkong." *Saturday Evening Post* 215 (16 January 1943): 28 ff.

Anonymous. "American Diplomats Held in Tokyo: Lives in a Virtual State of Suspension." *Life* 13 (7 September 1942): 24–25.

———. "Americans Return from Jap Prison Camps." *Life* 13 (7 September 1942): 23.

———. "Amerika no ippatsuya ga moku o tsuketa 'norowareta *Awamaru*' zaiho no shingan" [Truth or falsehood about the treasure of the 'doomed *Awa maru*' which the Americans sank with a single shot]. *Shūkan shinchō* 21 (2 December 1976): 143.

———. "*Awa maru* hikiage o Chūgoku ni yokodori sareta otoko no nesshin Nikkei-jin Minoru Fukumitsu" [The zeal of the man who was beaten by China in salvaging the *Awa maru*: the Japanese-American Minoru Fukumitsu]. *Shūkan yomiuri* 38 (20 May 1979): 160–162.

———. "Behind the Great Submarine Snatch." *Time* 108 (6 December 1976): 23.

———. "Fudōsanya made kaizai shi hajimeta 'takarabune' *Awa maru* sōdō sono go" [After the disturbance (over) the 'treasure ship' *Awa maru* they've even begun to go after the real estate broker]. *Shūkan gendai* 19 (1 December 1977): 41.

———. "Great Submarine Snatch." *Time* 105 (31 March 1975): 20.

———. "Jitsuryoku posto NiKa kyōkai o sute *Awa maru* hikiage netsu no gaimushō kōkan mibōjin: Tōkō Takeko" [Tōkō Takeko: widow of a high-ranking Ministry of Foreign Affairs official who, having given up a powerful position at the Japan-Canada Society, is eager to salvage the *Awa maru*]. *Shūkan taishū* (24 May 1979): 16–18.

———. "Kaimei no itoguchi hogusareru kōi ka guzen ka *Awa maru* gekichin no nazo" [Unravelling clues to understanding: (was it) deliberate or accidental? The riddle of the *Awa maru*'s sinking]. *Shūkan yomiuri* 32 (25 August 1973): 140–143.

———. "Mō hitotsu no *Awa maru* jōhō" [Additional intelligence on the *Awa maru*]. *Shūkan shinchō* 21 (23/30 December 1976): 24.

———. "Must be Presumed . . . : Loss of the *Wahoo*." *Time* 42 (13 December 1943): 68.

———. "Navy Ponders Its Atomic Future as Ships Head for Test Blowoff." *Newsweek* 27 (11 February 1946): 44–45.

———. "Sanjūyonen buri ni Chūgoku no te de hikiagerareta *Awa maru* no misuteri ni chōsen" [Challenge to the mystery of the *Awa maru* salvaged by China after thirty-four years]. *Pureiboi* [Playboy weekly] (12 June 1979): 63–64.

———. "Shijō saidai no higeki '*Awa maru*' gekichin no nazo Taiwan oki de hikiagerareru hyaku oku no takarabune" [The greatest tragedy in history: the riddle of the sinking of the *Awa maru* the hundred-million (-yen) treasure ship that can be salvaged off Taiwan]. *Shūkan bunjū* (13 June 1960): 54–60.

———. "Taiheiyō sensō mitsuroku no nazo o ou: *Awa maru* wa NitChū kokkō kaifuku ni torihikisareta to iu gekichin sanjūgonen me no shin suiri" [Pursuing the riddles of the secret records of the Pacific War: the *Awa maru* reportedly brought up in the restoration of Sino-Japanese relations; new suppositions thirty-five years after she was torpedoed]. *Shūkan posuto* (18 April 1980): 210–214.

———. "Trying to 'Swipe' a Russian Sub Is Just Part of CIA Saga." *U.S. News and World Report* 78 (31 March 1975): 16.

———. "Unregenerate Japan." *Nation* 161 (22 September 1945): 273–274.

Arima Yorichika. "Intabyū: nijūnenme ni: kekkon shiki o ageta jijō" [Interview: on the twenty-fifth anniversary: the circumstances of (my) wedding ceremony]. *Fujin kōron* [Women's review] (January 1969): 262.

Bellaire, Robert. "Tokyo Nightmare: Six Months of Terror and Starvation in Japan's Worst Concentration Camp." *Collier's* 110 (26 September 1942): 37 ff.

Chang Chih-k'uei. "A-po-wan'mi-chung chih mi" [The *Awa maru*: riddles within riddles]. *Hai-yang shih-chieh* [Ocean world] (May 1993): 30–32; (June 1993): 31–32.

Chihaya Masataka. *Awa maru* gekichin no fuhō o tsuku" [Attack the illegality of the torpedoing of the *Awa maru*]. *Jinbutsu orai* (8 August 1965): 148–163.

———. "Izentoshite tokenai *Awa maru* chinbotsu no nazo" [The riddles of the sinking of the *Awa maru* remain unsolved]. *Sekai no kansen* [Ships and warships of the world] (June 1980): 156–163.

———. "Sekai saidai no takararabune: *Awa maru* gekichin no nazo" [The world's greatest treasure ship: the riddle of the sinking of the *Awa maru*]. *Bungei shunjū* 34 (August 1956): 128–146.

Crowder, Robert. "An American's Life in Japan Before and After the Pearl Harbor Attack." *Journal of American-East Asian Relations* 3 (Fall 1994): 259–268.

Dingman, Roger, "Alliance in Crisis: The *Lucky Dragon* Incident and Japanese-American Relations." In Warren I. Cohen and Akira Iriye, eds. *The Great Powers in East Asia, 1953–1960*. New York: Columbia University Press, 1990: 187–214.

———. "The Dagger and the Gift: The Impact of the Korean War on Japan." *Journal of American-East Asian Relations* 2 (Spring 1991): 29–55.

———. "Farewell to Friendship." *Diplomatic History* 10 (Spring 1986): 121–139.

———. "Remembrances of Pearl Harbor Anniversaries Past." *Journal of American-East Asian Relations* 3 (Autumn 1994): 279–293.

————. "The View from Down Under: Australia and Japan, 1945–1952." In *The Occupation of Japan: The International Context*, Thomas Burkman, ed., Norfolk, Virginia: MacArthur Memorial, 1984: 98–122.

————"Yangtze River Crisis: A Reconsideration of the *Panay* Incident, 1937." In Gunji shi gakkai, ed. *Dai Niji sekai taisen: hassei to kakudai* [The Second World War: origins and enlargement]. Tokyo: Kinseisha, 1990: 95–124.

Duus, Peter. "Remembering the Empire: Postwar Interpretations of the Greater East Asia Coprosperity Sphere." Woodrow Wilson Center Asia Program Occasional Paper 54 (Washington, D.C.: Woodrow Wilson Center, Smithsonian Institution, 1993).

Field, James. "West to Japan: US Sub Sinks 70,000 Tons of Jap Shipping." *Life* 14 (15 March 1943): 84–86, ff.

Gibbon, Martha. "Food from Home." *Woman's Home Companion* 69 (November 1942): 68–69.

Gill, Brendan. "Thucydides Had Them in Mind." *New Yorker* 18 (17 October 1942): 49–50.

Gilmore, Alison B. "'We Have Been Reborn': Japanese Prisoners and the Allied Propaganda War in the Southwest Pacific." *Pacific Historical Review* 64 (May 1995): 195–216.

Hasrato, Stan. "Heroes Rising from the Sea." *Collier's* 116 (28 July 1945), 14–15, 50; (4 August 1945), 54–55, 73.

Hata Ikuhiko. "Going to War: Who Delayed the Final Note?" *Journal of American-East Asian Relations* 3 (Fall 1994): 229–247.

————. "Taiheiyō sensō ki no Nihonjin furyo" [Japanese prisoners of war in the World War II period]. *Seiji kaizai shigaku* [Political and economic history] 320 (February 1993): 76–98.

Hill, Max. "Tokio [*sic*] Christmas." *The New Yorker* 18 (December 1942): 42 ff.

Hill, Max, and William Brown. "Tell America What They Have Done to Us." *Saturday Review of Literature* 26 (9 January 1943): 5–7.

Holmes, Wilfred Jay. "On the Undersea Front: Manning the Submarine Tries the Courage of the Sailors." *New York Times Magazine* (10 March 1940): 4 ff.

Hoose, Harned. "Petrochemicals." In *Doing Business with China*, edited by William W. Whitson, 312–333. New York: Praeger, 1974.

Ikuse Katsuaki. "Kaitei no mitsuroku *Awa maru* o meguru nazo" [Secrets in the depths of the sea: riddles concerning the *Awa maru*].*Jidai* [The age] (15 November 1979): 156–163; (15 December 1979): 184–191; (1 January 1980): 182–189; (15 January 1980): 184–191; (1 February 1980): 184–191; (15 February 1980): 184–191.

Kenney, Capt. R.W. (USNR, Ret.). "'Mr. Lucky': Sole Survivor of the *Awa maru*." *The Retired Officer* (August 1974): 70–73.

Lockwood, Vice Adm. Charles A., Jr. "Nothing Can Equal the Atomic Submarine." *Coronet* 29 (February 1951): 37.

———. "U.S. Subs Out of Date." *Science News Letter* 51 (19 April 1947): 246.

Lockwood, Vice Adm. Charles A., Jr., and Percy Finch. "We're Betting Our Shirts on the Atomic Submarine." *Saturday Evening Post* 223 (22 July 1950): 26–27, 116–117.

———. "We Gave the Japs a Licking Underseas." *Saturday Evening Post* 222 (16 July 1949): 22–23, 116–119; (23 July 1949): 62–66; (30 July 1949): 30, 92–94.

Long, Frances. "'Yankee Girl': Adventures of a Young American Who Spent Five Months in Japanese Internment Camp at Manila." *Life* 13 (7 September 1942): 82–91.

Lowman, David D. "The Treasure of the *Awa maru*." U.S. Naval Institute *Proceedings* 108 (August 1982): 44–48.

Marshall, Andrew, and Toyama Michiko. "In the Name of the Godfather." *Tokyo Journal* 1094 (October 1994): 29–35.

Martin, Pete. "Tokyo Bound: Life on an American Submarine." *Saturday Evening Post* 216 (3 July 1943): 9 ff; (20 July 1943): 26 ff.

Matsui Kakushin. "Kūhaku e no chōsen: *Awa maru* no higeki" [Challenge to the void: the *Awa maru* tragedy]. *Asahi shimbun*, 30 September–31 October 1990.

Miya Tsugio. "Sude ni shinkoshite iru ChūTai gōsaku" [Cooperation between China and Taiwan is already progressing]. *Gekkan pen* (July 1973): 89–96.

Morris, F.D. "Seventy Million Problem Children." *Collier's* 116 (1 December 1945): 22 ff.

Nelson, Paul A. "Bowfin Park: A Dream Becomes a Reality." *Fore 'n Aft* (April 1989): 4–7.

Perkins, Dwight H. "Is There a China Market?" In *Doing Business with China*, edited by William W. Whitson. New York: Praeger, 1974.

Powell, John B. "Prisoner of the Japanese: Experiences in Shanghai." *Nation* 155 (10 October 1942): 335–337; reprinted in *Readers Digest* 41 (November 1942): 63–66.

Shimoda Kantarō. "*Awa maru* gekichin no iki shōnin" [A living witness to the sinking of the *Awa maru*]. *Bungei shunjū* 41 (November 1963): 262–270.

Speer, Richard T. "Let Pass Safely the *Awa Maru*." U.S. Naval Institute *Proceedings* 100 (April 1974): 69–76.

Talbot, J.E. "Weapons Development, War Planning and Policy: The U.S. Navy and the Submarine, 1917–1941." *Naval War College Review* 37 (May–June 1984): 53–71.

Voge, Rear Adm. Richard G. "Too Much Accuracy." U.S. Naval Institute *Proceedings* 76 (March 1950): 256–263.

Walter, John C. "William Harrison Standley." In *The Chiefs of Naval Operations*, edited by Robert William Love, Jr. Annapolis, Md.: Naval Institute Press, 1980.

Watanabe Ryōjirō. "Moto Gaishō hisshokan no kataru hitsuwa 13: Kodai *Awa maru* Toshohei chōnan" [Secret conversations of a former private secretary to the foreign minister, 13, Orphans, the *Awa maru* and Deng Xiaoping's eldest son]. *Jiyū* (October 1994): 131–144.

Wolf, Gillian. "Halliburton Company." In *International Directory of Company Histories*, edited by Adele Hart. Chicago: St. James Press, 1991.

Worden, William L. "Boarders from the Tyrant Fish." *Saturday Evening Post* 218 (1 December 1945): 38, 118–121.

Yamazaki Toshihisa. "Ōzeki repoto: Nittai ryokai ni nemuro yonsen gohaku oku en no zaiho" [Treasure report: the forty-five-million-yen treasure that sleeps in Japan–Republic of China territorial waters]." *Ōzeki* 3 (January 1973 special issue): 318–321.

PERIODICALS

Asahi Evening News
Asahi shimbun
Japan Times
Los Angeles Times
Mainichi shimbun
New York Times
San Diego Evening Tribune
Sankei shimbun
Tokyo shimbun
Washington Star
Yomiuri shimbun

VISUAL MATERIALS

"Full Fathom Five," episode 21 of *Victory at Sea*, Embassy Home Entertainment Special Collectors Edition, 1986.

"Gojūnenme ni *Awa maru* no chimbotsu" [On the fiftieth anniversary of the sinking of the *Awa maru*], Tokyo television program broadcast, n.d. March 1995.

Hellcats of the Navy, Columbia Pictures home video edition.

"Midori jūji no fune: *Awa maru*" [The green cross ship: *Awa maru*], NHK television program broadcast 7 December 1979.

Republic Pictures. "Cargo for *Crevalle*," "*Nautilus* Story," "*Sculpin* Story," "*Tang* versus Truk," episodes of *The Silent Service*.

Index

About the Author

Roger Dingman teaches American military, naval, and diplomatic history at the University of Southern California. He earned a bachelor's degree in history at Stanford University and went on to obtain the master's and Ph.D. degrees at Harvard University.

His special interest in Japan and things naval grew out of service in the U.S. Navy in that nation nearly forty years ago. His first book, *Power in the Pacific* (Chicago, 1976), dealt with the origins of naval arms limitation. His more than fifty articles, focusing on the history of American–East Asian relations, have been published in ten countries and five languages.

Professor Dingman has traveled and lectured extensively in the Asia-Pacific region. He has also served as visiting professor at the U.S. Naval War College and the U.S. Air Force Academy.

He and his wife reside in Harbor City, California, only a mile from the nation's busiest port, and they summer in Glade Park, Colorado.

The NAVAL INSTITUTE PRESS is the book-publishing arm of the U.S. Naval Institute, a private, nonprofit, membership society for sea service professionals and others who share an interest in naval and maritime affairs. Established in 1873 at the U.S. Naval Academy in Annapolis, Maryland, where its offices remain today, the Naval Institute has members worldwide.

Members of the Naval Institute support the education programs of the society and receive the influential monthly magazine *Proceedings* and discounts on fine nautical prints and on ship and aircraft photos. They also have access to the transcripts of the Institute's Oral History Program and get discounted admission to any of the Institute-sponsored seminars offered around the country.

The Naval Institute also publishes *Naval History* magazine. This colorful bimonthly is filled with entertaining and thought-provoking articles, first-person reminiscences, and dramatic art and photography. Members receive a discount on *Naval History* subscriptions.

The Naval Institute's book-publishing program, begun in 1898 with basic guides to naval practices, has broadened its scope in recent years to include books of more general interest. Now the Naval Institute Press publishes about 100 titles each year, ranging from how-to books on boating and navigation to battle histories, biographies, ship and aircraft guides, and novels. Institute members receive discounts of 20 to 50 percent on the Press's nearly 600 books in print.

Full-time students are eligible for special half-price membership rates. Life memberships are also available.

For a free catalog describing Naval Institute Press books currently available, and for further information about subscribing to *Naval History* magazine or about joining the U.S. Naval Institute, please write to:

MEMBERSHIP DEPARTMENT
U.S. Naval Institute
118 Maryland Avenue
Annapolis, MD 21402-5035
Telephone: (800) 233-8764
Fax: (410) 269-7940
Web address: www.usni.org